Second Printing - January 2000

ISBN 0-966620801

Publication Serviced by
Indiana Creative Arts
5814 Beechwood Avenue
Indianapolis, IN 46219

i

This book is dedicated to my six children
whom I slighted during the period it covers,
and to my grandchildren who may
some day ponder their roots.

Contents

Preface

Eight years ago I was interviewed by Abe Aamidor, an *Indianapolis News* reporter. When his article appeared in the June 28, 1988 issue I was in Europe. A copy of the article was mailed to Noëlle my oldest daughter who lived in Maine. What she read was completely new to her. She wasted no time when I returned home to reproach me for sharing my experiences with a stranger and for not having done so with my family.

The nature of my work was such that talking about it outside the compartment to which I was assigned was not a practice approved by the Army and other agencies involved in intelligence activities. Both my mother and father passed away without knowing what their son had done while in the military. Noëlle's feelings were hurt, because I had revealed to a member of the press what she felt would have been of interest to her, her kin, and her children. Not convinced that I had behaved wrongly, I decided nevertheless to make it right, and began to write my memoirs so that my grand children would know how grandpa managed his life.

For several years I had given talks related to my WWII experiences to my own Kiwanis club, to local churches, as well as to other local groups. Often I was asked if I had written anything about my experiences. This prompted me to embark on the writing project and encouraged me to complete a 560 page chronological history of my life.

It took about three years to complete the manuscript, and when finished James Haberman whom I had known for many years read it. He found the material very interesting and suitable enough to be a book, but required corrections in the language (too French) and filling in some additional details.

An outline of the manuscript was sent to approximately fifty publishers. Seven of them indicated an interest in its substance, and requested a copy of the manuscript. After examination all described the manuscript as "very interesting", however with one exception, for various reasons they found the manuscript unsuitable for publication. One publisher, the Presidio Press, returned the manuscript accompanied with a few specific valuable suggestions.

Although their guidance was welcome I realized that alone it would be difficult if not impossible for me to be objective enough to make the needed changes. Following the suggestions of the reporter who had written the article about my war experiences, I showed my manuscript and the Presidio

Press comments to Jim Powell Director of the Writer's Center of Indianapolis. He read the manuscript, liked it, and agreed to help me with its finalization. Following his recommendations I realigned all chapters eliminating or expending some of the material. Jim Powell went over the material and when it was ready I contacted Larry Muncie of Indiana Creative Arts (ICA) who had recently published a book about Fort Harrison. He agreed to help me with the publication of this book. His experience, persistence, and extraordinary skill are responsible for the final product.

This treatise is about my experiences as a young French emigrant who, without formal education, but with fascinating experiences, reached the rank of major in the United States Army. After serving in Europe and the Far East during WWII I was retained in the United States Army for twenty-two years. My successes in and out of the military were mainly due to an unusual amount of luck, and a degree of imagination acquired while growing up among great, but simple people. I believed that I was good at what I was doing. However, the lack of leadership of some of my superiors prompted me to be independent, critical and I was often accused of not being a "team player."

At forty-four, after twenty-two years of army life and by then completely disillusioned with the military, I looked forward to retirement. I had spent almost a quarter of a century in a field of activities that was supposed to help our elected leaders make sound decisions. Yet by 1965 the lessons we had learned in the past and the warnings raised by experienced men were ignored. This should not have surprised me, because I was told once by an American general that he ignored the estimate of his intelligence staff in favor of his own instinct which he believed was usually more accurate.

During the last twenty-three years following my retirement from the Army I choose to forget my past and concentrated on my family. When Abe Aamidor asked our family physician if he knew someone who was healthy. He was directed to me by our family doctor who gave me my annual physical but who was not fully aware of my past medical history. When I explained to the reporter that I had malaria, hepatitis, furonculosis and dengue fever, etc., and when he learned where I had acquired these tropical diseases he decided that my past military experiences were more interesting to his readers than my apparent great health. Thus on the 28th of June 1988, a full page article appeared on the Indianapolis News.

If some of the details described in the book appear to be too detailed to be based solely on memory many were extracted from official reports and, or from a diary kept at the time.

Before submitting my manuscript to publishers, I presented it to the Pentagon and to CIA. The Pentagon had no objection to it, but CIA censored two chapters. In addition, to protect certain individuals and their descendants mentioned in the book, I changed their names.

If some of the incidents described in the book vary with the recollection of the participants it is not intentional, but probably due to the author's creeping senility.

I Hope You'll Make It

In the cool, damp English night the Army major and I walked toward the aircraft, a B-24 waiting for me in the darkness. Only an occasional glow from the flashlights of the crew making their final check guided us to our destination. In the bulky brown jump suit I felt like—and probably looked like—an overstuffed Teddy Bear. We stopped underneath the twin vertical tails of the aircraft and faced each other. From his side pocket the major extracted a bright metal flask and handed it to me.

"This is good Scotch," he said. "It's to cheer you up and give you courage before jumping."

He stuffed his empty hands in his pockets and added: "It was nice to have known you! I hope you'll make it. I've escorted many agents to this base, but never have I seen one return. I probably won't see you again either!"

I could not see him clearly in the dark, but judging by his voice I felt that he needed the Scotch more than I did. I took the flask and stuffed it into my inside pocket.

For a while we did not speak, each of us lost in his own thoughts.

It was August 8, 1944, but I had no idea of the time. Time in those days was unimportant. I only knew that it was dark—extremely dark—due to the

Black Liberator (B-24 Serial No. 251211) used to drop author is shown returning to Harrigton air base after making a drop in occupied Europe.

1

Container storage area for the support of French and Norwegian resistance.

overcast, and I was hoping there would be moonlight at my destination. A member of the crew suggested that it was time for me to climb aboard. The escort officer shook my hand heartily, bidding me good luck and happy landing, and then vanished into the darkness.

Through a small hole in the bottom of the fuselage, I managed with the help of one of the crew to enter the aircraft. I sat on a package next to my parachute by the starboard gun port which was covered with Plexiglas. One of the four engines roared into action, soon followed by the other three. The plane shook as we rolled slowly toward the steel mat runway.

Only the dispatcher, a very young sergeant, and I were in the rear of the aircraft, behind the bomb bay loaded with containers of equipment, guns, explosives and ammunition. These were to outfit the unnamed French resistance group I was assigned to join. The dispatcher would make the final adjustment to my chute, and make certain the static line was properly hooked on the anchor point of the aircraft. He was also to relay the signal to jump from the cockpit. I was told there would be a tail gunner in the rear turret, but I had not seen him. Taxiing was like riding in a half-full van without benefit of a seat. The aircraft bounced over the rough ground and made it difficult for me to sit still on the pack which held my personal belongings. It contained items of clothing, well aged but neatly folded into two old French suitcases.

I looked through the window. The aircraft rolled slowly toward the runway between rows of other B-24s painted black like ours. With the earphone of the intercom, I listened to the conversation between the members of the crew. The pilot or the co-pilot was reading a check list and each member of the crew responded.

Suddenly, someone called out over the intercom, "Joe, hey Joe!"

The dispatcher pointed at me and hollered, "It's for you."

Until that moment, I had had no idea that the agents who were dropped behind enemy lines were not at liberty to reveal their true identity or their cover name to the flight crews. So the crews referred to agents like me generically as "Joes."

I acknowledged the call.

"Pass it forward," a voice said.

Puzzled, I turned to the dispatcher who said, "They want your flask."

Not knowing what to do, I handed the flask to the dispatcher who placed it on a slide that ran through the bomb bay to the cockpit. He gave it a push, then closed the opening.

After a final check of all four engines, the plane moved in the damp darkness onto the runway and started rolling. The clattering increased, then stopped as the wheels lifted off the steel mats and we began our climb. Despite my very uncomfortable position, I settled down for the three hours flying time to our destination. The purr of the engines lulled me into a half doze. How did I manage to get in such a predicament? I was satisfied with the quality of my training and confident in my nerve. "It was nice to have known you" the Major had said! Did he mean that none of us ever returned, or did he not know if any had come back?

How Is Your French?

Only a few months before, in late February 1944, I and approximately 150 members of my intelligence school graduating class waited in Fort Hamilton for a ship to take us overseas. During the weekends I was able to visit my parents' home, which was close by. Otherwise, we spent our time learning how to disembark using nets hanging alongside a ship anchored close to shore. One day after visiting my parents all passes were canceled for a final inspection. Our equipment was displayed neatly and everything was closely checked by an officer. A day later we were alerted and loaded onto buses. We did not know where we were going at first, but it soon became obvious that we were not going to the New York port, but to some other destination. We knew where we were once we saw the road sign announcing the City of Boston.

The ship that we and hundreds of other troops were to board was a Liberty ship, designed to carry troops. The hold was deep and stuffed with narrow bunks stacked close to each other five high. By the time we brought aboard our gear, there was not much room for us to lie in our bunks. The space between bunks was so narrow that while on my back in my bunk, my nose occasionally touched the back of the man above me. Turning over was impossible without disturbing him.

Before sailing, we waited in the harbor for a few days until all of the other ships which would make up our convoy were ready. Some of the ships came from other ports, so it was almost a week before we got underway.

Once the shore was out of sight, all we could see in all directions were other ships; some much larger than ours, others much smaller. Periodically small cruisers would pass us and go about their business of protecting the convoy from German submarines that lurked in the dark waters of the Atlantic. We zigzagged according to signals transmitted from one ship to the other by lights and/or flags. At night, we could occasionally see signals and all the ships would simultaneously change direction. I preferred to be on deck because the hold was hot and smelly.

After one week of this, we all had had enough of the ship. Some of us decided that playing poker would make the time pass faster. I did play a few hands and lucky for me I won. Playing cards was not my game; I preferred watching the other ships and guessing where a German submarine might appear. Although there was a watch on every corner of the ship and sailors manned the guns 24 hours a day, many of us strained our eyes trying to detect something. Invariably the "periscope" we sighted turned out to be the dorsal fin of a porpoise.

The second week passed without incident. The third week, we were getting closer to Europe. One evening, as we were watching the stars above, a red glow appeared on the horizon followed by a muffled explosion. Brief signals were seen from all the ships, then darkness returned. Ours changed direction, and the battle station alarm was sounded. Shortly thereafter we saw another red glare followed by another explosion. All hands were on deck ready to board the life rafts. We waited and waited, fully expecting to be next, but the sun came up and we were still in the convoy. We later learned that two ships of our several hundred ship convoy had been sunk with thousands of lives lost or missing.

On the 29th day a coastline appeared on the horizon. The green hills dotted with small white houses were a welcome sight. The powerful green topography proved it was indeed Ireland and several hours later we landed in Belfast. From there the entire intelligence unit was trucked to Lord Londonderry's estate to set up camp. Our quarters were former stables that had been cleaned, but to our surprise contained no bunks. Instead, wooden planks were laid on bricks and covered with a sack two feet wide and six feet long filled with straw! These so-called beds were the most uncomfortable sleeping accommodations I had ever experienced. No one had to get us out of bed in the morning.

Luckily the showers were great. Meant for grooming horses, they served our purposes well. We discovered then that the British took better care of their horses than of themselves.

We were permitted to go to town but there was not much to see. The many girls attracted to the newly arrived Yanks were anything but attractive. Thanks to the nightly blackouts, relationships flourished until the dawn. Under the daylight these Irish lassies did not look so good to the boys. We were ordered not to fraternize, but that was as foolish as saying do not drink to a GI. Army life as we knew it abruptly changed when we reached Ireland. To help the local economy, we were placed on British Army rations which consisted mainly of mutton and potatoes. The fish and chips we were able to purchase in town was not my idea of a gourmet dinner, but we learned to like them. With the first sip we even appreciated the warm beer after our weeks of forced abstinence.

Several days after our arrival, I was called to the orderly room where an Army Major was waiting to see me. He took me to a room, closed the door and mysteriously said to me, "How is your French?"

"It is okay, I suppose."

"How would you like to return to France ahead of the Allied Forces?"

He took me by surprise, but I was not entirely uninformed. I was aware that people were returning to France either to spy or to organize the resistance. I asked him how he proposed to send me there.

"Most likely, by parachute," he replied.

He did not request an immediate reply, but I gave him my answer on the spot. At that point he asked me not to talk to anyone about our meeting. He added: "When you reach England you will be contacted by a representative of the 1st Experimental Detachment." A few days later I received orders transferring me to London. I crossed the rough Irish sea aboard a ferry boat. We made it to Glasgow where I was contacted by an escort and from there we proceeded to London by train. Three of my comrades reached London about the same time as I. We were billeted in an old hotel located on Dever Gardens, the Prince of Wales. The management was composed of old ladies and of very young girls. The old ladies kept a strict watch over the girls to make certain there was no hanky panky with the customers, mostly young Yanks like me.

It was impossible to hide in the building. Mirrors were everywhere and one could see practically every door of the hotel from the front desk. I remember that one day a maid that we liked and gave chocolate to came to my room shortly before I moved on to another location. She was not in my room 5 minutes when the telephone rang. The voice said, "Do you have a girl in our room?"

I replied, "Who wants to know?"

The voice continued, "Get her out or she will be fired."

The girl with me could tell by the tone of my voice what was going on, and by the time I hung up she had left the room.

In late March, when I arrived in London, the city was under daily V-1 attack. The Germans had abandoned the use of conventional air raids, and were concentrating on their rocket attacks that they believed were psychologically more effective against the population. The V-1 sounded more like a motorcycle than a rocket, and would reach London at a relatively low altitude so that it could be seen and heard very clearly. As long as it was heard one was safe, but when the putt-putt stopped, it was time to duck: the rocket was falling.

A few days after my arrival, not knowing yet about the situation and what to do when the air raid alert sounded, I found myself in a taxi going to a meeting. The siren wailed, the taxi stopped, and the driver took off, leaving me in the middle of the street. I could see everybody running toward the same location when a woman said to me, "Get going Gov', they'll be here any minute!" I got out and followed her to what turned out to be the entrance of an underground station.

Down I went with the rest of the people, and I could not believe what I saw. All along the stairs leading below people were living there with what appeared to be all their belongings. When I reached the tracks, the space between the wall and the track was also occupied by people who had their bedding and personal belongings neatly stacked against the wall. There were old people and many very young children. There must have been thousands of people in the underground living, eating and sleeping as if they were at home. I learned that most of these people were homeless and that what they had with them was all that was left of their possessions. Some had been there for years, perhaps some of the children might have been born next to the rails. When traveling through London it was strange to see perfectly good buildings completely empty yet showing no sign of destruction. It was difficult to understand until one read the sign on the door that stated that an unexploded bomb was in its basement.

The all-clear sounded and I returned to my taxi. The driver had preceded me. I took my coat that I had left behind and left him standing by his vehicle. I supposed he knew what I was thinking. I walked the rest of the way.

One never knew when or where these "buzz-bombs" would fall. Psychologically, the population paid a very high price. On the surface most appeared brave and determined, however certain ones were not so courageous.

I managed to date one of the girls of the Prince of Wales. As prearranged, we met away from the hotel and went to the U.S. Officer's Club. We had a good time and were walking back to the hotel when the alert sounded. Almost immediately we heard the putt-putt of the bomb and saw the search lights looking for the intruder. My date, who up to that time had been as calm as could be, became hysterical. She pushed me down against a wall and, whimpering, she also lay down on the sidewalk close to the wall.

I never expected this kind of behavior. The all-clear sounded and after shaking the dust of our cloths we continue on our way. That was my first and last date in London during the blitz.

———————

Suddenly I was awakened by the rat-a-tat of the 50-caliber machine gun firing from the plane's rear turret. I bolted upright.

"No problem," said the dispatcher. "He's testing his weapon, just in case."

This was very reassuring! I felt more at ease and for a while I sat admiring the stars as we flew above a cloud bank. We had not reached the middle of the English Channel when the monotonous grinding of the engines made my torpor return.

You've Made It!

In London I eventually joined a group of 29 American soldiers who had, as I, recently emigrated from European countries or had been reared by emigrant parents and so were fluent in their native language. The 29 of us were told that we had been selected for special training because of our qualifications. Besides three of us graduates of Fort Ritchie, the others had been selected from already trained Army personnel. However, before the training stage, we would be going through an assessment program to determine our true qualifications and our eventual roles. We were driven 45 minutes from London to an old English manor with ivy covering the walls and loose gravel in the huge driveway. This was the beginning of the strangest situation in which I had ever found myself.

Before entering this new training program I was—as I suppose were all of our group— interviewed for about ten minutes by an officer by the name of Buckmaster, a typical gangly British Colonel. It was he who, at Churchill's request, had organized the French section of Special Operations Executive (SOE), the British wartime equivalent to our current CIA. We were told that, from now on, we were not to discuss our activities or to engage in discussion related to our past with no one. I do not know if the Colonel asked the same questions of all of us. In my case his questions were quite innocuous. Finally

Holmwood Hall, England. OSS Area H Main 413 Training location.

he asked me to squat in front of him and one of his aides. I was quite puzzled but I obliged. He had no further instructions and to this day I have no idea as to why he asked me to squat, but it must have had some value as an assessment tool.

One of our group was Dr. William Morgan, a captain who later would become a renowned psychologist and author of a book entitled *Assessment of Men*. His job was to monitor the British system of personnel appraisal. He would eventually return to the U.S. to organize the same system for our Army.

The British Intelligence assessment program was rather interesting. It lasted three days, and consisted of a series of situations that we faced either individually or as a group. These involved crossing a small stream without getting wet, climbing a wall too high to reach the top, and crossing a simulated mine field. I led a patrol through enemy territory. I was placed into a room in an old castle, forced to make a seemingly impossible escape.

For the final situation the entire group had to devise a game entirely different from anything we knew, and establish rules and direction. The fun really began and there were more arguments, and more bickering between us, than at any time. While this was going on, we had British officers observing us and taking notes without saying a single word. At the end we learned that we were not graded, only that some passed and others did not.

I was one of the fortunate nine selected for real training as a saboteur and guerrilla organizer. It did not make the Army very happy, because they felt that their selection and their training had been more than adequate That is when we learned that I and the other eight were assigned to the Office of Strategic Services (OSS) but under the operational control of the British. Thank God, because our pay was a lot better than that of the British!

Our training lasted over a two month period, spent almost entirely in Scotland in an ancient manor, the Traigh House, located close to Mallaig. The rigorous training was conducted by British

Traigh House, Scotland, SOE Commando Training School

commandos. At 5:30 a.m. we were awakened by an orderly—referred to as a "batman" by the British— who also brought each of us a cup of hot, bitter coffee. We each had our own room and our batman saw to it that our clothing was cleaned and pressed. This was the life, the kind of life that the officers of the U.S. Army had enjoyed before the war. It was hard to believe that only a few months before I had been peeling potatoes!

By 6:00 a.m. we were on the road led by a drill sergeant for a six to ten mile run. At first we ran without gear, then later with a full pack. Periodically we would stop for 10 to 50 pushups. In a week or so we were in real top shape. On our return, we had a hearty breakfast and we headed to the class room for instructions on the art of blowing bridges, destroying locomotives and communicating by wireless radio.

Once running on the road became easy for us, they took us to the shore and made us run in soft sand. That was murder on our leg muscles, but we improved our stamina and resistance. The obstacle course was one of the toughest I had seen. It covered more than a mile and involved activities from climbing trees, passing from one tree to another on two ropes, to sliding down a 100-foot cliff on an inclined rope. We were sometimes timed on the course in competition. In addition to the obstacles we had tasks to perform between stations. One task was to shoot at a target immediately after sliding down the rope from the top of a cliff. That required the use of a completely different set of muscles. At the final stage I managed two bull's eyes out of three shots which surprised the heck out of me.

All of us had to learn the basic technique of radio communication including Morse code. Every day for a couple hours we listened and sent class room messages until we were able to recognize the difference between a "dit" and a "dat" in the event our assigned radio-man was killed or incapacitated.

Of course, the time we spent in Scotland was not all work; we had our share of fun, particularly on Sunday which was always a day off for us. Some of us went to church, some slept late, but all were present at the luncheon that was presided over by the Commanding Officer, a Colonel, and one or more guests, mostly high ranking officers of the War Office or SHAEF Headquarters. Before we were served, the piper would play Scottish tunes walking slowing around the single long table. After half an hour of ear-piercing sounds, the piper would stop by the Colonel sitting at the head of the table and receive a tumbler full of Scotch whiskey. He would down it in one gulp, turn bright red, click his heels, salute the Colonel smartly, and leave, straight as an arrow. I could never understand how a man could do that, because at that time half a jigger of whiskey made me sick. The luncheon lasted close to two hours after which we retired to the small obstacle course located next to the manor to get rid of some of the calories we had accumulated during lunch.

Our training also taught us to operate small boats and row large fishing dories. The Royal Navy took us into one of the lochs and demonstrated the arts of sailing and navigating. One day when the sea was rough we took a large rowboat on the outlet of Loch Morrar. For a couple hours we had to row up the Loch, and by the time we reach our destination, the inside of our hands was full of blisters. I nearly became seasick, and was glad when we were ordered to climb a nearby mountain whose top was in the clouds.

A good portion of our training involved the handling and the use of explosives. The most popular explosive was Composition C, or plastic explosive. Unlike TNT or dynamite which are very sensitive, Composition C was very stable, requiring a special system to detonate. Because a detonator alone would not cause the plastic to explode, a primer was needed between the detonator and the explosive. To prove to us that the plastic was safe to handle, our instructor fired his pistol into it, and nothing happened.

One of our eventual tasks would involve disrupting the German's lines of communication. As the railroads were a most important part of their transportation, we would have to do something to either stop or slow their rail movements. Blowing the rails was one of the easiest and most effective way of doing it. We had a substantial supply of rails on which to practice. The ideal characteristic of plastic explosive was that it could be molded into any shape. It could be made to resemble a tool, a bolt, a part of a machine, even painted to match the area where it was to be used. In addition, the explosive was so powerful that only a small amount was needed to do a thorough job. For example, to destroy a rail it took only two small pieces the size of golf balls placed on both sides of the rail but positioned so as to not face each other. The explosion would bend one part of the rail one way and the other part the other way, thus shearing the rail neatly.

Another item on our training program was the destruction of locomotives. For this we were driven by lory to the railroad yard of Mallaig where we were shown how operate a locomotive. We even operated one just so that we would know what to do in the event we had to use one or steal one. The theory concerning the attack on a locomotives was to damage it enough to make it inoperative for a while, but not so much as to make it useless in the future. To achieve this it was decided that only one part of the locomotive, common to all locomotives regardless of type, would be destroyed. The same part, the right piston rod, would be ruined on all steam locomotives attacked. Before long, Germany would be without spare right piston rods, while they might have had a surplus of left piston rods. With less than one pound of Composition C, a locomotive could be sidelined for a long time.

To make our training more realistic, and get us used to operating under extreme conditions, often in the dark, we were ordered to wear welder's glasses. Even under the noon sun, it was difficult to distinguish one object from another, This was extremely dangerous when handling explosive devices. I am certain that our instructors, who were not wearing welder's glasses, watched us very, very closely.

The telephone was also a very important aspect of Germany's communication system throughout Europe. Cutting telephone lines was relatively easy, but lines were also easy to repair because one could see where the cut had been made. The recommended system was to do no cutting, but instead to discover where the cable could easily be reached. A small hole was made into the lead cable and a drop of water or acid dropped in the hole. Soon there would be a short. But it was impossible for the repair crew to find the short, and required them to dig up the entire underground cable.

The day of graduation came all too quickly. The banquet was unusually good, but the piper and the traditional speeches were the same. After the meal the Colonel decided to have Scottish dancing. Normally, these dances included girls. Having none available, the colonel decided that half of us would take their coats off and be the "girls" and those who kept their coats would be the "boys." Fortunately, the Scotch we had consumed helped kill the inhibition for most of us.

We had a ball and after the dancing, one of the guests, a Scottish officer wearing a kilt, decided that all present should go on the obstacle course. The course included a horizontal bar over which one had to pass by hooking one leg over the bar and swinging the other leg until one reached the upright position. That was the day when I realized that there was not much hidden under a Scotsman's kilt.

A few days later we were on the train back to London for some additional training.

Occupied France

A voice in the intercom said: "Look below, they're shelling the coast. Probably our Navy."

We had reached the continent, and, crossing over the coast of France, we could see the fires on the ground below. The Allied navies were shelling the German installations along the coast. So far, so good, but it did not take long for conditions to change. Suddenly small reddish puffs of smoke surrounded us. Our aircraft began to take evasive action—climbing, diving and zigzagging—to escape the anti-aircraft barrage and the searchlights which were relentlessly seeking us.

Without a proper seat, it was difficult for me to remain steadfast on my wobbly pack. I held on for dear life to a rib of the fuselage. The dispatcher did not seem affected by this dancing. Apparently he had been through similar situations before and stood like a sailor on a bucking ship. Thanks to our non-reflective black paint the Germans failed to visually locate our aircraft, and we proceeded to our destination.

We descended to obtain a better view of the ground below. Occasionally the moon would peak from behind small clouds and its light would reveal the ground below. Nothing appeared familiar to me! After all that zigzagging to elude the searchlights, I had strong reservations about our actual position. Through the dispatcher I questioned the navigator several times, but he assured me the area was as familiar to him as the palm of his hand and he knew where we were. Furthermore, as this was their last mission, he said that all would be well and not to worry.

My flask of "courage" was returned much lighter. Concerned with my destination, I stuffed it into my inside pocket.

A while later, the navigator announced that we were approaching our destination. The intercom instructed me and the dispatcher to get ready. I removed the earphones and stood up to get into my parachute. From that moment on I was in the hands of the dispatcher. He adjusted the harness of the chute to make sure that I was wearing it correctly. The cover over the "Joe" hole, located behind the bomb bay, was removed and a swish of cool air rushed into the cabin. The heavy crates to be dropped with me and my suitcases were brought up closer to the hole and the static line of the parachutes attached to each were hooked securely.

The sound of the engine changed. The aircraft began to fly a wide circle to divert the attention of the enemy and conceal the actual location of the drop zone.

Through the port hole and through the Joe hole, I could see the topography of the ground below bathed in the moonlight. None of the landmarks that I had carefully studied and memorized from maps and aerial photos were visible. The wind blast and grinding noise of the engines increased with the change of the pitch of the propellers as flaps and wheels were lowered to slow down the aircraft. I assumed the pilot had received the correct signal from the ground. I was the last cargo. One more check of my chute and I swung my feet into the hole. The ready signal showed red, then green. A pat on the back and I went through the hole.

It seemed that I had just left the plane when I was already on the ground—fortunately in one piece! When I left the aircraft, we should have been flying at an altitude of 600 feet, but judging by the short duration of my descent, I estimate our altitude to have been less than 400 feet. It was also fortunate that the release of my parachute had been governed by the static line, otherwise very likely I would not now be in a position to recount these events.

All around me I could see containers on the ground with their chutes barely opened. The noise of the engines faded and disappeared in the night. I was alone in an overpowering silence broken only by barking of dogs in the distance. I hoped that any moment someone would rush to me with a glass of good wine welcoming my arrival.

Where was my reception party? Where were those awaiting my arrival, as I was told they would be? Were they prisoners of the Germans? Were they dead? These and other equally frightening questions filled my mind.

In the semi-obscurity before me, I noticed a fence post approximately nine feet high, its tip as sharp as a pencil's! Behind me was another, and yet another, side by side. The field was covered with posts! Fortunately for me I had hit the ground between two of these. I thought, "It's a great start! René, you are lucky, you could have been skewered!" It was around 1 o'clock in the morning, the air was cool and windless. I reached into my junp suit for the flask - opened it. It was empty! I supposed the crew needed courage more than I did. They had to face flack on their way back to England. In semi-darkness and total silence I tried to remember what I was told to do in a case such as this . . .

––––––––––

One very important phase of our training took place at the British Airborne school of Ringway, near Manchester. Our training was quite different from that given at the U.S. Army airborne training school at Fort Benning. We learned that we would be wearing one parachute and not two as in the U.S. Army. We also discovered that we would have a quick release system with which to escape our harness very quickly. We also learned that we would be jumping out of an old bomber called the Lancaster. We were all in very

Dunham House OSS/SOE Secret training Station 51A near Manchester close to landing field at Tatton Park.

good shape, so it was not too difficult to keep up with the regular airborne troops training with us. Jumping from a ten-foot wall and rolling without breaking anything proved to be not so difficult.

The most frightening exercise we were put through was the "windbreak," a contraption installed on the fourth floor of an open tower. It consisted of a fan approximately four feet in diameter. Its blades were parallel to the axis of the fan to create resistance. Attached to the shaft was a drum two feet in diameter and one foot wide around which a cable was rolled. At the end of the cable, a harness—similar to a parachute's—was attached. In the center of the top floor of the structure was a hole four foot wide. Directly above the hole, the cable passed through a pulley before terminating at the harness.

Strapped into the harness and sitting with my feet dangling into the hole, I waited for the signal to jump. It felt like jumping into emptiness until the cable became taunt and gradually increased its tension (resulting from the resistance caused by the increasing speed of the fan) so that when you reached the floor it miraculously deposited you tenderly on a pile of sand. After the first jump I wanted to do it again just to experience the thrill!

The day of the actual training jump from the aircraft came, and our breakfast consisted mostly of a thick pudding which, we were told, was guaranteed to make us bounce in the event our parachute failed to open! It settled in my stomach and felt like a solid brick. The Lancaster was certainly not designed for airborne training; it was a bomber. Ours had been modified to hold as many as a half-dozen men. The bomb bay had been welded closed and in its place was a strongly reinforced hole approximately four feet in diameter. So low was the ceiling of the fuselage that it was impossible to stand upright. Our instructor checked our gear, making sure that everything was okay. He was not wearing a chute, but carried a small umbrella. As he jumped back and forth over the hole he informed us that he was so well trained that he did not need a parachute, that he could do just as well with his small "brelly."

The noise of the engines made it impossible to hear anything. Looking through the hole we could see the English countryside all green with white dots, probably sheep or perhaps cattle. Only four of us would jump at each pass over the drop zone. My turn came and I swung my feet into the hole and at the signal straightened my body and pushed myself into the middle of the hole. It happened so fast I did not have the time to realize what was happening. The noise of the engines faded away, and I was dangling below a huge umbrella, seemingly motionless. I looked below and watched the ground, the good old earth, coming toward me at an increasingly fast speed. I heard voices from a bullhorn telling me to bring my feet together, to bend my knees and to get ready to roll when I reached the ground. The pasture where we jumped finally reached me, fortunately rather gently.

"Boy, that was fun."

I was ready to do it that afternoon after a good luncheon with, for dessert, the leftover pudding we had for breakfast.

We jumped approximately one dozen times during training including twice at night. My most unforgettable jump was the one with a 60-pound bag strapped to my harness. The object was to jump and, once the parachute was open, to release the bag. The bag would then dangle below the jumper, greatly reducing the tendency to swing back and forth. When the bag hit the ground it would also break the fall, making the landing softer.

When my turn came I was in the ready position with my feet dangling into the hole of the plane. At the signal I tried to push myself into the hole but my chute caught the edge and held me back. I tried in vain to free myself. I motioned to the dispatcher and indicated my problem. He gave me a push, but instead of sliding smoothly down the hole, I hit the other side with my face and fainted. I remember hearing the bull horn calling my number and giving me instructions but I was in a daze. All I remember hearing is "Number 10 . . . Number 10 . . . NUMBER 10! Bring your feet together, number 10! Release the bag, number 10!"

I somehow managed to release the bag but was as limp as a rag doll and felt quite unlike the strapping paratrooper I had begun to envision myself. Those on the ground knew that there was something wrong with me, but they did not know what until they reached me and noticed my bloody face and the blood all over my parachute. They laid me down, the ambulance came and the doctor kept asking me questions: what did I have for lunch, what did I

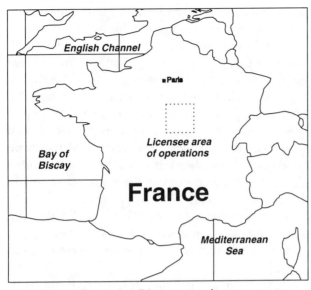

Operation Licensee territory

have for breakfast, what did I do yesterday. I could not understand what this had to do with my banging my nose on the side of the hole. They suspected a brain concussion. I was released almost immediately with cotton in my nostrils.

The most thrilling experience in jumping was night jumping. The night jumps were safer because you did not know when you would hit the ground. As a result one would be more relaxed and less apt to break a bone. We were told that in the event we were about to land on a body of water it was safer to release our harness before reaching the water. That way our parachute would not cover us and cause us to drown. We had a few small rivers in the area, but none so large that we would likely fall in it.

One night, the moon was full and the ground was bathed in moonlight. From 700 feet, the roads, particularly those covered with asphalt, reflected the light and looked like streams. That night we had one accident. One of our men, a fellow weighing well over 250 pounds, mistook a road for a river. He released his harness twenty feet above ground, waited until he was approximately 15 feet off the surface, and let go. Both of his ankles were broken. The war was over for him.

The Allies had already landed and were securing the beaches along the Normandy coast. Montgomery was held back while our own forces were trying to move deeper inland. Finally, a week later, I received orders to be ready to join a group in central France. The group I was to join already had an SOE agent radio operator. My operations officer gave me very little information other than locating the drop zone and telling me that my final instructions would come from the field. The individual I was to join was a French member of SOE whose code name was "Léon." I was given a detailed description of him and a recognition code to make certain that I would not be taken in by an impostor. I was also told that Léon had a scar on the corner of his lower lip. The supplies I was to bring along would be in containers, but my personal belonging would be in two seemingly well-traveled suitcases.

I had been measured from head to toes by two tailors who spoke with definite German or Jewish accents. The material they used was from France as were the thread and buttons. After several measuring sessions the clothes were made and they placed the suits into a machine to age them, adding some dust they had collected from European refugees. My documents were prepared with care using stamps that came either from Europe or had been duplicated by expert forgers. Once the documents were completed, they were also aged so that they looked well worn when I received them. I had clothes for all occasions, including a U.S. Army uniform in the event I had to rejoin the Allied Forces or had to impress someone with my position.

I was also provided with approximately 250,000 French Francs. The currency had been printed by the British, presumably utilizing printing plates either stolen or borrowed from the French mint, as the notes were indistinguishable from the real thing.

Experts helped me prepare a cover story that would match the documented information. I had to learn and remember what existed in the areas where I was supposed to have traveled. The latest information acquired through air photos or interrogation of escapees was provided so that I would be up to date with my cover story. In addition, I consulted maps and aerial photos of the area where I would operate. I located and checked the drop zone where I was to land to get an idea of the topography in the event I was lost. SOE headquarters was in constant contact with the field and the two commands had to agree as to when I would be dropped. The conditions had to be good so as to make the drop as safe as possible.

Finally, the date and the time were agreed upon. One afternoon I was alerted for final preparations. A coded message was sent to the field via the BBC advising them of my arrival that very night. It was to be hoped that they were listening and were making the preparations.

I had no doubt that during the training and briefings I had received all possibilities had been covered, except for my present situation! What does one do when there is no one to greet him?

Lost

I began folding my parachute when in the distance I heard faint voices. People were coming toward me. I palmed my little Colt 32 that was tucked in my belt and I waited. The voices were coming closer and becoming more distinctive, yet I could not recognize the language! It was not French, it was not German, and of course it was not English either. There were two individuals who spotted me and approached, pointing long rifles in my direction.

They were actually very small. At first glimpse, I thought they were children. Then, as they came closer, to my great surprise both seemed to be Chinese! They were definitely Asians. "Merde," I thought, "the flight crew dropped me on the wrong continent, I am probably in China." I knew it! Our navigator did not know where he was, and very possibly it was because shortly before jumping, my flask of "Fine Scotch" had been returned . . . empty! With their rifles pointing in my direction and appearing as surprised to see me as I them, the two Chinese motioned me to follow them while they mumbled something about "conteneur vivant" (a live container).

I grabbed my parachute, replaced the little .32 in my belt, and followed one of the Chinese while the other brought up the rear. We walked approximately a quarter of a mile from one field to another along the tree-lined edges until we reached a large oak tree. Underneath the tree stood an individual dressed in the light blue uniform of the French Colonial Army. Perhaps I was in Indochina! His presence reassured me somewhat. At least he was not a German soldier.

"Qu'est ce que vous faite ici?"

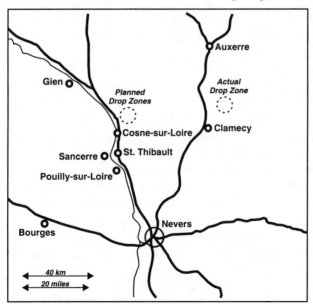

Drop Zones of Operation Licensee

(What are you doing here?)

"Est ce que vous m'attendiez?" (Were you waiting for me?)

"Non, où alliez vous?" (No, where were you going?)

I gave him my destination, the town of Annay. According to him I was approximately forty kilometers off course. At that moment I would have preferred to be in Indochina.

My host did not know "Léon," and he had never heard of him. Even my description of "Léon" meant nothing to him at all. This was most bizarre. What was my host doing at 1:00 a.m. in the middle of a muddy field under an oak tree. He stated that often when he and his group heard aircraft flying low in the area they would signal with flash lights. Sometimes they would receive container-loads of supplies; sometime they would not.

"Et votre radio?" (What about your radio?)

"On n'en a pas." (We have none.)

"Est ce que vous écoutez la BBC?" (Does your group monitor the BBC?)

"Quelques fois!" (Sometimes!)

I had a strong feeling that something was terribly wrong with all this and hoped that one day I would find out what was behind this confusion.

"What about the equipment that was dropped with me?"

"Don't worry, we'll take care of it. Come with me."

By that time, several members of the group had joined us under the oak tree. The leader who had greeted me wore a captain's uniform. He gave orders while I removed my jump suit and head gear and handed it and my parachute to one of his men. We left the oak tree and moved out along the fields. We walked another mile or so to a secondary road that led to a small village composed mainly of farm houses. We stopped by one of the farms close to the road and entered the court yard.

Quietly, the captain opened the back door. We went in and climbed squeaky stairs to the second floor. The room in which I was to spend the rest of the night was very small. Full of junk and very dusty, it must have been used for storage. A small cot stood in one end and a 25-watt bulb near the ceiling gave the room an eerie cast. I placed the Colt under the gray pillow. In case I had to move out quickly I decided to keep my pants on, along with the money belt that contained a large sum of Francs.

Alone in this miserable closet of a room, I tried to analyze my predicament. Finally, after familiarizing myself with the many noises of the house, exhausted and weary I fell asleep with one eye open, so to speak.

A short time later, I was abruptly awakened by a terrific noise coming from the road below my window. Peeking through the dusty curtains, what I saw caused my heart to rise into my throat. A column of trucks full of German soldiers was passing slowly on the road under my window not twenty feet away from where I was standing. The reality of my situation hit hard in my stomach. A few hours ago I had been surrounded by friends; now I was smack in the middle of the enemy with friends of questionable loyalties!

Was I dreaming? Not this time. I was fully awake, and my legs were shaking. My first reaction was to expect the worst. What would I do if the convoy should stop, and the German soldiers decide to come into the house?

I possessed two items that needed to be disposed of immediately: the Colt .32 and the money. I began to search the room for a hiding place, at the same time trying to think of an alibi although try as I might, my mind refused to formulate one. By the time I had figured out a passable explanation, the convoy had passed and silence returned. My breathing returned to normal and my heart assumed its usual location.

Lying awake on the cot, I began to wonder if the daily raids on London had been preferable to the close proximity of the German Army. I began to reflect on the training I had received.

Preparations

After the airborne training, wearing both the American and British paratrooper wings we had received, we returned to London. After having been discharged honorably as privates, four of us were told to report to the Supreme Headquarters Allied Expeditionary Forces (SHAEF). There, in a dark hallway, while an aide read the general orders, an American general pinned gold bars on our shoulders. We were now Second Lieutenants of the Army of the United States. General Eisenhower personally made the presentation, presumably because we were about to undertake what was expected to be a suicide mission.

At that point we were not aware of the dangers facing us. We were told only about the successful missions and advised that if we did as we were instructed we would be all right. Our confidence was very high. It never entered my mind that what I was about to do could be fatal! Unbeknownst to us, at that time the British were losing approximately 90% of their agents and so it was fully expected that few if any of us would return alive.

Then it was off to the Quartermaster for our new class-A uniforms! These consisted of dark green jacket and pink trousers. The bright shiny gold bars looked and felt mighty good on our shoulders. We were certain that the girls would notice us a lot more than before. The $120 clothing allowance did not

SOE Agents. From left to right: Lt. Michel Block, British Agent, Polish Agent, Lt. René Défourneaux.

go far, but the new pay—amounting to $250 per month that included the jump pay to which we were now entitled—made us among the best paid soldiers in the Allied Forces. This pay was almost the equivalent to that of a plain Brigadier General. Furthermore, we would soon also be entitled to additional hazardous duty pay.

We did not wear our uniforms very long. Our next order of business was to learn our "tradecraft," as the British would call it, before we could be assigned a mission. Wearing civilian clothing we were transported to a house located not far from London in the vicinity of Ruislip, close to a U.S. air base. We began by practicing the art of determining if we were being followed, and the methods to lose what we referred to as a "tail." During one of these exercises I was supposed to pick up a written message taped under a small shelf in a telephone booth. It was raining, and, wearing a raincoat, I walked on the sidewalk of a business section of a medium-sized town whose name I do not recall. I pretended to do some window shopping. Meanwhile, I watched the other side of the road in the reflection for someone doing the same.

Indeed, after a while I noticed an individual going through the same motions on the opposite sidewalk. Sure enough, he was observing me. I used several methods to lose him, but he evidently knew the town better than I did and he would constantly reappear. Exasperated, I decided to go ahead and retrieve the message from the telephone booth. I entered the booth as naturally as I could, but when I looked at the phone I realized that the system was quite different from the one with which I was familiar. I fumbled with the few coins I had in my pocket.

The booth was all glass and when I looked out, the man who had been following me was standing next to the booth looking at me. I ignored him, but felt certain that he knew exactly what I was doing. My raincoat was draped over my right arm. Carefully I slid my hand under the shelf and felt for the piece of paper that was supposed to be there. Sure enough I found it, rolled it into the palm of my hand, replaced the coins in my pocket and left the booth.

My escort was still behind me, but I no longer cared because I was certain that he had seen what I did in the phone booth. Eventually I returned to our base for the critique. When my turn came the individual who had followed me gave his report, stressing that I tried to shake him but that I had failed. He never mentioned the telephone booth other than stating that I appeared to have a problem with the telephone. He had not seen me picking up the message! That was the most important part of the operation.

Next I was given an assignment that took me to Bristol. There I was to find a place to live, and penetrate the offices of the BBC, through their garbage! Bristol was a busy place, full of many troops, mostly American, waiting to get into the war in Europe. When I reached Bristol, I found that hotel rooms were nonexistent. I walked the streets aimlessly until I became so tired that I sat on a park bench and tried to determine where I would spend the night. Next to me sat an individual who asked me for a light. He noticed my accent and asked me what I was doing. Of course I gave him my cover story. Then I told him about my problem, apparently not an unusual one in Bristol. He suggested that not too far from where we were sitting was a rooming house that might have rooms for rent.

I followed his advice and sure enough there was a sign, a small one I might add, which said only "Rooms." I rang the door bell and a woman in her forties opened the door. I asked if she had a room for a few days. She said that she did and showed me a very small room with a bed, a chair and a dresser. There was also a fireplace but it was covered by a piece of plywood. This was perfect for me.

The place had a living room that was empty when I first came in around three in the afternoon. By five o'clock several people, mostly GIs, and a few girls had arrived. They were drinking whiskey, which was very difficult to get in those days, and I soon discovered that they were buying it on the premises. The house had approximately a dozen rooms spread on three floors. I soon realized that this was not an ordinary rooming house.

The first night was uneventful. The next day was spent on a reconnaissance of the area and of my target, and in preparation of a meeting I was to have with a contact in a certain hotel lobby. The purpose of the contact was to pass on the information that I had accumulated up to that time. I proceeded to the appointed location at the time indicated, prepared with the signs prescribed for recognition. I was standing at the appropriate position when a good-looking girl in her late twenties came up to me. She addressed me by my cover name, shook my hand as if she had known me all her life! This was certainly not the way we learned to make contact with unknown individuals. I casually introduced the designated code words into the conversation, but got no response from her. She kept telling me that she knew about me from some common friends, and that she was very pleased to meet me and suggested that we have a drink at the bar. The time of the meeting had passed and I had no way of getting rid of her, so I invited her for dinner. She accepted readily and during the meal she kept asking me questions about myself. I gave her my cover story and went on the attack, asking her a multitude of questions before she had a chance to ask me more. I obtained her name, where she came from, what she did and where she stayed while in Bristol. She stayed in this same hotel in which we had met. After the meal we made a date for the following day.

I returned to my rooming house, which by that time was full of American soldiers and their respective girl friend for the night (or the hour). The next day I called the hotel and was told that the young lady I had been with the night before had checked out the previous evening. Very likely headquarters had sent her after me to see how I would react in an unexpected situation. I was carrying some very compromising material, so I decided to hide it somewhere, preferably in my room. After searching a while, I discovered a loose brick in the unused fire place. Better yet, it had a hole behind it! Every day when I left the room I would place my notes and codes in the hole and replace the brick and the wood panel.

Scotland Yard

On the third afternoon I returned to the rooming house. The landlady told me that she had need of my room and had moved my personal belongings to another. The new room was about the same size as the other—but without the fireplace! How could I get my papers from the other room, which by now was occupied? I went to bed, leaving this problem for the next day. At one o'clock in the morning, there was a knock at my door. Before I could open it, three men barged in, announcing that they were from Scotland Yard. "Do you have any identification?" they asked.

As two of them perused my false papers, the other made a thorough search of the room. "Would you mind getting dressed and coming with us," they said calmly. With wobbly knees, I got dressed, then they took my suitcase and all of my possessions and placed them and me in a waiting car.

We reached the offices of Scotland Yard in the early morning and I was placed in a cold, windowless cell with a hard steel bench in the center of the room. I was still sleepy so I lay down on the bench and listened to the noises of the building. I had never been in jail before and the isolation and the tenuous nature of my situation prevented me from relaxing enough to sleep. In my mind I kept wondering how they had found me. Did the landlady turn me in? Did she find the material I had hidden in the fireplace? Perhaps my arrest was only part of the training exercise? In my mind I kept going over my cover story, making sure that it was logical and believable.

I had no idea how much time had passed when I was led to an interrogation room. One of the individuals who had arrested me was alone to start the ball rolling. Name, date of birth, place of birth, etc. No problem with it. Then he began to ask some very specific questions about my activities of the day before, then of the day before that and the day before that, all the while taking careful notes. I was supposed to be an employee of Martin Aircraft Company in consultation with a British firm assembling aircraft engines for Martin. Fortunately for me he knew nothing about aircraft engines so I was able to convince him, or so I thought. Then the second inspector came and started all over again.

By noon I was exhausted and hungry, but no one offered food or drink to me. By one in the afternoon, the first inspector returned and said very sadly that I had been lying to them. They knew that I was not an aircraft engine specialist, and that I was in England illegally. In view of this I had no alternative but to admit that indeed I was not telling the truth. However, instead of telling them who I really was, I moved to my second cover story.

I told them that I was a Frenchman who had escaped from occupied France and made my way from Spain to Bristol on a freighter. Once in England I had jumped ship and met two Americans who were working for the Martin Company. I also mentioned that I had friends in England whom I wanted to join, but that I had lost their address. Indeed, the ship that I mentioned, a neutral ship, had touched port a few days earlier and had come from Spain. The ship had left so there was no way for Scotland Yard to verify my story.

They actually believed me. To make sure that I was looked after properly, as I was a French citizen, they decided to send me to the Free French Headquarters where I would probably be inducted into the Free French Army. This would pose a serious problem for me, considering the fact that I was considered to be a draft dodger by the French army. By that time I also realized that this was definitely not part of the exercise and that I had gone far enough with the masquerade. I asked the first inspector to call a number which I had memorized. When the individual answered the phone as Whitehall, the inspector turned to me and said: "Are you a British Agent?"

I said, "No sir, but I may be someday." They were told to escort me to the railroad station and to provide the office with a copy of the interrogation. After this was over. They asked me if I knew that the place where they found me was a house of ill repute. I had been unaware of this just as they did not know that the place was selling whisky illegally. We parted friends. Had they found my compromising code book and the messages I had hidden in the other room, they might not have been so kind.

A Taste Of What Is Coming

Our training was coming to an end. One of the final tests involved the penetration of a building held by "enemy forces" personnel. The case involved three of us who were to retrieve a cipher from a building occupied by members of the British Armed Forces. Allegedly, the building was owned by a friendly agent who had been arrested and incarcerated pending an investigation. Before being taken away he had managed to hide his code book in the second floor bathroom of his house behind a pipe that ran close to the ceiling. If the enemy investigators were to discover his code book, he would surely be killed. So, we knew we must find it at all cost.

About one o'clock in the morning, three of us located the house. We noticed that the window of the second floor bathroom was open, but covered with a blackout curtain. Fortunately for us the weather was warm. I was the lightest of the three, so I was the one to climb over the other two to reach the window sill.

I was about to push the blackout curtain away and climb into the room, when I heard the door to the bathroom open. I froze, hanging on as best I could, with my nose against the curtains and my toes on the shoulders of the man under me. Soon I felt the warmth of a body just on the other side of the curtain. I heard a falling stream of liquid, a couple bursts of passing wind, and a drop of solid into a pool of water. The odor reached me about the time I heard some complaining from my cohorts below me. I heard paper being crumpled then the water rushing from the overhead tank. The door finally closed and I held my breath as I entered the now empty toilet. I quickly checked for the code book and found it at the indicated location.

I dropped it to my friends outside and, as I was about to leave through the window, I heard foot steps in the hall way. I immediately took my pants down, sat on the john and grunted as the door began to open. "Excuse me old chap," the man said.

I stayed there a few more minutes and, after flushing, decided to leave through the front door rather than by the way I entered. If the individual was waiting outside he would expect me to leave by the door, and not by the window. The place was dark, it was early in the morning and surely no one would care who came out of a john.

So I passed by the individual who did not look at me. I quickly walked down the stairs to the front door and rejoined my two friends waiting for me on the road. We laughed and joked about what we did, and told each other that no one would believe us.

It was about one o'clock in the morning when we returned to our mansion. We went to bed tired, but happy with our success.

It seemed that I had just fallen asleep when I was awakened by someone shaking me roughly. Looking up, I could not believe my eyes. A German soldier armed with a Schmizer submachine gun was standing over me and in broken English said to me, "Get up!" Another German soldier was standing by the door. I got up and looked for my clothes. He said, "Don't bother. Move! We're going downstairs!"

Wearing only my shorts and a T-shirt I went downstairs and toward the dining room guarded by two more fully armed German soldiers. When the door of the dining room opened, I could not believe my eyes. I had gone through it a few hours before and it had been an ordinary dining room, but now the room was completely different. On the back wall behind a long table covered with a green table-cloth were German flags bearing swastikas. Sitting behind the table were six German officers in full uniform, Iron Crosses and all.. I stood before them and was told to stand at attention. When I did not move fast enough I felt a sharp blow to my back. I straightened my back and waited.

The German officers were speaking among themselves in German. I understood some of the words but could not follow their conversation. Finally one said in accented English: "Where were you tonight?"

I replied as best as I could, reviewing in my mind my cover story.

"You lie," he interrupted. "You are an enemy agent and we are going to prove it."

I protested as best as I could, telling the interrogator that I did not know what he was talking about. Then another German officer began to quietly ask me about my name, where I was from, what I did, etc., while the one who had opened the interrogation glared at me with contempt.

After half an hour of friendly talk between the second interrogator and myself the first officer (the "bad cop" of this "good cop/bad cop" process) jumped up and with an accusing finger said, "You are a liar. What you have just said is a pack of lies and we are going to prove it. What is your real name?"

I could feel the warm breath of the German soldier behind me and I felt a sharp blow between the shoulder blades. "Answer," he ordered.

I repeated what I had told the second interrogator.

"We want the truth, not your fictitious story," he repeated. Then the second interrogator returned with his soft but identical questions. I repeated almost precisely what I had told him initially. The fourth officer, who had kept quiet up to that time, jumped up and said, "You see, you are a liar, you changed your story. You are a spy; it is written all over your face." Then the fun began.

I was certain that I had not changed my story and that, if I did, it was something that was not very important. He started to pick away at my cover story bit by bit. I stood my ground and if I did not know the answer I stated that I did not recall or that I had forgotten.

"Put your hands behind your head," he ordered. Then he said, "Lift your right knee up . . . higher, higher."

Standing on one leg, I began to lose my balance. I brought my right leg down but my failure to follow instruction was abruptly pointed out to me with a tap between the shoulder blades. The interrogation continued for a while longer until, unable to stand, I fell to the floor. I could not believe this was happening to me. I did not know any of these persons. Exhausted, I was beginning to believe that I had been kidnapped and taken to the enemy camp. Perhaps England had been invaded, and this was the beginning of he end. I kept thinking, "This is not real, this is part of the training." But there I was, huddling half naked on the floor with a submachine gun-toting German soldier staring over me.

Finally, two burly German soldiers picked me up and took me out of the room. They dropped me on the floor of the hallway and returned to their post. Left alone I climbed the stairs to my room. There was not a sound in the building. It seemed that the house was completely empty. I fell on my bed and closed my eyes.

When I woke up the sun was quite high. Normally we were up at the crack of dawn. I had slept until nine in the morning. I was certain that I had a nightmare, that I had imagined all this. The batman came in my room with my uniform neatly folded. "Good morning, Sir. Did you sleep well? There will be a staff meeting in half an hour in the dining hall," he said casually.

I had nothing to worry about so long as the batman was not upset by my sleeping late. After cleaning up, I descended the stairs fully expecting a contingent of German soldiers. The dining room was the same old dining room! No German flags. A few members of our group were already there drinking coffee and laughing. They looked at me quite strangely but said nothing. Then a group of British officers entered the room. They were not our instructors. They were unknown to me until I realized that they were the German officers who had interrogated me and pushed me around the night before. [In fact, one of these instructors was David Niven, who would later become a well known actor.]

Apparently all the others in our group had been subjected to the same treatment throughout the evening, and this was to be the critique. "Gentlemen," one of the new officer began, "take your seats. We are sorry if we have caused you any inconvenience during the last few days, but it is necessary to give you an idea of to how it feels when you are subjected to this type of interrogation. Hopefully you will never be placed in this position in the course of your activities behind the enemy lines." Each one of us was told where we had done well and where we had failed. Fortunately all of us did well enough and were congratulated.

Our next, and last, location was an old but comfortable house in the vicinity of Bath managed by Captain R. H. Harris. This was a place where we could rest and wait for our assignment.

Que Sera Sera

In the French farmhouse daylight came and I felt reassured, able to see where I was and to assess my situation more clearly. Opening the door carefully I left my hiding place, reaching the landing to find three little girls ranging from six to eleven years standing in night shirts by an open window. They looked at me, surprised. The youngest giggled while the other two stared. Then a woman in her forties appeared and shooed them away. She motioned me to the kitchen where my host was sitting before a piece of bread and a bottle of wine.

They were as surprised as I by the passing of the German column. Someone had tampered with the road signs ahead, something apparently done often to confuse the occupation forces. Soon thereafter I was moved away because this location was too dangerous for a new arrival. From that point, I slept on the hard (and sometimes wet) ground under brush, or in a ditch. Thankfully, I had managed to recover my parachute, which became my main protection against the elements.

Quickly, it became obvious to me that I was in a situation where there was little I could do. This group had no contact with the official French resistance movement. The Captain, whose name I do not recall, was in his forties. Athletic and energetic, he appeared to be in full control of his group composed of a few local residents as well as several outsiders. They were mavericks, but with a purpose; a purpose I did not yet comprehend. I had no way of communicating with London. And the people I was to join, although only 40 kilometers away, had no idea where I was. So I decided to stay with the group which had received me, and make the best of a bad situation. This group of two dozen was not well organized and continuously bickered among themselves.

The two "Chinese" who met me at the drop zone were actually Indochinese soldiers, known in France as Annamites. They were members of a French colonial unit demobilized after France surrendered. On the evening I arrived they evidently only expected weapons and supplies. They were surprised by the appearance of a live person; hence their reference to "conteneur vivant," a two-legged "container" as it were!

Most of the Annamite members of this unit were demobilized French soldiers not taken prisoner by the Germans. A few had been taken prisoner, but had escaped. These Annamites did their own thing, living in the woods and stealing food from isolated farms. Others had joined resistance groups to participate rather than just hiding. From time to time they would go out at night looking for isolated German soldiers, killing them, stripping them of their boots and bringing back their ears that they proudly displayed to the others of the group.

What shocked me most about this group of resistance fighters was their handling of a situation that was actually none of their business. They were supposed to fight the German occupation forces and their French allies, not to render "civil" justice.

Using a tortuous path, they brought me to the group sanctuary located in a small clearing to a thickly wooded area. I was not prepared to see what I was about to observe. A few bearded men were there smoking or doing odd chores ignoring what was in the center of the clearing. Two women perhaps in their thirties were sitting on the ground their backs against the trunk of a tree. Their hands and feet were bound, and their heads had been completely shaved. They appear normal except for their bare legs which had been horribly burned. Charred skin remained at the edge of the burns and I could see maggots on the wounds of one of them. As I stood before them they lifted their bowed heads and looked at me with indifference, but I saw the pain and resignation in their faces.

When I asked for an explanation I was told that these two women were collaborators and that they allegedly had slept with German soldiers. In addition they had supposedly identified members of the local resistance to German occupation forces, who promptly killed them. To make the women talk, plastic explosive had been lit between their legs. Although their "plastique" was very powerful, it was very stable and would not explode in contact with a flame. A detonator was necessary to set it off. However it burned readily, releasing much heat. Thus the members of the group had acted as prosecutor, judge and jury, but did not worry about rendering justice. Both women were found guilty and there were lengthy discussions about what to do with them. The cruelty of these people was unbelievable. There was no trial. No one took the defense of these two girls. I was tempted to interfere, but was afraid that in doing so I may have shared their fate. Finally it was decided that both would be put to death, and that they would be buried in unmarked graves at the edge of the woods in which the group's command post was secreted. I did not witness the executions, but apparently they were carried out because I never saw the women again.

The people I was with did not form a very cohesive group. Strangers—French, Polish, men, women—would come in, stay a few days, then leave. I was never taken into confidence about these arrangements.

One day a casual member of the group—a physician who made the rounds of resistance groups to tend to their health—told us that he had attended a meeting of some of the resistance chiefs of the region. During the meeting of a dozen people, he had noticed an individual who had remained in the shadow of the room, saying very little. The Doctor believed that someone had referred to him as "Léon," and that Léon may have had a small scar below his lower lip. Furthermore Léon was wearing a British captain's uniform.

Was this my "Léon?" I asked the Doctor if it was possible for him to reestablish contact with the group. He believed he could and a few days later he advised me that a meeting had been arranged. He would take me to a small village approximately sixty kilometers away. Of course this was easier said than done!

The Doctor had an old 1938 Citroën that had been modified to burn fuel from a charcoal burner attached to the side of the hood. The burner was loaded with charcoal which would be lit, then sealed. After a while, the starter would grind and the motor would come to life. This very precarious system permitted the car to move at a rather slow speed, but move nevertheless. Using dusty back roads to avoid encounters with German patrols or convoys, we proceeded slowly to our meeting place. Several hours later we reached the small village where the meeting was to take place.

It was very hot. In the center of the square the traditional fountain was dry. With the exception of four unarmed individuals standing by the fountain, the square was deserted as in a western town prior to a fast-draw showdown. Windows of the nearby houses were shuttered tight.

We parked under the shade of a Linden tree. The Doctor and I disembarked and approached the group. By his scar I recognized Léon immediately as one of the four people standing there. Taking me by the arm, he moved me away from the others. Despite the password I softly uttered, and the large sum of money I gave him, he barely said "bonjour" to me and immediately led me to a barn. Locking me in a pigsty whose previous occupants had just left for the smoke-house, Léon left me behind with the pigs' characteristic perfume.

Alone, dejected and apprehensive, I could not understand why I was treated in such way. I had given the correct password and received the proper countersign: Why was I locked in a pigsty? During training we were told that the Germans had on occasion penetrated the French underground. The entire unit might be under the control of the Gestapo or, even worse, the dreaded French Milice.

What a way to return to the country I had left four years earlier! I decided not to let this bother me but to concentrate on my new identity and play my role.

Léon Prévost (Capt. Dupres)

Before nightfall an old woman came with some food. I ate, but was not really hungry. Later that evening Léon began a series of interrogations to determine if I was for real, or a German agent sent to penetrate his team, as had been the case in several instances in Northern France and in Holland.

The pilot of the B-24 had reported that I had jumped all right according to plan, and that he had received the correct signal from the ground. Léon had heard the BBC broadcast and had been waiting for me at the prearranged location. He reported that I did not show up. London immediately pushed the panic button. They were certain I had been taken prisoner by the Germans who would make a switch; the Germans would replace me with one of their own men after extracting from me as much information as necessary. For this reason, they advised Léon to be very careful in the event someone showed up claiming to be Daniel, my code name, or Julien Delpereaux of Lyon, my cover identity. Thus Léon had to make certain of my identity before accepting me.

A code name is used one time only as a means of recognition at a specific point in time. A cover identity is the one by which an individual is known in a particular locality, usually over an extended period of time. Cover identities were normally "borrowed" from real people. In this way, in the event the Germans would have checked on me in a cursory fashion (through telephone listings, birth records, etc.), they would have found that there was indeed a Julien Delpereaux residing in Lyon.

Unbeknownst to me and to add to the problem, the group who had intercepted me was not very popular with Léon, who suspected them—correctly I believe—to be a Communist organization masquerading as FFI (Forces Françaises de l'Intérieur). My presence with this group was doubly disturbing to Léon. I had firmly believed that I would be greeted as a hero for having reached my destination despite all adversities. Instead, I found myself in a pigsty, being treated as an enemy or worse. I suspected that something was very wrong. Judging by the questions Léon was asking me I realized that my identity was in jeopardy. I did not know what story to tell, not knowing what London was asking. Was I supposed to reveal my true identity or was I to stick to my cover story? After all, Léon was not the enemy!

At first I gave him my cover story and was promptly returned to the pigsty. The next morning I repeated the same but it did not appear to satisfy him. He kept asking about my mother, and my cover story had made me an orphan. After numerous sessions I decided that I should play it straight. I gave him my real mother's maiden name. Finally, after many hours of interrogation and numerous messages between Léon and our London headquarters, the door of the pigsty opened, and I was accepted with open arms.

I learned later that the area where I landed was populated by resistance groups not entirely supportive of the Western Allies. They were planning unilaterally for the time when the war would be over and France would be up for grabs. They hoped that France would become a Communist country as most of the eastern European countries would eventually become. Failing to obtain support from the Western Allies, and Russia being in no position to help at that time, these groups penetrated the resistance organizations supported by the British and the French. Stealing the codes for locations of the drop zones, they eventually collected large amounts of supplies, weapons and ammunition. To prevent such occurrence, a better system of communication was later established with the use of a rudimentary radar and S-phone which permitted the people on the ground to identify themselves and direct the planes to their proper destination.

As for the field where I landed, it had been an airstrip used by the Germans. They had abandoned it a few weeks earlier and—to prevent its use by the Allies' planes, gliders and paratroopers—they had planted sharpened posts as obstacles. London did not know of the existence of this airfield, and even if they had, it would not have been mentioned to the pilot who had not intended to drop me there in the first place. An error in navigation, compounded by the rogue band's duplicitous use of their flashlights, was to blame for my near catastrophe.

Operation Licensee

Throughout France, perhaps hundreds of small bands of French maquis-ards (resistance fighters) had organized themselves behind German lines. Some were recognized and supported by SHAEF, while others were not. A London-based French General by the name of Marie Pierre Koenig was in command of the FFI and was responsible for coordinating the efforts of the various Maquis with SHAEF.

"Licensee" was the code name assigned the resistance group that had been organized by the famous American operative, Virginia Hall, known within the French resistance only as "Diane." Diane allegedly made several trips behind German lines and was known by many throughout France as a person of exemplary courage. After the War, she was revered throughout France. Despite all of this, I was not even aware of her existence prior to hearing her name referenced by various members of our band. In listening to their glowing descriptions of her, I could not understand how an individual with no military experience could be so astute in organizing the resistance. Only later, when I had to opportunity to meet her, did I comprehend the depth of character she possessed, which enabled her to make such a strong impression on those who knew her.

Members of the Maquis Dubois of operation Licensee a Buckmaster's net. 4th from the right "Léon". Next Captain Dubois. Behind both: Father Norac.

At the time I joined them, my group consisted of approximately 12-15 men (although by the time of the final German retreat from our region of France we numbered close to 500). Once I became acquainted with the group, I quickly appraised each member's ability. These men were quite different from my initial group. Several of them had some military training as regular French soldiers or officers. Captain Dubois a reserve officer who had seen combat and had been released after France surrendered to the Germans was in charge of all the resistance groups north of the Nièvre Department. He was a good-looking individual, extremely devoted to his spouse and daughter Nicole, who lived at Cosne-sur-Loire. He was particularly concerned with my safety, and watched over me like an old hen. I took it for granted that he knew all those who were with him. Unfortunately, this was not the case as we learned to our sorrow later.

Capt. Dubois (Vic Calvat)

By military standards, the group's command structure was, to say the least, unusual. It consisted of an informal executive committee composed of Captain Dubois, Léon, myself and, later, Father Norac. While we did not always agree initially, we always managed to come to a consensus. Léon was nominally in charge of planning and communications (as he was also a radio operator), Dubois was responsible for operations and I held sway over training, equipage and the collection of intelligence.

Probably through Diane, Captain Dubois had been in contact with Buckmaster, the Chief of the F-Section, SOE (Special Operation Executive) and from them he had received a small amount of material by air drop that had been carefully hidden in the some of the fields and farms of the area. One of his hiding places was a thicket on the edge of a field close to a road. The supplies were camouflaged beyond suspicion in the dry grass and the thick underbrush. Unfortunately, the man responsible for the maintenance of the road did what he always did that time of the year. He put a match to the dry grass and when the flames reached the thicket the supply of explosives and ammunition went up to the great surprise of the road worker as well as the local villagers.

Apparently Captain Dubois' idea of a supply hideout was not so hot! He was keenly aware of his shortcomings specifically concerning the use of the material SOE had sent him. To him some of the weapons were unknown and the type of explosive and its utilization was alien. It was for this reason that he had requested an agent capable of training his men.

Léon Duguet, whose real name was Paul Duprés, was a French officer of Eurasian ancestry. Wounded in France in 1940, he had been taken prisoner but released for health reasons, at which time he joined the Vichy police. Suspected by the Gestapo, he hid in Lyon and eventually escaped to England through Spain and Gibraltar. There he was recruited by SOE. He passed himself as a British Captain, occasionally wearing the uniform with three pips on his shoulder straps. He identified himself to Dubois as Colonel Léon Prévost. It was Léon who had interrogated me when I reached the group. He had parachuted at Ivoy-le-Pré near Sury-en-Lère in the Cher region as a radio operator and organizer a few weeks before me at the request of Diane.

My sense at the time was that Léon was not completely forthright regarding all of his activities. Léon spent most of his time away from our group; I assumed he was either with a girl friend—which made Dubois very nervous—or involved in some schemes he did not share with us.

Léon had recruited Pierre Boitier a young Frenchman as a radio operator to relieve some of his burden and improve communication safety. Messages that would have taken more than fifteen minutes to send were divided in two sections and were sent from two different locations. The Germans had sophisticated equipment capable of locating transmitters very rapidly but not in under fifteen minutes. One day our radio operator was sending a message from an isolated farm surrounded by open fields. Why he selected this place is unknown to me but it seemed a stupid choice. Probably the farmer had a good-looking daughter! The message he sent was rather short. He left immediately after hiding the radio and hopped on his bicycle.

He was not 100 meters from the farm when a German plane came over, dropped a bomb and leveled the building in which he had been a few moments before. No one was hurt, but the farmer was quite unhappy and probably wondered why his farm had been singled out by a lone German plane. We did not have the heart to tell him that the enemy could detect radio communications a lot faster with aircraft than with their direction finder trucks, which had to use triangulation to locate a transmitter from the ground.

All messages were coded using a one-time pad. This was a slow and tedious job, especially when the sender made errors or when the radio operator did not copy the signal properly, yet we managed quite nicely.

One of our most important jobs was to train the people in our group. Some were willing, but most of them had no idea as to what to do with the material we were receiving on a nearly weekly basis. They knew what dynamite was, but Composition C was new to them and they had no idea how to use it. A small amount did go a long way if one knew what to do with it.

One of the weapons we had to assemble in the field was the Gamond Grenade. It was composed of a detonator with a safety device and a skirt made of strong material which was wrapped around plastic explosive the size and the shape of a large grapefruit. The lower part of the skirt had an elastic band which held Composition C in place. The grenade had to be assembled because the amount of explosive varied according to the target. We always received the detonator and the explosive separately.

My job was to instruct a few men from our group in the construction of this device.

One day I was in the dark basement of a farm with three of our men. I had all my material spread out on a table while I showed them how to shape the soft plastic into a usable ball, when one of the men complained of a headache. I was not surprised because I almost always had a headache when I handled explosive. I had learned that it contained a chemical that enters the body through the skin and could cause a severe headache. To eliminate this problem, one had to take a small amount in his mouth and chew on it like chewing gum. So I told those who were with me to do just that.

As soon as the one who complained of the headache placed the explosive in his mouth he fell to the floor in convulsions. Foam came out of his mouth and he jumped like a carp on the dirt floor. The others were as mystified as I. I was sure that I had unintentionally killed the fellow. We tried to hold him down but to no avail. He was strong and we did not know what to do.

As we were struggling with him, one of our men came in and said: "I see Pierre has had one of his epileptic seizures." Eventually he calmed down and we placed him on an old bed frame until he was completely recovered. That was the last time I asked anyone to chew on Composition C!

We had all the latest weapons imaginable, some of which could not be used for training because the sound of fired ammunition or an explosion would alert either the Germans, the French police or their agents. All I could do was conduct dry runs with the PIAT, a device developed by the British similar to the bazooka but operated with a strong spring. Captain Dubois preferred the bazooka, but the PIAT was better than nothing. We also received silent weapons called "Welrods" capable of firing 32-caliber bullets from a short distance without making a sound. This was to be used against fat ruddy German officers on crowded streets. Their death would appear to be from a heart attack and give the assassin time to get away. We never used this weapon and I kept it until I returned to the United States.

We had automatic weapons such as the British Sten gun which looked more like a plumber's tool than a gun. It was simple and effective, but also dangerous if one did not know how to use it. To this day I am still uncertain as to why none of our men were shot accidentally. I almost killed a young French girl as she watched us pass by at full speed in our Citroën. The Traction Avant model had a windshield that could be opened and moved forward, enabling us to place a weapon's muzzle through in case we had to fire quickly.

One day I was riding shotgun, the barrel of my Sten through the windshield with the safety on—if one could call it a safety. The lug of the bolt was placed in a recess and as long as it remained there nothing could happen. Going through a small village the car hit a chuck hole, bounced pretty hard, and the bolt of the Sten disengaged, firing a round. I must have had my finger in the trigger for the entire magazine went off, bullets hitting the ground approximately fifty feet ahead of us. The young girl was standing by the side of the road. I could see the puffs of dust made by the bullets hitting the road less than a foot in front of her. I don't believe that she knew what had happened, but all of us in the car did. That was the last time I placed the Sten through the windshield.

That same day we had to meet the leader of one of the adjacent groups. It was a gray day and was raining lightly. We reached a straight road which was in pretty good condition. On either side the ground was flat and even. On our right was a series of electric poles, composed alternately of concrete and wood. The road was so good that our driver decided to gun it. All of a sudden, a hundred meters ahead of us, a man with a rifle stood in the middle of the road and aimed his weapon at us. Our driver panicked. He applied the brakes with all his might, but the gravel road caused our vehicle to slide. Fortunately, there was no ditch at that part of the road. We kept moving to the right towards the poles. I was ready for the impact. We passed one concrete pole, thank God, and I closed my eyes, expecting to hit the next pole. We kept on going. When I opened my eyes, we were still moving but the wooden pole was in front of our car's radiator, moving right along with us!

The car stopped and we all got out to inspect the damage. To our surprise, we discovered that the front bumper had wrapped itself around the completely rotten pole and was holding it straight up. We had completely forgotten the man with the gun, but he had joined us, shaking his head and laughing at our luck. This could have been a bad situation, because from a distance we thought that he was a German soldier, and because of the type of vehicle we were driving, he thought we were the French police and was ready to open fire on us. The poor fellow was just an ordinary farmer who had never shot anything except a few rabbits. The only damage was to the front bumper and to the speedometer/odometer cable.

Besides training the group in the use of some of our more sophisticated weapons, one of my missions was to collect information about the German armed forces in my area; another was to gather information about French collaborators. Neither mission was an easy one. For the most part, the Germans in the area had maintained a good behavior relying on the French police to do their dirty work. The people I was with had a very good idea as to who the collaborators were, but they kept that information for the future. There were a lot of rumors about who had collaborated, but no one in the area had been openly accused of the crime. That was not the case where I had landed initially.

Soon after his arrival at Cosne-sur-Loire Léon became acquainted with a good-looking local girl. Before long he was spending much time in her company. Capt. Dubois, aware of the danger, investigated the girl and learned that she was also close to the local German occupation forces, and in all probability she reported to the Gestapo. Dubois had trouble convincing Léon that it was to his interest and ours to stay away from that girl. But, reluctantly, Léon relented.

Although the Germans occupied France entirely, they were few in our area. To maintain law and order they relied primarily on the French police who were much better equipped to detect the presence of strangers than they were. Fortunately for us, a few members of the police had friendly relations with the resistance. Yet the bulk of the French police force represented a threat to those involved in anti-German activities.

If my French was without reproach—although occasionally sprinkled with American idioms such as "OK" or "shit"—that was not the case with my eating manners. In the span of four years in the United States I had managed to Americanize the way I fed myself to such a degree that it was observed by the SOE training staff. I was told it was imperative for me to stop using my fork with my right hand and switch it from one hand to the other. I was encouraged to push food into my fork with the knife, a la Europeans.

At times some of us had to mingle with the local population. Fortunately for me I was closely supervised and instructed by the members of my group who had survived four years of Teutonic occupation. I was told that, if asked for identification by a German soldier, I should always look directly into his eyes. Never look down. When in a crowd, always look as if you are searching for someone and, if in a restaurant or café, look as if you own the place and stare at people before settling down to a table. They assured me that most people would look away, and no one would ask me what I am doing for fear that I, a blond fellow, might be a German agent.

Our travel was done primarily by bicycle. Those we would requisition were not the ten-speed type, but were heavy and hard to handle. Pedaling uphill was impossible. One had to push the thing to the top and hope that going down the other side would save time.

Once I was accepted by the group, Captain Dubois asked me what food I liked best. I replied that milk and steak were my preferences. He was surprised to learn that wine was at the bottom of my list of foods. I drank milk practically every day until one day we stopped at the home of a member of the resistance who offered us lunch. There was no milk, the water was unsafe, and it was extremely hot.

A bottle covered with mud was brought in. Capt. Dubois insisted that I try a glass of this fine Pouilly Fumé, a famous local nectar which up to then had been buried in the garden with drums of gasoline to keep it out of hands of the occupation forces. I was not familiar with this wine and all the other wines I had tasted did not suit me. I drank one glass, then another, for I was not only thirsty, but it tasted mighty good. After the third glass it was time for us to go. I was told later that I had cycled up the steepest hill in the area without stopping. From that time on I had abandoned milk for Pouilly Fumé.

Our area covered one of the best wine regions of France. Sancerre was the center, but the small village of Pouilly was known for the quality of its wines and it was on our side of the Loire river. One of the best places for us to hide was into the underground caves located beneath the vineyards. The entrances of these caves were hidden within the wineries and caves of the different wineries were connected by underground tunnels. One could enter into one of the caves and travel several kilometers passing through one winery after the other without surfacing. The locations of these caves were well protected from the German who would have loved to move their precious contents to Germany. But the caves were dangerous for another reason.

Once we held a meeting with several local winery owners who were also members of the local resistance. Once the meeting was over it was decided that tasting the wine of the owner of the cave was in order. Unfortunately, there was only one glass for the six of us. We each took a sip before moving to the next cave. Same procedure there, but two sips instead of one. In the sixth cave, which thank-god was the last, we found a pile of straw on the floor. Before long all of us were comfortably resting until the effect of these famous crus had disappeared.

The woods were our best hiding places but it was difficult to practice minimum body hygiene. Slit trenches were used for normal evacuation, but washing and shaving were problems. For this reason many in our group sported heavy chin growth. For days we could not wash, nor even brush our teeth, and when we did it was usually at a village fountain or at the hand pump of a farm's cistern.

At times I felt that Capt. Dubois was over-protective. When going into an area which might prove dangerous, he would leave me in a safe place and retrieve me on his return. Once he left me in an isolated farm house in the care of a woman in her late forties. Unlike most French farmers' wife she was not rotund, nor did she wear the traditional drab working dress and apron. Her flowery dress and her short hair made her look younger than her age.

She was alone and spoke French with a slight accent which I did not immediately identify. We talked for a while and she told me that a year earlier her husband had been taken by the Germans as a laborer. She had no idea where he was, and she was managing the small farm alone. Then she said: "You are not French. You are British!"

"Pas du tout," I replied.

But she insisted and finally she told me that she was from England, and was hoping that I would be from her own country. Then, probably because I did not appear to be very clean, she asked if I would like a bath. How could I refuse such an offer? French farms were not known to have shower rooms, but I did not question her proposal. She immediately busied herself heating large kettles of water on the wood-burning stove. Then she brought into the spacious kitchen a large flat basin about four feet in diameter. Once the water was steaming, she poured it into the basin, tested it with a finger, and added cool water until she felt that it was the right temperature. In my mind I was wondering how this operation would proceed. Making sure that all was in order, she stood facing me. As I did not move and sensing that I did not know what to do she said: "Take off your clothes."

I removed my shirt then, hesitating and somewhat self-conscious, I first stared at the steaming water, then at her standing on the other side of the basin. She said: "I know what men look like, but since you are embarrassed I will leave you alone."

Taking my shirt and without closing the door, she left after placing a bar of soap and a towel on a stool nearby.

I continued undressing and sat in the basin. This was heavenly after so many days in dusty barns and other filthy hiding places. I could not see the woman, but I sensed that she was watching me. As soon as I was dried and had my pants on, she reappeared, carrying another shirt. She had been crying.

Sniffling, she said: "Please tell me you're an Englishman."

Feeling sorry for her, but not wanting to lie, I replied: "No, I am not an Englishman; I am an American."

She smiled and said: "I knew you were not French. This is one of my husband's shirt; I will wash yours."

When Captain Dubois retrieved me, quizzically after seeing my new shirt he asked: "Did you have a good time?"

I replied, smiling. "I had a bloody good time!"

The situation in our area did improve. By this time, Patton was moving across France with his armored division. We were very busy planning operations against the German units west of us trying to return to their homeland as the situation deteriorated in favor of the Allies. We knew of two German Panzer divisions located in the center of France, west of the Loire river. Our job was to prevent these two divisions from hitting the south flank of Patton's forces which for lack of fuel were stuck north of Orleans. The logical solution was to blow the bridges on the Loire river and prevent them from crossing for a while. Patton must have had the same idea because he sent two of his officers to our area to tell the resistance units to knock out all of the bridges on the Loire! Because I was the link between the Allied Command and the local resistance, I became involved not only as an interpreter but as a participant.

Members of other groups could not understand why all the bridges had to be destroyed, because they felt that they were fully capable of protecting them. On the other hand, we were receiving our instructions from SHAEF and not from General Patton. There were resistance teams that operated on the other side of the Loire, and these needed the bridges to cross the river back and forth to conduct operations. I translated during the heated discussion between the two messengers of General Patton and several resistance leaders including Capt. Dubois. It was agreed that mining the bridges was the most practical thing to do. If the Germans decided to use the bridges, we could destroy them easily before they were able to cross. We mined the bridge of St. Satur the best bridge to handle heavy tanks on a logical route of escape for the Germans, and waited. Unbeknownst to me at the time only my objection was reported to General Patton, who apparently took a very dim view of this so-called American agent operating in the area. He contacted London in an attempt to learn my true identity, but failed.

It was also decided that it would be better if some of the small bridges were destroyed to prevent the German Panzers from using secondary roads, which they often did with smaller units. The local people used a ruse to confuse the German convoys which apparently had very poor maps of France. The road signs—for the most part heavy concrete signs—were either removed or altered to show a different direction. It was not unusual for German units to go round in circles until they realized they had been fooled. Even the kids watching German convoys were told to give wrong information when asked.

It was decided that a bridge crossing a small stream in a heavily wooded area would be destroyed. It would then have been impossible for heavy vehicles or tanks to cross on either side. It would probably have taken several days for the Germans to repair the bridge or to bypass it. One night six of us came to the target on our bicycles with enough explosives to destroy the Brooklyn bridge. The stone structure was old, probably built during the Roman occupation. It was approximately five meters in width with an arch of three to four meters in diameter. I had never seen bridge of this type and our instructors did not cover it in our course on bridge destruction. I figured that if I could demolish the keystone, the bridge would collapse. With pieces of lumber to support the explosive, we placed the Composition-C underneath the keystone and, after introducing the detonator with a ten-minute time delay, we moved to a safe distance out of sight and waited.

We heard the explosion, congratulated each other and went to our respective hiding places. The next morning two of us hopped on our bicycles and took to the road leading to the bridge. We were laughing and joking about the big hole we would find. When we reached the curve of the road which opened a view to the fruit of our labor, we could not believe our eyes. The bridge was still there, intact! We could see only a small bump on the road in the center of the bridge. But on either side of the road the trees had lost all their leaves. In effect, the bridge had acted as the barrel of a huge gun and directed the force of the explosion toward either side of the road, reducing the trees to their bare branches and creating a hundred-meter-long tunnel. My reputation as a saboteur and a destroyer of bridges also went down that day. I had to do something quick to live this faux pas down.

I sent a message to our London office describing the result of our attempt and waited for a reply. It did not take long. Their answer was short and to the point, but I could tell that they must have had a good laugh at my failure. Their instruction was to place half the amount of explosive on the road in the center of the bridge and cover the entire thing with sand bags. That would do the trick! A few nights later we returned to the bridge and did exactly what London suggested. This time we did not wait until the next morning to see the results. As soon as we heard the explosion we rushed to the sight, and what a sight it was! Instead of a bridge, there was a huge crater! We returned to our base and had a glass of wine, or perhaps two or three. My reputation was reestablished.

It was also decided that another bridge should be destroyed. Unfortunately, this one was well guarded by the Germans. We had learned that they had mined some of the bridges to retard the advance of the Allies should it became necessary. The traffic over the bridge was rather sparse; only a few local people crossed on foot. The news about the Allies' invasion was getting more and more encouraging as the BBC told the world that the Allies had secured their landing beaches and were now moving across France. Brest had fallen, and we could occasionally hear artillery firing in the distance. We could not approach the bridge ourselves but the local people could, so we decided to trick the Germans into believing that the Allies were close by and that it was time they took off for the homeland.

A few locals were instructed to come from the west and cross the bridge with wheelbarrows, bundles, suitcases and anything they could carry so they would appear to be refugees. They came to the bridge and, when asked where they were going, replied that they were running from the fighting. The Allies were right behind and would be there at any time. A few shots in the air by the Resistance created a very believable situation. The Germans decided that it was smarter for them to go too, so they blew up the bridge and headed east. I believe that we were credited for having blown that bridge!

In our area, between the Loire River and the main highway, lay a railroad marshaling yard, a key rail center well protected by the German Army. We could not get near it without being seen and although we had destroyed the communication system of the railway we decided not to try the yard itself. One day, poised on a hill overlooking the yard, awaiting a German convoy, we heard aircraft approaching our area. Almost immediately air-raid sirens gave the alarm. We took cover and waited. The aircraft hugged the ground until they were approximately four or five miles from our position, then climbed a couple of thousand feet, described a circle, and all five of them dove to the marshaling yard and dropped their bombs. In a matter of minutes it was over. Not a single bomb had fallen on the nearby roads, on the river or on the railroad station, but the entire yard itself was in a shambles, burning and exploding. The planes left the area, again hugging the ground, and disappeared in the distance. We recognized the Mosquito bombers and only later we learned that they were Canadian fighter bombers.

At other times, the Allied Forces were more of a threat to us than the German Army. Our own Air Force had no idea what was going on behind the German lines. Every day, based on their own intelligence, they arbitrarily drew a line across their map and anything on one side was friendly and everything that moved on the other side was fair game for them to attack. In reality, there was no "line"; it was actually a constantly moving, wide, blurry band. Since we were on the other side of "the line" most of the time and they had no way to tell the difference between a German vehicle and a friendly car, we were hit a few times, but fortunately for us without casualty.

The locations of our ambushes were always carefully selected, usually on the edge of a wooded area so as to allow maximum cover and the escape. We placed sentries to alert us once the enemy convoy was spotted. The participants were dispersed in a V formation with the opening toward the enemy so as to fire on the convoy without shooting each other. At the base of the V, we placed a PIAT whose purpose was to hit the first vehicle disabling it, thus forcing the whole convoy to stop. Most German convoys were preceded by a single vehicle traveling a mile or so ahead. If it were attacked, the rest of the convoy would have time to organize a defense and counterattack. That is why mines were not used for that purpose. We would let the scout vehicle pass, then attack the real lead vehicle.

On one occasion, we were about to ambush a convoy, when the German column was suddenly strafed by a flight of P-47s. All we could do was watch and stay put for fear that we would be strafed also.

Our own Air Force caused us all kinds of difficulties. Shortly after the convoy incident, a high altitude bombing by a squadron of B-29s completely missed its target. All of the bombs fell on the small village of Neuvy-sur-Loire, destroying it and killing more than half its population in a matter of seconds. The people of the surrounding villages were up in arms. They knew that Germany had no air power left and that the only ones capable of doing this kind of damage were the Allies.

They were more than upset, they were outright hostile. When I met them they gave me an earful, reminding me that during the entire German occupation they were never subjected to such treatment. I could not understand our forces lack of care either. So I did the best I could to excuse the incident, telling them that it was impossible to guide a bomb from 10,000 meters and that, occasionally, due to various factors such as wind shift, bombs would drift and miss their target. I tried to convince them that this was not intentional, but only a few believed me. I learned, forty years later, that to this day some of the people of the village still believe that the bombing was intentionally done to destroy a small factory making rubber washers, even though there is no evidence that their production in any way benefited the Germans. And, instead of blaming the U.S. Air Force, to this day they ostracized the local family which owned the washer factory: a major miscarriage of justice.

Another odd incident involving our own Air Force occurred in our area. A lone P-47 on a search and destroy mission lost its propeller approximately thirty kilometers from our base but several hundred miles behind the German line. The pilot had parachuted safely, and was picked up by members of our group and taken to our headquarters. The bombs attached to the plane which crashed did not explode, probably because they were not armed. We exploded them and the plane was thoroughly burnt. Meanwhile the young pilot, who was now escorted by a couple of black-bearded resistance fighters, was in shock. He did not speak French and his escort did not speak English, so that he was relieved when I met him and was able to talk to him in his own language. Under the cover of darkness we took him to a hotel at Cosne-sur-Loire and settled him into a room overlooking the main street of the town. We told him to stay there, and not to move until we could take him back across the lines to friendly forces.

We had other things to do, so for a while we went about our business, forgetting our pilot. When the time came to return him, after several days and careful planning, I went back to the hotel and found a wreck of a man, unshaven and almost incoherent. He was petrified because he had seen some German soldiers on the street below, and was fully expecting to be turned over to them by the local people. We loaded him on a vehicle we had borrowed, and off we went toward the fighting lines. It took us several hours to locate a friendly unit. When we did, our vehicle was not yet fully stopped when the pilot jumped out and rushed to the first American soldier he saw and began hugging him, much to the surprise of the soldier. After thanking us abundantly, he continued telling anyone who would listen about his escapade. We left him to return to our area of operation without further incident.

In order to move quickly from one part of our territory to the other we had to use vehicles. Some were borrowed, some were requisitioned and very few worked properly because parts and maintenance were very scarce. One day a member of our group came up with the news that he had located a big American car in a garage owned by an old lady. The car had been left behind by an American businessman who spent his vacations in France. From the name of the individual and his profession, he could have been a member of the Mafia. This car was a Dodge and it was the biggest Dodge I had ever seen. Between the back seat and the front were two small jump-seats that disappeared when folded. It was an ideal car for our operations—waiting for German convoys at cross roads, then hitting them with everything we had and take off. The Dodge was so long that during long expeditions we could set a fifty-five gallon drum of gasoline behind the back of the front seat and still have enough room to sit on the back seat with legs outstretched, barely touching the drum with our feet.

The top of the Dodge was cut out so that two individuals could stand and fire their weapons in different directions. We filled the floor of the car with hand grenades, and for long expeditions, all we could load. The problem with the Dodge was its temperament. Sometimes it would not start, and would require a thorough cleaning of the gas filter which was full of something which looked like rust. We blamed the gasoline which had been buried in the ground since the French surrender in 1940. Even straining the gas through a chamois did not help. Gasoline drums and cases of wine had been hidden buried in gardens for future use by the local people who did not want to share these precious items with the German occupation forces.

Our "armored car" was usually driven by a professional chauffeur who was also a fair mechanic. I was not allowed to go on the type of expeditions for which the car was eventually often used, probably because I would have discouraged this type of often counterproductive activity. The German response to these attacks was to arbitrarily select some of the local inhabitants, line them up against a wall and shoot them in front of the rest of the population.

Typical of these operations was an oft-repeated one which had been devised by a young man in our group. It involved harassing the Germans by creeping along side their convoys and heaving grenades into the trucks as Sten magazines were emptied into the sides of vehicles. By the time the convoy realized what was going on the Dodge was gone in a cloud of dust. Our car was anything but inconspicuous, and yet the target convoys were nearly always caught unaware. This was because they were only passing through our area on their way back to Germany and had not heard of our car or its earlier exploits.

I say "nearly always" because one day a convoy commander realized quickly what was happening and ordered his vehicles to move to the left. The Dodge ran out of road. Our people had enough time to jump out with the exception of 20 year old Marcel Supliciau the young man who was in charge. He was killed and left where he fell. The car came to a rest upside down in a ditch, although it was later retrieved and repaired.

I happened to be nearby with Captain Dubois. Normally we never engaged the Germans so close to our hiding place. We had no idea what the heavy shooting was all about. Both of us hit the ground and crawled away with bullets whizzing over our heads. We returned to our base and learned about the incident. The Germans had left the body behind, so we retrieved it and planned a funeral befitting a hero. Because of the presence of Germans in the area and our inability to determine who was friend or enemy, we decided to bury our comrade in the forest and place a marker so that he could be moved later. After a brief but somber ceremony comprised of my few words and a eulogy by Captain Dubois, the pine box was lowered into the hole and covered with dirt, leaves and branches. He was the only casualty we had so far and I believe that his death made a strong impression on the rest of the group.

It was obvious that with time, the Germans would have learned about the activities of the resistance in the area. The few friends we had in the French police kept us informed through their contact with the German occupation forces. The only way to escape detection was to avoid routine activities. We never slept in the same place twice in a row. To go from one place to another we never used the same route and we tried as much as possible not to repeat our movements or establish a pattern. We spent much time in the woods under makeshift shelters. Occasionally we would slip into a farm, find a pile of straw or hay and, rolled into a parachute, sleep with one ear and eye open.

One night after a long and difficult day we reached a farm I had not visited before. Captain Dubois and I climbed into the barn and settled on top of a pile of hay. We felt quite safe and sleep came to us readily. All of a sudden, I felt a sharp pain on my neck. I woke up and looked into the business end of a pitchfork. On the other end was a woman with fire in her eyes. She was quite good-looking, if a typical farmer's wife. She asked, "Who are you, and what are you doing in my barn?"

I looked around for my friend Captain Dubois, but I was all alone. I was not prepared for this. I mumbled something, hoping that someone or something would get me out of my predicament. She kept poking me with her pitch fork, repeating her question. Finally she said, "Stay where you are. I will be right back."

I felt apprehensive as I fully expected her to return with reinforcements. I also discovered that my weapon was gone and that it was daylight. I was about to take off when she returned alone without her pitchfork, but with a cup of hot ersatz coffee and a piece of black bread. She was now smiling and was even more beautiful.

"Were you scared?" she asked.

I was about to reply when Captain Dubois came in, laughing. The woman was Eugenie, the wife of Jean Guillot, the one that I liked the most. I was very relieved when I realized that they had arranged this welcome for me as a joke. We became very good friends and had the opportunity to visit them often and taste her wonderful cooking. Fortunately for these farmers, life was not as difficult for them as it was for the city folks. They had chickens which laid eggs, pigs that grew fat on garbage, and milk from their cows. For coffee, they roasted wheat and, believe it or not, it wasn't too bad. It was devoid of caffeine, an unimportant factor in those days, and the bread was made with whole wheat flour not appreciated by the French people, who loved their white and crispy baguettes, but which are far less nutritious. The meals we had at the farm sometimes lasted until the wee hours of the morning.

The resistance in our area became more and more important. The need for equipment and supplies increased. At times we had several planes unloading their cargo in our drop zone at the same time. This activity required a lot of planning, because it was summer and the nights were short. There was very little time between the drop and sunrise. The selection of the drop zone was important because the Germans knew that large open expanses of terrain were potential drop zones to be watched. We were fortunate to have so many options that it was impossible for the Germans to watch all of them at any given time. When our request for supplies was accepted by our London office, we had to listen to the BBC for our code which would tell us when the drop would be made and how many planes would participate. Our code was the giraffe, and the planes were designated as monkeys. When two monkeys would climb on the giraffe, we knew that evening two planes would come and drop containers of supplies to us.

In the beginning, we marked the field with bonfires or car headlights, and signaled with a flashlight in a prearranged Morse code for positive recognition. The planes would describe a wide circle to mislead any would-be observer and prevent pinpointing the drop zone. Once the pilot was certain that the reception party was in place and ready he would drop his load and return to his base. Depending on the size of the drop, we would have ten or fifteen men at the site. One plane would hold 12 cylindrical canisters, each measuring six feet long and two and half feet in diameter and holding 150-200 pounds.

Some drops would involve two planeloads simultaneously. In theory this was the way it was supposed to work; unfortunately, it was not always so perfect in practice and on several occasions the supplies fell into the hands of the Germans, or into the hands of other groups that were not supposed to receive the goods. This usually occurred after someone obtained our code and set up a drop zone a short distance away from ours. We learned later that a Communist group had penetrated our organization in order to acquire supplies. We knew who the infiltrator was but there was very little we could do about it, short of banning him from our group.

Subsequently, through the development of high-tech equipment, the drops became safer and more successful. In order to help the pilot locate the drop zone and prevent the capture of our supplies, we were given a small radar device called "Eureka". It sent a signal that was intercepted on an instrument aboard the aircraft called "Rebeka". When the plane was approximately twenty miles away, a blip would register on a cathode ray indicator showing the position of the plane in reference to our position. When the plane came directly over our instrument, the "Rebeka" shut off. At that time the pilot would release his load and all the containers would fall within our drop zone, or very close to it.

In addition, to make the drop even more secure, we had a radio phone called the S-phone with which we could communicate with the aircraft and direct it to our location should the radar fail. The S-phone operated on line of sight so it was virtually impossible for the Germans to detect. All these very sophisticated instruments operated on large batteries and unless they were fully charged their effectiveness was unpredictable.

In one instance, we were expecting a drop around two in the morning. I had set up the Eureka and had the S-phone strapped on my chest, a series of wet batteries around my waist, the microphone encased in a mouthpiece so the sound of my voice would not be heard for more than a couple of feet. Shortly before two in the morning, we heard the plane. We knew that he must have been close to nine miles away, flying low. I kept calling him, but received no reply. All of a sudden I heard voices, but they were not calling me. It was a casual conversation, apparently between the pilot and the navigator. I was listening to the intercom of the plane and the crew never knew it. Unknowingly, the pilot or copilot had switched to my frequency, allowing me to hear but not be heard.

The conversation went something like this: "Pilot to navigator, do you see anything?"

"Navigator to pilot, I don't see a thing."

A little while later: "Pilot to navigator, do you see anything below?"

"Not a damn thing."

In the distance we could hear the purring of the engines, but we could not see the plane. I kept calling using my code designation, but to no avail. The pilot kept asking the navigator and the tail gunner whether they saw a light but the reply was always negative. Why didn't he switch on his listening button? Finally I heard him say, "Let's drop the stuff anywhere. They'll find it eventually."

That is when I really got mad. I hollered at the top of my voice, "You bastards, I'll get you for that."

Those who were with me knew that something was wrong. Even though they did not understand English, they knew I was very upset, but had no idea why. As I was about to explain, the pilot must have switched his button to the listen position, because he heard me. He also learned what I thought of him and his crew. However, we were then able to communicate. He followed my directions and soon thereafter he unloaded his cargo and headed for home.

Sometimes we would wait for a long time for a drop and nothing happened. Either the pilot was lost, or for some reason the plane had never taken off. One fact was certain: if the containers were dropped without a reception party, the next morning a German patrol would find containers hanging by their parachutes on trees or on telephone poles, and the village which happened to be located the closest to the drop would suffer the consequences. At a minimum arrests would be made and at times, summary executions would serve as example to the rest of the population.

Once we had stripped the containers of their contents, we would bury them in holes that had been prepared ahead of time. The Germans had dogs trained to find the buried containers, so to prevent the dogs from digging them up, a few of us urinated on the burial site. When dogs would come to the spot they would do the same. None of our containers were ever discovered.

The supplies were loaded on carts, or cars waiting close to the drop zone. We checked the field carefully and a count of the material was kept by one of our people. One day after a drop, I noticed that a dozen 45-caliber pistols were to have been part of the shipment. But when I checked the inventory, the pistols were missing. We had a thief in our midst! I assembled the reception committee in one of our safe houses and, placing my weapon on the table, gave them fifteen minutes to bring the weapons back to me, or I would start shooting. In less than five minutes someone discovered the pistols. That was the last time we lost any of our supplies.

There were several individuals I shall never forget. Jean Guillot, whose specialty was the destruction of communication cables, was one of these unforgettable men. The telephonic cable holding 945 lines between Paris and Marseille was a priority target. Cutting a cables with an ax was fast and effective. Once they discovered it, a service crews could repair the break very quickly. Jean decided that in addition to severing the cable he would cause a disruption elsewhere far more difficult to locate. Tracing a cable under a road culvert on his back, he managed to crawl into the narrow duct where he found the cable encased in a steel pipe. The following night while the area was secured by his team of saboteurs, with a hand drill he made a small hole into

Jean Guillot and family Eugenie was the one with the pitchfork

the steel pipe. Penetrating the lead cover of the cable with a sharp tool, and using a baby syringe, he laboriously injected water into the cable. Satisfied, Jean and his team left the area, but not before making an obvious cut with their ax some distance away. It took a long time and much digging for the PTT to discover the problem.

Besides Jean, we had another that defied all description. He was a contemplative monk of the Benedictine order who had been sent to the resistance to function as a chaplain to our group. His arrival in our camp caused quite a stir because he was wearing black leather pants and coat, and riding a motorcycle. At first glance he looked more like a member of the Vichy police than a priest. He was a friendly fellow, very gregarious and full of a wide knowledge of things. For a while, when we were camping in the woods, he would get up early in the morning, set his chalice and wafers on a tree stump and say his mass alone. Afterwards, he would replace everything in a bag and attach it to his cycle. He did this every morning until it was decided that we might as well attend mass with him. All of us would stand behind him—Catholics, Protestants and perhaps a few Jews—watching the miracle of the mass.

He was known as Father Norac although this was not his real name. It was difficult for me to believe that this man, so outgoing, could be a contemplative monk. His order was known for the silence and deep contemplation of its members. In any case, after we discovered that he was a former officer and that he had served in the French Foreign Legion, we took advantage of his knowledge and involved him in all of our activities. He told me that he came from an old Brittany family and had many brothers and sisters. His mother had been very disappointed because none of her children had gone into the priesthood. So he decided that he, the last son in his family, would become a priest. I learned later on that this was not exactly his only reason. In fact, he was a reformed alcoholic. Nevertheless, he was a tremendous asset and when things got boring he would tell us stories that I remember to this day.

He had attended the Sorbonne University as a pre-med student. His stories involving dissection were hilarious. When he recalled these incidents as we waited close to the drop zone in the cool night for the planes to bring us supplies we would laugh so much that we could be heard miles away. One of his tales told of a student who hated to go to a local coffee shop because it was so crowded that he could never enjoy a cup of coffee quietly. Very likely he himself was that student! One day, the student removed an index finger from a cadaver they had been dissecting and, after ordering a cup of coffee, slowly took the finger from his coat pocket and started to stir his coffee. In about ten seconds, the place had emptied. It was this same student who removed the penis and the testicles of a cadaver and pinned it to the outside of his pants. Wearing a long coat, he went to a paper stall and ordered a local paper. As he was fumbling in his pocket, his coat opened, revealing his appendage. The lady who was holding her hand to take the money saw the organs and, pointing toward his fly, said, "Monsieur, Monsieur!"

He replied with assurance, "Ah—do not worry madame." With a pair of scissors, he casually snipped the organs and stuffed them in his coat pocket. When the lady regained consciousness and recounted the incident for the police, a search was organized for a young man probably bleeding to death.

One day I asked Father Norac, "Don't you feel bad killing Germans? After all, you are a priest."

He replied, "Not at all. I give them absolution with one hand and knock them off with the other!"

Actually, I don't believe that he had killed anyone, but he always gave a good account of himself in planning some of our more creative operations.

Although local groups were supposed to make up the main resistance in our area, I soon began hearing reports from the locals about the existence of a battalion-sized unit under the command of a Canadian colonel which was ensconced in a rough mountainous area south of our position. The Colonel did come to see us occasionally, probably to stock up on wine. I don't believe that they did much of anything, and if they did it never came to my attention.

In addition there was a British SAS unit consisting of 15-20 men based approximately fifty kilometers northeast of our area. It was commanded by a Captain Davis. They had jumped behind the German line at approximately the same time I had. They dropped seven Jeeps with the team, which was very unusual during that time, but only five survived the drop. They used the unfortunate two for spare parts.

One day, Captain Davis invited us to follow his Jeep and visit his position which was in a wooded area. The black top road passing through the thick woods was relatively straight and devoid of crossings. At one point, Captain Davis' Jeep stopped and he honked twice. To our surprise the hedge on our left parted, revealing an entrance and a dirt road. The Jeep proceeded and we followed, then the hedge closed behind us.

Approximately half a mile away we came to a camp fully equipped with kitchen, tents and a repair shop. While our super Dodge was admired by all the members of the SAS team, we discussed other things with Captain Davis. He did not have to worry so much about being shot as a spy by the Germans, because he was in uniform and he had fire power unequaled by the Germans. His Jeeps were equipped with twin Vickers machine guns, intended for use on fighter aircraft, capable of spewing lead at a terrific rate in all directions. Later, we would meet occasionally, but we never coordinated our activities.

As the war progressed, more people felt the need to participate in the resistance. Those who had assumed a passive, neutral position, or had even mildly collaborated with the German occupation realized that it was to their advantage to get involved now that it was obvious the Allies were winning and it was relatively safe to do so. We kept in touch with newly formed groups and provided them with supplies and guidance.

One day we were traveling from one group to another in a soft rain. We were approximately one hundred miles from the front, on a straight, flat stretch of road running along a steep, sloping hill, with a barbed wire fence on our left and on our right a lake edged with willow trees. Approximately one kilometer ahead of us appeared a military vehicle with the barrel of his cannon pointing upward. We were not moving fast. As soon as he saw us he leveled his gun at us and our driver panicked and abruptly stopped. We grabbed our weapons and headed for the lake which fortunately was shallow and bordered by heavy brush. In the water up to our belts we slowly and quietly followed the road approximately 200 meters back and reached a dirt trail bordering a thick woods. After determining our best escape route, we took our position under cover and waited.

We decided that we could probably inflict some damage before retreating into the woods. We waited and we waited, but the enemy did not come. Soon thereafter we heard the horn of our car. One of us said: "The Boches are playing with our car."

Finding this rather strange, I moved toward the edge of the road and peeked in the direction of the abandoned Dodge. It was surrounded by a bunch of soldiers wearing helmets and long green raincoats. Their vehicle was stopped next to ours, and they kept looking in our direction. Slowly we approached, taking cover until we were close enough to identify them. I realized that these were not Germans, they were American soldiers. What were they doing here so far from the front? They greeted us in French but they were surprised that one of us replied in English. They wanted to know where we got this Dodge. The hood was open and they were all peering into it with great interest. That was when I mentioned the mechanical problem we had with it. Before we knew what was happening, parts of the engine were on the road, tools were spread all over and the entire patrol was at work on our car. In less than fifteen minutes the Dodge was purring like it never had before. Among other things, they had cleaned the gas line and the carburetor.

I wanted to know what were they doing this far from the Front. They claimed to be an Intelligence and Reconnaissance platoon which had become lost! I did not believe them. Chances were they were on a mission the nature of which they were unable to reveal to us, or involved in activities which the military would not have approved. In either case, we accepted a couple of cases of C-Rations (which came in handy later) from them and sent them on their way.

By the middle of September the Allies were making good progress despite all adversities. We knew that Patton was racing across France toward the Rhine, but his fuel supply was severely curtailed. Some of his tanks were bogged down, some in very dangerous situations. Once, as we were crossing the front line, we came across an armored unit that had run out of fuel and was bivouacked—I should say stuck—in a small wooded area. Fortunately for the unit, the German air power was, by now, completely gone, otherwise they would have been sitting ducks because their "hiding place" was the only clump of trees for miles around. We pointed this fact out to them but they only shrugged their shoulders and continued the maintenance on their armored vehicles.

The British SAS were not the only ones operating in our area. The French equivalent, or Commando Units, occasionally appeared in small groups equipped with British weapons and uniforms. They wore the French flag on their sleeves and the traditional beret. While the British kept well hidden when they were not involved in actual operations, the French Commandos spent a great deal of their free time in restaurants and cafes, eating, drinking and telling their exploits to the girls. To us they seemed to be a bunch of free-lancers without specific goals or purpose. However they were interesting and, after all, they were those who had fled France rather than accepting the

German occupation. They appeared well trained, probably by the British, and their confidence was unsurpassed.

The German garrison of Cosne-sur-Loire had fallen back to Nevers and joined their Army corps. Large contingents of enemy troops searching for a route to Germany had crossed the Loire at La Charité. It was imperative to keep them away from Cosne-sur-Loire and force them to go south east through a rugged area where well-equipped resistance units could successfully harass them. Several resistance groups using hit and run methods blocked their way toward the north without suffering casualties, but inflicting some to the enemy. When the Germans brought their artillery into play it shook up the leadership of the local resistance. Captain Dubois and I proceeded to Briare where a contingent of French paratroopers was located. At 23:00 hours, we reached the Hotel du Grand Cerf and awakened the notorious but tired Colonel Bourgoin to ask him for help. Without a moment of hesitation he agreed to send a portion of his unit to our area to even up the score. We rushed back to our units which had abandoned their defensive positions and urged them to return to their forward positions.

The following day a couple of Jeeps and a half-dozen French Béret Rouge (red beret) paratroops commandos rushed through town and settled in the restaurant on the main street, ordering food and, of course, wine, and soon they were singing and laughing loudly. They had been at it for a couple hours when news reached the town that the Germans had taken over a bridge south of our position and that they were in control of both sides of the river. It meant that large units were about to cross, and since there were two Panzer divisions on the other side, it was suspected that these intended to cross at that point. This was not exactly our territory, for we had nothing to do with the protection of that particular bridge. Ours were mined and ready to go up at a moment's notice. When the commanding officer of the Commandos heard the news, he decided that it was time for them to do something. He rallied his troops and, singing a war song, led them to the bridge to "teach the schleu a lesson." With screeching tires and kisses to the girls who stood by with their mouths opened in awe, they were off in the direction of Pouilly.

One hour later only one of the two Jeeps returned with the dying Captain and the four survivors of the team. The attending physician told us that a piece of the hood of the Jeep had penetrated his chest. He was still singing the Marseillaise, the French National Anthem, when he died on the operating table as they were removing the metal. They had ignored our warnings that the Germans had at least one 88-caliber field gun which they used as shot guns with unbelievable accuracy. Indeed, when the Captain led his team to the attack, driving in the middle of the road towards the bridge, one round had hit his Jeep, killing the occupants instantly except for the Captain. This was a sad day for all of us, not only because of the casualties, but because it had been so useless and foolish. Yet the German did not move toward Cosne-sur- Loire. The French paratroopers with the help of Capt. Davis' SAS commandos convinced them otherwise. German units including Panzers crossed and moved east toward the Rhine. We heard that to avoid attack by the resistance, they had taken hostages from the villages and walked then on either side of the convoy

Many of the German service troops did not leave the central regions of France. Approximately 20,000 enemy troops—including Ukrainian soldiers who, in the initial stages of the war, had allied themselves with the Nazis—were captured by the resistance and turned over to the Allies. The process of moving them to a prisoner of war camp became a serious problem for the Allies who learned that some French resistance groups were waiting in ambush to kill as many Germans as possible as they were marched unarmed to camp. Thus the command decided not to disarm the German soldiers until they reached their destination, which made the French very unhappy.

There were German stragglers or deserters all over the area and these would be picked up by the resistance and treated as prisoners. I am certain that most of the resistance participants had heard of the Geneva Convention concerning the treatment of prisoners of war, however for all intent and purpose the Convention had been suspended by the Germans and therefore the resistance did not feel obliged to respect it. I heard that some local resistance groups had been using German soldiers to clear mine fields and that at night, after drinking parties, some of the locals had gone to the jail where the prisoners were held, and used them as punching bags.

I witnessed an interrogation conducted by Léon which made me sick. As a minority among people who had lived for four years under the Germans' boot heel I was powerless to intercede as Léon questioned a young German soldier who kept saying that he did not know the answers. Léon grabbed a metal fireplace poker and hit the young soldier across the face. Most of the prisoner's teeth fell on the floor, and blood oozed from his mouth. I had to merely walk away, but reported the incident to London.

A few weeks later we were visited by a British Captain who had crossed the line specifically to inquire about the alleged atrocities committed by the French resistance. Of course he warned all of us that should any of the Germans report abuse when they returned home it could be very embarrassing to the Allies as well as damaging to the resistance's reputation. He suggested that it would be better if none of the prisoners returned home; this would be the safest way to handle the matter.

Unfortunately, among the prisoners was a German Navy Captain who had been captured while making his way back to Germany to join his family. He was very cooperative and of course he maintained that he was not and had never been a Nazi. He claimed that he despised Hitler and the entire Nazi system, that he was a professional Navy man who only had done what he was told. Unlike the other German prisoners, he was well educated, he spoke French fluently and, at the first opportunity, shed his uniform and escaped from us. That was very unfortunate, but perhaps he was telling the truth. As far as I know nothing was ever officially reported. Not surprisingly, out of the hundreds of German prisoners who I had contact with, not one claimed to be anything other than an ardent anti-fascist.

The bridge of St. Thibault at St. Satur, which we had mined earlier, was eventually blown up. We had no problem with it because of its relatively recent construction. One 130-foot span fell approximately 20 feet. It would require a major operation to repair it. Occasionally German units would appear on the west side of the Loire and shoot at anything that moved on the other side. A few members of the local French resistance would return the fire, but it was a waste of effort. They felt pretty safe from that distance and they would be able to say that they fought the schleu!

During a three months period of operation Licensee 19 Liberators (B-24) brought 707 containers, and 311 packs, enough material to equip 1200 men.

Bridge over the Loire river at St. Satur destroyed by "Julien".

Simone

One of my missions, not known to the rest of the group, was to investigate certain persons who were expected to be involved with the future French Government. One of these personalities was Mr. Gadoin, a well-known banker, the former prefect of the Nievre region where we operated. Having asked some of our partisans about him I discovered that he lived in a house very close to one of our hideouts. Only a small park separated the two buildings, but socially and practically more than distance separated us. I wanted to meet him and talk to him, however I had no opportunity. I had heard that his house had been occupied by high-ranking German officers and it was rumored that his wife, a pretty woman with Latin blood, had been suspected of having affairs with these officers. Nothing was ever proven, but in small towns rumors travel fast. I learned that the Gadoins had a sixteen-year-old daughter, Simone, and that she was quite friendly with the wife of Captain Dubois. I arranged to be introduced and before long we were pals. She invited me to her home and there I was able to meet her father and her mother, a charming lady with a lot of class.

Although her mother was dark, Simone was a tall blonde and could have been taken for a Swedish or Norwegian girl: friendly, inquisitive, sometimes aggressive, but reasonable. Because of my motive, I never thought of her other than as a friend and a means to learn about her father. Of course, she knew what our group was doing in general, but she never participated in any of our activities. Her father was not officially a member of the resistance, but he was a trusted member of the business community who had held a high political position in the Department equivalent to that of a governor

Our safe house was so close to his that Simone would come to visit Dubois' wife and daughter almost daily. I was fortunate to have the occasional use of a room with a large bed but no chair. When I was around, Simone would come to my room and, sitting on the bed, we would talk. It took a while before we even kissed, even though French girls kiss for any occasion. I was twenty-three, and my hormones had been suppressed too long. Before we knew it we did more than kissing, but petting was the limit.

One day the girl, who knew we were receiving supplies by parachute, asked to witness one of the drops. At first we resisted, but eventually we relented and told her that we would pick her up around midnight and take her to the drop zone.

At the appointed time and place we picked up Simone in our Citroën and traveled the thirty kilometers to the drop zone. We parked our vehicle under a tree and told her to stay there until we were through. She would be able to observe what was going on even though it was quite dark. The planes came as planned and the containers came down from what seemed to be all directions. I was looking in the direction of the car to make certain that Simone was all right when I heard her voice next to me. She had decided to come closer to the field and, as we talked, a container came down a few feet from her and almost knocked her over. Eventually the planes left, and our job began. By five o'clock in the morning the field was cleared, the supplies were on their way to their hiding places, and it was nearly six in the morning and daylight when I returned the girl to her home.

Two days later I received a note from Simone's father who wanted to see me urgently in his office. When I entered, I noticed his daughter sitting against the wall, smiling like the cat who swallowed the canary. Her father, looking every bit the powerful banker behind his enormous desk, was very courteous, but to the point. He informed me that he had learned that Simone had been out all night with me. She had been seen returning home with me that early morning, and her reputation was completely ruined in the community. The only honorable action for me to take was to marry his daughter.

I had received some very thorough training during my short army career but none of it dealt with a shotgun wedding. I felt that I had been had, and asked our headquarters for advice. Their reply was brief and to the point, "Do nothing, we will advise you later."

I did nothing of course, but the die had been cast and as far as Simone was concerned we were engaged. Marriage was the next step. I tried to explain to her that I was in the military and had no idea where I would be sent next, but it made no impression on her at all.

By late September our area had been cleared of German troops. Our safe house next to Simone's home had become our headquarters. I decided to wear my uniform as I did not have to hide my official position. Despite great difficulties, a group of young girls managed to create a superb American flag which was attached to the rear of our car.

Patton was at the door of Germany and the French had landed on the Riviera and were moving north along the Rhone river. I felt that having returned to France without seeing my relatives would be unthinkable. So I mentioned my desire to Captain Dubois who suggested that we take the Dodge and a 200-liter drum of fuel, and go east in the direction of my home town. We did fine for the first part of our trip. However, when we reached the area near Besançon, the roads became so full of military traffic that it was almost impossible to proceed further. We had believed that the entire area had been liberated, but it was not so. At a crossroads manned by a black U.S. Army MP we were questioned as to where we were going and why. I identified myself as an American Army officer and explained our mission. The MP politely suggested that we return from whence we had come. He told us that there were pockets of Germans between our location and our destination. Finding no place to settle and rest, we slept overnight in the Dodge with the gasoline fumes and all. We returned disappointed and sad.

Shortly thereafter, in November, I received orders to proceed to Paris where I would be reassigned. With the retreat of the Germans, the French were organizing the resistance groups in our area into regular—and large—army units. Once it became obvious that the Allies had the upper hand the French resistance fighters came streaming out of the woodwork. Our initial group composed of a dozen partisans quickly increased to a company and eventually a battalion-sized unit. Paris had been liberated a week before so Capt. Dubois, his wife, Léon, another man from our group and, of course, my "future wife" Simone—who was never very far away from me— decided to accompany me.

The trip to Paris was uneventful, but when we arrived, the biggest party I had ever seen was in progress. We found rooms in a small hotel and settled down before going to a restaurant owned by a friend of one of our group. We ate and drank until the wee hours of the morning then returned to the hotel. I shared a room with Simone but, not wanting to make the situation worse, respected her virginity. It might have been a mistake on my part for this was the reason she would later track me to the other side of the world. The next morning we heard some commotion in the hallway and, looking outside, noticed the French and American MPs escorting two individuals from the hotel to waiting vehicles. We learned later that they were Gestapo agents who had been hiding in the hotel, probably in rooms next to our own.

One evening, while I strolled near the Arc of Triumph in uniform with a friend who was waiting for a return plane to England, two French girls approached and, thinking that we were American, asked in broken English if we wanted to have a good time. Probably because I replied in French, one of the girls said, "They are French. They don't have any money!" We were unable to convince them otherwise.

There was nothing for me to do in Paris. Now that the war was almost over, the number of those who had served in the resistance (or now claimed to have done so) was suddenly overwhelming. In the streets of Paris it seemed that every Frenchman was wearing an "FFI" arm band, or a World War I uniform. Strangely enough, I had no inclination to remain in my home country. I felt bad for not having seen my uncles and cousins, but OSS had another job for me on the other side of the world, where the war was not going so well for us.

We were in Paris three days during which alone I reported daily to our headquarters at the Hotel Grillon for preliminary debriefings. There I met some of my SOE buddies, but in the afternoon I did return to our hotel and spent the rest of the evening with my resistance friends and of course my shadow, Simone. On the third day I was told that a plane would take several of us back to England.

I did not want my friends especially Simone to know that I would leave the following day because they may insist on a going away party including an engagement ceremony, and very likely emotional good-byes which I dreaded. Thus I spent my last night in Paris in Simone's room. I had casually mentioned to Capt. Dubois that the war might not be over for me, but if after the war he receives a box of chocolate without a return address it would mean that I made it in one piece. On the forth day bright and early I tip toed out of the hotel with bogus travel orders I reported to Orly Transportation Office where I met Capt. Hornaday our escort Officer, A few hours later we were back in our London Office. As for my resistance friends I suppose that once I failed to show up, they realized that I had gone on to another assignment.

When I reached our London headquarters, there was a lot of kidding about my adventures. The Roman bridge episode was a big joke, and the shotgun engagement was, to my colleagues, very funny. But what they wanted to know more than anything was what did I do to make General Patton so upset. They told me that he had requested the name of the individual who had prevented the destruction of the bridges along the Loire river thus leaving his flank completely exposed. He promised to give the individual a chewing out and perhaps worse when he found him. I do not know how true their story was, but it was logical, and for a while I felt quite apprehensive, because I was aware of Patton's reputation.

```
                              9 Septembre 1944.


Chère Mme. Défourneaux,

        Votre fils René nous a demandé de vous donner de temps
en temps de ses nouvelles, étant dans l'impossibilité de le faire
lui-même, ayant été posté loin de Londres.

        La correspondence avec le Lt. Défourneaux sera donc établie
par les moyens suivants: nous vous enverrons mensuellement de ses
nouvelles, car nous sommes constamment en contact avec lui.

        Votre fils se porte à merveille, et remplit consciencieuse-
ment son devoir.  Vous pouvez être fière de lui.

        Recevez, Madame, l'expression de mes sentiments les meilleurs.


                              Charlotte Norris

                              Charlotte Norris  (Mrs.)

                              For the COMMANDING OFFICER,
                              1st Experimental Detachment,
                              A.P.O. 887, c/o Postmaster,
                              New York, New York.
```

Letter of reassurance sent to Author's mother.

Translation of letter:

Dear Mrs. Défourneaux,

Being unable to write to you himself because of his assignment away from London, your son René has asked us to provide you with news concerning him from time to time.

Thus the correspondence with Lt. Défourneaux will be conducted in the following fashion: Every month we shall send to you news about him as we are in constant contact with him.

Your son is in good health conscientiously accomplishing his assigned duty. You should be proud of him.

Madam, accept the expression of my sincere feelings.

Mairie de la Ville de Cosne

(NIÈVRE)

Le Comité de Libération pour reconnaitre
les immenses services rendus à la libération de
notre ville par l'Officier Américain DANIEL,
aux applaudissements de la population convoquée
sur la place de la Mairie, lui décerne le titre
de "CITOYEN DE LA VILLE DE COSNE SUR LOIRE".

Fait à Cosne le 26 septembre 1944
Le Comité de Libération :

Certificate by the Liberation Committee of Cosne nominating Daniel (Julien) a
citizen of the town of Cosne-sur-Loire.

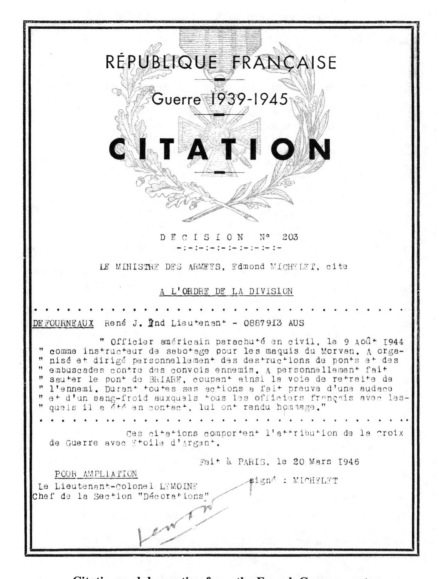

RÉPUBLIQUE FRANÇAISE
-
Guerre 1939-1945

CITATION
-

DECISION N° 203
-:-:-:-:-:-:-:-:-:-

LE MINISTRE DES ARMETS, Edmond MICHELET, cite

A L'ORDRE DE LA DIVISION

. . . .

DEFOURNEAUX René J. 2nd Lieutenant - 0887913 AUS

      " Officier américain parachuté en civil, le 9 Août 1944
" comme instructeur de sabotage pour les maquis du Morvan. A orga-
" nisé et dirigé personnellement des destructions de ponts et des
" embuscades contre des convois ennemis. A personnellement fait
" sauter le pont de BRIARE, coupant ainsi la voie de retraite de
" l'ennemi. Durant toutes ses actions a fait preuve d'une audace
" et d'un sang-froid auxquels tous les officiers français avec les-
" quels il a été en contact, lui ont rendu hommage."

. . . .

              Ces citations comportent l'attribution de la croix
de Guerre avec Étoile d'argent.

                    Fait à PARIS, le 20 Mars 1946

POUR AMPLIATION
                           signé : MICHELET
Le Lieutenant-Colonel LEMOINE
Chef de la Section "Décorations"

Citation and decoration from the French Government
Translation: DEFOURNEAUX René J. 2nd Lt. 0887913, AUS, an American officer parachuted in civilian clothing 9 August 1944 as sabotage instructor for the Maquis of Morvan has personally organized and directed the destruction of bridges and of ambush operations against enemy convoys. He personally destroyed the bridge of Briare thus cutting off the retreat of the enemy. During these actions he displayed an audacity, and coolness for which the French officers with whom he was in contact gave him credit. This citation carries the award of the CROIX de GUERRE with silver star.

Note: The maquis was in the Nievre and not Morvan, and the bridge was the bridge of St. Thibault and not of Briare.

Translation of Léon's report to FFI HQ

SUMMARY Of THE ACTIVITIES OF THE "LICENSEE" (LEON) NET
IN THE COSNE (NIEVRE) REGION

ARRIVAL OF CAPTAIN LEON: Parachuted in the vicinity of Lere (Cher)
  early July 1944.

RECEPTION OF WEAPONS: Following the request of Leon and with the aid of
  Captain DUBOIS (Calvat) chief of the maquis responsible for the
  protection of the region of Cosne the net received 12 parachute drops on
  the drop zones of "Rouget" at Entrain, "Anguille" at Annay, and
  "Barbillon" at Arquian. Despite the close proximity of the enemy these
  operations were conducted from the 20 of July to the 5" of September
  1944 without incident.

ORGANIZATION OF THE UNITS: From the first weapon drop the net was
composed of two (2) maquis at Arquian and Entrain each composed of 250
  men, and five local sabotage teams each composed of 10 men.

OPERATIONS CONDUCTED BY THE NET:

SABOTAGE: From the 25th of July repeated sabotage operations effectively
  caused the permanent isolation of Cosne a regional hub of all telephonic
  railroad communication. Specifically the destruction of the underground
  telephonic cable Paris-Marseille and at Tracy the capture of an enemy
  train with 320 head of cattle.

COMBAT: From the 5" of August the goal of the net was the protection of
  the right flank of Patton's army and the canalization of the retreating
  enemy columns coming from the south west toward the Morvan passes
  such as:

a) Occupation and interdiction of the bridge of St. Thibault on the Loire
  river, the only remaining bridge above Never, and on the 1st of
  September the mining and destruction of the bridge faced with a sizable
  enemy force. The unit lost 2 officers and three men in the defense of
  the bridge.

b) Harrying of the retreating enemy columns with many ambushes,
  specifically the spraying of several convoys of enemy vehicles with
  automatic fire resulting in an undermined number of casualties, then on
  the 24 th of August the complete destruction of an enemy convoy
  including a armored vehicle and the capture of 20 prisoners. Losses to
  the unit included: One NCO and a vehicle.

c) To prevent enemy columns crossing the Loire river at Nevers and
  moving north a plug was created at Pouilly. From the 1st to the 4th of
  September an enemy column of about 3000 men supported by artillery
  and mortar fire conduct day and night attacks against units of the net
  composed of 600 men spread over a 5 km front. Because of the
  incomparable guts of the men and the clever maneuver of the command
  the enemy exaggerating the importance of the force facing them decided
  to take to road toward the Morvan where terrain permitted other maquis
  to attack them. In these operations the enemy lost 30 KIA and 3 vehicles
  destroyed. The maquis had 3 KIA 5 wounded and two vehicles destroyed.

d) Clean up operations in the area: Up to October 1, 1944 (end of the
  mission o the net) the enemy suffered 7 KIA and among small enemy
  groups escaping or in sabotage mission 1 1 were taken prisoners.

Continued on following page

e) Intelligence activities: In addition to information related to the general situation in the area transmitted daily to London, between August 24, and September 25 th 1944 a special team reported on an hourly basis enemy troop movement within a radius of 50 km around Cosne. Counterintelligence activities allowed the discovery and the arrest of several Gestapo agents preventing several operation by the local enemy forces.

Note: The net was reinforced on the August 10 with the arrival of Lt. Julien who had been requested by Leon.

Diane

I was delighted to learn that all nine members of my intelligence school class who had served as "Joes" had returned safely. One day, while comparing experiences with one of them, I happened to mention the challenge I had in trying to fill the shoes of Diane.

"Have you ever heard of this woman?" I asked.

"Do you mean to tell me that you've never met Diane? Well, you're in luck! She's in London now. I'll arrange for us to meet her for lunch tomorrow."

The next day, I went to Grovenor House, the London Officers' Club, across

Diane (Virginia Hall)

from Hyde Park. There I was to meet my colleague and Virginia Hall, which turned out to be the true identity of "Diane". I arrived a few minutes early and took a seat in the ornate lobby to await the two of them. Sitting next to me was a woman who appeared to be past her 60s, wearing an elegant black dress and a stylish black hat with an expansive brim. She appeared to be a typical upper crust Brit. I presumed that she was there as the guest of a General or some such person, and paid her no further notice.

Just then, my friend arrived. As he walked up to me he said, "Ah, I see you two have already met!"

Astonished and a little embarrassed, I replied, "No." He introduced us and, after exchanging pleasantries, she immediately began asking about particular people in my group whom she had known. After a few minutes of conversation, we rose from our seats to move into the dining room. As she began walking, I was flabbergasted to notice that "Diane" had a prosthetic leg. How in the world, I wondered, could a woman with this type of disability have parachuted four or five times behind enemy lines and done the things that she had.

Virginia Hall was a well-educated, Amelia Earhart-type American who had been living in France when the War broke out. She escaped to England where she was recruited by SOE to go back to occupied France. In fact, she never parachuted into France. She and a radio operator were landed by rubber dingy on the northern French coast. The Germans were well aware of her and had posted a large reward for her capture. As a result, she had become a master of disguises, something she continued to practice, for reasons not known to me, here in England. Far from the sixty years old which she appeared to be, in reality she was at that time in her forties.

During the course of our discussion, my friend and I had made reference to the fact that we were to be awarded the Silver Star for our mission in France. To this she entered into a half-hour-long discourse on America and patriotism and how we had not performed our mission for a medal, fame or other recognition, but for our country. I later learned that for these reasons she had refused the Congressional Medal of Honor. Virginia Hall was one of the most courageous, memorable people I have ever known. Our paths would cross several times after our initial meeting, primarily at the CIA at which we both would eventually work. She did marry my fellow "Joe", Gaston Goillot, who had introduced us!

Memories

This was my second arrival by sea in the United States. On my first crossing, embarked for the new land, I never dreamt that five years later I would be on a troop ship returning from the battle fields of Europe. I had known that something was about to happen, but when and how was the big question.

"Never again will the German Army set foot on French soil," the French people had said. On two occasions, in 1870 and in 1914, German troops had invaded France. The French believed that the Maginot Line, the incredibly expensive, complicated and comfortable underground fortress, would without question prevent the next Teutonic invasion! All along the German border miles of tunnels connected fortified artillery batteries whose pieces faced Germany. The air within was pumped through an elaborate filtering system, and large quantities of ammunition and supplies planned for the troops to survive almost indefinitely.

The famous Maginot Line was completed by the mid-thirties. It was a marvel of engineering. No nation in its right mind would ever attempt to cross it by force. It was originally designed to extend from the English Channel to the Alps. However, under this plan the northern-most portion would not actually face Germany, but Belgium, one of France's allies. It was felt that to extend the Maginot Line along the Belgium border would have been an insult to the Belgian people who were no threat to France, and who claimed that they could hold the Huns. The other end of the Maginot Line was to face Switzerland. Who in his right mind would attack Switzerland? So in the south, the Maginot Line ended in the heavily fortified region of Belfort where we lived. The French were correct in the Swiss case, but wrong about Belgium.

In addition, conventional wisdom held, the League of Nations, with or without America, would unite all European nations to prevent future wars. Those feeble-witted Boches might be able to fly their Zeppelins to America, but they could not produce butter! In the 1930's this was the prevailing attitude among many people, especially those who ignored the warnings.

Meanwhile, Spain was being used as a military testing ground by both Germany and Russia, the Soviets on the side of the legitimate government and the Germans on the side of Generalissimo Franco. And, after making certain that Italian trains ran on time, Benito Mussolini invaded Ethiopia.

Emperor Haile Selassie was betrayed by the do-nothing League of Nations. Ignoring the Treaty of Versailles, Hitler moved his troops into Saarland. In Germany, glider pilots were improving their skill. While German workers were busy building Hitler's war machine, the French government was preoccupied with social experiments.

To tease or appease their northern neighbors, on a bridge at the border the Swiss placed stacks of butter, an extremely scarce commodity in Germany. By 1938 Mr. Chamberlain assured the world that Hitler would not invade other countries and that "Peace in our time" was at hand.

Even though my father had immigrated to the United States in 1927, I was not too concerned with the New World. Two of my uncles, who had gone to America with my father, had returned five years later completely disillusioned.

By early 1939, Europe was on the verge of a war nobody wanted, particularly those who twenty years earlier had fought the great war, the war that would end all wars! It was inconceivable that twenty years later anyone would think another conflict possible: the last one had cost so much pain and destruction to so many throughout Europe.

My own father had served in the war and was gassed in Salonica during the Greek campaign. His two brothers, as well as practically every man in our small town, had served in the grande guerre (Great War.) To make certain that those who had fallen for the "Patrie" (homeland) were not forgotten, an imposing monument had been erected to their memory in the center of town. The names of the fallen had been engraved on the stone. Veterans organizations were popular, and soldiers returning home after November 1918 spoke of the War with reverence because it had been a great sacrifice for them and their families.

The French people were divided along undefined political lines. On the extreme left were the communists, who wanted to establish a system of government similar to that of the Soviet Union. Toward the center were the Radical Socialists, which included Socialists and some of the other splinter groups, who favored strong government control of the life of the people.

The right was composed of a multitude of small parties that were so busy fighting each other they did not represent a serious opposition to the left.

I sympathized mostly with a group called "Croix-de-Feu" (Cross of fire). This organization was founded by bitterly anti-German veterans considered by many as extremist because they were in favor of fighting Germany immediately and against appeasing Hitler.

Although it had been officially disbanded in 1936, its members had many followers even among those who had never been in the military. In the late 30's France, which had sided against Franco in the Spanish revolution, had later inherited many of Spain's communist leaders. Labor unrest was common. The unions wanted to cut the work week to 35 hours, while Germany's war-building industry was working 60 hours a week. French labor's position did not make sense to most of us who were concerned with the tense situation of those days.

I was born in 1921 at Lebetain, a small French farming community on the Swiss border where my Swiss grandfather on my mother's side had a farm. In 1918, my father, before his discharge from the French Army, was in command of a surplus military supply depot near Nancy in Loraine. In 1920 he returned to Lebetain, his birthplace and, after marrying Emilie Monnot, my mother, he obtained work at Delle, the county seat, as a mechanic in a local garage. We lived nearby in an upstairs apartment at my Uncle Lucien's farm house where my sister Marcelle was born three years later.

The prevailing wisdom at the time was that America was the pinnacle, the land of opportunity, and my dad immigrated there in 1928. I was seven years old. He, my uncles Achilles, and Lucien with his wife Marcelle, went to America to make their fortunes!

Economically, this was not a very good period for France; however, it turned out to be worse in the United States, and by 1929 the depression was in full force. Five years later my two uncles returned to France to resume their farming while dad stayed and tried his luck. Jobs were scarce, but his skill as a toolmaker enabled him to survive quite well. He might have believed that it was easier for him to support his family from the United States, or other reasons may have caused him to remain there and wait for an opportunity to bring us over. But remain he did. Unfortunately, for twelve years that opportunity to bring us over never seemed to present itself.

After my father and uncles had left for the United States, we moved to another lodging because my uncle's farm had been sold or leased to someone else. Mother found a two room apartment in a house owned by the grandfather of a school pal of mine. Mr. Nathan Ulman was a kind old Jewish man who resided next door. He was probably not older than sixty which to me was very old. I used to take the rent money and watch him sign the receipt with a flurry of lines punctuated with two dots even though this name had none. When I asked him why, confidentially he said "This is a secret code". I was impressed. So I grew up without a father, but my many uncles compensated for it.

The three of us were poor by today's standards, but we were not aware of our precarious economic situation. What we lacked did not seem very important at the time. To me, my father was only a symbol, not a person; whereas my uncles, aunts and cousins were my family.

The money that my father periodically sent, along with items around Christmas such as clothing, crayons and coloring books, did not compensate for his absence. Character and values—these qualities ascribed to us by others—were much more important than any material concerns.

At my uncle's food was plentiful and well prepared especially at my uncle Lucien's farm who had moved to another farm when he returned from

America. His farm was a walking distance from our apartment (4 km) allowing me to help with the chores including cooking and baby sitting my two little cousins. After a hard day's work my favorite snack was raw bacon hanging from the rafters of the smoke house. With a long knife my uncle Lucien would slice a thick piece and give me a good portion with a big piece of bread. We would chew and chew washing it down, he with a glass of *vin ordinaire*, and I with a glass of milk until it was gone.

My sexual education began before my father left for America at a nearby mattress repair shop managed by a young Jewish fellow. I used to watch him making mattresses, a most professional skill. He asked me once if I had ever seen "un jet" (a jet, as in water jet). I shook my head "no". So he showed me! It was not exactly the game I used to play with some of my friends when we tried to see who could urinate the farthest. Later I learned that he was "pédé" as the uncle of one my school friends, and that he was different. I did not learn about the difference until much later.

When we moved to our new lodging I was 7 or 8 years old, and surrounded with girls of my age. They all lived in our neighborhood and were always playing together. As the only boy the same age in the area, I was often invited to join them. I did not mind. Although they took advantage of my good nature and inexperience.

It took several years for me to appreciate the attention of the opposite sex. Only later when playing hide and seek in the dark did we have the opportunity to know each other better.

Our family shared the second floor of the building with Monsieur Naver, a bank manager. His family consisted of two girls, Denise and Gilberte, and one boy, named Georges. Another girl, Jeannine, arrived after we had moved in the new apartment.

Monsieur Naver was an obese individual whose religion was eating. His altar was the dining table upon which he practiced his sacred rituals under the watchful eyes of his acolyte and cook, the mousy-looking Madame Naver. Every meal at the Naver's home was punctuated by gourmet cheese and a fruit followed by a cup of strong coffee.

Georges, who was a couple years older than I, became my closest male friend. Since I had no father close by, Georges' dad adopted me. With or without Georges he took me hunting, fishing, and on outings in his auto, which was a company car. Denise, the older daughter, was a hefty girl who was engaged to Rick Barthoulot, a local boy attending college in a nearby city.

Gilberte, one year younger than I, was my pal. We spent a lot of time together investigating each other and discovering the real difference between boys and girls. I could not understand why she was so friendly and receptive on regular basis, while at other times she wouldn't even let me come near her. On the winter evenings, sitting in our living room under a 25-watt bulb with our homework spread on a large table, she would sit close to the table and fondle each other which gave me an indescribable pleasure that I am sure she shared.

Periodically she would reject me and sulk alone on a chair away from me. I knew that there was something bothering her. I did not know what was the cause—her period, of course—but I did not insist. I waited until she got over her mood. We knew the rolls of our sex organs and how babies were made, and that marriage was the prerequisite to the act of reproduction. The mystery that surrounded this activity was to us very attractive.

Georges was the smart one; he knew everything and was given everything he wanted by his father. He had two guns—an air gun and a .22 rifle with which we used to kill rats and birds. Together we built a club house out of old lumber and scraps of all sorts, and held conferences in its sanctity.

The two apartments shared a single john, and when old man Naver used it everyone knew it. He spent a long time in the small WC with a newspaper. Many times I waited impatiently for the sound of the flush to rush to the toilet, holding my nose. The Navers had five rooms and a kitchen, whereas we had two rooms including a kitchen. Marcelle slept with Mother and I slept in the kitchen on a folding bed. We had no bathroom nor bathtub. I washed in the small kitchen sink.

Occasionally mother would boil water in the building's laundry room at the back of the house, and fill a large wooden wash tub with warm water for me to bathe in. In the summertime, we used the river for bathing. The Naver girls used the laundry room for bathing more than we did, and they became upset when Georges and I threatened to peek in the room's dirty window.

Next door lived the Fleury family. Michelle, the oldest daughter, was my age. After the Navers moved away she was the only girl left in the neighborhood. Unlike Gilberte, she was only interested in kissing which we did often in her darken hallway.

In the fall, the river that ran behind our house would overflow its banks, fill the valley and would reach the retaining wall behind our house. When the temperature dropped to freezing, the entire area became a huge natural skating rink.

It remained frozen until spring, when the warm south winds would blow away the snow clouds. Then the melting snow and ice from the mountains would once again swell the river.

Occasionally subterranean noises could be heard. On the Swiss side of the border, a huge hole at the base of a hill led to an underground cavern. In the spring, water would gush out of it. We were told that a large underground river flowed from the Alps to the English Channel, and that during the melting season there was so much water that it filled the entire cavity, occasionally bursting out onto the surface. The river's noise scared some of the local people, who were sure that it was hell grumbling below our feet.

School was difficult and demanding. By the time I reached the eighth grade I had walked a total of over 10,000 miles, going from home to school twice a day. My favorite subjects were art and technical training, while my worst were chemistry and physics. By the time I was twelve I had reached fifth place in a nationwide art contest. My art teacher was the wife of the principal. She and I got along extremely well. As my mentor, she encouraged me to improve my drawing technique while the other teachers were not so kind, probably because I was a disruptive factor in my other classes.

After all, not every kid had a father in America. I felt that I was special and I expected everyone to know it.

During recess, a few of my followers and I would gather in a secluded spot between two buttresses of the church next door. I loved to clown for my friends, imitating the teachers we did not care for and telling jokes. Unfortunately, some of my friends repeated my jokes for their parents, and to avoid a reprimand, they admitted that they were only repeating what I had said. My jokes eventually reached the school staff and that was one reason why I was very much disliked by some of the teachers, who probably celebrated my departure after I left for America.

Literature was all right by me, as long as it dealt with adventure and mystery. Mother would read adventure stories to my sister and me that excited my imagination to no end. Racine, Molière, and even Voltaire made very little impression on me. But Victor Hugo's father was my ideal personality; Mr. Sagin's adventurous goat was my favorite goat; and La Fontaine's Maitre Renard was my favorite fox. Not only was he mischievous, he was also clever. Georges' father was known to have killed one of these smart creatures. In the cold months, his mother would wear its pelt around her neck for warmth. I could not imagine Mr. Naver having been smarter than a fox!

At school, in order to check our writing ability and imagination, we periodically had to write our own stories. One time we were encouraged to be especially creative and concoct a different story. I could not think of something different and waited until the last minute to write it. Then I settled on a gangster story taking place in America. I was certain that I would get a good grade, probably an A.

Instead, the next day the teacher asked me to stay after school. He seemed very upset. Abruptly he asked me how I dared to write a gangster story in which the gangsters were depicted as the winners. Without meaning to be sassy, I replied that he had asked us to write something different, so I did. I didn't know what hit me, but before I realized it I was on the floor and the teacher was pounding on me with his fist. Confused and hurt, I went home and complained to my mother about it.

Instead of sympathizing with me, she slapped me hard. "If the teacher beat you it was because you did something wrong and deserved it," she said.

Although father sent money periodically, mother found it difficult to make ends meet. She decided to seek work and found a job operating a overlock knitting machine for a local man who was also a locally esteemed artist. I was fascinated by his charcoal drawings. At first I thought they were photographs, since I could not believe that it was possible to make such accurate drawings using charcoal. Seeing my interest in art he gave me some charcoal sticks and showed me how to use his technique. From another friend I learned how to make industrial drawings, and fully intended to be a draftsman. But events prevented me from achieving this goal.

My village had a particular historic significance because it was there that in 1914 the first French and German casualties occurred. A German horse patrol coming from Alsace crossed the border only a few miles away and reached a farm house where a French squad under the command of Corporal Peugeot was bivouacking. A young girl gave the alarm. The Corporal aimed his rifle while the German Captain aimed his pistol. Both fired at the same time and killed each other. Two days later war was declared and the slaughter began.

A cross had been painted on the door of the farm house with the corporal's blood. Twenty years later the cross was barely noticeable, but could nonetheless still be seen. One of our young priests would take us on periodic hikes in the countryside. When we would pass in front of the farm house, after crossing himself, the priest would remind us of the cowardly deed, and of by whom it was committed!

There was also some bitterness toward the United States which was requesting French repayment of war debts while allowing Germany, which had lost the war, to go scot-free. The French victorieux felt very much the losers, and many war veterans looked over the Rhine with fear and apprehension. By 1938 France was under the control of the Socialists, and remained sharply divided. The rightists, fearing the Communists more than the Nazis, were accused by the leftists of being pro-Hitler. The French government embarked on a huge social program. The CGT, a Communist-controlled union condoned by the government, began a series of strikes to demand less work for the same pay, and then more pay for the same work. The thirty-five-hour week demanded by the CGT paled beside the German sixty.

The French public school system, under the control of the central government, was bent on indoctrinating its students in Socialism. Many of the teachers were on the left of the political spectrum, and those who were not kept their mouths shut for fear of losing their jobs. Socialism was praised and capitalism decried.

One of my teachers, of history, was a communist who in his spare time trained some gullible people to sing "l'Internationale," the communist anthem. I am certain that he did more than teach them to sing. His version of the French Revolution was along the Communist Party line. I had developed a strong dislike for this man who had no sense of humor and appeared to prefer Russia to France.

Fortunately, most of us of high-school-age, the post-World War I baby-boomers, paid little credence to our teachers' ideological bias. Those having the greatest influence on us were our parents and relatives who had fought the Great War, and our priests, who were bitterly anti-Communist.

While growing up as most boys of my age I enjoyed an amazing amount of freedom. While my sister as all girls— with a few exception— lived under strict rules, I largely did what I pleased, at the great dismay of my mother. I had many friends, some poor, some very rich and influential, but most all very smart. I was always involved with some project, ranging from building a club house with Georges to building a plane that would fly with André Bauman, the local genius. I made model airplanes and gliders, and drew plans that I sold for pocket money.

My friend Georges learned to pilot a real plane. I went with him to a nearby airport when he took his final test, which consisted of flying a series of figure-8's without losing altitude. He passed with flying colors but was not yet allowed to take up passengers. Francis Kohler, the owner of a large factory and an accomplished pilot, occasionally took me up in his Farman. We even landed in the wheat fields of Delle, which was not an easy thing to do as there were no landing strips or markers. Francis was the motivator (and, in many instances, the financial supporter) of our small group of aviation enthusiasts. He and André Bauman collaborated in the construction of a very small ultra-light plane called pou du ciel, or "sky lice". André was a farmer by trade, but could repair an aircraft engine as well as make a propeller out of raw wood. Aircraft engineers came to him for advice. I learned much from both individuals.

I enjoyed the good things in life; especially hunting jack rabbits with the fat bank manager and Georges. I did a lot of hiking not only around my home town, but in the Jura mountains of Switzerland. I knew many of the mountain trails and was able to easily move about them at night as well as during the day.

Our family life revolved around three areas: the Cheval Blanc Inn of Cornol in the Swiss Jura, and in France my uncle Victor's farm at Etupes, and l'Enclos Roland (my uncle Lucien's farm, which he leased from its owner and operated with his brother, my Uncle Achilles). We were always welcome in all three places, but my favorite place was Etupes because there I would be the youngest family member, unlike at l'Enclos Roland, where my three cousins were younger than I. In both places, in order to obtain acceptance, I had to work hard and follow very strict rules.

During the school summer recess I would go to Etupes to live and work on my Uncle Victor's farm. I loved the farm, the animals, the good food, even the hard physical work. My Uncle Victor was my idol. Tall, wearing a luxuriant black mustache, he was a very handsome individual. In addition, he was smart, and could talk about any subject. His knowledge of animals and farming was boundless. His live stock consisted of twenty-five milk cows and three draft horses. Of course he had two dogs, a compliment of chickens and some rabbits. But no bull! Thus periodically one of my cousins and I would take a cow ready to be inseminated to the lucky village bull and help him with his duty. I often wonder how cattle managed in the wild! At times the bull was so excited that he missed the mark entirely and one of us had to grab his slimy penis and place it in the correct aperture! Then, shaking with anticipation, the bull would ram his "verge" into the cow who would arch her back in either pleasure or pain.

I grew older and stronger, and by the time I was fifteen, I was old enough to be assigned more responsible duties. I was given the job of watching the cattle as they fed in the field after the hay had been collected and a new growth of grass had appeared. The field had no fences. I had to keep the cattle in my uncle's fields. The two sheep dogs were my helpers. In the late summer, when the increasingly colder days announced the coming of winter and the sky would turn gray with heavy clouds, I would build a fire and collect a few potatoes left in the field and cook them over hot ashes. These were the best potatoes. Never have I tasted anything as good since. The pastures were located next to a canal that linked the Rhine and Rhone rivers. On this masterpiece of engineering, huge flat barges called "péniches" moved along carrying loads of coal, stone, cement and other commodities. A few of the barges were still pulled by teams of horse or oxen, but most were by then self-propelled by diesel engines. Occasionally a beautifully painted barge carrying passengers, many of them American or British, would glide by. Holding a glass of je-ne-sais-quoi in one hand they would wave at me from their rattan chairs. I would wave back, happy to know that someone had noticed me. I also knew that they were not French because the French never waved at anyone!

Life on the farm was not always fun. In between the pleasant times, we had some very difficult work. The days were long and the work hard, but I never heard a word of complaint from anyone.

Cornol is a small Swiss village located at the foot of the Jura mountains. One of Cornol's three auberges (small inns) was the "Cheval Blanc" (White Horse),owned by our cousin Alcide Gérard, his ailing spouse Emilie, and aunt Mathilde, Emilie's sister who had once lived in Nice on the French Riviera.

Mother had spent the first World War as a waitress at the Inn that was the Headquarters for the Swiss Army defending the region. Since then, mother had kept in contact with our cousins. After father's departure, our relationship with the cousins became closer, with frequent visits and longer stays during school vacations.

Cornol was a predominantly farming community on a strategic route between central Switzerland and France. From the French border to Cornol the land was rather flat and devoid of natural obstacles. Immediately after the village, the Rangiers, the western-most range of the Juras, presented the first serious barrier to any invasion of Switzerland. To celebrate the Swiss determination remain strong, if neutral during World War I, a huge statue representing a Swiss soldier was erected on the fork of the road above the village. Locally It was referred to as le Gros Suisse (the big Swiss). Unfortunately, instead of facing Germany, the statue faced France. This seeming distrust made the French very unhappy, and upset even the local Swiss, who were predominantly pro-French. Eventually, once the Jura region assumed the status of a "Canton" (County or District) separating itself from the Canton of Bern, which was predominately German, the statue was destroyed by persons unknown, but definitely not pro-German.

Unlike my uncles' farms at Delle and Etupes, I had no close pals in my age bracket at Cornol. My cigar-smoking, wine-drinking, and card-playing cousin Alcide was my closest friend and playmate. We called him and his wife "uncle and aunt" rather than cousin, as a mark of respect and close relationship. Together we would take long walks, sometimes in the mountains, and at times to nearby villages where he knew many people and everyone seemed to know him. He was always well dressed, including tie and vest, and sometimes spats and cocked hat, and he acted as a debonair. In his seventies, he was a good walker and an interesting individual.

The rumor was that he was a Freemason, which in a mostly catholic community was not a very good recommendation. On Sundays, he would dress up and go to church, but always late so that there was no room to sit, which was his excuse to go across the street to "Au Boeuf", a small inn, for a cup of coffee or something stronger. Once the mass ended and the people left the small cemetery surrounding the church he would return to the Cheval Blanc where a bubbling cheese fondue and little square pieces of bread were waiting for the customers coming for the traditional Sunday "apéritif".

Sometimes these so-called apéritifs lasted until it was time for the farmers to leave to milk the cows, or until the late evening for those who had other occupations.

Uncle Alcide treated a lot of people to drinks, which made Aunt Emilie very upset. For a few hours the restaurant was a lively scene of talking and joking. Beer and wine were served, and occasionally some hard liquor. In summertime the basement ("la cave") was the only cool place where beer and wine could be kept. The wine was stored in barrels and the bottled beer in a large metal basin full of water and a block of ice. But it was also where absinthe, a forbidden elixir produced from the plant roots, was served illegally to those who were known to be discreet. In the cool damp basement an ounce of absinthe was placed in a tumbler, and water was poured over two sugar cubes held over the glass on a fork.

The only individuals to be feared were the "Gendarme" (town police) and the "Garde Champêtre" (constable), law officers who could issue a "contravention" (fine). When clients were in the cave (cellar), my job was to watch for the law and give the alarm in the event they came too close to the Inn. Funny thing though, when everyone was gone, one or another officer would come down the cellar for his own glass of absinthe!

Although we were young we were given beer and wine, and at times, if we had done something special, a small glass of Malaga wine was our treat. This was a dark, sweet, thick Spanish wine which made our heads light!

From my vantage point I was able to observe our customers, some of whom were pillars of the community—such as the school principal and the Mayor—and see them under the influence of alcohol. Watching them stagger from the Inn, even sometimes falling down, and listening to their incoherent speech made a lasting impression on me. I swore then that I would never be in that position.

During the week, while everyone was busy and the Inn was empty, Uncle Alcide and I would go to nearby villages. One in particular was the small village of Charmoille where my mother was born and her family lived. It was said that half the village had immigrated to the United States.

My grandfather was a "Cantonier" (road maintenance man). He was responsible for a stretch of road leading to and from the village. This was a government job with some perks. He owned a cow that he used to keep the grass on either side of the road mowed. This free pasture provided forage to the cow and the cow provided free milk to the family.

My mother's grandparents owned a saw mill operated by a mountain spring which originated on my great grandmother's property. It became the Alaine, the river that passed through Delle and eventually ended at the Doubs river. My grandfather's house was across the street from the mill and one of our many cousins, Poupon, lived next door. Poupon was a tall good-looking fellow and an officer in the Swiss Army. His Kirsch was the best in the region, which was probably why we would go often to see him.

Occasionally I would go up the mountain on my own, and get lost. Fortunately for me, my sense of direction always came to the rescue. Sometimes I would find some unusually scenic area and return there with my water colors and pad, sit on a warm rock and sketch and paint for a few hours.

There were so many things to see, to hear, to feel. In some specific places the mountain would talk back to me. Facing a certain ridge I would cup my hands to my mouth and in a loud voice say my name. Before the last syllable I could hear in the distance a voice saying: "René.é.é... Défourneaux.o. o. o." I loved the mountain, not only because I could do what I wanted to do, but because it was overwhelming, full of obstacles, constantly changing but always beautiful. My water colors were displayed at the inn by my proud Aunt Emilie.

At Delle, Sunday mass was a major production. The church that was completed in the eleventh century had a choir loft with a terrific organ operated by boy power. The bellows had to be manipulated during the service so that the organ could be played. I would go up on the choir loft and help the boy pump the bellows. I loved watching the people below us and to see the Suisse (in European catholic churches, the gaily uniformed individual who maintained order during the service) in his Napoleonic uniform nudging sleeping parishioners with his long halberd.

Tough-looking sisters in black robes and hobnailed boots taught us catechism. They prepared us for our first confession and first communion. We learned that thanks to our baptism, our original sin had been wiped out, but since then we had accumulated a plethora of venial (not to mention a few mortal) sins, which had to be divulged to the priest so as to get his absolution and a clean bill of health for admittance to heaven. When I told the priest what I did with Gilberte I expected the worst. To my surprise, ten "Notre Père" did the trick. What I did was not so bad after all! I did not tell him what had gone on at the mattress shop; after all the fellow was Jewish, and had his own rules.

The Old Testament was difficult for some of us to swallow. But we went through the motions, learned the basics and promptly forgot it all after our first communion.

Occasionally the old priest would take the place of the sisters to explain to the boys the very serious aspects of our religion such as having sexual intercourse before marriage and "se branler" (masturbating). These two were a sure way to hell unless the absolution was given prior to your final voyage. I did not know what the sisters or the priest told to the girls, for they had nothing to masturbate with, and they were seldom left alone with the boys.

Visiting missionaries would also entertain us with tales of their activities in foreign countries and with the past exploits of saints, hoping that some of us would get the calling and volunteer for the seminary. Few did, and these did not remain very long.

I was fascinated by the dedication of some of those saints who had lost their lives in the promotion of religion in the most primitive countries. I even toyed with the idea that it would be worthwhile to travel to deepest Africa and spread the gospel, but did nothing with the idea.

The town's clothing store was owned by a Russian refugee. We were friends because my Aunt Elaine had married a Russian who had come to the community about the same time. Whereas my aunt had married a Cossack, Daniel, the owner of the clothing store, was a businessman. He was of medium height, pudgy and spoke French with a slight but distinct Russian accent. Both Uncle Elia and Daniel began their business ventures in about the same way. With a baby carriage loaded with socks and other accessories they would go from house to house, selling the goods they had purchased at a bargain.

Before long each had made enough money to purchase a small vehicle and expand their territory.

My friend Daniel was Jewish and probably had some financial backers because it was not long before he was able to lease a small room on the street level of the building next to the butcher shop. I would go there periodically to watch his wife, who had dyed red hair and fake eye-lashes and spoke mostly Russian so I would not understand. The two liked me and occasionally would ask me to watch their store while they went shopping at the market. Being tall and skinny, I even modeled some of their clothes for their customers.

One day Daniel asked me for a favor. One of his Swiss clients had purchased a suit from him. In order to return to Switzerland with the suit, the client would have to pay a substantial import duty to Swiss Customs, which the Swiss had imposed in order to protect their own industry. Daniel asked if I would cross the border while wearing the suit and deliver it to the client. I agreed and for me it was my first experience in international trade and the beginning of a life of crime.

Smuggling was illegal, but many people did it to various degrees. I was fortunate because I was well known in the area.

I lived next door to the Inspector responsible for the border guards and occasionally I baby sat with his two small girls. I took advantage of the situation and nosed into the patrolling schedule of the douaniers (border guards), which he usually left unattended on his desk.

I did a lot of walking in those days. I knew all the trails in the hills, I knew where the patrols were and when I wanted to avoid them it was easy for me to do so. Occasionally I would daydream, forget where I was, and come face to face with a Border Guard. I would need to quickly think of a reason to be where I was at that time.

Once I was caught just as I had crossed the border near my uncle's farm. In my coat I was carrying a few packs of Swiss cigarettes, enough to get me into deep trouble. It was warm so I had hung my coat over my arm. The officer knew that I was up to something. He decided to search me. While he patted me down on one side I moved my coat to the other side so that he never felt the pockets. He reprimanded me for being out so late, then let me go.

Occasionally I had to dump what I was carrying in the bushes, and return later to retrieve it.

My Uncle Lucien's farm was very close to the border. During inclement weather the officers would stay in his barn to keep warm and my Aunt Marcelle made sure that they had a hot cup of coffee. I do not believe any of my relatives were smugglers. My mother was the most scrupulous person I have ever known. Had she known what I was doing she would have killed me.

The smuggling was a secret I did not even share with my close friends. One of my many cousins was the train conductor on the Swiss side. By taking the train in Switzerland, I avoided the regular customs inspection when crossing the border. I used one of the trails and walked to the Swiss station. One day as my cousin was punching my ticket, he looked at me and said, "René, you seem to be gaining weight."

Indeed, I was wearing two suits for a good customer!

From our back yard, I could be in Switzerland in less than two minutes. The back of my uncle's farm came up to the border which was indicated by a line carved on the top of a lone stone marker: on one side of the stone was France; on the other side was Switzerland. The locals never took notice and only an occasional douanier (customs officer) would patrol the area, weather permitting.

I never had an actual allowance. I earned a few francs now and then by washing glasses and clearing tables in my cousin's Inn of the White Horse in Switzerland. My watching over the absinthe sipping in the cellar also brought me a few sous (pennies).

By age thirteen, one other enterprise that earned me a few francs was to distribute fresh fish in our largely Catholic town every Thursday. Our town was approximately 1,000 kilometers from the nearest ocean and in those days there was no established distribution. Every Friday by telephone I placed an order for delivery to an organization run by the Church. They in turn contracted with fish wholesalers in Normandy or Brittany. The following Thursday around five o'clock in the afternoon, I would go to the railroad station and pickup up a large, heavy, iced box of fresh fish that had traveled all night. It was my equivalent of a paper route.

Eventually I was put out of business by local merchants who began stocking fresh fish throughout the week.

By 1938, the situation in Europe had severely deteriorated. France was positioning a few troops along its borders. There were maneuvers in our area and strikes continued to plague the struggling industries.

When I turned seventeen, over my mother's objections I left school and went to work for a large automobile manufacturer, Peugeot, where my uncle Paul, one of my mother's many brothers, was a director. I joined a union called

CFTC (Confédération Française des Travailleurs Chrétiens) which was a Christian union opposed to the CGT, the Communist-led union. Early every morning I took the bus to Sochaux, some sixteen miles away. At first I became an inspector of parts, then I was given the opportunity to operate a grinding machine. But there was a lot of labor strife.

One day when we reached the factory we were surprised by thousands of people standing in the street in front of the main building. They had been bussed in from other towns for a demonstration against the plant. Inside the plant all seemed calm until members of the CGT began to shut off the electric switches controlling the production lines. We waited, and most of us were happy when the demonstrators left, the power was restored and the machines once again hummed. The next day when we arrived at the plant we were met by an angry mob who would not let us get off our bus. The police came and made a path for us to the door. The strikers tried to attack us as we filed into the plant between two lines of police officers. It was obvious that most of the mob were outsiders; the plant appeared fully occupied and yet there were thousands of people in the street!

The government tried to maintain order through the local police, but in vain. Then they brought in the army and the tanks. Pretty soon, the mob was on top of the tanks and the soldiers refused to shoot. So they brought in the Republican Guard, the republic's own police with their short carbines. The mob had placed women in front of them, thinking that they would be safe behind the females. What Frenchman would hurt a woman? They learned very quickly that one does not fool around with the Republican Guard. With the butts of their weapons they knocked out a few teeth and the mob action ended, but not before a few Guardsmen were killed inside the plant. Some demonstrators had climbed the scaffolds of the smelting plant carrying heavy metal ingots. When surrounded by the Guards, they dropped these ingots and some landed on the heads of the pursuers, killing them instantly.

The company wanted to deal with our union, but we were too insignificant. Despite our efforts to recruit new members and to convince those non-communist members of the CGT to join us, we were overwhelmingly outnumbered. Distributing handbills at the door of the plant was the primary means of informing the workers of their options. The communist union, which considered us to be "scabs," did not appreciate our efforts and tried to stop us by any means. This included beating those distributing the handbills. A friend and I became the object of the attention of some thugs so it was obvious why people were reluctant to join us.

No one had told my Uncle Paul that I was working at the plant. Mother was unhappy and a little ashamed that I had left school and so had not spread the news to our relatives. One day as I was busy at my tasks, I heard a voice calling me saying, "Qu'est ce que tu fous ici?" (What in the hell are you doing here?)

Turning around, I faced my uncle who appeared very unhappy, and let me know bluntly that I should have told him before applying for the job. From that time on my life at the plant was never the same. I was related to one of the directors and even the supervisors treated me with deference. I had not wanted my coworkers or anyone else to know about my uncle for that very reason.

To be accepted by my co-workers, I decided to take up smoking. My preferred brand was called "High Life" which was pronounced "eeg leef" by most of us who did not know the English language. Unlike Gauloise, which tasted like burnt rope, these cigarettes were aromatic and mild. I also smoked a pipe and occasionally rolled cigarettes with loose Swiss tobacco. I began to grow a few whiskers which became the object of many jokes on the part of my relatives and co-workers. I was told several times not to buy a razor; instead I should open the front and back doors, stand in the draft for a few minutes and my beard would blow off my face. I was sure that to shave every day, religiously, would encourage my beard to grow.

By 1938 the French National Conscription was accelerated but had not expanded to include older or younger men. I was seventeen, not yet an acceptable age for military service. Many of my older contemporaries were in uniform. Georges was deferred because he was attending college studying aeronautics, but Denise's boyfriend was already in the Air Force.

With mixed emotions, in the fall of 1938 I received the news that we were finally going to America. Why had it taken twelve long years for my father to send for us? Now I would be leaving a multitude of friends to go to a father I barely remembered, to a place I did not know. Still, I looked forward to the voyage with both anticipation and no small fear of the unknown. We were about to leave a relatively comfortable existence for an adventure full of expectation. I felt that once I left the shores of France I would never return, and that all I had experienced up to that time would be erased forever.

I was leaving those who had been close to me and it was difficult for me to imagine that I might never see them again. I had a girlfriend in the Swiss village next to ours. She was the daughter of an old boyfriend of my mother. She was a tall, blond, healthy-looking girl I had met one day at a sport meet when the Swiss team beat the pants off our team.

Her father, Mr. Berger, a school teacher, was the coach of the Swiss team, and an athlete well known in the community. His daughter and I usually met at night along the river which crossed the border because girls were not supposed to meet boys without a chaperon. I had liked her immediately because she reminded me of my own mother, and perhaps by then I might have been in love with her!

She was nothing like Gilberte, the banker's daughter, or Michelle, our neighbor. Holding hands and a goodnight kiss were the extent of our romantic activities. Of course her father was not the kind of man to tangle with! It was very difficult for us to meet during the day. I knew that she would be airing the household bedding around 9:00 in the morning, so when I had the time, I would climb the hill overlooking the village, sit on a rock and watch for the sheets and eiderdown to appear in the open windows. When I would see an arm waving to me I would stand up, wave for a while and then run down the trail whistling a happy tune. Our final rendezvous came on the bank of the River Alaine on a moonless night. Holding hands, we promised to write each other faithfully, and shed a few tears.

In April 1939, my mother, sister and I obtained our passports and went to the American Consulate in Strasbourg for physical examinations in order to obtain our visas to the United States. Then, in the middle of May, mother packed our belongings, giving away to our relatives what we could not carry. We traveled by train to Paris and then by Micheline to Le Havre where we embarked aboard the SS Manhattan.

Back Home

My trip returning from the war was a lot faster and more comfortable than on the victory ship going over. The few of us lucky enough to go back home were loaded aboard the Queen Mary berthed at Glasgow, Scotland. On the 21st of December as we were about to get under way, the ship loudspeaker announced that Germany had counterattacked and had surrounded our troops near the Belgium town of Bastogne. Apparently the war was not yet over! Some of us fully expected to be unloaded to help. But it was not to be. The Queen quietly left port and we headed home. I was walking the promenade deck when someone approached me and said: "Aren't you the fellow we dropped in France a few months ago?"

I replied to the affirmative trying to remember his face. He continued: "I am the one who assisted you before you jumped."

There was so little light in the tail end of the aircraft that I did not have the opportunity to observe my companion very carefully. Indeed he looked familiar, but it took a while for me realize that he was the one who had helped me with my parachute, he made certain that every thing was ready for my jump. He was the one who had taken my flask of "good" scotch and pushed it forward to the cockpit. He was the one who open the cover of the hole through which I was to jump. He was the last American I would see for several months, the one who said: "Go", and I went!

"What about the rest of the crew?" I asked.

"They are on the top deck" he replied.

"Do you want to see them?" he added.

"You're damn right I want to see then."

But I did not tell him why I wanted to speak to those who dropped me at the wrong place. When I showed up on the upper deck I could see the surprise on their faces. Indeed they were the ones with whom I had shared a cup of coffee before leaving. But never before had they seen a Joe back from behind the lines. Actually I did not have the heart to tell them that they had missed their target by 40 kilometers. They would not have believed me anyway. Sgt. Roy Korrot the dispatcher gave me his address because he was from Philadelphia which was close to my home town.

After passing Ireland we went through the worst storm ever faced by the Queen Mary. At times the ship listed so badly that even the Captain was scared. He told us so, but only after we reached calmer waters. It was wonderful to reach New York in one piece and to set foot in the best country in the world.

S E C R E T   Report 1512

1. Squadron _788_ A/C # _211_   Date _8/9 Aug._

2. Name of Operation _LICENSEE 2_ Alt. _____
   Country _____ FRANCE _____

3. Crew: Pilot _SECCAFICO_   Disp. _KORROS_
   C.Pilot _LAUZON_   R.O. _DAHLKE_
   Nav. _MILLER_   Eng. _RUH_
   Bomb. _POU_   Gunner _WERSEL_
   Pass. _____   Pass. _FARMAN_

4.

	J	G	P	N	PK
Load Carried	1	12	10		
Load Dropped	1	12	10		

5. Result of Operation. _COMPLETE_

6. Time of Take Off _2229_   Landed _0355_

7. Was Exact Pinpoint Found? _YES_. How was point identified? _____
   "C" TYPE FLASHING "R"

8. Estimated Dropping Points _A LITTLE LEFT OF LIGHTS_
   & THEN FELL
   TWO PACKAGES STUCK IN HATC ABOUT ½ MILE
   EAST OF TARGET ON 1ST RUN

9. Bombardier and Dispatchers Report. _TWO RUNS - ALL OUT_
   O.K. EXCEPT PACKAGES MENTIONED ABOVE

10. Target Area From _0101_ to _0118_. Time Dropped 1ST. _0111_
    2ND _0118_
    Height above ground 1ST 650' 2ND 400 Course 1ST 110° 2ND 240° Min. 1ST 133 2ND 131

11. Routes - Time, Altitude and Point of Crossing English and Enemy.
    Coasts _LITTLE HAMPTON - 2311 - 9000 - ELETOT - 2338 - 9000_
    - ELETOT - 0236 - 8600 - LITTLE HAMPTON - 0302 - 7500'

12. Leaflets dropped _NONE CARRIED_

S E C R E T

Squadron 788 Mission Report N° 1512 Aircraft N° 211, dated 8/9 August 1944 following the return of the crew in support of Operation Licensee. The back of this mission report is continued on following page.

13: Load or part of Load Jettisoned: What was jettisoned? _____

_____

Place _____ Altitude _____ Time _ ____ _

14. Enemy Opposition (give A/C position, time and altitude, and what happened)_____

*NONE*_____

15. Weather. How did weather affect mission: In Route: _____

_____*O.K*_____ At Target: *GROUND HAZE -*

*ABOUT 1 MILE VISIBILITY*_____

16. Captains personal report *VERY GOOD RECEPTION*

_____
(INTERROGATION OFFICER)

DECLASSIFIED
Authority *NND 745005*
By ___ NARA Date 3/9/98

INTELLIGENCE OFFICER,
CARPETBAGGER PROJECT

Crew of B-24 Number 211 for Operation Licensee, August 8/9, 1944.

Pilot . . . . Capt. James A. Seccafico
Co-pilot . . . . 1st Lt. Russel J. Lauzon
Navigator . . . . 1st Lt. George F. Miller
Bombardier . . . . 1st Lt. Charles D. Pov
Dispatcher . . . . . . S/Sgt. Roy L. Korrot
Radio Operator . . . . . Cpl. Albert Dahlke
Engineer . . . . T/Sgt. Eugene A Ruh
Gunner . . . . S/Sgt. Harold J. Wersell
Passenger . . . . Cpl. Steve Forman
J = Joe (Author)

While many of us did not make it back, those who did were doubly thankful, knowing they were either extremely lucky or that someone up there was watching over them. Unlike many of my companions I was not excessively religious. Before falling asleep, I occasionally said a prayer—if I remembered to do so. I could not imagine this old man shown in our catechism with Jesus Christ on one side and the holy Ghost on the other side keeping an eye on all of us. I was sure he did miss a few. I had a rather philosophical approach to life. When my time would come, it would come regardless of my wishes. So I never feared dying or being hurt. Yet we were told by the sisters that we should never laugh on Friday, because sure as hell we would be crying on Sunday. This myth remained with me a long time. For many years I stifled a Friday laugh for fear of offending the one who made the rule!

Yet after receiving such a mild punishment for playing with Gilberte's treasure, I doubted that sex was considered such a deadly sin, as long as the result was not a new life.

My main concern was to make sure that whatever I did I would have at least a fifty-fifty chance of survival.

So far it had worked for me.

My first stop was to see my father, mother and sister in New Jersey to show them my uniform and the gold bars on my shoulders. I could see their pride for me in their smiles, and they were overjoyed to see me after all these months of silence. They had known that I was involved with something special because the FBI, in arranging my security clearance, had interviewed our friends and neighbors, asking all kind of questions. Some of our neighbors were sure that I was in trouble. But my parents knew better; their faith in their son never wavered. While I was in France, SOE's London office had been very kind to my family. They wrote mother that I was not able to communicate with her, but that they knew where I was and that I was all right.

It felt good to be back and I decided to see some of my friends, our neighbors, and those with whom I had worked prior to joining the Army. I went to see the Bennetts, whose son Lowell Jr. had been captured after his plane was shot down over Berlin. As an AP news reporter, he was covering the night bombing of Berlin. He had parachuted to safety but was eventually captured and interned in a prisoner of war camp. His sister, Georgette, had joined the Navy and was stationed at Hunter College, attending a course sponsored by the Government. His other sisters, Mimi and Charlene, were at home. I wanted to see Georgette more than anything else, probably because she wanted nothing to do with me! When I would get close to her she immediately lifted her shoulder in a shrug that meant "bug off".

After over a year absence it felt good to see and talk to the "ma and pa" storekeepers of the neighborhood who knew me and were surprised to see me in an officer's uniform. Before reporting to Washington, I took some of my clothes to be dry cleaned down the street. A dark good-looking Italian girl waited on me. She was working alone and I had nothing to do, so we talked for a while, then she invited me in the back of the store. The room was dark and bare of furniture with only a shoulder-high shelf and a pile of clothing on the floor. She asked me for a lift and she sat on the shelf, her skirt rising half way up her thighs. What happened then I shall never forget.

Then the doorbell rang, she jumped off the shelf, adjusted her skirt, and moved to the front of the store. When she reappeared and said: "She is gone! You may leave now."

Slowly I walked back home around the corner. The cold January wind brought me back to reality. It dawned on me why my American friends always asked why the French fought with their feet and f—ked with their face! Would I ever forget this strange encounter?

The neighborhood had not changed since we settled there five years earlier after leaving France in middle of May 1939—but I had.

Nouvelle Patrie

I shall never forget my first meal aboard the SS Manhattan. It was breakfast, a typical American breakfast with funny-looking chips that the waiter called "corn flakes". I thought that this strange new food was the best thing I had ever tasted. And eggs, bacon—the works. They could not fill me up. The food aboard was wonderful and plentiful, however I doubt that I gained an ounce the whole voyage.

Aboard was a large contingent of Jewish refugees from Germany and other emigrants from all parts of Europe. There must have been a dozen languages spoken on board the ship, but French seemed the most commonly used. Conversations among the passengers were lengthy and sometimes emotional, with the comments from people who had experienced the realities of Hitler's regime. These remarks had to be translated into two or three languages for the benefit of all in the group. Excitement built among the passengers and one could feel a sense of euphoria growing as we approached the shores of the United States.

But a certain tension among the passengers also mounted. Day by day we felt an increased excitement within the group of émigrés, never before away from their homes yet hoping their dreams were about to come true. We were to arrive very early in the morning and sail past the famous French lady, the Statue of Liberty, created by August Bartholdi, a fellow Frenchman from Colmar, the same sculptor who created the famous Lion of Belfort on whose tail I had scratched my initials several years earlier while visiting with my school class.

On the day of our arrival I was up before dawn, but I found the upper deck already filed with passengers ready for the spectacle. At around 6:00 in the morning we entered New York harbor, and slowed down to accept the pilot, who was to guide us to our berth on the west side of Manhattan.

As the sun rose over the horizon, the extended arm of the statue appeared brighter until her entire form was bathed in the early morning light. As we sailed by, a strange silence replaced the excited conversations of the passengers. This was America. She was freedom personified, especially for many of those who were fleeing from persecution. And although this was not my case, I was emotionally impressed just the same, and proud to see this symbol, presented to the United States by the country I was abandoning.

We landed on the 24th of May, 1939, on a bright sunny morning, another relief from rainy Europe. My dad picked us up at the pier where our luggage was lined up for inspection. After a few questions by the Immigration and

Customs officials, we were free to be on our way. We loaded dad's big car and drove through the cavernous streets of New York. I could not believe the height of the buildings. We left Manhattan via the Hudson Tunnel and proceeded to New Jersey. We were to stay with friends who had a house in a woody small town called Floram Park, near Morristown, New Jersey. The temperature was balmy and when it came time to assign each of us a bed, I volunteered to sleep on the porch on a cot. The porch was screened, which was something I had never seen before. In France, flies were part of the environment and it was difficult to imagine a world without them.

I finally went to sleep and began to dream. I was dreaming about France and the forthcoming war, when I experienced a strange sensation. A peculiar odor was enveloping me and made me gasp. I was certain that war had started and that we were being gassed. My consciousness had not yet realized that I was no longer in France but in the United States. The next morning I told everyone about my nightmare. Our host burst out laughing. He said that night, a skunk had visited the area and that the local dog had scared him.

The next day our friend took me to the small tool shop where he worked as a supervisor. He put me to work immediately and from that time on I was making $18 per week, a fortune to me. I gave most of it to my mother and some to my sister, who was not working at the time. I was not a trained toolmaker but I had some very good teachers, most of them German. The shop manufactured tools and fixtures, such as jigs, for the aircraft industry.

Before long, I was holding my own and trading jokes with my coworkers. My sister and I went to night school to learn the language because it was soon apparent to us that unless one could speak English the future would be very gloomy.

We moved into a nice two-bedroom apartment which my father had rented on the first floor of a row house on 21st Street in a suburb of Newark called Irvington. Mother and Father had one bedroom, my sister had the other, and I slept on a divan in the dining room. There were a few young men of my age in the neighborhood. With a few exceptions they treated me well, even though I was "Frenchy" to them and had some difficulties with the language. They took upon themselves teaching me the correct way of speaking English.

Boys being boys, they soon indoctrinated me with a wide variety of American slang, without always explaining its full meaning to me. Instead, they would teach me a few choice words and send me over to try them out on a nearby group of girls. After being slapped a few times, I quickly got an idea as to the real meaning of these phrases.

"What did I say?" I would ask my friends, rubbing my stinging cheek.

"Oh, don't worry. You did very well, very well," they would reply.

I had my face slapped several times before I realized that they were pulling my leg and making me say things they would never say themselves.

One of my friends had an old Model T with a rumble seat. Four of us would pool our resources and on weekends buy fifty cents worth of gas and tour the countryside. This was fun and useful because I discovered many places that I would never have seen if I waited for my father to take us. He preferred taking his friends on trips over his family, which led to occasional confrontations and harsh words between me and my father. I was the one doing most of the talking while my father sat and said nothing. Mother did not like these confrontations. On the surface she accepted her situation rather well, but at times I felt that she missed France, Switzerland, her friends and relatives. Her husband, my father, was a stranger to us, and we were probably the same to him.

Mother treated him as another of her children. She did everything for him, even removing his shoes and putting on his "pantoufles" (slippers). On Sundays at noon she would prepare a meal fit for a king, after which my father would sit in the parlor and sleep until supper time. Little by little he grew fatter and became lazier and lazier. But he was always full of ideas. He invented several items, one of which he could have skipped entirely. He designed a self-lighting cigarette dispenser. As a chain smoker, he discovered that he was wasting too much time taking cigarettes from his pocket, from the pack and lighting them. Thus he designed a box that, with use of a button, would send the cigarette out already lit and ready to be puffed on. He failed to realize that eventually smoking would kill him.

On Saturdays I went to the movies. For ten cents I could sit in a theater from 11:00 a.m. until closing, but by 4:00 in the afternoon I had usually had enough and was ready to step into the sunshine. I learned a lot more English at the movies than at night school. I learned to understand the various accents, including cowboy dialect.

When I called my friends "pardner" they would burst out laughing. I would see the same movie two or three times if I did not understand the plot immediately.

It was very easy for me to go to work by bus and I did so for approximately one year. By that time my salary had increased to $25 per week. I felt that the experience I had acquired on the job over the previous year was worth more than $7 per week so I asked for a raise that was promptly refused. I quit my job, ignoring the warning of my friend and boss who said, "You will never get another job. You will be back, mark my word." He was correct, for indeed I did return, but only to tell him that I now had a job paying me twice what I had earned with him. We parted company but we remained friends.

When I left my first job, I actually did not know what I would be doing. I was so used to getting up in the morning that I rose even though I had no job to go to. I decided to look around in an area new to me. Passing in front of a shop, I saw a "Help Wanted" sign, walked in and met the foreman. He was a man of few words. Placing a piece of metal and a file in my hands he said, "Square this for me." I did so quickly and he told me to report to work the next day which I did, but not before telling my friend the good news.

The new company was owned by two Hungarians. The foreman too was of Hungarian ancestry, but had been born in the United States, while the bosses were emigrants as I was.

As in most of the tool shops in the area, a majority of the employees were German, Swiss or Italian. There were very few Frenchmen. Most of the French people that I knew were either chefs, cooks or retired police officers! As a result, I was quite a novelty in the trade. Although the main activity of the shop was mold-making for the plastics industry, the time came for us to join work for the national defense. Our bosses sought and obtained Government contracts, and we became a subcontractor of Republic Aircraft Corporation.

This immediately posed a problem because I, like several others in the company, was not a citizen of the United States and as such was not supposed to work on defense contracts. One of our projects was the design and manufacture of tools and jigs to make gun mounts for the P-47 fighter aircraft. Two other employees—one German and one Spaniard—and I were considered security risks. Of course we were not, but the regulation was unbending. So the company built an annex behind the main plant, and stationed the three of us there to do our own thing.

By 1941 we were very busy. I was working 10 to 15 hours per day and with overtime pay earning $120 per week—an extremely good salary at the time. We started each morning at 8:00 and on some evenings did not go home at all if the job was on a tight deadline. I would catnap on the bench and remain in the shop for two to three days at a time. Despite my salary, I was not happy. Most of the friends I had acquired up to that time were called to serve in the Armed Forces. Pretty soon, I was the only male in his 20's left in the neighborhood. The six eggs and chopped meat which mother fed me every morning did nothing for me. I weighed 140 pounds soaking wet. I was working very hard and felt more and more tired. At the shop were I worked most of the employees were old men with whom I had very little social contact. I did not mind some of them, but I felt isolated and at times unhappy.

Fortunately I had Jeanne, my one and only girlfriend. A couple years younger than I, she was the sole daughter of a couple who appeared to live together but have separate lives. She was the only one with whom I could share my feelings and find moral support. We were introduced by a teacher friend of mine who knew her mother, also a school teacher. She suggested that I help her with her French, the language she was trying to learn at the local high school. Her mother was a charming, dark-haired, striking woman known to have a local police chief as a lover. Her father was a stiff collar attorney much older and quite boring. The only thing the two had in common was their allegiance to the Republican party and a deep hatred for Roosevelt.

As her mother Jeanne was tall, dark, and seductive, and reminded me of Michelle, one of my French girl friends.

We became close from the very start but not intimate and met as often as possible, between her homework and my own work schedule. As a rule, and weather permitting, we would stay in the dark hallway of her house. There I kissed good night without attracting the attention of her parents.

Our relationship changed abruptly after an evening out. It began rather innocently. Close to midnight one evening returning

Author with first American girlfriend

from a party where alcoholic beverage were not consumed, I escorted her back home only four or five blocks away from our apartment. In the dark hallway I leaned toward her to kiss her good night when with her entire body she pushed me against the wall. Surprised by her action I had no time to consider my move when I felt her tongue searching mine. She was panting and appeared very excited, much more than I.

She kept pressing her abdomen against mine and we went further than we had anticipated, but played safe. Less impressed by what we did than I she went up the stairs to her apartment while still confused by this encounter I slowly walked home. Later on, without telling our parents, we even spent a weekend at Asbury Park. It was not as great as I had anticipated.

The War was getting closer to us. One of our employees, a German, was caught in an alleged act of sabotage. He supposedly had damaged an expensive lathe and was arrested at the plant by the FBI and taken to a prison.

The war was not going well for the Allies. France had given up, and England was about to be invaded. It was touch and go, and to some Americans, "neutrality" was merely a code word for a pro-German position. Once the war touched the United States directly, this attitude changed somewhat, but there remained an element in our area that was pro-German, if not pro-Hitler.

Irvington had a very heavy German population, much of which seemed to be sympathetic to the Nazi regime in their fatherland. A German Bund hall, resplendent with swastika banners and other Nazi regalia, had been established at a park in the center of tow. The hall had a park enclosed by a high wall. It was more than a social setting; a regular forum for pro-Nazi political meetings. These Nazi sympathizers were not very popular with those of us with non-German ancestry. One of my best friends was Polish and the son of the local chief of police.

One day, my friend surreptitiously obtained several tear gas bombs from his father's store room. We hopped into our Model T Ford, which together we supported in gas, and headed for the Bund hall, where a large gathering was taking place in its walled outdoor garden. We cruised by and lobbed the canisters over the wall. In no time, the place emptied.

From 1939 to 1941, the situation in Europe had been very bleak. By 1942 it had deteriorated completely. Hitler had invaded the low countries and occupied half of France, signing a peace treaty with Petain and preparing the invasion of England. It became bleaker after the Japanese attack of Pearl Harbor and the active participation of the U.S. into the conflict.

The pace of rearmament increased daily. Months of non-stop work was taking its toll. I was constantly fatigued, but taking a vacation was out of the question. I must have looked pretty bad for one day my boss suggested that I go home and stay there a few days. While at home resting, I realized that I was not doing what I really wanted to do. Earlier, a friend of mine who had been an Army Intelligence Officer during the war of 1918 suggested that I consider joining the Army. I had doubts about my qualifications, and despite his reassurance I ignored this possibility until I was able to think about it away from the shop and its problems. I abruptly made up my mind and told my boss of my decision. He suggested that I take an additional week off but eventually realized that I was serious.

Perhaps I decided to enlist because of a reoccurring dream that I had after my arrival in America. The same dream visited my sleep for several months after the War started: I had returned to my hometown by parachute and I was helping my friends in their fight against the Germans. After a while the dreams stopped, yet occasionally I would remember them and ponder.

It was difficult for me to explain to my folks why I wanted to join the Army and exchange $120 a week for $21 a month. My boss thought I was crazy, but accepted my decision. My Dad stated that I was nuts, and my Mother only worried. However my girl friend told me she thought I was doing the right thing, probably because she was tired of me.

In December, 1942, I reported to the Draft Board of Essex County, and being careful not to tell the Board what I was doing for the war effort, requested to be assigned to the infantry. Of course, their preference would probably have been to send me to the psycho ward. For who in his right mind wanted to be in the infantry? The Marines, yes; even the Navy or the Air Force, but not the infantry. I wanted to return to France and in my mind I felt that this was the best way to do it. I had some paramilitary training in France and was familiar with guns. I had heard many stories about the American infantry, the queen of battle, which had helped to win the previous war. Of course I had also been influenced by the exploits of the French veterans of the Great War, especially those of the foot soldiers. Both of my uncles on my father's side had been in the French Army, serving in the camel corps in Tunisia and Algeria. I can still remember my uncle René coming home on leave, wearing his bright red baggy pants with a million pleats, his blue vest, white burnous and red chechia (similar to an open-top fez) cocked to one side of his head. Too bad the U.S. Army did not have a camel corps—I might have considered it!

The Army Years

On February 10, 1943, a trainload of young men from New York and New Jersey, myself among them, headed for Fort Dix. A young but very important corporal greeted us as if we were the lowest kind human beings in this world, cursing us one minute and making us the objects of his warped sense of humor the next. He warned us to be wary of the famous "hook," a mythical, exaggerated version of a syringe. The corporal vividly described to us a procedure that would cause intense pain and disfigurement.

Then he asked for volunteers; first, those who could type. These disappeared. Of course, when he asked who spoke French, I lifted my hand and promptly was whisked to the mess hall and given a knife and directed to a ton of potatoes. That was my last instance of volunteering.

A few days later we lined up for our physical examinations. First came our injections. Fearful of the "hook" so vividly described by the corporal, a number of the recruits passed out cold. Next we had the "short arm" inspection by physicians. The entire barracks stood naked in the center aisle. While passing in front of the doctor we were ordered to hold our penis with the index finger and thumb and to "milk it" to determine if there was any oozing (which would reveal a venereal disease). For most of us this was the most demeaning aspect of the Army, yet some of the men seemed almost to enjoy it. Assembled in a large theater we were shown motion pictures describing the results of various venereal diseases. This did not sit well with some of the recruits who threw up. Then an impressive corporal told us that unless we took precautions we would be court-martialed.

The weather was terrible. We lived in tents, eight recruits to a tent. It rained and snowed continuously from the time we arrived. The cold, the smoke-filled tent and the heat of the kitchen probably all contributed to my coming down with a beauty of a cold that turned into pneumonia. At sick call I was given some APC tablets (similar to aspirin) and I was told that since there was no room at the hospital I should return to my tent and remain there until a bed was available. Every morning, a doctor would check me and within a week I was back on my feet. A few days later I was on a troop train moving slowly through snow-covered country to our final destination, Texas, a secret kept until we had safely crossed the border.

The troop train was not equipped with a diner car. Instead, a boxcar had been transformed into a field kitchen. The gas burners were placed over wood frames filled with dirt so there was some insulation between the burners and the floor of the boxcar. We did not have KP duty because we were fed in our mess kits and had to wash them in a series of three 55-gallon drums filled with hot water. The first drum was full of soapy water while the others were for rinsing. The going was very slow. We spent much time on sidings as faster trains passed us. After a week we reached our destination, Camp Wolters, Texas, an infantry training center.

Up to that point, we had been a part of the Army in name only. Except for a few NCOs who escorted us, we were a bunch of recruits who barely knew our left from our right. This changed in a hurry once we reached Camp Wolters.

On my application at the selective service office, I had indicated that while in France I had had some paramilitary training and had fired a rifle. This had apparently been duly noted and passed on because I was made an assistant squad leader and guidon bearer. Perhaps I was selected because I was tall and could maintain an even pace. My platoon was primarily composed of New Yorkers, Jerseyites and Texans. Those from the eastern United States spent their time complaining about everything. The Texans complained about one thing only—the guys from the East, and they were particularly upset with me. They could not understand why a foreigner who could barely speak English was their assistant squad leader, while they, who could shoot a fly at fifty paces, had to scrub floors while I watched. I was certain they were hoping for, if not plotting, my earliest possible demise.

Fortunately for me, our platoon leader was aware of the situation and made certain that their plans never came to fruition. Smiling Jim Atwell was a full-blooded Cherokee Indian and a fine platoon sergeant. I learned a great deal from him. Although he treated me the same as the others, we were friends from the very beginning of our training. I could not understand why they called him "Smiling Jim" (something we had learned from the rest of the cadre) until one day after we had completed our basic training. I saw our platoon leader at Mineral Wells, a small town renowned for its mineral water, Crazy Water. Smiling Jim was all smiles, red as a beet, and not walking very straight. I was told that he never indulged during the training period, but once it was over, look out!

Washington D.C.

A few days after my return from Europe I had to go to Washington and reported to OSS Headquarters, which was located in a temporary two-story structure built along the Mall. I was told that I would be reassigned to the Far East but given no specific information. I was wearing my class A uniform: "pink" trousers (though actually gray in color, for reasons unknown to me they retained this name), dark green jacket and shiny paratrooper boots. Along with four other members of our unit I assembled one day in one of the OSS buildings to receive a decoration from I believe General Al Gruenther. The General's aide read the citation. I could hardly believe that what he was reading was about me, and that I was given the Silver Star. I had received the second highest decoration for valor, yet I remembered the words of "Diane": "You only did your duty as an American." Yes, I did my duty, and this decoration was a token of thanks from the American people. I felt that now I had earned my citizenship.

Presentation of the Silver Star to Author by General Grunther.

I did not spend much time in Washington except for the routine of the military. We were billeted in the Congressional Country Club, an exclusive club where members of the U.S. Congress came to relax and play golf. The OSS, had taken over the entire facility and had transformed it into a military camp. The rooms that had held one congressman or senator, now held several of us in bunk beds.

Back in Washington we occasionally went out in the evening. Three of us usually went to a restaurant for a change in our diet. Once, we were having a drink at the Willard Hotel when three good-looking girls sat down at the table next to ours. Immediately we decided that we should become acquainted and their smiles of encouragement prompted one of us to invite them to our spacious table. They suggested that we come to their table to which we immediately agreed. We stood up holding our drinks when all of a sudden we were surrounded by four big fellows who politely asked us to place our drinks on our table and to leave. They proceeded to escort us bodily out of the hotel. It's hard to believe now, but at that time Washington D.C., like many states, had a law prohibiting moving from one table to another with drinks. Once on the sidewalk we toyed with the idea of returning for a practice session of hand-to-hand combat using the techniques we had learned with the British, but cooler heads prevailed.

I returned home once to see the family and check on the Italian beauty. She was still operating the store but this time she did not entice me to the back room. Instead, she invited me to her home to meet her mother and have a good Italian meal. She was the spitting image of her mother except that her mama was 5'2" and weighed close to 200 pounds. I realized then that pasta had done her in, and the same thing would happen to her daughter. I could tell that both were salivating at the prospect of a husband for the young one. However, I was not about to marry into that family. That evening we went to a movie and sat in the balcony, but that was our last date!

While at home, I touched base with Jeanne's mother and learned that she was attending college at Philadelphia. Although she had been my only girl friend, I did not expect to marry her then or in the future. She used my knowledge of French to improve hers, and I used her sexual desires to satisfy mine. Petting seemed to be more fun and safer at the time. Had she given me the treatment of the Italian beauty I might have reconsidered!

Since Philadelphia was close to Washington, I decided to surprise her after obtaining her address from her mother. I should have stayed in Washington, because I discovered very quickly that I had been forgotten, and that she had not even bothered writing me a "dear-John" letter. She kept the fact that she had a new boy friend a secret until I came to see her. It was rather awkward for both of us, but I did not believe then that I had lost a great deal.

RESTRICTED

HEADQUARTERS
EUROPEAN THEATER OF OPERATION
UNITED STATES ARMY

GO 61   12 Apr 1945

SILVER STAR. By direction of the President, under the provisions of AR 600-45, 22 September 1943, as amended, the Silver Star is awarded to:

Second Lieutenant René Défourneaux (Army Serial No 0887913), Army of the United States, for gallantry in action as a member of the Special Operations Branch, Office of Strategic Services., European Theater of Operations,.United States Army, from 8 August 1944 to 30 September 1944. Lieutenant Defourn'eaux was parachuted into France., in civilian clothes, as an organizer and director of French resistance forces. By exercising tact and diplomacy, he.successfully organized resistance forces and led them in sabotage activities. Bridges across the Loire were destroyed and German convoys were harassed by a series of ambushes, forcing them to turn back or to change their routes, Lieutenant Défourneaux took an active part in the reception and distribution of arms and munitions with which to supply the resistance forces and procured and delivered valuable intelligence information to the United States Army. Entered military service from New Jersey.

BY COMMAND OF GENERAL EISENHOWER:

Catalina

Shortly thereafter, in early January, 1945, came the order for me to proceed to Catalina, a small Island off the coast of California. Mr. Wrigley, the chewing gum king, owned the island that had been requisitioned by the OSS for sea and survival training. The island was reached by boat from Newport Beach. The main city, Avalon, was off-limits to us but the rest of the island was our training ground. We had instructors who had been famous hunters and well-known mountain climbers, people who had been in practically all the mountains and jungles of the world. With well-qualified instructors we practiced mountain climbing on the rugged cliffs of the island. We hunted goats, set traps to capture wild game and dove into the surf in search of abalones.

With Navy personnel and boats we practiced landing on beaches. Our final test was a week in Lands End north of the isthmus separating the northernmost part of the island from the main section. This area was the most desolate part of the island and only oak trees, cacti and a sparse grass covered the rocky soil. A small herd of cattle fed on this meager forage, and a few goats managed to survive in the small hills and cliffs. We were briefed on our mission, which was to survive for one week living off the land, and were advised that the cattle were off-limits. They put each one of us on a scale and recorded our weight. Evidently they wanted to grade us according to the amount of weight we ended up losing. To make certain that the game was played fairly by all we were told to empty our pockets.

Then they gave us a 7-inch sheathed knife and a GI blanket, and on a sunny afternoon deposited us via landing craft on a desolate beach of Lands End.

Six of us—one major, three junior officers, and two enlisted men—made up the team. The major came from a well-to-do East Coast family whose ancestry had been in the silver trade. Either he received a direct commission, or was the product of the ROTC program. In any case, all his life he had been sheltered and, if I may be facetious, he was born with a silver spoon in his mouth. Finding himself with only a hunting knife for an eating utensil was more than he could stand. The rest of the group was composed of veterans who had seen fighting in Europe and accepted the situation with good humor— and as soon as we were left alone on the deserted beach, it became obvious that we were not caught unprepared. Out of our socks, boots, sleeves and other hiding places came chocolate bars and other emergency sustenance, enough to open a small PX. Only our Major had not had this forethought. The other members of the team displayed a complete lack of fair play. Survival was the name of the game and if one was expected to survive he would normally take precautions, whether it was in training or for real!

The first day passed without incident. We found cactus pears which we peeled carefully and ate. We were not to remain in one spot during the length of our stay. We had to follow a course, marking points. In a hidden box at each point we would find instructions to direct us to the next point. Without a compass and using only the sun and the stars to guide us we had a tough job to stay on course. However we managed and eventually we reached a part of the island where there were very few cacti but many oak trees. The acorns were plentiful but not very good to eat in its raw form. They had to be roasted to eliminate the tannin and then boiled. We did find some old cans, and soon we had a can-full of a grayish paste which tasted not unlike burnt pea soup. This was all right for a while but it only increased our hunger for real food. By the third day, the chocolate and candy were gone. Conversations continuously revolved around food. Some of us took this philosophically, but some of the others, particularly the Major, became obsessed. At times he seemed nearly delirious.

Finally the majority of the group decided that this was unnecessary—no one has to learn how to starve to death. Food had become the most important aspect of our lives. It was suggested that one cow among so many would not be missed.

Carefully we approached a small herd and as a pack of wolves surrounded the panicking cattle and directed them towards a cliff. By the time most of the cows reached the edge they veered to the side and escaped. However one old cow, probably too sick to stop on a button and spin, went over the cliff and broke one of her hind legs. She lay mooing in despair, but managed to roll over, trying without success to stand up on her broken leg. Our starving pack reached her and without a word our Major grabbed a rock, and began to hit her head with it. Of course he was hitting her between the horns where her skull was the hardest and the rock did the least damage. She mooed in pain which made the Major more determined to end her misery. I was watching all this in amazement. Finally I suggested that with his knife he could easily cut her jugular vein and let her bleed to death. That he would not do, or could not do, but another of the group did it and before long we had a dead cow in our hands.

This was all well and good, but how would we get to the prime ribs, the filet mignon, etc? Where would we start?

Fortunately, I had been raised in a farm and had even lived over a small slaughterhouse. During my youth I watched many cattle and horses going to their just reward. Our knives were not the kind normally used for dressing an animal, but they had to do. I suggested that the most nutritious part of the cow was the liver. But most of our group hated liver. The next easiest part to use was the leg. We managed to detach one of the cow's hind legs and cut thin slices small enough to hold over a fire to broil. We ate our fill and slept quite well. The next day, cheerfully carrying the severed leg of the cow, we continued on our course. It was amazing how a little food could change the attitude of some people. From that time on everything was great. Food became the least of our problems.

Of course there were others, rattlesnakes included, but the physical aspect of our operation was no picnic. Some of our targets were located on points located at the top of rocky ridges almost impossible to reach. Fortunately for those of us who had been reared in mountainous regions of Europe, this did not pose a serious problem. For some of the others, it was a grueling and terrifying experience. Happily, the weather remained friendly, and warm enough to sleep on the ground without too much discomfort.

We completed our course without further incident, and waited to be picked up by our sailors. As soon as we reached our base we were placed on the scale again, and what a surprise! Some of us had not lost any weight at all, and others had actually managed to gain a few pounds! As a rule, all of the earlier groups which had participated in this survival test had lost weight. What had we done to gain that much weight? They separated us for interrogation and one then the other stuck by the story we had decided to give. We had captured a goat. Finally, since this was most unusual because goats are not easily captured, they asked one of our group how we had managed to grab a goat. He explained that the goat was grabbed by the tail and secured that way. Unfortunately the goats that inhabited the island had no tails!

That opened Pandora's box. Now they were aware that the details of our stories did not match. As far as the command was concerned something was really fishy. They soon realized that we must have killed one of Mr. Wrigley's cattle. A flight over the island by the local command verified the existence of a carcass. We were caught and severely admonished. Then the Major came in handy, pulling weight enough to get us out of this predicament. He probably was a personal friend of Mr. Wrigley.

The survival training continued but not without further incident. We did go hunting for the elusive goats with rifles equipped with scopes. At one time we had to traverse an almost vertical steep rock to reach a dead animal. Using our toes and fingertips we started across the vertical wall separating us from our game. Halfway across one of our men froze, paralyzed with fear, and clung tightly to the rock. One of the instructors had to reach him at great risk to talk him out of his trance. Eventually we all made it to the dead goat. Because the animal was too heavy to carry in one piece, we began dressing it. We noticed that it was afflicted with a serious infection as evidenced by a pocketful of pus in the intestinal cavity. Not knowing the cause of this, it was decided to leave the goat to scavengers rather than bring it back to our base. This made the return trip much easier.

After the completion of the month-long training we returned to Washington via the Santa Fe Chief. Railroads were the main means of transportation in those days, and I must admit that it was a pleasure to go from one end of the United States to the other in style even if it took several days to reach our destination. Some well known entertainers were also on the train, going to Washington to celebrate the birthday of President Roosevelt and to participate in the annual March of Dimes activities. Kay Kaiser and his band were practicing almost continuously. Jane Wyman was also aboard. She was very friendly and after a while several of us were playing Gin Rummy with her.

Back in Washington we received our orders to the Far East. I expected to return to the West Coast, the normal way to the Pacific Theater of Operations, but instead we were directed by train to Miami! Only years later I was to learn why: OSS was apparently not welcomed in General MacArthur's turf!

The Hump

Prior to our departure for China, at the Cha-Boa Air Base in India, a junior officer briefed our assembled group on the nature of the flight we were about to take. As we sat in a Quonset hut, he stressed the seriousness of the information, because we were to fly over a portion of the Himalayas referred to as "The Hump".

"Gentlemen, in a few hours you will be on one of the most dangerous flights of your lives! To avoid the attention of the Japanese Zeros based in Burma, your flight will be over the tallest mountains in the world. Your aircraft will not be pressurized and above the 10,000 feet level you will be on oxygen. You will have two enemies to contend with—the Japanese fighters and the lack of oxygen. Our Air Force will handle the Japanese, and there will be no smoking during the entire trip!"

He continued: "It may be bumpy up there. If you get sick make sure that you remove your mask before vomiting. Any questions?" There were none. We proceeded to the next building where we drew our parachutes and oxygen masks, then we loaded aboard a C-46.

So, this was the most dangerous flying we would ever do! They did not know that some of us had dodged the Luftwaffe, and anything other than a combat jump we considered a joy ride.

With our gear tightly secured in front of us by nylon nets we settled into our bucket seats and buckled our seat belt. The crew chief secured the door, verified all seat belts fastened, and after the usual checks we took off.

A half hour later as we were climbing both motors died! Instinctively we all stood up, ready to evacuate the aircraft, then a few seconds later they started again. The Crew Chief told us that the reserve gas tanks had been accidentally disconnected and reassured us as we continued our ascent.

When we reached 10,000 feet, wearing our now indispensable oxygen masks, we cruised for half an hour flying above a sea of clouds. From time to time violent turbulence shook the aircraft. I looked at the twenty-odd passengers, and none appeared sick. So far so good!

We continue to climb to our cruising altitude. It was cool in the plane, but not uncomfortable. Through the small windows I could see some of the highest peaks of the Himalayas, and way above the clouds, reflecting the sun rays like a diamond, Mount Everest. The monotonous roaring of the engines almost lulled me to sleep but the vibrations were more than usual. Soon the door leading to the cockpit came a bit ajar and eventually it opened. From my position I could see the entire cockpit, but could not believe what I was seeing.

The pilot was stripped to the waist, and so was the co-pilot. Each had an oxygen hose in his mouth, and between them sat a small tray. They held cards and were playing while I, like most of the other passengers, was shaking in my boots. The sun shining through their windows made the cockpit very comfortable while we were freezing in the cabin. They had the plane on automatic and were relaxing, while many of us were expecting the worst.

We realized that to our pilot and crew, this "very dangerous flight" was not as bad as we had been told. Indeed, for each of the few aircraft that did not make it over the Hump, many did, bringing tons of supplies and thousands of personnel to China.

While there is no question that the air crews flying the Hump had one of the most hazardous jobs during the War, they rarely complained and served with distinction. That is, until some of the missions requested of them proved to border on the absurd. One story in particular involved a request by Madame Chiang-Kai-Shek that a spinet piano and several cases of Kotex be transported to her at her husband's headquarters in Kunming. The crew assigned to the "mission" evidently decided that this was not an appropriate cause for which to risk their lives. After loading the cargo, taking off from their base and reaching the mountain range, the crew declared an emergency condition. In an emergency, the standard procedure was for the crew to jettison all cargo. The door of the plane swung open and out went the piano, dropping several thousand feet before crashing to the rocks below. Upon returning to their base, the pilot feathered one of the props as he landed and informed the group commander of the unfortunate occurrence.

The now reassuring purr of the engines brought back memories of my European adventures and of my subsequent movements . . .

The Other War

The first leg of our trip to the CBI (China-Burma-India) theater had taken us by train to Miami. After a few days at the Fleetwood, one of the best Miami hotels requisitioned by the Army, we reported to the airport where we boarded a C-47, the work horse of the Army. Sitting uncomfortably in bucket seats, our gear piled under nets, we took off on the second leg of our journey—to Puerto Rico— then on to what was known then as British Guyana. George-town, provided our initiation to the real tropics, and landing there was like entering a steam room. We stayed only overnight to refuel and for the crew to rest.

Our next leg took us to Belem, on the east coast of Brazil, but not before we crossed the mighty Amazon River, so wide that from the north shore of the river it is impossible to see the south shore. There we were to stay a couple of days and change aircraft because the C-47 could not make the trip across the Atlantic with a full load. The monsoon was in full force as we arrived. I did not know what real rain was until we reached Belem! The temperature was in the nineties and it rained and poured, then rained again. On the base in the evening, the only entertainment was the outdoors movie. The projector sat on a platform protected from the rain with a tarp. The seats were logs lined up in a semi-circle, and the screen was a piece of thin white material resembling a bed sheet. The show began with half the seats filled with GIs in their ponchos, while on the other side the natives watched the action on the rear of the semi-transparent screen. I would see this arrangement repeated throughout the Far East, and the results stayed the same: one side of the audience laughed while the other was silent, oblivious of the jokes, then, when the action was exciting, these others, also oblivious of the dialogue, were the ones screaming with joy.

Eventually we received our departure orders. This time we would fly in a converted B-24, its bomb bay removed, and regular seats installed from the cockpit to the tail section. I sat at the center of the fuselage under the wing section. We took off and had been flying for approximately half an hour when I felt something cold on my right pants leg. I thought it was moisture dripping from some of the pipes running along the ceiling, but a strong odor of gasoline attracted my attention. I realized that the drip was not water but fuel! I brought the situation to the attention of one of the crew and the decision was made not to return, but to leave the no-smoking sign on the rest of the trip. Our first leg took us to Ascension Island, a volcanic island located between South America and West Africa. This was the most desolate place I had ever seen.

No vegetation existed on the island. The only tree, a palm probably imported from Brazil, was located in front of the Officer's Club. The landing strip had been virtually cut through a mountain, and it was more like landing on an aircraft carrier than on terra firma. Both ends of the air strip ended over the rocky shores of the island. Taking off, we could see below us the carcasses of aircraft that had not made it! I prayed that ours would not end up as these did.

Our next destination was to be Accra, the capital of Ghana, a British colony. The airfield was hot and dusty. We went to town to see what was of interest, but the main activity took place outside the city in a huge market where people from other villages came to barter or sell their goods. Accra was bisected by two main roads, and a lone policeman directed the traffic consisting mostly of buffalo-drawn carts, bicycles and pedestrians. Only a few cars and trucks, mostly military, were visible.

We did not linger in Accra or at our next destination, Khartoum in the Sudan. We refueled there and shortly were on our way to the Island of Mazirah, a small stretch of sand a few feet above sea level located on the southeastern coast of Saudi Arabia. There we landed in the afternoon to a temperature of 105 degrees. We were directed to a supply room and given a couple of blankets because we were to spend the night in a tent village nearby. Why the blankets? we asked. We could have used a fan or a bucket of ice! But around 2:00 in the morning we understood why we were issued blankets. The temperature went down to 50 degrees and with the cold moist air flowing through the tent, we were freezing even with our two blankets. This island was even more desolate than Ascension. There was not a single rock bigger than a golf ball. The extremes in temperature contributed to the cracking of the stones and the winds did the rest.

I hoped our human conditioning proved us more flexible in tolerating the forces of nature.

India

Karachi, in eastern India, was our next destination. From there each of us was to be assigned to various parts of the Theater. Karachi was one of the dirtiest city I had ever seen. We were billeted near the military air base away from the teaming populace. We were told that the old city was worth seeing. Because of the many shops on narrow crowded streets, the only way to go in and out was by horse-drawn coach. Five of us—including Major "Cow Killer"—decided to try it. He had recovered from his survival trauma, but this was a new experience for him. The odor which permeated the old city mixed sandalwood with urine, feces, and God only knows what else. It was too much for our good Major who walked around, nose covered by his handkerchief soaked with Chanel No 5.

Our coach driver was a young native wearing a long white robe. His English was passable and his gift of gab excellent. He gave us a tour of the town, explaining everything with humor and passing along jokes he had picked up from earlier passengers. When we had enough, we decided that the center of the old town was a good place to call it quits. We asked our driver to go back but instead he got down from his coach and, standing in front of his horse in the middle of the street, smiled broadly. He told us that it was not very safe to stop anywhere within the old city. So we urged him to carry on.

Instead, he calmly squatted and remained in front of his horse for approximately two minutes. Then he got aboard again, and with his whip put the horse in first. With another crack of the whip we were in second and on direct drive to our destination, the Gim Khana Club. Looking back from were we had stopped, I could not help noticing the stain on the ground where the coach driver had squatted. He had relieved himself in front of us surrounded by hundreds of people and no one had seen anything. What a strange way of doing things! Indeed, there were not public toilets (or as in Paris, *pissoirs*) where one could relieve oneself. People did their business on the street, anywhere, and no one seemed offended!

One afternoon we were invited to the home of the local OSS representative. He lived in a beautiful house that had belonged either to a British businessman or to a high government employee. It was decorated with great taste and the gardens were manicured by the many servants. We wore our khaki summer uniforms. The temperature was far above one hundred degrees in the shade, but only ceiling fans moved the superheated air.

I was not used to drinking water, as a matter of fact I very seldom drank water. But we had been warned that because of the dryness, one could dehydrate very rapidly. That day I felt rather weak and cold despite the temperature. Someone asked me where I had been. The back of my shirt was white as if I had been in a flour mill. Our host immediately ordered water and encouraged me to drink it. In addition he gave me a couple of salt tablets. The white powder on the back of my shirt was not flour, but salt resulting from my perspiration. From that time on I watched my water intake very carefully.

At that point, no one knew what they would do with me. From Karachi, several others and I were sent to New Delhi. It was the capital of India, where the Viceroy and the Governor resided. We visited the Red Fort and hitched a flight to the Taj Mahal located near one of our air bases. I was somewhat disappointed with the Taj Mahal. It looked so great in pictures, but up close it more closely resembled a garbage pit. The architecture was magnificent. Unfortunately the Indian tourists were slobs and left all their garbage behind. Apparently no one bothered to remove it.

Calcutta was our next stop. What a city! I had never seen so many people in all my life. We were housed in the center of the city in a hotel that had been requisitioned for our use by the local authorities. We were told that because of the lack of supplies we could wear the type of clothing worn by the British soldiers. The bush jacket seemed to be the most logical apparel, because it was not tucked into the trousers. It left plenty of space for the air to circulate around your middle. Most of us bought one, but some splurged and purchased the typical Gurkha hat along with the traditional Gurkha knife. We took a tour of the area which included a trip up the river. On the return leg we passed by the burning gates where the local people cremated dead bodies. The cadaver was placed on a pile of soft wood approximately six feet in length, three feet wide and four feet high. Before long, the body was engulfed in flames. On that day, several bodies were being cremated.

At one point, probably due to the heat, one of the bodies sat up. It was an omen to the mourners who prostrated themselves before the pyre. The ashes were thrown into the river afterwards.

Ceylon

Having seen the ceremonies for the dead, I had nothing left to do in Calcutta and was relieved to learn in late March that I would be going to Ceylon. Approximately three weeks after arriving in India, several of us were flown to a British air base at Ceylon. From there we were driven by lorry to a small OSS base near Galle situated on a beautiful tropical bay surrounded by palm trees and populated by huge lizards. The town of Galle had been a Portuguese colony and its architecture was typical European. Its people had maintained some of the characteristics of the Portuguese in their dress, food and religion.

Although the majority of the people were non-Christian many were practicing Catholics. The area was rich in fruit of all types and I became fond of the papaya which grew in large numbers and in great sizes throughout the island. Every meal had papaya either as desert or fried as in French fries.

There were lizards and snakes, but we welcomed another local animal because it kept the snake population in check. Mongooses are among the fastest animals in the world and that is probably why snakes are incapable of hurting them.

At our base, we kept a pet mongoose. For some unknown reason, it had been abandoned by its mother and had been raised by the personnel of the base. The mongoose was a friendly playful pet. When we sat or lay on our bunks she loved to curl up against us, hide in our pockets and even make her way into our shirts, crawling into the sleeves. If one would grab the tip of the her tail, in a flash she would have his fingers into her jaws. But never did she bite. She knew it was a game and loved it. Occasionally we would see her mother, a much larger animal, strolling on the edge of the camp. Our pet would join her and play with her for a while, but she would always return to where the food was.

One day a group of newcomers arrived. One of them I had known in Europe. It was his first time in the Far East and he did not know much about the animals and flora of the region. As it was extremely hot during the day, between noon and two became a quiet time when all activities at the camp stopped and we were encouraged to take a siesta. Our new arrivals were only too happy to comply. So, shortly after lunch, we all retired to our respective huts. These were made of bamboo and palm leaves with plenty of space between the bamboo sections to let air circulate. Of course our mongoose had the run of the place, and this time of the day was also her siesta period. She would normally climb on a cot and curl up to someone's warm body. That particular day the mongoose decided that this new fellow would make a very comfortable bed. He was already fast asleep and snoring happily when she jumped on his cot and curled up on his chest. The weight of the mongoose awakened him, and when he saw it he let out a yell that woke up the entire camp. He kept on yelling as if he was being murdered.

We all rushed to his hut and found him flat on his back, the mongoose looking at him with interest even as he yelled "Get that thing off me! Get that thing off me!" We all laughed at the sight, but he did not think it funny at all. He never became friendly with the mongoose, and the mongoose tended to stay away from him as well after that.

What was I doing in Ceylon, when no one on the island spoke French? It was obvious to me that I had been selected for another job, another mission. It became clearer to me when I realized that the camp was a training base for the use of one-man submarines. I was a paratrooper, not a sailor. Why would I end up in a submarine? Obviously it was for a good reason. My training as an intelligence specialist and my having learned the composition of the enemy armies would have qualified me as an observer anywhere. And that was what was planned for me. I was to travel to the coast of Sumatra on a real submarine and from a safe distance, I would approach the coast in the smaller craft. After scuttling it I would establish an observation post along the mountain range and with a radio report on the movements of the Japanese fleet passing along the coast. But before reaching that stage I had much more to learn about what I was to do. Instruction was given during the week, but on Sunday we usually had the day to ourselves. We had access to boats of various sizes and we were encouraged to stay in the water and do a lot of swimming. Our beach was off limits to all on the island, so we usually swam naked. The boats were tied to buoys a few yards from the shore.

One Sunday three of us decided to take a ride on one of the boats. We swam to the boat, detached it from the buoy and started the engine. It was fun. This was not an outboard engine, only a small inboard, two-cylinder gas engine that allowed a speed of 10 to 15 knots. We aimed our boat into the bay expecting to go no more than a mile from shore, but suddenly the engine stopped. We tried to restart it, but in vain. For an hour we struggled with it, but no luck. We even took the engine apart with the tools that were aboard, but nothing would make it run. By that time, the sun hung right above us. We were naked and resembled well done lobsters. The only thing left for us to do was to use the oars and return to the buoy by muscle power. It took us two hours to return to the place of anchor because we were fighting the tide.

Eventually, we were close enough to tie the boat to the buoy. We found the line dangling from the front of the boat but when we pulled it we encountered some resistance. One of us jumped overboard and underneath our craft he discovered that the rope was wrapped around the shaft and that the propeller was frozen. That was why we could not start the engine! It had no clutch, only a direct shaft to the propeller.

All three of us were sunburned in places where the sun rarely reaches. We reported to the dispensary. The doctor listened to our sad story and, feeling sorry for us, decided not to report us for what would have been a court martial offense. Instead he sent us to the kitchen for vinegar that he then splashed all over our bodies. It took a few days to recover, but recover we did.

The Allies' situation in China was not very good. The Japanese were moving inland, and the Chinese army did not appear capable of containing them. The one-man submarine no longer appeared to be appropriate duty for me. So in May I was on a C-47 on my way back to Calcutta, but only as a stopover. I was glad to land in Calcutta because I was traveling with a cargo of one million eggs and some were rotten. The smell plus the roughness of the air along the eastern shores of India made this flight the worst I had experienced up to that time.

Detachment 101

Calcutta was not my ultimate destination: that was Cha-Boa, the base from which all the flights to China began. However neither Cha-Boa nor China were to be my destination as yet. By that time, the meat diet that I had on Catalina Island and poor mouth hygiene began to take their toll. My gums began to bleed and the pain became unbearable. Every day I had to go to the dentist to have my gums scraped. This lasted for two weeks. By mid-April I was finally reassigned to Detachment 101 located near Mazirah south of the Cha-Boa Air Base for jungle survival training.

Detachment Headquarters was located on a tea plantation in the Assam region of India. Known as K-Camp, it consisted of several bamboo huts constructed for our convenience. Included in the deal was the luxury of an Indian cook!

Our meals consisted of two or three meats and five or six vegetable dishes, dessert, beer and coffee, and, of course, tea, which we ignored completely. Simply put, it was the best cuisine I had had in the Army, and for 80 cents per week! It was a steal, but not as much fun as the specialized training we were getting.

Tea Plantation serving as HQ for OSS Detachment 101, Mazira, Assam.

OSS Detachment 101, Assam, India. Survival training.

At K-Camp we learned the advantages and the pitfalls of the jungle. Our base was situated at the base of the Naga hills which were populated by former head-hunters known as Nagas. When dealing with them, I inwardly hoped that their idea of a gourmet dinner had changed, and that white meat was no longer part of their diet.

The jungle has a wealth of food if one knows how to get to it. We learned to survive in an environment much different than Catalina. Unlike the natives who enjoyed insects and grubs they found in bamboo sections, we preferred the meat of monkey and fowl. The natives told us that monkey meat tasted almost the same as human flesh! We took them at their word!

It was the dry season and the weather was great. In the morning, wearing a sarong, I sunbathed. We had no inspections so I dressed a la Burmese in a bright-colored skirt and a turban to pro-

OSS Detachment 101, Bamboo hut quarters.

tect my head from the scorching sun.

According to my buddies I had "gone native", but really had only adapted to local circumstances because this type of clothing was light and comfortable. My skin gradually darkened, not to brown but to copper, and my hair next to my tan seemed lighter.

On the 27th of April several of us received travel orders. We left K-Camp at 8:00 in the direction of Cha-Boa. There we were billeted at the Polo Grounds where I finally collected three months of pay and waited. I had completely forgotten my birthday which was on the 29th of April.

At noon on the 31st of April 1945, during lunch, we were finally told that we would be flying to China that afternoon. At 3:00 p.m. a truck took us to the Cha-Boa Air Base . . . .

A change in the sound of the engines startled me out of my reverie. Some of the passengers had removed their masks. We must have descended below the 10,000 feet level, and left the Himalayas range behind.

China

Once we had passed the mountain range, we returned to our normal altitude. By then we were over China. Moments later, we began our descent toward a high plateau and the Yunnan capital of Kunming. It was late afternoon and sundown when we landed in a cloud of dust. Already the air base was in the dark, and lights of the runways were on even though I could see the blue sky over the distant mountain peaks.

After landing, the most vivid impression that I had of the area was the tremendous change in the prevailing odors, completely different from those of India. I was not the only one of our group who remarked that China smelled like an outhouse. I wondered what our Major would do or say when he reached this area!

We were driven to a dirty restaurant close to the air base, where we doubly appreciated what we had left at Detachment 101. A single large bowl filled with small pieces of meat and vegetables was placed on the table beside another full of steaming rice. Instead of knives and spoons we were given two pieces of bamboo! Our China indoctrination had begun. Dogs waited everywhere for customers to throw on the dirt floor chicken bones which the dogs then devoured noisily. Presumably they served as the restaurant's garbage disposals!

Once fed, we loaded our gear on a truck and proceeded to our headquarters a few miles outside the city of Kunming. We were then directed to what they referred to as the "Country House." Tired but glad to have reached our destination safely, we went directly to our sleeping quarters. As a junior officer, I inherited an upper bunk, and after placing under my pillow the Colt .32 that I had carried since France, I went right to sleep. When I awoke early the next morning my pistol was gone. During the night, someone had taken it!

We were all supposed to be officers, gentlemen by an act of Congress. One of us was a thief, but which one? This was not the only thing that was stolen from me during my stay in China. I learned later that the OSS had recruited individuals with certain abilities useful for covert operations from inside the U.S. prison system. These individuals, I am certain, had a distorted view of honesty.

Since my arrival in China I had felt nothing but disappointment, probably because Detachment 101 had been such a good place for me. The Chinese were so uninteresting that I began to wonder why I was risking my life for such people! Since I had volunteered for the job, I resigned myself to fate and decided to do my best so as not to be discouraged.

Except for a few of us who had seen action in Europe, most of the people in our compound were new to this type of business. Some had never jumped in their lives and it was necessary to train them. The area was not the best suited for airborne training. The elevation and unusually strong winds made it very difficult if not outright dangerous. One of our colonels, a trained paratrooper, was injured when the wind smacked him into the side of a ditch. However this did not prevent ground training and its jumps from a 10-foot wall to test the strength of our ankles.

Occasionally we went to town, although Kunming had very little to offer except food and rice wine. During one of these trips I observed the way the Chinese Army trained their recruits. When I first noticed young men marching in groups of ten to twelve, each man wearing a steel collar and linked to the next by a chain, I thought that they were criminals being sent off to jail or to the penitentiary. I later learned that these were army "recruits" from neighboring villages. They had passed the preliminary test— that is, they were caught after their village was surrounded by a "recruiting" company or, depending on the size of the village, a battalion.

Once captured, to make certain that they would remain faithful, they were tied together in groups and marched to the training compound. This treatment did not prevent the recruits from deserting at first opportunity, which usually came after completion of their training when on leave visiting their families. Many did not return and we were told that some took their weapons with them!

As soon as I arrived at Kunming I was assigned to a group whose members I did not know. The others who had been with me at Detachment 101 stayed together and were joined by Major Roger who had reached our compound soon after we had. Almost immediately they left for their assigned station. I remained behind for one important reason: my teeth needed further attention.

A few days after arriving in China I was called to the orderly room. When the company clerk handed me a telegram my heart skipped a beat. I thought something dreadful had happened to my family. But when I opened the cable I discovered it came from France—Simone! How has she found out where I was?

A few days later a letter from my mother wanted to know why, when I returned from Europe, I had not mentioned to her the fact I was engaged to be married. Simone had written to her telling her the good news! Her son was to be her future spouse!

If Simone was able to find out my real name, my address, and that of my mother, and she now knew my location in China, she might well decide to show up in Kunming to tie a knot using the strings she had pulled thus far. I casually mentioned my dilemma to our company clerk, a sharp corporal whose specialty was to make certain none of us got in trouble.

"No problem Lieutenant. I can fix it so that she will never write to you again," he said. I did not ask what he was planning, and wrote my mother that the news about a marriage was premature and warning her that she might not hear from me for a while.

Among the officers in our unit, one in particular was a great fellow. He came from middle-European stock and had seen action in Yugoslavia before reaching China.

One day we were in the orderly room when he showed me a small metal tube that I recognized as a "Stinger", perhaps the smallest weapon one could hold and be effective. It held a small-caliber shell with a firing pin that could be released by pressing a trigger on the side of the tube. Holding the Stinger in his right hand, my friend came to me and said, "I understand that when one pushes this it goes off."

At that moment he pressed the release and the Stinger fired, the bullet striking the floor between my feet! You should have seen the face of my friend. You should have seen mine.

Throughout the war, the Japanese had respected the French Vichy puppet regime's dominion over France's Indochina colony. The Vichy government agreed to an arrangement (actually, they had no alternative) whereby Japanese troops could be stationed there as a jumping-off point for further incursions in the region and for R & R. On March 9, 1945 (by which time the Vichy Government in France had been relegated to the dustbin of history), the Japanese commanders throughout Indochina summoned the top French officers to supposed receptions. During the course of the events, Japanese officers, after offering a toast to their guests, announced that from that moment the French officers in attendance were prisoners of Japan. Some resisted and were brutally executed. Others were marched off to prison camps. Many wives and children of French soldiers were killed, and others were publicly raped by Japanese soldiers.

The news about Indochina was not very good. After the Japanese takeover, the French troops that had managed to escape the Hanoï basin and those who had been stationed in outposts throughout the Tonkin region streamed across the China border in great numbers. Most had no food, water or other provisions. These troops were composed of French colonial army personnel and of Indochinese serving in the French military and holding French citizenship. Many of these troops were accompanied by their families. If left behind, they would have been subjected to the wrath of both the Japanese and of some of the collaborating local people who believed that Japan held the key to their liberation from the French.

Up to that time, these troops had overtly remained faithful to Pétain and the Vichy Government although some officers had covertly worked with the U.S. armed forces. Now that they were pursued by the Japanese, their status had suddenly changed in the international scheme of things.

Until early May, in our Kunming headquarters, I had many routine tasks to perform, from folding parachutes to censuring letters. I discharged my duties without complaining. Then I, and several members of our organization, learned we were to be sent to Kay Yuen near the Indochina border where the escaped French colonial troops had been assembled to await their disposition. There my job would be to mix with them and collect pertinent information from the escapees.

Our trip south to Kay Yuen was by train, and what a train! From Kunming, the railroad had to cross a range of mountains passing through steep canyons and through more than twenty tunnels, some close to a mile in length. The coal-powered locomotive needed the help of an auxiliary engine to reach the highest elevations. The going was slow and at times they had to let the engine rest before restarting it. At one point, the engineer stopped the locomotive outside a tunnel, forgetting that some of his passengers were still inside breathing the engine's sulfur-laden smoke. Once we had abandoned the auxiliary locomotive the train raced down the mountain slope toward our destination.

The train was filled with passengers to three times its capacity. In addition to humans we had live chickens, ducks and pigs held in bamboo baskets. At each station, venders enticed us with broiled chicken quarters and bamboo sticks filled with rice. The markings on the train were in French, and so were the signs at each of the stations. It appeared that the French had built this railroad and had used the same design as in France. It was rather strange to see a characteristic French railroad station surrounded by typical Chinese houses. The track was a narrow gauge and it did not go past the Chinese border, where the Indochinese railroad on the Tonkin side picked up the passengers on another train which operated on a different gauge. The powers that be had decided that using the same gauge on both sides of the border might encourage an invasion! We reached our destination near the China frontier, across from the Indochinese town of Lao-Caï. There we visited the French troops. With them were many Indochinese who had followed for fear that their past association with the French might not be looked upon too kindly by the Japanese. Most of the soldiers and their dependents had suffered much during their escape. They had to hide not only from the Japanese but also from the local populace that would have turned them in to the Japanese for a reward. The official representatives of the newly reestablished legitimate French government were on hand in Kunming. They helped their own and did as much as they could to convince the Americans and the Chinese to give their support to the refugees. Some food and clothing had reached the refugees.

As a group they appeared quite miserable. Their clothing was a mixture of French, Chinese and American army uniforms. They could not understand why they had not been welcomed with open arms by the Allies. They had forgotten quickly that the government which they had served had, in fact, been a collaborator with, indeed an ally of, Germany, Italy, and the Japanese. The fact of the matter was that these wretched souls had been dealt a lousy hand by the events of the past few months and had not been given many options. Unlike their brethren back in France, many of whom were able to either escape to nearby England to regroup and prepare for the liberation of France, or who joined the French Resistance, these troops were based in an extremely rugged, isolated area, thousands of miles from home.

Accompanied by Burley Fuselier, an Air Force intelligence specialist assigned to General Chennault's Flying Tigers, I went among the French refugees to determine which of them had the most information potentially useful to the U.S. Military. I spoke French as well as most of them (and sometimes better), and had no trouble passing as a French friend. Rapidly I gained their confidence and learned a great deal more than I would have as an American. Together, Burley and I identified those with the best information and, after removing them from their compound and treating them to good food and drink, escorted them to the Headquarters of the Flying Tigers where intelligence officers debriefed them, particularly about the effects of our bombing effort in Indochina, and where our flyers were held in Japanese prison camps. Kept in isolation, the French informants were not mistreated, but they understood that they were being held under "protective custody" and that they were no longer free to return to their group. We did not want them to mingle with the rest of the escapees telling them about our interests and in the process staining the information we might acquire from other sources.

This went on for a few weeks after which the remaining French leadership among the refugees realized that several of their men had disappeared and were last seen in company with my associate and me. The word got around very quickly that we two nosy fellows were not to be trusted and that all should stay clear. That marked the end of this operation, for me anyway.

In Kay Yuen we had very comfortable quarters located close to a silk factory built by French investors from Lyon. We met them occasionally and soon discovered that the mulberry trees they used to feed the silk worms had a fruit that did not go to waste. The French talent for making intoxicating beverages was immediately apparent when they treated us to their "wine." They offered us some which we transported to our quarters in five gallons

Jerry cans. Periodically, we returned for a refill—because the water in that area was filthy and very dangerous to drink.

We were fortunate enough to have a Jeep to take us to various places, officially, or, in many instances, unofficially. I did not know much about driving, but the other officers who had apparently driven all their adult lives were very good at it. One day one of those expert drivers flipped our Jeep into a rice paddy. Fortunately, no one was injured but only because the top had been removed and the windshield folded forward so that all the occupants were able to get out unharmed.

When my associates learned that I had never driven a car, they convinced me that our area was a smart choice for lessons because there was no traffic on the dirt roads in and out of our compound. One day, accompanied by one of our enlisted men, I went for a spin into the countryside. The road was stone-covered and on either sides were bushes and a few trees, including bamboo. Hanging from the trees over the road were thin vines. They appeared to be harmless and we passed through them but after going through a rather serious accumulation of vines I looked at my assistant whose eyes almost came out of their sockets.

Pointing his finger at my face, he said, "Lieutenant, lieutenant what happened to you? You'd better stop!"

I had no idea what he was talking about. With a shocked expression he said, "You're bleeding!"

I stopped the Jeep and as I did so I saw that my pants were covered with blood. About that time I felt a sharp pain on my chin. I had a cut of about three inches running horizontally approximately one inch below my lower lip. What could have done have done this to me and yet spared my friend, sitting right next to me? While I was holding my loose chin with both hands, my friend took the wheel and we returned to our base.

Still wondering how I could have sustained such a deep cut, we stopped to examine the vines that were hanging from the trees, some stretching across the road from one bush to the other. Grabbing one of the vines, I understood immediately what had happened to me. The vines were covered with tiny needles no more than 1/32 of an inch. These vines were like saw blades and even more effective. I reported to the local clinic, but they did not have the necessary equipment to stitch the gaping wound. They suggested that I hold my wound together until it mended itself. Fortunately for me it healed rather quickly and before long only a scar remained visible.

Up to that time the military situation in China had not improved. The Japanese were moving into the hinterland and the Chinese resistance was becoming weaker and weaker. The remnants of some of Merrill's Marauders had joined us and from them we heard some very disturbing stories about the Chinese fighting ability and its effectiveness.

During their training by American instructors, the Chinese were told that the effective range of their U.S.-made rifles was 1,000 yards. As a result they very carefully kept 1,000 yards away from the Japanese, fired all their ammunition at God-knows-what, claimed a victory and immediately requested additional ammunition. This technique was not well received by those who had come thousands of miles to deliver them from the Japanese.

Eventually it was decided that the Japanese had to be stopped and that reinforcements as well as supplies would be shipped southeast to block the Japanese advance.

On the 17th of May some of us were ordered to return to Kunming for a very important mission. We were all very happy as we had begun to despair.

The return trip was as bad as the earlier one which brought us to the Indochinese border. The smoke in the tunnels was even worse. With sighs of relief we reached the clean air of Kunming on the 20th of May.

It was then that I learned that I was to be part of a team which would cross the Indochinese border and, with some French troops, conduct guerrilla operations against the Japanese in the Tonkin area. Major Allison Thomas was to be the leader of our team. Two enlisted men, Sergeants Vogt and Zielski—the latter having seen action in France and the former having lived in China a long time—and a Chinese interpreter, Mr. Lee, were to be part of the team. Captain Mike Holland was to lead another group going in to the same general area as an advisor to a Chinese unit.

We were given three days to get ready and form a convoy before proceeding to Poseh, our advance base. There we would be briefed by Major Davis and Lt. Martineau, his radio operator, who were already in contact with the Chinese general commanding the region.

Before meeting our leader, I was told by a member of the team that Major Thomas had once accidentally shot himself while demonstrating to fellow officers the characteristics of his sidearm, an Army issue 45-caliber pistol. He was explaining that, when one pushes back on the barrel of a .45 with one's hand and a round is in the chamber, the pistol will not fire. The backward force blocks the mechanism and prevents the round from discharging. This technique is taught in training as an act of desperation in hand-to-hand combat when an opponent has a gun and you do not.

In theory the technique works, but once one releases the pressure on the barrel, and the finger squeezes the trigger, it fires the pistol immediately—a fact Major Thomas learned very quickly when the round passed through his hand and leg, fortunately without causing much damage to either.

It was difficult for me to imagine that an Army major would shoot himself accidentally. A private or even a corporal without experience could possibly do it. Those who did it usually wanted to go home and as a rule their toes were the victims. They never shot their hands and legs accidentally! I wondered what kind of team I was joining, and what was in store for me! I should have known!

To the Rescue

While in South Yunnan, I allowed my mustache to grow to eight inches from tip to tip. To stiffen the ends and keep them from drooping, I used beeswax. When I returned to Kunming my new whiskers were admired by some but scoffed by others, including Major Jack Shannon who decided that the brush under my nose had to go. I ignored him, but finally, with the help of four junior officers holding me spread-eagle, wielding a huge pair of scissors he leaned over me ready to snip the stiff extremities of my pride and joy. Suddenly he stood up and walked away while the others dropped me on the ground. Asked why he did not cut off my mustache, he said "When I saw tears in his eyes, I could not go through with it. It meant too much to him."

The author with handlebar mustache. South China - 1945

But I ran out of beeswax, and the tips of my mustache began to droop. One day these unruly extremities got tangled with the food I was eating and caused me to almost swallow them. That was the end of my king-size mustache.

My first meeting with Major Thomas was brief because an emergency had occurred and I was ordered to drive a supply truck to Poseh, several hundred miles southeast of Kunming. I was never asked if I could drive. After the few times I had driven at Kay Yuen, I felt pretty comfortable behind the wheel of a Jeep, but a truck was another matter. Nonetheless, Second Lieutenants were expected to obey orders, come what may.

After three days of preparation with the other team commanded by Captain Holland we left Kunming. Our convoy consisted of two trucks, two trailers, and one jeep. A photographer and a medic would join us later. Fortunately for me both sergeants who were with me were familiar with automobiles, but not necessarily with trucks. On a gray foggy morning we left our compound on a 6 x 6, 2 ½ ton truck, the backbone of the U.S. Army, while Major Thomas flew to Poseh, our destination, on an L-5. Of the three of us, I was the worst driver due to my lack of experience. This was a learning adventure for me and a very scary experience for my two companions. As long as we traveled on flat even ground the going was easy. However, when we reached the practically vertical mountains and had to negotiate twenty-nine hairpin curves to reach the top, my skill left much to be desired. Because of our large turning radius of our vehicle, at each curve we had to back up several times with our tail hanging over an abyss before we moved again to the next hairpin. Once, the right front wheel of our truck was hanging over the edge. My two companions jumped off, leaving me alone in the cab. I leaned to the left, as if that would help, and gunned the engine. The truck moved enough to bring the right front wheel on solid ground. I stopped, too shaky to go any further, and looked out over the 1,000 foot drop. I saw a truck, very much like ours, which had not made it. Actually, it was the carcass of a truck because it had been stripped of everything that could be removed.

The road on which we were traveling was one lane wide and any traffic coming from the other direction had to be carefully avoided. Sometimes there was no room between the edge of the road and a rice paddy full of water. Built to accommodate buffalo-drawn carriages, the road was very narrow, and narrowed more passing through villages. In one of the villages, the eaves of the houses extended over the road approximately level with the top of our truck. We were rolling at a fairly good speed when we realized too late that we could not avoid the roofs. We did not stop, and looking behind we could see the tiles and pieces of lumber flying in all directions. People ran after us shaking their fists. We did not stop, having been told that even if we had an accident, to keep on moving in a hurry.

Another time we reached a village where an outdoor market was in progress. The fruit and vegetables were displayed on flat bamboo trays which extended to the edge of the road. Again they were too close to the side of the road and our wheels hit the edges of trays and flipped them and their contents into the air, some of the fruit and vegetables landing in our truck. Again we gunned the engine and left the area as fast as we could.

It was not unusual for army trucks to kill Chinese. Surprisingly enough, many more might have been killed if the trucks had been driven by Chinese, who felt no obligation for the "truck's actions"! When driving through towns or cities, people waiting on the side of the road would rush to the other side a few seconds before the truck reached their position. I learned that the reason for this behavior was the villagers' belief that the bad spirit behind them would be crushed by the truck and they would be liberated from its evil influence!

Because of our lack of experience we soon discovered that we were lagging behind the rest of the convoy. We traveled alone on the road which in places had only recently been built and in others was still under construction. Men and women carried stones in baskets hanging on the ends of their yo-yo sticks. They placed each stone carefully on a prepared spot on the road bed and with a long-handled hammer they drove the stones into place. With nothing even remotely resembling a steamroller, they built the road entirely by hand.

We reached our destination on the evening of May 26th. Because we were eager to arrive there and get rid of our truck, we drove on past sunset through dark streets with only our headlights to guide us as we hoped we were on the right road. Eventually, at 4:00 a.m. and nearly out of gas, we came to the end of the road and faced a rather wide river. We could see the reflection of our headlights on the water, and on the other side there seemed to be activities with lights and the humming of generators. It was the air base at Poseh, but how to get there was another matter?

A Chinese appeared with a small motor boat and before long we were across the river, then making our way to the lighted hut which seemed to be the site of most of the activity. When we reached it only a lone and sleepy CQ (Charge of Quarters) greeted us. We were not supposed to be at the base, but at the OSS HQ, a compound 8 miles from Poseh, where the rest of the convoy had arrived. To refuel our truck we had to return on the other side of the river. Fortunately for us, the duty officer suggested that we use their 3/4 ton truck which was parked next to the building.

We immediately noticed that this truck did not handle as we thought it should but, eager to get going, we ignored our worry and headed towards the river where a ferry was anchored. We drove to the center of the ferry and shortly thereafter reached the other side. As soon as the ferry boat was secured, we started our truck and began the steep climb on the side of the river.

We were half way up the bank when the truck started to slow down, then stopped. Even in low gear it could not negotiate the steep bank of the river. As a matter of fact, the truck started to slowly slide backwards because the brakes could not hold it.

Before we knew it, the rear wheels were in the water and I began to wonder what I was going to say to the officer who had been kind enough to let us borrow it! We could not understand why the rear wheels did not do their job until one of my companions looked underneath and discovered that the rear drive shaft was missing. We were running the truck in front wheel drive only! With as much manpower as we could recruit we managed to push the truck to the level portion of the road.

By 6:30 a.m., we reached our final destination and met Major Davis, Lt. Whallen and Lt. Martineau. Sleeping quarters were assigned and the very tired men fed. I promised them the afternoon off but could not keep my word because Capt. Holland's truck had to be unloaded. Reluctantly they did the work, showing me that I could count on them when necessary.

The following day was Sunday. It was very hot and raining. We rested or went to church. In the morning Major Thomas flew to Tsing-Hsi, leaving me in charge of the team that now included Sgt. Alan Squires, a photographer, and Pfc Paul Hoagland, a medic. The Major gave me 80,000 CN (Chinese Dollars) for the team's expenses with instructions to join him on foot within a couple of days. He had set up a radio schedule between Zielski, our radio operator, and Martineau, the base radio operator at Poseh.

The following morning, Major Davis ordered me to unload our truck. It was very hot and muggy. Coolies were not available and I did not want my men to carry these large heavy boxes, so there was no unloading. At noon I was again told to unload. Very unhappy, the men did not move until they saw me struggling with the heavy boxes, and immediately came to help me. Up to that time we did not know the nature of our load. It turned out to be mostly high explosives!

In the process I accidentally caught the ring I wore on my small finger on the edge of one of the boxes and bent it. Hoagland, who had come to help us, also cut his finger and bled. We attracted the attention of local children who watched us from a safe distance. I managed to get the attention of one of the adult onlookers, and with 1500 CN, bribed him to help us.

The two enlisted men who were with me the entire trip and I had become quite friendly with one another. While unloading the two and a half tons of explosive, we discovered that a box of detonators had been placed in the center of the load in such a way that had we crashed, the entire truck could have been blown to smithereens. This brought us even closer to one another.

While working together, rather than calling me by my rank, they would often call me "René". The day we were unloading the truck, while unbeknownst to us, Major Davis was watching from a distance. He sent Lt. Whellen to warn me that my men were too friendly with me, and should show more respect by not using my first name. Moreover, I should not be sharing their work!

The men were highly trained personnel with a very important role on the team. Because of the lack of close-by replacements, losing any of these men would have jeopardized our mission. Carrying heavy boxes when help was available was to my way of thinking not only unrealistic, but stupid. I told Whellen to mind his own business.

After we were finished Major Davis sent for me and in the sanctity of his office chewed me out royally because the men had called me by my first name and because I was working rather than supervising. He raved for a while and then asked for an explanation, hoping that I would apologize and repent. Instead I told him that I did not give a damn what my men called me as long as they did the job to my satisfaction. I should have known better. It was not what the Major wanted to hear, and unfortunately for me he was the one who rated me. I would not be promoted from First Lieutenant to Captain for seven years.

The Deer Mission

On the 28th of July, after a quick breakfast, we took a CID Jeep from the air base to Poseh where I reported to Major Davis. With his usual sarcasm, Davis greeted me: "What took you so long to get here?"

I did not reply. Recalling his previous admonition, I thought it would be better for me not to offer an excuse. He explained that on July 16th Major Thomas had parachuted in to join a Vietminh group in the Tonkin region of FIC. With him were Pfc Henry Prunier, our interpreter, 1st Sgt. William Zielski, our radio operator, Lt. Montfort, a French officer, Sgt. Logos, a French Eurasian, and Sgt. Phac, an Annamese.

Then Davis announced: "You and the rest of your team—together with Holland and his boys—will jump tomorrow! Thomas is expecting you and the remaining members of his team, but there is a serious problem. The Vietminh refused to accept any member of the French army even as part of Thomas' team. Montfort, Logos, and Phac are being forced out."

Casually he added, "With a name like Défourneaux, you may have a problem, too! It may be wise to change it to make the team as Anglo-Saxon as possible."

"What about Prunier? That is not exactly an Anglo-Saxon name!"

"He speaks Annamese, and they could tell that he was no Frenchman."

I did not have much time to think of a name so I decided that Raymond Douglass, a name I had used during training in England, would be fine. To account for my ability to speak as a native Frenchman I would have a French mother. I was to make up the other parts of my new identity as needed.

The rest of the team consisted of Staff Sgt. Lawrence Vogt, a weapons instructor, Pfc Paul Hoagland, a registered nurse who was to be our medic, and Sgt. Alan Squires, a photographer who was to record the team's activities. Hoagland had already made a name for himself before joining our group. Rumor stated that he had conducted an emergency appendectomy on a fellow soldier using only his pen knife! The patient had survived and I felt relieved having such an individual on our team.

Capt. Holland, Sgt. Stoyka, and Sgt. Burrows were to jump with us. They composed another team that was to operate in an area adjacent to ours. John Stoyka was an experienced OSS agent who, like me, had seen action in Europe.

Supplies for both teams had to be readied. Some had been packed in cargo nets by the members of the team who had left earlier. The remaining supplies were my responsibility. It took a 2 ½ ton truck to move all of our supplies to the air strip. The same old ferry took us across the swollen river.

Major Davis in his inimical way was running supply and ground transport for the operation. Behaving as the proverbial fly helping the coach, running around our stacked supplies, he gave orders, then countermanded them. On the edge of the fields several tiger-faced growling P-51s stood guard over us and the lone olive-drab C-47 with its cargo-loading door wide open. Our gear was in square packs wrapped in cargo netting, each with a parachute attached to its webbing. By the time our supplies were aboard, there was very little room for the passengers.

In addition—and to our surprise—a full colonel, a major and several others decided to go along for the ride. The pilot was a veteran of the Chinese campaign, and so were his copilot and navigator. However, I remembered that, a year earlier, a equally experienced crew had dropped me—forty kilometers off my designated destination!

The rough calculations on the weight of the cargo made everyone, including the crew, nervous. Perhaps we were overloaded, but Major Davis decided otherwise. By the way, he was not flying with us. Of all the members of our team, only Bill Zielski and I had ever jumped before in a combat situation!

In France, Bill, a radio operator, had devised an ingenious method for avoiding detection of his radio transmissions by the enemy. The Germans would locate unauthorized transmitters through the use of a series of fixed and mobile detection stations known as DF stations. When a transmission would occur, three stations would fix their revolving antennas on the signal. Then, by triangulation, the location of the transmitter could be pinpointed. Bill was fortunate enough to spot one of these fixed DF stations close to his hiding place. He could actually observe the rotary antenna searching for illegal broadcasting. He could tell when the station was locking on his transmission by the direction it would point. As he began transmitting, he watched the DF station's antenna. When the DF antenna revolved near his position, he would cease transmission, making it impossible for the Germans to get a fix on his signal. This frustrated not only the Germans, but the London OSS radio operators, who could not understand why the keyed (dot-dit-dot) transmission would suddenly pause, only to restart moments later. Bill was later commended for devising this novel approach.

Poseh was located in a saucer completely surrounded by mountains between three and four thousand feet in altitude. The air strip was short, designed for the takeoff of light fighter aircraft, but long enough to accommodate a Dakota known as C-47. We taxied to the end of the runway and locked the wheels; the pilot revved the engines at top RPM before releasing the brakes. We began to roll, rapidly increasing our speed, but not enough for a lift-off. None of us were strapped into the bucket seats which had been folded back to allow more space for the cargo. We held on the static cable above our heads. The door had been removed to facilitate our exit and we could see the runway and the field without obstruction.

We passed the half-way marker wheels still firmly on the runway. At runway's end the wheels were no higher than one foot above the surface. I watched the right gear retract under the engine gondola as bushes flashed by a few inches below. Slowly we gained altitude, circling around the valley until we reached enough height to fly over the mountain range to our destination.

To reach cruising altitude, the plane burned a good portion of its fuel, which made it lighter and improved its climbing ability but reduced its flying range. Heading south, all we could see was the mountainous landscape of northern Tonkin, a series of steep ridges separated by narrow valleys, many of them totally blind, and covered by thick vegetation. Nowhere could we see a suitable landing site for a team of paratroopers.

As we proceeded farther south, the landscape did not improve much. Occasionally we spotted a few rice paddies in the bottom of the valleys. The navigator took us to the general area where a "T" marker placed on the ground by the advance party of the team was to greet us. It was obvious to most of us that if something went wrong with the aircraft, only those who had a parachute would survive. Captain Holland, a devout Irish Catholic, was not looking at the countryside; he was on his knees saying his Hail-Marys and Our-Fathers.

Sgt. Aaron Squires, our photographer, a very nice fellow and the smallest of our group, was probably wondering what he was doing with this bunch of nuts who, despite having seen the horrors of combat, were telling jokes and laughing instead of praying. This was too much for him so he needed the toilet to relieve himself. Of course there were no toilets aboard, only a funnel at the end of a hose with the other end leading to the outside of the fuselage. The contraption had been designed strictly for urinating and nothing else. When we learned of his predicament, we offered numerous suggestions. One was that he should extend his rear-end outside the aircraft while we held the rest of his body inside. He did not appreciate this method. We had all kinds of canned food with us, including many number ten tin cans. Someone suggested that we empty one of the cans and let Squires use it as a miniature john. The can was opened quickly and the contents disposed of. As we looked the other way, our photographer relieved himself then threw the can overboard. The joke of the moment was "What will the fellow who finds the can think when he compares the contents with the label?"

After three and half hours of futile flying, we realized that time was short and we might have to abandon our search. All eyes were on the ground as we hoped to spot the red "T". We knew our fuel was limited and that some was needed for the return trip. We circled the area watching for smoke which was to guide us to the marker, but saw none. The terrain was so rough that it was impossible to see anything from a distance. Only when exactly above a landmark could we identify it. At times, the plane flew so low into valleys that, looking up, I could see banana plants on the top of ridges rise higher than my eye level.

About the time our pilot thought of giving up, someone spotted what appeared to be red smoke. We flew toward it and sure enough in he bottom of a small valley we saw the red "T" and three white parachutes. Besides showing the location of the drop zone the colored smoke also indicated the wind direction.

From our altitude, the drop zone looked about the size of a postage stamp. It was a small valley, no more than a quarter of a mile wide and three miles long, completely occupied by rice fields, and on either end was a high ridge. It was decided to first drop some of the supplies to see how much time we could spent over the DZ and how much space we had before reaching the side of the mountain. For the first pass, the pilot lowered the wheels and the flaps and descended to four-hundred feet above the ground. As soon as the test load left the aircraft, the pilot retracted the wheels and began a steep climb so as to clear the top of the ridge ahead. He returned several times until it was time for us to go.

I chose not to jump first because I wanted to properly check everyone's chutes. When it was Holland's turn, the All-American froze at the door. With both hands on the side of the door he stiffened and locked his knees. We had to take another pass. This time we knew what to do and just pushed him out. He fell with a yell that must have been heard ten miles away and it was not "Geronimo!"

Everything seemed OK below, I was the last to exit the aircraft. Coming down, I faced the C-47 as it flew away from the drop zone. I could see the top of the aircraft, its engines straining to get above the hills and the banana plants.

The Tonkin Jungle

The landing field selected by our reception party was no ideal drop zone for paratroopers. With little time to guide my chute, I assumed the landing position, hit the ground, and rolled as I was supposed to. Fortunately for me, I fell on a narrow path between two rice paddies full of muddy water.

My other companions were not so lucky. Most were covered with muck and one hung on a tree until he was rescued. All of us were all right, no broken bones and no injuries except to the pride of the wet ones. As I gathered my chute, I noticed an individual on the path ahead of me. I thought I was imagining things. The man, an oriental approximately five feet six, wore a white suit, black tie, black shoes and a black homburg. We were in the deep jungle of Tonkin and there he was, dressed as if he'd come from an embassy reception or the board meeting of a bank. He introduced himself as "Mr. Van", explaining that the "Chief" of his group was ill in a nearby village and that Major Thomas was away on a reconnaissance trip. Along with Sgt. William Zielski, who had set up the drop zone, in single file we followed Mr. Van to our lodging some distance away. Walking on a narrow trail lined with bamboo we reached what were to be our temporary quarters, a group of huts built on stilts approximately eight feet off the ground. Their floors were also made of flattened bamboo strips interlaced into a rather springy surface. The roofs were made of palm leaves. The huts were accessed by means of wide ladders. We would soon learn why these huts had been built in such way.

A streamer at the entrance of this jungle development proclaimed: "Welcome to our American Friends!" A shocking sight in the middle of the jungle! Later we met Lt. Dan Phelan and Frankie Tan, a Chinese-American, members of AGAS (Air Ground Aid Service) an organization responsible for the rescue of 14th Air Force pilots shot down over French Indochina. Both were instrumental in bringing the first section of the Deer Team to their location.

It was Frankie Tan who had established an escape route for US airmen of the 14th in that area. Phelan had joined him shortly before our own arrival.

The hut we occupied was barely large enough to accommodate both teams. We did not mind and, if I recall properly, we were a bunch of happy fellows. There was a sense of relief on the part of those who had never jumped before, and in the case of the praying Captain a new sense of bravado as he was now convinced more than ever that prayers do pay!

The beer we were given enlivened the discussion far into the night when all of sudden we heard a growling coming from below the floor. Our conversation stopped abruptly. Someone suggested that the noise be investigated, but no one volunteered to go down the ladder. One enterprising member of our group spread the bamboo strips and directed the beam of his flashlight underneath the floor. The eyes and the grin of a tiger appeared for an instant then disappeared almost immediately. We knew then why huts were built so high off the ground!

In sleeping bags on the springy bamboo floor of a native bungalow most of the group fell asleep. Lying there yet still unable to relax, I marveled at the way our roof was constructed with interlaced palm leaves. I had been in many houses and shelters in China, but none as original as the one we were in.

As I recalled our pains to reach this very spot I was boggled. Now the Deer Team was finally in place, ready and eager to do what it was created to do. But I could not help thinking about our wasted efforts, our lack of direction and leadership. Had our preparatory China adventures really been necessary to get us this far?

On the French Indochina Border

Several weeks earlier the day after we had reached Poseh, Major Thomas sent word through Chinese Combat Command (CCC) HQ communication channels for us to proceed to Tsing-Hsi, our jumping-off point to French Indochina (FIC). However OSS-Kunming headquarters had to concur before we could move. We finished packing and loaded our two trucks. We hoped that some of us might be airlifted, but learned to our sorrow that no L-5 was available. We decided to leave the following morning.

We were up at 6:00 a.m. and on the road by 9:00 a.m. Before reaching the ferry we discovered three flat tires on one of the trucks. Lt. Whallen, our transportation officer, had failed to check the vehicles the day before our departure! We unloaded the equipment to another truck and finally left at 11:00 am. By then, having had only a cup of coffee for breakfast, we were hungry. But Major Davis refused to feed us and rushed us on our way.

On narrow dirt roads Whallen recklessly drove 21 miles at top speed. Exhausted and hungry, we arrived at Tiang-Tung at 2:00 p.m.. It was inconceivable to some of us that one of our leaders, with all the means at his disposal, could send men on a mission without adequate sustenance, but he did!

On the first of June we were ready to leave at 8:00 a.m. This was as far as our trucks could take us so we would now rely on porters known in China as "coolies." The coolies hired for us came from 10 miles away and they only showed up at 9:30 a.m.! Looking over our supplies, the Chinese officer in charge of our transportation decided that there were not enough porters for the amount of supplies to transport. Coolies were not supposed to carry loads in excess of 60 pounds, but Davis had figured on a 120 pound load per porter. Even the U.S. Army does not expect a soldier to carry 120 pounds in the field. Apparently Davis was not aware of this. Since we did not have enough coolies, Capt. Holland, the senior officer, decided to wait another day before continuing to Tsing-Hsi.

We were in the dark about this operation since all its details had originated at our HQ without any input on our part. For example, we did not know that coolies only traveled a given distance from their base, and that another set of coolies had to be acquired when they reached the limit of their territory. This demanded a rather sophisticated planning by someone having knowledge of the local situation. This someone was nowhere to be found among our leaders.

With 80 loaded coolies we left Tiang-Tung at 9:30 a.m. on a rough mountain trail and began climbing between large rocks. The going was very slow. Even with 80 coolies some of the loads were way over the recommended 60 pounds. Exhausted but happy we reached Po-Hong at 6:00 p.m.. While the coolies prepared their rice and chicken in large woks we cooked our own meal, then retired in our sleeping bags for the night.

On the 4th of June we took the trail at 8:00 a.m. The first four miles were on a treacherous mountain trail leading to a valley where we crossed the main road from Tien-Pao to Poseh. The hard-top road was covered with obstacles and tank traps every three hundred yards. At 4:30 p.m., after walking over 24 miles, we reached Tien-Pao and were met by Captain Yo of General Lee's staff. General Lee invited us to a welcoming party that very evening.

To maintain good relations with the Chinese, we were expected to attend social events when invited. These were, for the most part, drinking parties. I shall never forget the party General Lee gave at his home. There must have been twenty Chinese officers and approximately six of us led by Mike Holland, the ranking officer in our group and well suited for this position. Apparently famous in the world of sports as having played football for Notre Dame, his Irish ancestry seemed responsible for his unquenchable thirst and his great capacity to hold his liquor. It seems that these parties were calculated to place us at a disadvantage, force us to relax, and perhaps to lull us into a false sense of security.

The large round tables held approximately ten people and the food was served Chinese style. One plate full was placed on a lazy Susan in the center of the table, and the guests attacked the food with their chopsticks. Right there we were at a disadvantage, because chopsticks were still new to us but very old stuff to the Chinese who usually cleaned the plate before we had one mouthful.

The first part of the meal went fine, but if by chance we made eye contact with one of the Chinese guests, he would lift his cup full of rice wine and say, "Gambay," to which we had to reply the same, then down the contents of our own cup. We were told that to refuse a "Gambay" or fail to empty our cup was rude and that our interlocutor would lose face. So the four of us at one table faced six Chinese who seemed to be having much fun getting us drunk. It was useless to feign emptying our cups, because after each toast we had to turn the cup upside down to show that we had emptied it. We learned later that the pork fat served as entrée was not to curb the appetite, but to coat the stomach and permit a greater intake of alcohol. That was the accepted norm followed by all the Chinese who entertained us. I managed to avoid the gaze of most of the Chinese guests, but our Captain did not. Before long his sun-tanned face began to glow.

Mr. Lee, our interpreter whose services we seldom used, managed somehow to translate what our Chinese friends were saying, but we doubted his accuracy. After much drinking and some eating, the Chinese general, who had not touched a thing (we were told that he had eaten before the party so that he could concentrate on his guests), got up and made a speech. It must have been a good one because all the Chinese officers present stood up, some with much difficulty, and applauded. We did the same. Then, they all looked at us because they expected one of us to respond. Our captain got the message and stood up but, weaving somewhat and with a smile, he began to say the craziest things to our host and the assembly.

He began by calling them "little brown bastards", explaining that we had come to save their f—ing necks, and for ten minutes he insulted our host, the Chinese army, the Chinese government and everything else Chinese. I looked at our interpreter whose English was not good enough to understand all that was said, and watched the Chinese to see their reaction. Most of them appeared too drunk to care. They applauded our "ugly American" and continued their drinking.

One fat Chinese officer, a particularly heavy drinker who did not need a "Gambay" to empty his cup, had two of his enlisted men standing behind him. After hoisting one drink too many, the officer keeled over. However, just before hitting the floor, the two men picked him up, one by the feet the other by the shoulders, and carried him out feet first. The Chinese General left and everyone else followed suit. I was still worried about our Captain's speech when one of the Chinese officers approached me and, in perfect English, said, "He is very funny, your friend."

I knew that the jig was up and that we would have an international incident on our hands. But the Chinese continued, "Don't worry, the others did not understand. I am a doctor and was educated in the United States and frankly I agree with some of your friend's comments." I knew then that we had an ally, and that we were very lucky. Later on we had the opportunity to exchange ideas and information.

Something else occurred during the party which proved that we also had a friend among the Chinese enlisted men who served us food and refilled our cups with rice wine. Halfway through the party I realized that I was no longer drinking rice wine. I was actually drinking a weak tea. While the waiter was serving real rice wine to our hosts, he was serving us tea! Why was he doing this and who had instructed him to do so, or was it his own idea?

The primitive facilities placed at our disposal were not the best in the world. They lacked the most basic conveniences such as showers and flush toilets. Fortunately, a nice river flowed nearby and we used the clear water for our daily baths. We found an ideal place where the river was so shallow that one could cross it by stepping on flat stones which stuck a few inches above the water. This fording was used by the local people as there was no bridge over the river. We had no bathing suits, so most of us wore our underwear except for our famous Captain, the jock, who preferred to strip completely to show off his anatomy of which he seemed very proud.

Once, after a hot day's work, we decided to go for a refreshing dip in our favorite hole. We were soaping ourselves in the clear water when a Chinese girl in her early twenties loaded with two baskets of dry water buffalo manure on a yo-yo stick began to cross the fording stones. She stared at us but more so at the anatomy of the Captain who was unusually well endowed, much more than Chinese men, we were told. Stepping from one stone to the next demanded special care, as they were not placed evenly. The girl missed her step and into the water she fell, taking the basket of dry manure with her. The manure began to float down stream, and all of us rushed to the rescue. We lifted the soaked girl back on the flat rock, and after recovering most of the manure, helped her on her way. She kept looking back at our Captain who was showing off even more.

The next morning we received a written communication from the Chinese general telling us that, from now on, we were to bathe north of the village, far away for the gaze of the Chinese maidens. Someone, probably a member of the General's staff, had seen the incident and informed the General.

Perhaps the Chinese officials felt that it was not smart to show their women the difference between the sexual accouterment of American and Chinese men, if in fact there really were any.

We were at the mercy of Chinese General Lee, the only one who could supply coolies. Those we had employed up to Tien-Pao had returned to their base. General Lee invited us to another party, but Holland declined telling him that we would cook our own meal. He was then told that was not the correct thing to do and in order not to lose face he should invite the general and four members of his staff. After an uneventful meal the General took us to an outdoor theater presentation, the equivalent of a USO show for our own Armed Forces. A stage had been erected in the center of a large field and a few chairs placed in front of it. These were for the General, his staff and his guests to enjoy the screeching of the actors and the off-tune music, drums and bells. This was no doubt the most boring spectacle I had ever attended. However our Chinese friends seemed to enjoy it, laughing periodically, until halfway though the third act, when we were pelted with rocks as large as my fist. Behind us stood a couple of thousand soldiers grinning at us, and from within this human mass rocks came toward us at an ever increasing rate. We did not know if these rocks were intended for us or the Chinese officers sitting with us. However the show was immediately canceled. Later we sang American songs and Aaron Squires, our photographer, entertained the troops with his muscle tricks to the great delight of the Chinese soldiers.

While we were enjoying the attentions of the Chinese, Mr. Lee, our interpreter, managed to line up 80 coolies and 14 horses.

By 10:00 a.m. the next morning we left Tien-Pao, each one of us on a horse, though it was still too late to reach Tsing-Hsi the same day. In addition to horses, the Chinese unit escorting us had mules. These, imported from Missouri, were used to transport heavy weapons and cases of ammunition. Most of us chose to ride on the backs of the small Chinese horses, which unlike the mules trotted continuously, causing great pain and discomfort to the unaccustomed rider. I was one of them. While the horses were equipped with leather saddles, the mules only had a wooden rack designed to hold a load of supplies. One could sit on this makeshift saddle with some padding to absorb the shock.

To be in the saddle on either a horse or a mule while climbing a mountain was all right, but the technique was not recommended during the descent. We reached the summit and could see in the distance the broken Chinese countryside, rice paddies clinging to the steep hills, norias spinning slowly and the haze over the villages. Absorbed by the sight, I relaxed on the saddle when abruptly I found myself on the ground looking at the mule from below. She did not pitch me over, all she did was lean forward, almost on her knees, and down her neck I went. The Chinese who was responsible for her feeding and general welfare was following not far behind. He saw the whole thing and laughed, telling the other mule-keepers and starting a laughing session among the other Chinese. Since that time I have never trusted a mule.

We stopped at Doe-On and after a good meal retired for the day. Up to then we were all in good shape. We drank only boiled water, had a cup of coffee in the morning and ate a full meal in the evening. We only covered 18 miles that day.

At 8:30 a.m. we left Doe-On with our complement of horses and mules. That day, unfortunately, the mules had other ideas. It appeared that the dozen or so of them had taken a crush on a white horse that was part of the unit. Everything was well in the conduct of our expedition as long as the white horse was ridden to the same destination as the mules. But if for some reason the white horse had to go to a different destination, we faced a serious problem.

Leaving Doe-On, we had to follow a very dangerous stretch of mountain trail. Our sure-footed horses would have had no trouble negotiating the trail, but the loaded mules might not have an easy time. The convoy was divided so that the horses would follow the rough path while the mules would take a longer but easier trail. We left the mules on their own while the horses took the short-cut, the white horse bringing up the rear. We were not gone twenty minutes when we heard shouting behind us. We stopped and watched in amazement as a line of mules in full trot came toward us with their Chinese keepers in hot pursuit. The mules did not pass us but instead surrounded the white horse. I only wished that I understood their language! No amount of shouting or beating could move the mules. The only solution was to let the white horse lead the mules to their destination while we continued on without him.

We had to climb a mountain range which, though not very high, was very steep. We followed a trail that had been cut by caravans thousands of years before. Periodically, we would pass small shacks where one could stop and order a bowl of noodle soup. These stands consisted of a counter behind which a Chinese would greet the customer with a smile and a joke, a Chinese joke. Most non-Chinese laughed as is if they were able to understand Chinese. I never got the jokes and our interpreter was not able to translate them because he did not understand the dialect!

On a narrow table behind the counter, a stack of cold noodles was normally kept in a bamboo basket along with some green onions. Over a charcoal range hung a pot of boiling water. Hanging on the rafters immediately above the table was a variety of dark meat and sausages, smoked or naturally cured. These were usually covered with flies which preferred meat to noodles. In front of the stand a long piece of lumber served as a bench. Chinese travelers came to the stand to order their soup. The waiter took a handful of noodles, placed them in a colander and submerged them in the boiling water. While the noodles warmed up he unhooked the meat selected by the customer and sliced small pieces from it which he chopped with a sharp cleaver. It was unfortunate for the flies that were not fast enough to escape, as they ended up in the soup with the meat.

A few inches of green onions followed the meat onto the chopping block. By then the noodles were steaming hot. The cook lifted them from the boiling pot, let them drain and filled the bowl to the brim. With the chopper, he collected the meat and the green onion, and sprinkled them over the noodles. On the stand three or four dirty bottles contained various sauces including Soya, and a small jar held used bamboo chopsticks. The customers selected a matching pair of chopsticks and after sprinkling various sauces, gobbled the soup with the required sound effect to please the smiling cook.

When the going was rather hard and hunger took over, I was glad to reach the noodle stand and order a hot bowl of soup. My teammates could not believe that I would not only eat this food, but actually enjoy it. The noodle soup was very tasty, and probably very healthy. One of our team actually threw up when he saw me eating with the coolies. Strangely enough, I was the only one in our group who did not contract dysentery while in Asia. All the other members of our team did, and one almost died from it.

We continued our journey toward the Indochinese frontier and reached a most interesting valley. It was peppered with hills which looked very much like sugar loaves. One could go completely around them without climbing one foot.

The hills were covered with small trees and bushes and inhabited by wild goats. The trail that we followed paralleled a river no more than one hundred yards wide. The valley narrowed somewhat and we could see villages at the base of the rolling hills on either side.

In establishing camp, we preferred as a rule not to stay in villages for a number of reasons. First, the old Chinese warlord system was still the de facto rule of the day, and in many cases we did not know the true allegiance of the people of the area. In addition, with our lack of grooming, we did not physically resemble a conventional military unit. Finally, we wanted to disassociate ourselves from the way Chinese units on the move temporarily dislocated entire villages in order to provide shelters to their troops.

At 4:00 p.m., 21 miles later, we reached Tsing-Hsi where we reported to Major Thomas who was with Captain Babineau and Mr. Thiercy, the French Consul.

Later on that day I joined Major Thomas, Capt. Holland, Capt. Boggs, Capt. Baudenon, and Lt. Tersac on an inspection tour of the French Indochinese troops at Sinh-Hu, a short distance from Tsing-Hsi. Although ill-equipped and poorly clothed, the unit had ten sections with a total of 125 officers and men. They appeared well trained, even snappy, and their morale was very high. Each section was composed of one French officer with two to three noncoms commanding the Annamese troops.

Back in Tsing-Hsi, Thomas and Baudenon planned our next move. They decided to send an advance party of 25 men under the command of Thomas and Lt. Langlois, while the rest of the French troops were to be trained close to the FIC border.

When the question of logistics was brought up it became obvious that it would be impossible to conduct a successful operation without the strong support of either the U.S. Army or the French. The French had nothing to offer, so Thomas decided to give to the 25 men the excess uniforms and supplies from his and Holland's teams. The French had no shoes nor uniforms. We managed to scrounge enough clothing and weapons to equip the first group of twenty-five.

Since escaping Indochina the French officers and NCOs had not shaved for some time. Most of them sported heavy beards. If they were to pass as Americans for the benefit of the local people, Thomas decided that the beards had to go. He wanted them to look more like GIs rather than foreign legionnaires.

Poseh advised us by radio that Capt. Ebaugh and his team would be joining us shortly. It was midnight when they reached our position. The following day they began training the Chinese. Mr. Thiercy invited all the officers to a party, probably to celebrate the formation of the first French unit to return to their Colony.

We did not want the Chinese to know that we were arming the French. Thus, on June 12, using coolies, I brought additional material to CCC HQ, then using FIC troops I quietly transferred the material to the French Military Mission. Under cover of darkness I brought the rest of the equipment to the French camp. Meanwhile Thomas had asked the Chinese General for an authorization to select an area in his territory where we might train the French troops. Feverishly we prepared for our departure, making sure that we had everything we needed. Sgt. Zielski was finally able to receive messages from Poseh and Kunming and he was still decoding messages past midnight.

On June 13th, after a light breakfast, we reported to Thomas at 4:45 a.m. The French had already moved out and only Lt. Montfort remained behind to guide us. We had left many of our personal belongings behind, but we still had too much to carry. Fortunately, daylight began just as we departed. We passed the first three arduous miles on a muddy and slippery trail and at the first village hired coolies to carry our packs to the next village. Although by then our marching route was easier it was not pleasant. Our men were very unhappy, not only because they had to get up early after working very late the evening before, but also because Major Thomas was not with them to enjoy the trip!

We joined Lt. Langlois and his Group at Low-Son and bivouacked together. I reached the conclusion that night travel in this area was too dangerous. Several members of the unit which had left early in the dark were injured on the treacherous trail. To be effective and safe, our men should not have had to carry more then 5 pounds over and above the weight of their weapon and ammunition. Field radios and their equipment were too heavy for this type of terrain.

With empty stomachs we left Low-Son for On-Ning, 6 miles away. We reached our destination at 11:00 a.m. At the gate of the village the secretary of Mr. Chan-Tsu-Minh, the local Tou-Pan, greeted and hurriedly directed us to the local school house. It was market day in the village and the traffic on all trails was very heavy. He told us that it was a bad day for us to be in the village because of the probability of Japanese agents mingling among the people. So we stayed indoors until the following day when we surveyed the region to locate a possible training area and a drop zone. Our search proved to be fruitless. It was a mountainous region in which all the valleys were covered with rice paddies, and construction material was not locally available. The few possible training locations were too near main trails, and we were too close to the Indochinese border where Japanese patrols ranging from 2 to 400 men roamed at will.

We advised Thomas of the situation and sent a runner to head off the main group who had left Tsing-Hsi in the morning to join us. We were ignored and told, probably by Davis, that an air drop was planned for June 18!

On June 16, Capt. Baudenon and Major Thomas reached our location on horseback. Apparently Thomas did not believe that an officer with airborne training and combat experience could determine the suitability of a drop zone! He came to verify our findings himself. Our cold reception did not phase him. He agreed with Holland and I that the entire group had to withdraw to Tsing-Hsi and search for another training location.

The first phase of our mission was a complete failure. We had to start over from a solid base. Finding a suitable training area where the entire unit could be moved to was our main concern. On June 17 we received a very strange message from OSS-Kunming Headquarters. We were ordered to stop issuing material to the French! What is going on? I relayed the message to Thomas by runner. Then we received orders to return to Ti-Tiou immediately.

When we reached An-Ning we saw several bodies on the street. This was most unusual and, even stranger, their skin looked almost black. The people were packing and leaving the village in all directions. Medic Paul Hoagland immediately identified the problem. These people had died of the dreaded cholera. We contacted our headquarters who immediately sent a medical team with serum and needles by L-5, a light-weight aircraft designed for extremely short take-offs and landings. As best as we could, we convinced the remaining villagers to line up and be inoculated. That was the easiest part of the job for us, as we could not convince the population to stay in one place so as not to spread the disease elsewhere. We had no problem with the inoculation because the residents seemed to enjoy being injected with whatever we had.

The rain made it difficult to move rapidly, but we reached Low-Son and settled in the school house. The lack of organization and our leaders' inability to intelligently plan anything affected our men who had volunteered for this mission. Upset, they began questioning the leadership of the team.

The three of us, loaded like mules, took the road leading closer to the FIC/China border. For some reason our leader decided to remain behind, stating that he would join us soon. We had strong suspicions that he did not come with us for some reason he did not want us to know. After a couple of days march, we decided to wait to see if he would catch up with us.

Indeed he did. But unlike the three of us, who were straining under the load of our gear, he was riding a horse and a coolie trotting behind, carrying his equipment. I do not believe he knew that we saw him. Right then our leader lost the confidence and the respect of the rest of the team. We did not believe that his decision not to march with us had anything to do with his wounds. Had he mentioned any wound-related disability to us, we would have been the first to suggest he use a horse and a coolie to carry his pack.

Capt. Holland and I tried our best to make our enlisted men understand the complexity of the problems. We officers were in the same boat as the men and suggested that anyone unhappy should request a transfer back to Kunming. But there were no takers, and life went on.

We reached Ti-Tiou the following day. Lt. Sourice escorted us to the village of Po-Ka-Hao, 2 kilometers north of Ti-Tiou, where we were to occupy two houses selected by Major Thomas. These were so filthy that we decided to bivouac outside. Capt. Popper and one of the US Annamese interpreters mentioned that he knew the whereabouts of a great bivouac area, as well as a drop zone.

Following his suggestion we moved to a raised pine-covered cemetery approximately 2 km north of Po-Ka-Hao. Stone tablets and pillars stood between the pine trees and the distance between trees seemed ideally created for hanging our hammocks.

We, or I should say I, decided that this was a good place to spend a few days. As we set up sleeping accommodations, our radio operator checked the area to determine the best location for his antenna. As we worked, we were interrupted by a local inhabitant of advanced age. By his gestures we guessed that he was not very happy. Our interpreter, though unfamiliar with the man's dialect, managed to understand the gist of the old boy's complaint. We had located ourselves on top of the burial ground of the ancestors of the nearby village! This was a major no-no and we must leave immediately or find ourselves subjected to all kinds of supernatural calamities. He left us unconvinced and determined to stay where we were.

A few moments later, as I was talking to one of my men, one of the stone columns fell right between us. I thought that our radio operator, stringing his antenna, had somehow caused it to fall, but he was nowhere near it. We examined the base of the stone which weighed at least a ton and could find no logical reason for it to have toppled. This worried us a bit so we decided to be more careful and to take turns on guard during the night. A fog came up from the river located approximately a half mile away. I took the first shift and two hours later, at approximately 10:00 p.m., I slid into my hammock. I had no trouble falling asleep.

Twice a day we walked to the village to share a meal with the French troops as we had no rations of our own. Their food was locally acquired as C and K rations were unknown to them. The French colonial troops had developed a ration that was more like their cuisine than ours. Using yeast from the fermented rice, and rice flour, they made small individual loaves of bread. Before baking these in a field oven made of rocks and mud, they filled the center of the dough with small pieces of cooked pork or chicken and sometimes vegetables. Once baked, the small hard crusted loaves would keep several days even under unbearably hot temperatures and high humidity.

In combat the call of nature could place a soldier in a very awkward if not dangerous position, so the French colonial troops used opium to freeze their innards. They ingested the residue scraped from opium pipes. For days they did not have the urge to relieve themselves, but this obviously contributed to the addiction which showed up in many.

It seemed that every mealtime was taken by radio communication requiring both of our teams to be present to help turn the hand generator. This scheduling resulted in cold food, and many gripes from our men.

From a security point of view, our camp was located in an excellent location. It was also a good area for our communication which up to that point had been iffy. We received and sent our messages to both Kunming and Poseh with ease. On the evening of June 23rd a mean storm reached our area. Lightning illuminated the countryside and thunder echoed through the valley. We had hammocks designed by Abercromby and Finch for big game hunters. Besides having a plastic cover, each was equipped with netting for protection from mosquitoes. Once tucked inside, one was supposed to be protected from the rain and insects. In our oasis we felt pretty secure and comfortable. The rainy season was approaching and this area was subject to the monsoon. The rain started rather slowly, but increased in intensity until instead of drops sheets of water came from all directions, soaking everything.

By 2:00 a.m. the rain had subsided somewhat. We tried to dry our clothes as best we could over a fire that I had managed to make. Several of the enlisted men returned to their hammocks, but Hoagland and I stayed up until sun up. By then I felt a little feverish but it disappeared that evening when the French had a party in the honor of St. John, the patron saint of Lt. Gourg, one of our French officers.

The following evening around 11:00 p.m. we heard in the distance the sound of a plaintive horn coming from a distant valley. In the still of the night it was mournful, urgent and very strange. It stopped, then started again, but seemed nearer to our position. Again it stopped and restarted in the same lugubrious tone, still moving closer and closer to us. Eventually it faded away the same as it had begun. Intrigued, we queried our interpreter as to the meaning of the horn, but he did not know. Then I remembered a story that I had read about China. In the old days this was the way the Chinese villages warned each other of pirates or bandits roaming the countryside. Were there bandits in the area (or perhaps Japanese) or was it merely some kind of drill, as someone suggested? Worried somewhat, we went to sleep hoping our guard was alert. An official explanation was never given!

We decided to maintain a high state of alert as we were on the path of the approaching Japanese. We established a lookout on one of the hills dominating the valley, and with our thirty power telescope, we looked for possible Japanese troop movements and observed the activities in the valley below us.

This was rice planting season and we could see lines of local women bent over, planting green rice in the flooded rice paddies.They had their pant legs rolled up to their knees as they bent down in unison under wide brim bamboo hats.

It was early one morning when I was awakened by one of our team who said, "Have you heard what happened Lieutenant?"

"What happened?" I asked.

"Paul Hoagland shot someone or something last night."

"He what?"

"Someone came to our camp last night but the fog was so thick we could not see what it was so I shot it," Paul said.

"Why didn't you wake me up?" I wanted to know.

"We tried but we couldn't wake you," he replied.

I was sure that they were joking or pulling my leg. By 8:00 a.m. the fog had lifted to reveal an open corn field nearby. After determining the direction of the shooting, I walked a short distance and came to a small, dark red puddle! It was thick and it seemed to be blood. The ground was hard and dry.

The few red drops formed a trail that I followed, but soon ended. I did not see footprints because the soil was so dry. I returned to the camp and we all agreed that if one of the villagers had been shot or one of their buffalo injured, we would soon hear about it. No one came to protest so we felt that it might have been a wild animal, perhaps a goat, or better yet a Japanese!

The monsoon was now really upon us. We woke up one morning and could not believe our eyes. The river, which had been a quarter of a mile away, was less than 50 feet from our wall. The recently planted rice fields were completely submerged. A local man standing on a bamboo raft passed near us. He was collecting rice plants washed away by the flood and now floating on the surface, piling them on his makeshift raft.

By mid-morning, the water had reached our wall and the rain had not let up. The nearest village, approximately a mile from us and higher on the side of a hill, appeared to be out of danger. I made the decision to leave and move to higher ground. The men and I began packing, planning to move toward the village. I was the last one to leave the clump of trees and the ancestral burial ground which had been our refuge. By the time I left, the water was up to my knees. I was carrying a heavy pack and when I reached the village I went to the first hut built on stilts and climbed up the short ladder to the bamboo floor. I looked for a place to hang my hammock, but never finished the task because I apparently passed out.

I do not remember much of what took place afterwards, except that periodically I would see a face close to mine which reminded me of the devil. There was a strange odor accompanying the vision, an odor I could not identify, but which proved to me that I was in hell. Some time later I apparently received a reprieve because I found myself holding a hot bowl of soup. My men were around me laughing and glad to see that I was back to normal.

What they told me was very difficult to believe but I am sure that they were serious.

They told me that as I was about to hang my hammock on one of the rafters, I fainted. My men finished the job and tucked me in, not knowing what to do. I then became delirious. I cried and wanted to kill myself, or someone else, and became impossible to control. So they tied me into my hammock like a sausage and left me to rave. The owner of the hut was not very happy. He did not want me to die in his house because by custom he would have to bury me and that was an expense he was not happy to bear. So he placed incense sticks around my hammock and periodically would peer over my face, wipe my forehead with a cloth and repeat incantations.

Four or five days later Lt. McCarthy, a French officer, came to see me. Based on my men's description of my behavior, he immediately knew what was wrong with me. He left a handful of quinine tablets with my men and instructions. A few days later I awoke to discover that I had missed a few days due to a malaria attack, despite the fact that I had been on Atabrin (an anti-malaria drug) for almost one year. The "devil" that I saw in my delirium was our host, and the odor was that of the incense. Once more, the prediction of the old Chinese priest appeared to have come true.

Meanwhile, our training of the French troops continued, while members of our team were becoming more and more unhappy and restless. Arguments often broke among them, and it took both Capt. Holland and I to maintain peace and keep things under control.

On July 1st, after four months in China, I had hoped that I would be promoted. But no such luck. I felt much better as long as I took quinine and had a little chum (rice wine).

Eventually a message from Major Thomas directed all of us to proceed with the French troops to Poseh for parachute training. The French were delighted but Capt. Holland did not like the idea. It seemed that every day we received messages which contradicted each other. Finally, no one was going to Poseh; instead, everyone was to go to Tsing-Hsi. At 6:30 p.m. on July 4th we reached Tsing-Hsi where Major Thomas presented us with his plan.

A group including Lt. Langlois and one American officer was to proceed to FIC overland. He did not indicate who was the lucky American officer, but I had a pretty good idea who he would be! The following day Thomas identified the location of the rendezvous point where we were to meet the main body of troops who would parachute behind the Japanese lines.

The overland party composed of 26 individuals including Lt. Langlois and I was to be known as the "Group Tersac"!

On July 7th Major Thomas and I went to see Mr. Hu-De-Ban, the local Tou-Pan, to obtain the necessary travel permits allowing the French to march from Tsing-Hsi to the Poseh Air Base. Then Major Thomas left us, giving me the command responsibility over the Tsing-Hsi operation as he flew by L-5 to Poseh.

The following day I met Major Revole, the ranking French officer. He was ill and very upset with Major Thomas who, while planning the use of French troops, had ignored him and failed to share his plans with him, most specifically the question of a guide.

After some serious discussion, Revole and I reached an understanding and his promise of full cooperation.

At Tsing-Hsi, besides the French Consul, Mr. Thiercy, whose consulate office was a few miles from the frontier, the French had several representatives who included a military presence referred to as MMF. Lt. Langlois and Lt. Depin were part of this mission. Together we met at the office of French Consulate to prepare a detailed plan for our next move. A few hours later we had a completed a plan of action that should have been prepared months earlier.

To make certain that we were on the right track, the three of us presented our plan to Major Revole who agreed that it was an excellent plan. But he cautioned us not to implement it as yet. I had the impression that Revole, an old colonial officer, knew a lot more about the situation than he was telling us. He felt that the Vietminh question was a factor to be seriously considered. Up to that time no one on the American side had acknowledged the existence of this factor.

On July 10th the Chinese Command identified a Japanese regiment from the 22nd Division moving toward the FIC/China border and immediately asked the US Army command for air support which was promptly refused. Mr. Hu-De-Ban advised us that this Japanese action was probably a movement prior to their withdrawal to Hanoï. Major Revole confirmed this information and added that the Japanese were also moving out of Cao-Bang and Lang-Son. Among the Tsing-Hsi population it was rumored that the Chinese were about to attack, a sure sign that the Japanese were withdrawing! It was said among the China experts that the Chinese only occupied a town after it was completely evacuated by the Japanese!

After the Japanese had taken Long-Chow, Chinese troops moved into Tsing-Hsi and again they asked the U.S. command for air support which was again refused. On the evening of July 12th, Captain Ebaugh invited me to a dinner attended by General Linn and Simon Yu, who sat next to me. All evening Yu tried to find out what I was doing and to determine my relationship with the French. Linn wanted to know why some of our troops had moved to

Poseh while others did not, but he learned nothing from me simply because I did not know.

Major Revole's illness did not subside. A serious case of dysentery kept him in his quarters. When I met him he was usually in his bed. With the help of his aide-de-camp, every few minutes he would shuffle to a portable toilet close to his bed and eliminate what sounded like liquid. He had lost so much weight that he more closely resembled a cadaver than a live major. On July 13th one of our planes evacuated him to a Nanning Hospital.

The military situation in that area was very confusing. We received information from both the Chinese and from the French who had diplomatic and commercial representation along the Indochinese border. I maintained contact with the French Consul, who probably was an intelligence officer. He invited me to stay in his house as we got ready to proceed to Indochina with the Group Tersac.

The stark room the Consul assigned to me held a bed with a mosquito net, a table and a chair. The roof was the ceiling, and the windows had no panes, only shutters. I shall never forget my first night. We typically held discussions far into the night, so it was always past midnight before we retired.

With the Consul was Alex, an Eurasian who seemed to be maintaining a close liaison with the Chinese. His main duties were to intercept and interrogate Indochinese refugees crossing the border and provide them with documentation so that they could either continue on their way to other parts of China or remain in the area. The three of us had long discussions about the political and military situation in the Tonkin Area. The Consul and his associate were much concerned with the activities of Indochinese communist groups who had been organized by native Annamese and who apparently collaborated with the Japanese for the sole purpose of ridding the region of the French. One name kept coming up: Nguyên-Ai-Quoc, who was also known as Ho Chi Minh. They believed that this known communist trouble-maker was somewhere in China but out of their reach. The French had not given up trying to capture him, but they had thus far failed.

One of the Consul's jobs was to identify any possible members of the outlawed Viet-Nam-Doc-Lap-Dong-Minh, also referred to as the Vietminh League, and to turn them in to the Chinese Nationalists. It appeared to me that the French were more concerned about the activities of the Indochinese people, both in and out of Indochina, than the activities of the Japanese. By then, they had learned to live with the Japanese and knew what to expect, but they were well aware of the anti-French sentiments of certain elements of the FIC population.

I recorded what I had learned from my contact with the French and gave it to our L-5 courier pilot for our Poseh Headquarters, hoping that Major Thomas would see it prior to his departure.

On the 14th of July, an important French holiday, Lt. Tersac invited all the American officers and the same Chinese crowd including General Linn and General Chow to a banquet at the Dragon Lady's Place, a local restaurant. As usual there was a lot of drinking and some of the guests left the restaurant feet first.

The following day, July 15th, Captain Babineau flew in to see Captain Ebaugh. I briefed both so that either could explain the situation to Davis and Thomas and asked that either one confirm their acceptance of our plan with a note.

Lt. Tersac again invited only the French and American officers for supper. While eating, we were interrupted by Chinese Col. Tinh who requested the presence of both Capt. Ebaugh and Capt. Guinn at a conference given by the Chinese generals. They claimed that the situation had become very serious: one thousand Japanese had taken Luong-Ban, 3 km inside Chinese territory. They were fighting only 18 km away and moving in the direction of Tsing-Hsi.

The majority non-Chinese opinion was that it was a diversionary move on the part of the Japanese, however no one was about to take a chance. A general alert was declared.

The following day Lt. Tersac located a local guide who knew the territory where we were to go. Not entirely satisfied with the man's ability, he left for Lung-Ban to look for a guide better qualified and at the same time pick up information related to the situation which might influence our operation. He was to maintain communication with me by radio through the French Military Mission.

While he was away, three members of the Group Tersac showed up at Tsing-Hsi. They were Picaude, his wife, and Gleron. They expected to parachute into FIC with Capt. Baudenon! This was news to us. Obviously someone was making decisions on their own without advising those in charge!

Capt. Guinn left his post long enough to provide me with the local Japanese order of battle according to the Chinese! The situation appeared very complex and the Chinese loudly maintained that they would not be able to stop a Japanese advance on Tsing-Hsi with only 200 men who were running out of ammunition! They asked Capt. Ebaugh to help with the defense of the town!

The 17th of July was a bad day. It was the day Thomas was to jump! Lt. Langlois, my most trusted friend, had a very bad attack of malaria. He would be out of action for some time. On that same day, surprise of surprises, a Lt. Bougier arrived from Kunming. He told me that he was working with OSS and would be in charge of northern FIC for intelligence and administration. Who was he? French or American? Why wasn't I told that he was coming?

He seemed to be very familiar with what was going on in this part of the world, but knew little of our actual activities. Thus I briefed him on our plan after which he declared: "This is a damn good plan, I will be very happy to work with you. Together I am sure that we can do a good job." Based on his enthusiasm and supposed experience, I agreed with him.

Picaude had been snooping in the countryside and reported that he saw Chinese transporting thousands of American overalls toward the front. These coolies were not Chinese military coolies, they were business coolies! What did it mean? Apparently the situation was normal!

More bad news that day. Captain Guinn's L-5 crashed at the new Fo-Tong air strip and I learned indirectly that Major Thomas had jumped the previous day and had been received by the Vietminh without incident. Lt. Tersac left in the morning. I was to join him in four days at the designated rendezvous point.

The military situation in the area was not improving. Most of the information we received came from the Chinese who made a concentrated effort to keep us isolated and in the dark. They insisted on controlling our movements and it was impossible for us to go anywhere without obtaining a travel permit from the local Tou-Pan (regional administrator). Very quickly it became apparent that the Chinese officials monitored and controlled our movements and invariably knew our plans long before our arrival to destination. This prevented us from getting an accurate picture of the situation. I discovered that one way of preventing the Chinese from knowing our intended destination was to give them several options. This way they would not know exactly where we were going and would make their spying more difficult.

I remember an old Chinese Tou-Pan, the one who gave us the travel permit, asking me one day, "Lieutenant, how come when we ask the other Americans where they want to go they always know their destination, but you never know except when you are about to leave?" I supposed that the old boy had never read the fables of La Fontaine and perhaps the Chinese foxes were not as clever as French foxes. This method enabled us to obtain information which we otherwise would not have been able to acquire.

To rejoin Lt. Tersac in the vicinity of Soc-Giang I had to obtain a travel permit from Mr. Hu, the local Tou-Pan. He discouraged me from going, telling me that there was fighting in the area. I insisted, so that he gave me the pass, but it was good only on the following day!

I went to see Capt. Ebaugh to warn him about the possibility of hostilities between the Vietminh and the Chinese. I had trouble convincing him, but he finally agreed that the possibility existed.

Davis contacted me and strongly suggested that I hurry up and get going. After designating a new rendezvous point with Tersac far enough away from Soc-Giang, I awaited his instructions regarding the best way to cross the border.

The wives of the French NCOs made American regulation insignias of rank for all the members of the Group Tersac—we would be an American unit! Only three of us could really pass as American. The others might have passed as American Indians if they could manage to kept their mouths shut.

The French colonial troops that had escaped the Japanese were without support and hoped to be fed and equipped by the Americans. They had to purchase their food on the Chinese market from funds they received through their Kunming Embassy. On June 11, authorization to support the French with clothes and weapons arrived. A few days later the French departed for their jumping-off point at On-Ning, close to the Indochina border. They had decided that this would be an excellent location for training, and for planning their return to the Tonkin area.

I maintained contact with them and was able to learn and appreciate their feelings and concerns. I also learned their plans and dutifully reported these to our headquarters. They planned to return to their colony, not so much to fight the Japanese as to reestablish their control over that part of the world which they considered theirs. I believed that this was important and reported it, however someone in the upper echelon thought otherwise. One day Major Davis, who had earlier chewed me out royally when we unloaded our truck full of explosives, called me and ordered me to go to the French unit to tell their commanding officer they must return everything that the U.S. Army had just given them. He did not tell me the reason why this was done, but apparently the French already knew it.

When I arrived at the French compound, I instructed the French commanding officer to collect all the equipment we had given his troops and return it to the U.S. Army. When a circle of armed French officers slowly closed around me and pushed me against a wall, I knew that I was in a very precarious situation. I tried to tell them that I had nothing to do with the decision, but they were upset by the fact that I had ratted on them earlier. They really believed that only I could have told the U.S. Command that their primary aim was the securing of their colony. They might not even have had to guess—Major Davis probably let it be known that I was the one who reported their intention! The fact that I was an American officer was immaterial. To them I was a Frenchman and I was a traitor. One of the junior officers suggested that I be shot on the spot. However Lt. McCarthy, the senior officer who had given me the quinine, interceded and told them that this was not the way to handle the problem. He advised me to get out of their compound and not to return, and he promised that some day they would get me. I could not understand the logic of sending me to bring this bad news to the French, knowing full well that they would suspect me of betraying their confidence.

I had learned a lot more from listening to their conversations than their actual revelations to me. It did not take them long to figure that I was the only one close enough to them to have learned of their true intentions as I was the only one with whom they could converse without the aid of an interpreter.

On July 19th I received a message from Davis ordering me to hold everything because Thomas had recommended withdrawing all French and Indochinese troops from U.S.-planned operations. This was not very clear, so I decided to wait for further instructions. I felt that if not allowed to walk to FIC, I would have to jump in order to join Thomas. To complicate matters even more, a garbled message from Simon Yu through the Chinese communication system advised me that Major Thomas was "ordering me and my Group to return immediately to Poseh!" I was not able to decipher the rest of the message.

At 9:00 a.m. the Tou-Pan came to warn me about the Vietminh and the French, but he was quite surprised when I told him that I knew all about it. I asked him to help me decipher the message. He offered to put me in contact with the Vietminh, and there was a great possibility that they would help! I wanted to go to FIC overland, not because I did not want to jump, but because I felt that someone should reconnoiter a possible withdrawal route in the event withdrawal became necessary. After all, unlike the others who had never jumped, I had seventeen jumps including a combat jump.

We were all very discouraged and the lack of information from above made it worse. There was very little hope for us to know the Vietminh, and as far as the French were concerned their involvement in this operation now appeared to out of question. I felt that we were making a mistake as big as that of the French. I decided that my opinion did not matter and that I should keep it to myself. I felt that no one would be able to deal with the Vietminh successfully. They would not keep their promises because their main goal was not to chase the Japanese out of FIC, but to acquire as many weapons they could and attempt to control the Tonkin. They knew that sooner or later the Japanese would leave Indochina, so why should their risk their lives for a forgone conclusion? From the French I learned that most of the known communists in FIC had attended political schools in Moscow.

On the 21st of July, I was still waiting for a word from one of our headquarters hoping that Major Thomas would have reconsidered his position. Apparently the situation around Tsing-Hsi was serious, so serious in fact that the Chinese were taking a collection for a big party for any American who brought in large quantities of supplies so they could hold the Japanese for a couple of weeks. According to the Chinese, while I was trying to establish a contact with the Vietminh, the Japanese had moved slowly along the border toward Tsing-Hsi. With only 200 men available, the Chinese claimed that they could not possibly stop a Japanese thrust toward that city.

Captain Guinn got all excited, as did the CCC. The Chinese immediately received their ammunition. Waves of transport planes came and unloaded tons of ammunition and weapons in a field prepared for that purpose. They did not always use parachutes, but dropped their cargo as they flew very low over the field. As a result, some of it was badly damaged.

The rumor was that the Chinese wanted the ammunition for their future struggle against the communists. The Chinese had depicted the situation much worse than it actually was, and we had no way to check the veracity of their information because they controlled all our movements. Once Mr. Wou told me: "The Japanese will never attack Tsing-Hsi; any one with a little sense will see that."

Some time later, while on one of our journeys, we came across a line of coolies under the command of the Chinese Army, traveling in the opposite direction away from the so-called front. The supplies they were transporting were the same as those that had been dropped a few days earlier. Where were they taking them? It was and is my feeling that the Chinese army was stockpiling this material for later use in the inevitable post-War clash with the Chinese Communists. Official U.S. policy would never have permitted this, given our status at the time as faithful allies of the Russians.

According to Mr. Wou, it appeared that no one in Tsing-Hsi was able to put me in contact with the Vietminh. The Chinese had problems with the Vietminh claiming that they were helping the Japanese, while the Vietminh said that the Chinese stole and raped in their villages and Chinese agents are poised along the border to enter FIC.

Thanks to the quinine, I survived my third attack of malaria, but could not leave without travel orders from Mr. Wou. Lt. Tersac was also ordered by his own command to proceed to Poseh. We had a few things to settle in Tsing-Hsi so we decided to leave in a day or so. I felt that something was going to happen. I had better be close to the policy-makers.

Finally on the 24th, the Tou-Pan sent us our travel permits. I moved in with Langlois, because Thiercy was supposed to return that day. He arrived at 6:00 p.m. and invited us to a going away dinner at the consulate.

The next day, July 25th, accompanied by Lt. Victor, we left Tsing-Hsi. After stopping at Captain Ebaugh's HQ to pick up the official courier, we joined the Group Tersac on the trail a short distance away. Picaude was in charge of the unit and his wife was carried on a sedan chair by four coolies. We reached Doe-On where Chinese officers invited us to stay for a Gambay party, which was just an excuse for them the get drunk. We didn't accept!

At 6:00 a.m. the following day, we left in the direction of Tien-Pao. Langlois wanted to stop at 10:00 am to feed his men. Unfortunately rice was not available, so we went on Tien-Pao which we reached at 1:00 p.m. I checked in with Col. Marris at CCC HQ and learned that four planes had landed at the new Air Strip. Believing that these were CCC planes, I did not go to the field to see them. Subsequently I learned from one of the passengers, a Major I knew, that these planes had come from Kunming and that they had missed Poseh! I felt that something was going on but had no idea what it was.

On July 27, Lt. Tersac, Lt. Villesange, two coolies and I left Tien-Pao at 4:00 a.m. and at top speed headed out along a trail that would take us across the first mountain range.

We traveled light, only carrying our weapons. The rest of our equipment was carried by the coolies. Fortunately it was cool when we started, but by midday the temperature had reached 90 degrees.

We let the coolies take the lead as they knew the trails better than we did. Initially, the terrain was rather flat and the first few hours were easy going. We followed the course of the river that we knew all too well, having been flooded by it. By this time it had receded and we could walk along its bank.

It was not long before we realized why the river had flooded the valley so quickly. The river flowed through a cave and into a mountain! Under normal conditions, the water had no trouble flowing through this channel, approximately fifty feet wide. There was even enough space on either side for a trail upon which men, horses and even pack-mules could pass in order to reach the other side of the mountain and the next valley. However, when it stormed, the space under the mountain was not large enough to accommodate the volume of water. As a result, the water backed up rapidly, flooding the cave and the entire valley until the rain stopped when the river would return to its normal banks.

We probably gained several hours by going through the cave for approximately two miles. To light up the path, our coolies ignited wood torches. We followed, watching for bats and protruding rocks. Had it begun raining again, we would have had a major problem, but the local "weather reporter" had assured us that it was to remain clear for the next several hours. It felt great to reach the other side of the mountain and see the sky again. We were moving at a good pace behind our coolies, who as usual were trotting along with our baggage suspended from their yo-yo sticks. We stopped occasionally for a break, a cigarette or a swig of water from our canteens. By mid-afternoon we had slowed considerably and so had our coolies, who by that time were behind us, at times far behind us.

We decided to stop for a rest at Po-Nong where a caravansary offered food and lodging to travelers. This large compound had been in existence for centuries. It was located on the silk route and was used as a stopover by the caravans bringing silk and other products from China to Europe, and European civilization to China. There were stalls for horses, mules or camels, and places for men to rest or sleep. Food was prepared continuously for travelers who stopped night and day. We joined our coolies in a tasty Chinese meal, the first good meal we had since our breakfast.

We had walked twelve hours without stopping. Our coolies were tired and so were we, however we still had a long way to go. It was decided that after a couple of hours of rest we should take to the trail again and move on. When we explained our decision to the coolies, they balked. They stated that was as far as they would go that day, and that they would resume the trek only in the morning. This was not exactly what we had expected. First we offered them more money. They still refused. One of us had an idea. We always carried Benzedrine with us, a drug which was used to keep us awake and ease our anxiety. We offered some to our coolies who, like all Chinese, loved any kind of pills. We didn't tell them what it was, but by nine o'clock that evening, one of the coolies advised us that they were ready to go; they couldn't sleep anyway. Our trick had worked.

We took to the trail again under the stars. The going was extremely rough. Our coolies were ahead jumping from one rock to the other talking and laughing with each other as if they were on a joy ride. We, on the other hand, stumbled, huffed, puffed and lagged far behind. We decided that perhaps it would be to our advantage to take the same medicine, which we did.

It was amazing how effective these pills were. Very soon, we caught up with our coolies. The trails, which earlier seemed so difficult, became smoother. Our ability to see at night improved tremendously. Our agility increased miraculously. No more stumbling, no more hesitation; we were on cloud nine, just as happy as our coolies.

By the next morning we had traveled almost as much as the whole day before. Yet we still had a long way to go. The second range of mountains was not as bad as the one before. We knew that our destination lay in the next valley. This was enough to edge us on even after sundown. It was past ten o'clock in the evening when we began our last descent to Yien-Yang to cross the river. The moon was high in the sky, which made our travel easier. We had exhausted our water long ago and dehydration was beginning to take its toll. In the distance we could see the lights of CCC HQ ahead of us, and a shimmering body of water appeared. We rushed downhill to the cool, refreshing water and, ignoring our better judgment and responding only to our human craving, dunked our heads in it. Later, we had no recollection of what we had done. I felt a lot better afterwards.

The last few miles were uneventful. When we reached our headquarters, we discovered hat we were not expected. They did not believe that we could travel close to 62 miles in two days on a mountain trail. But we did it. I do not remember much except that as soon as we arrived, we hit our cots and slept until noon the following day. Upon awakening, I was curious and asked about the body of water in which we had satisfied our thirst. I was told that there wasn't any. There were only rice paddies! Later on I was to pay dearly for this error of judgment . . . .

The Vietminh Training Center

Finally I fell asleep as had the others.

The following day, we visited the nearby village to meet local dignitaries who seemed to enjoy our visit. There was much hand-shaking and singing, and the local food was great.

Later that evening Major Thomas and Prunier returned from their reconnaissance of the fort of Cho-Chu, which was occupied by the Japanese. From a distance, they had noticed only a few Japanese soldiers moving in and out. They could only guess the real size of the complement within the garrison.

When Hank had the opportunity to speak out of the Major's hearing, he told us what had occurred. He could hardly keep a straight face telling how the Major had gone completely beside himself when with his binoculars he observed a Japanese soldier leaving the confines of the fort. He jumped up and down laughing and saying: "I saw a Jap, I saw a Jap, I saw a Jap!"

Prunier thought that this was indeed a strange behavior on the part of a US Army Major, a leader of men!

On the morning of July 31st, after all the supplies had been separated, Captain Holland left us with Sgt. Stoyka, Sgt. Burrowes, native guides and porters. It was the last we saw the three until the war ended and they joined by us in Hanoï. A day went by before we realized that Holland had left his maps behind. By the time we noted the mishap he and his team had gone too far for us to reach them, and in any event we had no idea as to the road they had taken, although we knew where they were headed. On the 1st of August Lt. Montfort, Sgt. Logos, and Sgt. Phac, all unwelcome guests of the Vietminh, left to join French refugees in a nearby village. After capturing a Japanese concentration camp, a local Vietminh Group supposedly under the leadership of our host had freed these prisoners. Lt. Montfort was to arrange the evacuation of the women and children by air, while he would lead the rest to China on foot. Apparently all French people as well as French sympathizers were no longer welcome in this area!

When we arrived, Mr. Van had told us that he was not the head of this group of Indochinese. The leader was a Mr. Ho. His name rang a bell, but I did not immediately connect it with the individual the French were looking for all over Asia. In this part of the World, Ho is a common name. Thiercy, the French Consul, and Alex, his Eurasian sidekick, had told me about a Nguyên Sinh Cung also known as Nguyên-Ai-Quoc, also referred to as "Ho Chi Minh." They considered him ruthless, clever, and very dangerous. Previously associated with the French Communist Party, and indoctrinated by the Soviets in Hong Kong, he had created the PCI (Parti Communiste Indochinois) (Indochinese Communist Party). The Consul had never mentioned Mr. Van to me. Incidentally, much of the information I had obtained from the Consul had been transmitted to our Poseh Headquarters for Major Thomas and to SI-OSS at Kunming. Apparently, Mr. Ho was too sick to see us just yet. He was in a village nearby, and when he felt better we would meet him.

After our supplies had been stowed away, Mr. Van and I went to check the area he had selected for a training site and for our living quarters. Later, Aaron Squires (we called him Alan) and I walked to the village to photograph points of interest. There a woman was introduced to us as a Vietminh hero. During a battle she had won her place among the great of the great, but we never learned what was battle to which they were referring. Was it against the Japanese or the French?

Later on that day our team was invited to the dedication of the Political Reunion House, a large bamboo hut, and then to the clean cool hut of the village chief for an official dinner. Afterward we attended a local theatrical presentation. The first act was entitled: "How the Japanese deal with the population and the reaction of the Vietminh", and second act was called: "The rescue of an American pilot". I did not understand what was going on, but many red flags were waved about! I wondered how many pilots had been rescued by these people! Considering the time and location it was a very good production, completely unexpected in the middle of the jungle!

From that time on our two main daily meals did not vary much. They consisted of rice, chicken, duck or water buffalo meat with bamboo shoot soup supplied by our host. Our meals were supplemented with coffee and jam from our C-Ration or 10-1 combat rations.

Because my boots had taken the appearance of green velvet, I decided to ignore them for a while and go barefoot to toughen my soles. Except for Mr. Van, one or two of his men, and the members of our team, everyone else there was shoeless.

On the 3rd of August the temperature had declined slightly and it was raining so the humidity was close to 100%. We moved some of our material and equipment to the training area approximately 3 km north west of the village of Kim-Lung. I met the individual responsible for the construction of our living quarters and of the huts to be used as classrooms at the training site. I gave him instructions as to our needs.

The roof of the building was made of interlaced palm leaves and was almost completed. Natives brought stacks of leaves either on their yo-yo sticks or on their heads. The builders were slow. The workers discussed things constantly between long periods of idleness.

164

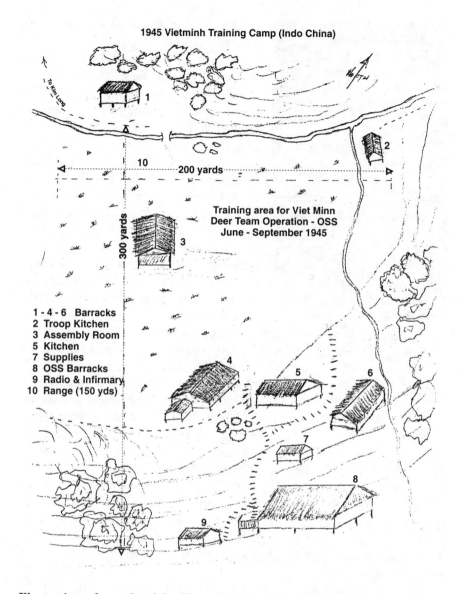

1945 Vietminh Training Camp (Indo China)

To Kim Long

200 yards

300 yards

Training area for Viet Minn
Deer Team Operation - OSS
June - September 1945

1 - 4 - 6 Barracks
2 Troop Kitchen
3 Assembly Room
5 Kitchen
7 Supplies
8 OSS Barracks
9 Radio & Infirmary
10 Range (150 yds)

Illustration, after a sketch by Henry Prunier, of the Vietminh training camp in the Jungle of Tonkin.

165

Ho Chi Minh (1945)

Having nothing to do the rest of the day, we took this opportunity to go the village and see Mr. Ho who was still very ill. Paul Hoagland, our medic, came along to see if he could help. We found Mr. Ho in the corner of a smoky hut. He was partially covered with what appeared to be rags. His eyes were closed, his yellow skin stretched over his skeletal body, and a few stray hairs hung from his chin. He certainly did not give me the impression I expected of a fierce leader of men. I did not recognize a ruthless and dangerous individual, only a weak old man about to join his ancestors. Out of respect for the patient, I left the hut so Paul could do his stuff and determine if anything could be done for the poor man.

After a while, Paul joined us outside the hut with his prognosis. As best as he could determine, the patient had a multitude of problems including malaria, dysentery and perhaps other tropical diseases. Left untreated, they would eventually do him in. We had plenty of medicine with us, and we could get some more if necessary by air drop. Paul gave him some medicine and from that time on looked after him periodically.

On August it was still raining softly. I accompanied Major Thomas to the training site to check the progress made on the construction of the buildings. He took along some of his equipment. I'd been there before, so I didn't carry anything because the trail leading to the training site was so bad that fording the several streams was difficult. By the time we reached our destination we were soaked to the skin.

On August 6th Hank and I went to the training area to speed up the construction of the buildings. When left alone the workers did not do much. Someone has to encourage them or prod them.

While on the slippery trail we met a few girls who seemed out of place. Unlike the local peasants who wore dark clothing and blackened their teeth with lacquer or betel juice for beauty or to kill the pain, these girls had white teeth and were wearing the traditional Indochinese long pants and flowing slit skirts. Who were these beauties so far from civilization?

166

When we arrived at the hut that was supposed to be our home, we found only four walls, a floor and a roof. This would not do! Partitions had to be erected and tables and chairs made for our convenience. Unlike the natives who squatted automatically when resting we had to find a place to rest our behinds. Up to now we slept on the floor in our sleeping bags with our parachutes as extra cover. We asked the builders for additional bamboo to make our quarters more livable.

Hank, a very ingenious fellow, designed and built the longest communal bunk I had ever seen. It consisted of two twenty-foot bamboo poles. Across them, hung from rungs, was a series of seven frames, each two and one-half feet wide and six and half feet long, separated by a one foot space to permit access. The rungs were tied solidly to the two long poles with nylon ropes. The nylon netting used to drop our cargo was stretched within each frame giving the appearance of a stiff hammock upon which we would recline. Then a few shelves were constructed using bamboo and lines from our parachutes.

To minimize the time wasted going back and forth Hank and I decided to stay in our unfinished quarters until the following morning and retired for the day listening in the dark to the singing of the few individuals already at the training site. We were in a political school where young men came from every part of FIC to be indoctrinated by the Vietminh. They were taught patriotic songs so that, when they returned to their village, they would teach these songs to others and spread the Vietminh doctrine. These young men were happy to be together without restraint, to talk among themselves, and to learn from each other. Under French rules even to assemble for a funeral required a special permit!

By 8:00 a.m. on the 7th of August we were ready to go, but our workers were not. I kept pushing them, but with no apparent success. They made tables while Hank and I made a bench and covered one of the table with heavy cloth taken from the containers. One of the walls held our maps and additional shelves were constructed.

The training camp consisted of several huts. Unlike ours, they were directly on the ground adjacent to an open field. At one end of the field a tall bare tree held a Vietminh flag, a red banner with large gold star in its center. This was to be the assembly point for morning reveille and for special formations.

According to Mr. Van the Vietminh represented a variety of ethnic groups. Their main objective was the elimination of the Japanese control of the area. This may have been their immediate and pressing goal, but there was no doubt in my mind that Van's true aim and that of Mr. Ho was to establish a new political order in the region, along the lines of Communism. We were there to instruct this select group in the use of the weapons we were providing and to train them in the fine art of guerrilla warfare! For that purpose, Major Thomas had brought along a barracks bag full of U.S. Army field manuals. These covered every conceivable type of weapons and military circumstances except for one—guerrilla warfare—because, up to then, none had been written. At that time, the U.S. Army did not recognize guerrilla warfare as viable a military tactic. In fact, only Bill Zielski and I had seen action with guerrillas.

In the afternoon of the following day the Major, accompanied by Larry and Paul, joined us. They admired our handiwork. Larry and Paul immediately pitched in to put up our mosquito bars over the communal bed so that each section was covered with netting to keep the nasty bugs away from us. While this was not the most comfortable sleeping accommodation, it was an improvement, much better than sleeping on the floor.

After a good lunch we were ready for a conference with Quang-Trung, the leader of the 110 recruits assembled at the camp. With Mr. Bach, our interpreter, we discussed the training program and the selection of the best recruits. Unlike the other students who were typical Mongoloids, Mr. Bach with his light hair and skin had very distinctive Caucasian features. French or European blood must have flowed in his veins.

It was decided that a 6-hour work day would be adequate, but if need be, we could increase it to 8 hours as a few of these persons had not had any military training! They were very eager to start and already they requested their individual weapons. It was decided that the weapons were to be issued only after the selected students had completed their training. We retired for the day ready to begin training in earnest the following morning.

The day began on the parade ground with a report from platoon leaders, the singing of the Vietminh song and the closed-fist salute to the flag. I was

Deer Team with a formation of Vietminh guerrilla and Kim Lung. Lt. René Défourneaux, Sgt. Aaron Squires, 1st Sgt. William Zielski, Pfc. Henry Prunier, Pfc. Paul Hoagland, and S/Sgt. Larry Vogt (Photo taken by Major Allison K. Thomas)

168

Triangulation practice. Lt. Défourneaux sitting on target third from left.

quite familiar with this salute, having seen it where I grew up in France: it was that of the Communist Party. The gesture was particularly in evidence when the Internationale was sung at their reunions. When members of our team attended these formations none but one of us saluted the red flag.

After we selected forty of the most promising recruits we asked Quang-Trung to show us the drilling method he would use to train his troops. He gave the commands, but it turned out to be a miserable performance. Selecting one recruit who appeared to know what he was doing, the Major asked him to demonstrate, instead Quang-Trung gave us, and his troop, a snappy demonstration of the American manual of arms! Quang-Trung could even speak some English, a rare skill in this area. One of our brightest students, he had full responsibility over the others, probably placed in this position of authority by Mr. Van himself, or Mr. Ho. Evidently he had some military experience, either with the French army or, as the Major suggested, in some capacity in contact with a U.S. unit in China. He wore leather gaiters, a Sam Brown belt and side arm. The Major requested a demonstration of "Port Arm" and "Inspection Arm," and Quang-Trung gladly complied. Compared with my past activities with the French resistance, this operation was quite unusual, not so much because the enemy was not the same, but because the concept was completely different. We were training recruits for conventional warfare while contemplating guerrilla operations. The most important factor for a successful guerrilla operation is the knowledge of the terrain. This was certainly not within our range of expertise. The people we were training could operate throughout Indochina without fear of being identified as other than natives. In no way could we, Occidentals, convince local people to take arms and resist an invading power. The other important factor for a successful guerrilla operation is the attitude or conviction of the individual guerrilla. These recruits had two good reasons to strengthen their convictions: the elimination of the Japanese occupation, and the liberation of Indochina from the French. They did not need us to increase their fervor, and indeed they knew that we had initially been working with the French. All they needed from us were weapons, and training to use of these weapons. After the morning formation, we took over the instruction which consisted mostly of material from U.S. Army field manuals including the field stripping, maintenance and firing of the weapons. We were all amazed by their ability to learn, and at times we wondered if this was just a refresher course for some of them! Our period of instruction lasted approximately 50 minutes followed by a ten minute break. During these breaks, while the Americans smoked or otherwise relaxed, our students gathered in front of one of their own who appeared to be a very proficient speaker. This was the political break during which they were told that they should pay close attention to our instruction, but never forget who was the enemy. They should not be influenced by our political views or lack thereof. I suppose they did not care that only one of us understood their language.

I had not shaved since we left Poseh and I was sporting good-sized whiskers. I decided to let my beard grow, along with a bushy mustache I soon looked more like a pirate than an officer of the U.S. Army.

Next to our hut was a smaller structure where Bill, our radio operator, stored his equipment, including the generator. He did not participate in the training as he had enough to do with his own chores. Keeping his equipment operating under jungle conditions was not the easiest thing in the world. The only electric power we had came from a hand-operated generator intended solely for the operation of the radio. We took turns turning the crank. It was not too bad when receiving, however when sending messages, the demand on the generator required much effort. This necessary duty was not a pleasant one. We had to keep in touch with the world and we were in constant communication with our headquarters in Kunming, and Poseh. Outgoing messages were painstakingly encoded, and those incoming decoded. The humidity played hell with our equipment, especially the radio. Fortunately, we had a clever radio operator who could repair and maintain his equipment under the most difficult conditions. Bill's radio shack was eventually completed and Larry had started the construction of a firing range, but heavy rain forced him to stop. We settled into a daily routine. For breakfast we had our own GI instant coffee and biscuits. Then we were well cared for with two meals a day, same as the students. The meals consisted of local products such

170

as chicken, rice, and bamboo shoots served at 10 o'clock in the morning and at 4 in the afternoon. After a good dinner we usually played cards and drank coffee.

The only convenience missing was a hot shower! Unlike our camp in Assam, we did not have the luxury of 55-gallon drums, nor rubber hoses to construct a makeshift hot shower. However the local people had brought water to our camp from a distant mountain source by a very ingenious method. Sections of the bamboo so abundant in that region were split in halves, and transformed into gutters.

From a higher elevation the first piece of bamboo was placed into the water spring. The collected water was then dropped to the next section of bamboo, then to the next until it reached a distance of several kilometers. The sections were supported by bamboo trestles all along in such a way that a gradual slope allowed the water to flow smoothly to our camp. There the end of the conduit was approximately six feet high, and the water fell to the ground. It was our shower, though at times a very cold one!

It was difficult for me to embrace the concept of giving military basic training to a bunch of natives who, thanks to their individual wits, had escaped the attentions of their Japanese colonial masters and managed to survive. If our purpose was to make foot soldiers out of these ragamuffins why not bring drill sergeants to do the job instead of guerrilla warfare experts. When training French resistance fighters, I did not care if they knew the difference between "port arm" and "inspection arm," or if they could shoot a target at 100 yards. My main purpose was to teach them the art of unconventional warfare. If these men were to be organized in regular platoons, companies, and battalion size units, although we were able to do it, we had no business being involved in the building of an armed force for the purpose of fighting "the Japanese."

The Major was determined to manage his team as a regular Army unit. Periodically he would call for a staff meeting in our headquarters, a one room hut used as sleeping quarters, dining and recreation room. In front of the enlisted members of our team he would give me orders starting in this fashion: "Lieutenant, I want you to tell the men that . . ."

I presumed his request was directed at me because he thought that I was his only staff! At first I thought he was joking. No, he was deadly serious. The first time he did this I asked the men if they heard the instructions. A movement of their heads assured me that they had, which was good enough for me. When the Major persisted in calling staff meetings, I decided that I might as well go along and instead of asking the men collectively if they heard the instructions, I called on the ranking NCO and gave him a same information; I then advised him to instruct the next ranking NCO of the orders. Each member carried out his instructions until the last one our lone Pfc's, who said: "Who in hell you want me to tell this crap to?"

This was our last staff meeting for a while!

On the 9th of August, with the exception of Larry who had trouble waking, we were up at 5:00 a.m. and by 7:00 were at the training site for morning formation, the flag raising and the singing! Our first class was the demonstration of the intricacy of the US Army M-1 carbine. While Larry took one carbine apart I described its composition in French while Mr. Bach translated into the local language.

The twenty minute lecture made a hit with the Major. We then divided the students into three groups. I took one, Larry took another, and Hank handled the third. My group took the carbine apart and put it back together very quickly which surprised me because I had seen American soldiers struggling with more instruction by a lot better instructors. In the afternoon they were shown the care and cleaning of the carbine, and afterwards we brought some rusted Thompson submachine-guns for them to clean. They also took these apart and Quang-Trung, familiar with the weapon, demonstrated how to reassemble it, explaining each step carefully. He was a very good officer who knew how to handle his men, and these men had been well selected by him! The rest of the afternoon was spent in triangulation, a method used to teach aiming with a stationary weapon.

By then we were fully settled in our quarters and Hank had supervised an excellent supper to inaugurate our new home. It included some of our gourmet C-ration, chicken, chocolate, fruit cake, and rum from our hosts. After supper we met the leaders to plan the program for the following day.

Before retiring we played cards; gin rummy was our favorite. We played constantly. At night we used the solid alcohol blocks that were supposed to warm our food. If we became bored with the card game, we could always watch the huge ants trotting along the wall of our hut. They were the biggest ants I had ever seen, some at least one inch long. For fun, we would create an obstacle in their path so that they would have to construct a bridge to go from one twig to the next. This was fascinating. Occasionally, we would spot a praying mantis. These were also gigantic compared to the familiar ones at home. They where at least one foot tall.

On the following day after the morning formation I gave the students a 20-minute American-style calisthenics that amused them immensely. Then I instructed the recruits on the importance of the trigger squeeze and on the aiming position. Quang-Trung handled the technical side of the instruction in his own dynamic way, making our job a lot easier. In the afternoon we continued with triangulation after a short address by the Major who promised a pack of cigarettes to the student who created the smallest triangle. All the students did well, some making triangles as small as the eraser end of a pencil.

We were interrupted by the arrival of a plane with additional supplies. The Major rushed to the drop zone while we continued our instruction. At the end of triangulation we discovered that a young boy—barely fifteen-years-old—was the winner, but he refused the cigarettes.

The Major returned with the mail. I had three letters, one from my sister, one from a friend, and another from Simone! I guess Simone had not yet heard the news! This was good for the morale of the entire team who by then appeared to get along fine. If the Major had some good ideas, we had our own and did not share them with him! Our quarters were adequate and the food was good. As long as we collected our pay and per diem on our return, all would be fine.

I do not recall the exact date, but one day Ho appeared in our camp. He was shaky and weak, but alive. He assured us that he was okay and that from now on he would handle his own medication. He sent some of his boys after a certain jungle deer which was known to have very potent antlers. He collected some jungle herbs and with it made a potion from a recipe he knew or obtained from a local herb dispenser. Nevertheless, this seemed to be effective and he regained his strength and visited us more and more each day.

Before leaving Poseh we decided that the name Raymond Douglass would be a good one for me to go by. I had built a cover story to fit my new name in case someone questioned me. No one had trouble remembering my name as "Ray," although they usually called me by my rank.

It turned out that the only one who ever asked me about my background was Ho. Judging from his questioning, it was obvious that he suspected me of being a Frenchman because I spoke French as fluently as a native language while the others did not do as well. Although he spoke English quite well, he preferred to converse with me in French and proceeded to ask me some very personal questions about my mother, my father, where I was born, where I went to school, etc. Then a few days later he would ask me the same questions again, probably to see if I would give the same answers. Evidently, Ho's intelligence net had failed to link me with any of the French refugee groups or French officials in China. After a while he relaxed his efforts and our conversation turned to himself and what he was attempting to do.

He was a good conversationalist with a wide range of knowledge. He spoke often of Indochina, not just Tonkin where we were, but the entire Indochinese peninsula that included the Tonkin, Annam, Cochinchina, Laos, and Cambodia. He was particularly impressed by our relationship with the Philippines and by the United Nations declaration of self-determination. He kept saying that the Indochinese people must be self-determined. The French had abandoned them, he said, and once the Japanese were dealt with, the people of Indochina should be allowed to choose their own future. He even intimated that he would accept a transition period during which the French would train and eventually turn over the responsibility of government to elected Indochinese.

Unlike Mr. Ho who was quite talkative, Mr. Van was non-communicative with me. His role within the group was not very clear, but was clearly important. When Mr. Ho was not available Mr. Van was in control. From the comments made by some of our students, I believed that he was or had been a teacher. For this reason he was highly respected by the members of the group, more because of his past profession rather than his current position. Except for three or four of our students, the rest kept a respectful distance from us, probably because they had been told to do so by Ho, Van or the political commissars. Those who had the most contact with us were better educated and somewhat fluent in French. Of course among them was Quang-Trung.

While Ho visited us often, Van would disappear for days, then reappear, however very seldom in the company of Ho. Only when we had an official function or a social engagement would they both be present. One such occasion was the presentation of an Indochinese production by a local theater group, which resembled those we had seen in China. The screeching was just as bad; the drum and bells and the local flute just as loud. Only the language was slightly different, but to my ears sounded the same. We did not understand the plot, but it must have been political as the Vietnamese flag was always prominently displayed and their national song sung. These were about the only times that I saw Ho and Van together, and then not always next to each other.

Once I observed something rather strange. During one of these presentations, an individual, probably a runner, casually approached Van. Surreptitiously the man passed something to Van but I did not see what it was until much later when Van opened his hand, unfolded a small piece of paper, looked at it intently. He then crumbled it, stuffed it in his mouth and chewed it. I concluded that Van had something going on his own and that he did not share it with Ho, at least not at that time.

In any case, we discovered that they had translated the U.S. Constitution and Bill of Rights, provided earlier by Phelan, from English into French and that one of theirs who was a native priest had translated it into the local language, Indochinese. Apparently some of the native priests were in contact with Ho and were collaborating with him. Eventually this led to the Vatican's decision to sever their relation with the Catholic hierarchy of North Vietnam.

My early dealings with the communists in my former country and my experience with a communist Maquis in France, caused me to wonder as to our function in the jungle of Tonkin. Were we active participants in a local revolution or innocent bystanders? Ho Chi Minh had made it clear to me that his goal was the unification of FIC. It meant that those independent countries such as Laos and Cambodia with their kings would be part of a new state under the leadership of the Vietminh. Unlike Tonkin, Annam and Cochinchina, Laos and Cambodia were not colonies, they were protectorates, independent nations under the tutelage of the French Government. I wondered how Ho Chi Minh would convince the rulers of Laos and Cambodia to abdicate! I doubted that our own leadership, military or political, knew anything about this area's complicated situation.

On August 11th, Hank, Alan and I started the actual target practice on the range. It was a sunny day and although the targets were adequate, the shooting was poor. We had a few bulls-eyes, but the majority of the students who had never fired a gun failed to qualify! Actually firing a gun was new to them.

Despite the great help of their leader and our interpreter Mr. Bach, it took two hours for 30 students to fire 5 shots each.

The End of the War

During the afternoon break, an excited Dan Phelan came to the training site. "The war may be over soon," he announced. "The U.S. dropped a super bomb on Japan. The Japanese have been asked to surrender."

We were stunned. We hoped it was more than a rumor. Why hadn't we been informed of this by our own headquarters? Dan and his radio operator remained with us, while we continued our firing instruction. The rain started again so we canceled the firing and asked the students to clean the weapons we had received the day before. In addition to weapons and ammunition, the Major's typewriter, such a useful item in the jungle of Indochina, had also arrived!

Later on the Major confirmed the news that the war might soon be coming to an end, and added that Mr. Ho or his assistant Mr. Van would be going to Kunming to meet a French delegation. Mr. Ho wanted to communicate his views, not only to the French officials, but to the Americans, whom he regarded as the leaders of the world. On several occasions he asked us to send messages to our headquarters for transmission to Washington, from whom he repeatedly requested recognition, or to the French. However the responses he was getting were not exactly what he had hoped for. The French obviously wanted nothing to do with him, and Washington, unwilling to upset their French and Chinese allies, did nothing.

Ho was smooth and able to convince us of his good intentions, such as insisting that his party, the Vietminh, was the most popular movement in Indochina. But he could be intimidating when things did not go his way. He had stated to me that he had "friends" who would help him, and he intimated to me that the Soviet Union might well be of one them.

Although it was Sunday, on the 12th of August I was up at 6:00 a.m. After conducting the usual PT session—including a few push-ups—I joined the team for a cup of coffee. Taking advantage of a clear day, we returned to the firing range to qualify the few students who had not yet made it. As usual it was a very slow process, lasting all morning. While I was busy with my whistle on the firing line, the Major was teaching others the correct way to throw hand grenades. Then he briefed a reconnaissance squad before sending it to seek information about the nearby Japanese.

Later that day high Vietminh Party members from Hanoï visited our training site. They were amazed by our progress, but so shocked by our slovenly appearance that they offered us razors! We declined their offer, explaining that our beards were of our own choosing, and not due to a lack of razors. It was our first chance to do what we damn pleased, and we wanted to take full advantage of this opportunity.

Fast firing went no better—only a few did well. We closed the range at 5:00 p.m. and returned to our hut for a shower and a late supper. By 7:00 p.m. the rain preceded a mean storm. Lightning hit the ground all around us, accompanied by deafening cracks of thunder. Everyone was in the sack except the Major and I, he typing, and I scribbling on my diary. We had heard nothing more about the war.

In the morning the rain had subsided. Normally I was up before anyone else, but that day Hank had to awaken me. I gave a 20 minute PT to the troops, and as the rain started again we decided to keep our instruction indoor. Quang-Trung gave a lecture on the Thompson and afterward the three groups went to their respective quarters to study and practice. In the afternoon it was still raining and I gave instructions on the Bren after which each group under the supervision of their respective leader took the gun apart and studied its functioning. At 4:00 p.m. the Major gave his lecture on the light machine-gun.

Under the circumstances, we were all doing pretty well, except Larry who was upset. He did not like what he was doing. He wanted action. He had volunteered to kill Japs, not to be a drill sergeant. This seemed a normal reaction after hearing the news that Japan might possibly surrender.

Mr. Ho sent us a bottle of rum, supposedly to cheer us. The training of the group continued. Some of our students went on patrol on their own, looking for Japanese. We were told that in one of these patrols, they encountered a small Japanese unit which was probably looking for food rather than a fight. The story they recounted was hard to believe. The patrol had come face to face with a Japanese convoy composed of a few trucks. The patrol waited patiently until the Japanese column was close enough to attack. One young man, about the size of a 12-year-old American boy, was carrying the bazooka. He stood up, aimed his weapon at the lead vehicle and fired. Unfortunately he had not locked the two sections of the bazooka together properly.

As a result, the rocket got stuck in the tube, and the launcher went forward with the shell, ripping his shirt. The propellant of the rocket was normally enough to send the shell at least one hundred yards, but the weight of the tube caused it to go less than half that distance. Apparently unconcerned, our young guerrilla stood up, ran to his weapon, retrieved it, removed the shell from the tube and, realizing the problem, reloaded it with a new shell and again fired. The round fell short approximately ten feet in front of the vehicle and ricocheted smack into the radiator, causing it to explode with a terrific bang. The Japanese were so surprised that they did not immediately react. The patrol was able to escape and return to our base with the details of their escapade.

Mr.Ho's health had improved noticeably, however we did not know if this was due to the medicine Hoagy provided or the potions he himself was making. One day, we were shocked by the arrival of a half dozen girls dressed in colorful native dresses. We knew that these were not farm girls and suspected that they probably came from the finest houses of Hanoï. We later learned that indeed they had come from Hanoï and that they were courtesans brought in for the pleasure of Mr. Ho and his inner circle, not to assist directly in the upcoming battle against the Japanese.

The construction of a storage building was almost completed and supplies were already inside. As the rain did not subside, we decided to remain in our hut and after many card games we retired for the day.

On the 14th of August we followed the same routine. After a chocolate breakfast, I gave the students instructions in the use of the Bazooka and fired a phosphorus demonstration round that became the topic of their conversation for a long time thereafter. Then Hank gave a lecture on the 60mm mortar while I helped with the operation and nomenclature of the weapon. I usually introduced each period of instruction because I was the only one who could speak French well enough for the our interpreter Mr. Bach to understand. Then the Major and Hank gave a demonstration on the proper way of throwing hand grenades. When Hank and one of the student threw two live grenades, the rest of the students were much impressed.

Henry Prunier conducting 60mm mortar training at the Vietminh camp.

Author loading a bazooka for Sgt. Larry Vogt.

After a lunch featuring goose on the menu, the Major and Larry demonstrated the use of rifle grenades until 3:00 p.m. when I took over for a course on booby traps. I tried to make it as interesting as possible and included some humor about this rather sinister subject. I ended the lecture discussing the use of incendiaries. We closed the day as usual with supper and card playing, then on to the communal bunk.

The next day, August 15, it was still raining. Not feeling well, I did not get up as usual, so Hank handled the PT for the troops. We did not do much except issuing guns. The Major was talking about going to Cho-Chu to check on the fort occupied by the Japanese. That afternoon he went to see Mr. Ho.

Our men appeared dejected and unresponsive. The unmistakable happiness displayed by the Major made them very suspicious. Three months earlier all had wanted to fight the Japanese, but now they felt that the Major was at fault for not having given them the opportunity. I was not aware that before leaving Kunming the Major had said that he would not risk anyone's life, he would only fool around until the war was over. Our men had heard him, they remembered, and resented his attitude as their opportunities for combat shrank.

After noon the Major left and I issued more supplies to the students. We continued training, with Hank handling the mortar, Larry the light machine-gun and me the Bazooka.

The few practice mortar shells we had were fired without activating the charge. This was not as dangerous, but we still took every precaution to avoid any mishaps. It was a good thing that we did, because Mr. Van decided to be involved at the mortar practice though he had not bothered to attend the period of instruction. He only wanted to fire one round. He took the shell and placed it head first into the tube. He then found himself suddenly alone with the mortar as all the students hurriedly vacated the area. Fortunately, one of our team was there to stop his procedure and show Mr. Van how to do it properly. This incident was particularly ironic considering that I learned later that "Mr. Van" was actually the nom de guerre of none other than the future famed North Vietnamese general (and later Deputy Premier of a unified Vietnam), Vo Nguyên Giap. In 1954, Giap led the Vietminh to victory against the French at the famous battle of Dien Bien Phu. However, prior to our training mission in 1945, Giap appeared to know very little about armaments or military tactics. Or did he know more?

The students did pretty well so I let them practice fire the Thompson submachine gun, a weapon more to their liking, and better suited for guerrilla operations.

During the supper, around 4:00 p.m., I received a very strange message from the Major. We all felt that he was about to do something that would either bring him glory or get him in a lot of trouble. When he returned later that evening he told us that the hostilities had stopped at 12:00 noon, and that the war was over! Why didn't his earlier message include this information? At 8:00 p.m. we celebrated the end of the war by shooting our flares to illuminate the entire area. Our students sang their patriotic songs and Paul drank too much of the Major's whiskey.

On the Way Back

On August 16th the Major was up early while the rest of us slept until 7:00 a.m., one of the team with a beautiful hangover. I felt good because the decision to return to our Kunming base had been made by our headquarters. But at the insistence of the Major, we would not go before two of our students had fired the M-1! The Major issued ammunition to the students while we packed our equipment. By 10:00 a.m. he left with a 12-man patrol for a destination known only to him. Quang-Trung and Mr. Bach were supposed to wait for the rest of our team at Kim-Lung. We bade good-by to our jungle home at 11:30 a.m. I was still barefoot. An hour and a half later we reached Kim-Lung where the first Vietminh Congress had been held and where important people from Hanoï and other parts of FIC were assembled with Mr. Ho. There we met a 77-year-old woman who had walked all the way from Hanoï to meet the new leaders of her country. In the crowd I spotted the Major who was with Mr. Ho. When he saw me, he grinned and gave the thumb-up high sign. Then, taking me aside, he told me that before leaving he would have to give a speech. And what a speech it was! He looked so comical that we all laughed.

Finally we left Kim-Lung, following a trail on the clay soil made very slippery by recent rain. For the first time I noticed that young girls who had not been part of our student body had joined our group. Although they did not appear to be local farm girls, they wore black peasant clothing and carried French rifles almost as long as they were tall. The face of one of the girls was red, and when I held her hand to help her on a steep climb, she felt very hot. Obviously she had a high fever and no business on a trail, but she refused to stop and continued the rough march with us. The jungle's thick cover reduced the intensity of a bright daylight to minimum. Hungry and exhausted we kept on going until it was as dark in the clearings as under the jungle's canopy. Dead tired, we reached the village of Lay-Hong. I climbed the ladder to the polished bamboo floor of a clean hut, and collapsed. After a good meal during which I consumed the traditional seven bowls of rice to please our host I slept on the floor close to the fire.

Any time that we passed through a small village, we would be surrounded by children who, while interested in our weapons as were all children, were more interested in our physical appearance. They were fascinated by, and would touch, the hair on our arms and our chests because the native males were devoid of body hair except under their arms and in the pubic region. Apparently, to them we more closely resembled monkeys than men.

After a restful night on August 17th we were ready to take the trail to Thaï-Nguyên. The Major suggested that we swing by a village not on our route where, according to him, 20 Japanese prisoners were waiting for us to escort them to our destination. This was contrary to the specific instructions we had received concerning our dealings with the Japanese.

With a single platoon the Major and Mr. Van left at 8:00 a.m. and at 10:00 the remaining party and I left Lay-Hong with coolies carrying our equipment. Two kilometers out of town the trail improved and led us to a hard top road we followed for a while. We passed by a ruined village allegedly burnt by the Japanese and continued on our way. Bridges had been destroyed and we had to ford the small rivers or wade through them when they were not too deep. Two kilometers before Hong-Trung, we took to the trail again and went through several areas flooded with water up to our knees. We managed to pick up a few leaches and after examining each other for these hitchhikers, we continued until we reached the Major who was on the trail waiting for us.

He took me aside to brief me on the situation, but I did not listen because he did not make sense. Realizing that he was not reaching me, he called Bill. Then he lost his composure and behaved like a spoiled kid when told that there was no message from Poseh or Kunming. Bill sassed him back, explaining that if the radio was not working, how in the hell could he send a message! The Major left in a huff with his Vietminh platoon.

An hour later, following two scouts, I gave the order to move out. Two miles later Quang-Trung, waiting for us, told me not to proceed but to wait a while. Because the Japanese were close by, he sent a patrol ahead and directed the rest of us onto a different trail that turned out to be the worst of our trip. Sticky mud made the going very difficult. We crossed several streams in water up to our waist, and collected more leaches. The Vietminh without shoes had a rough time. By them I had changed my mind about going barefoot. Even wearing my boots I found the trail to be the most difficult. We joined the Major at Trung-Ninh at 7:00 p.m. He briefed me on the situation and asked me to do the same to our men who were standing nearby. He just could not get through his head that a team is one single unit and not a battalion! I was sick and tired of it and I told him: "Why don't you tell them yourself?"

On the 18th of August, the Major, with Larry, left Trung-Ninh at 8:00 a.m. on his way to Hung-Son where he would meet the Indochinese Guards, who were under the control of the Japanese. He told us that he did not intend to ask the Japanese to surrender! He only wanted to talk to the Indochinese guards. I declined his invitation to join him, and the rest of the team chose to continue with me to Thaï-Nguyên.

We left at 10:30 a.m. for Co-Wan where we were to rejoin the Major. For three kilometers we followed the trail, then hit the main road to Thaï-Nguyên. In tactical formation behind the first section we covered the ten kilometers

Five members of the Deer Team crossing a swollen stream on their way to Thai Nguyên.

rapidly and arrived at Co-Wan at 1:30 p.m. With a couple of beers and bread-fruit offered to us by local people we waited for the Major. Wondering about his delay and imagining the worst we were told by one of the Vietminh leaders that we were waiting for him at the wrong place, and that we were to move to a village closer to Thaï-Nguyên, but not on the main road. We left Co-Wan on a difficult trail and by 5:30 p.m. we arrived at Lan-Ngo in the outskirts of Thaï-Nguyên. After a good dinner we retired to our sleeping bags while Bill fiddled with his radio. Lo and behold he fixed it, and was able to send and receive messages from Kunming and Poseh.

On the 19th of August at 8:00 a.m. we received a message from Poseh. The Major came in just as the message was being deciphered. The message stated:

"Chow to Deer: CEASE ALL OPERATIONS. DO NOT. RPT NOT. ACCEPT SURRENDER OF ANY JAP UNITS. YOU WILL PREPARE TO MOVE TO Hanoï. BUT DO NOT START UNTIL YOU GET ORDER FROM THIS HQ. NO CHINESE OR ANNAMESE TO GO WITH YOU EXCEPT THOSE NEEDED AS GUIDES. DON'T DISPOSE OF ANY EQUIPMENT UNTIL I GET KUNMING DIRECTION."

The message came too late and did not impress the Major. On his order our supplies had already been distributed to the Vietminh. He decided to help the Vietminh capture Thaï-Nguyên anyway. He told us that we did not have to follow him and left with Mr. Van who appeared to have full control over our leader. I decided that we had no alternative but to go along as our goal was to go Thaï-Nguyên anyway. Behind a huge red flag, we followed a rough trail until we reached a Buddhist temple where we rested. The Major, who had reached the temple before us, took me aside to tell me something he said was important. But he did not say much except that he had apparently again changed his mind and he would only follow the Vietminh to Thaï-Nguyên, then leave them to do their own thing. I was in full agreement.

But soon thereafter I noticed that he was still very much in charge of the Vietminh escorting us, and kept close to Mr. Van, obviously not giving a damn about us. As usual, he was still very much in charge of the Vietminh escorting us, and kept close to Mr. Van, obviously not giving a damn about his team.

I felt rather useless, having been replaced as an assistant team leader by Mr. Van.

Finally we reached Tan-Ninh where the entire Vietminh unit was assembled to wait for darkness before entering Thaï-Nguyên. At the staging area we were given adequate quarters and good food. Unfortunately, static interference did not permit partial radio contact with Poseh or Kunming. Bill was only able to send a portion of a message, and it did not include our actual location.

There was a celebration in the village where we stayed. A water buffalo was sacrificed. Its neck was severed with a small knife and blood was collected. The head was displayed with burning scented sticks in its nostrils and offered to the local god or gods by the village chief.

Up to then the Major was rather calm and restrained. By 7:30 p.m. he became nervous and restless. He rushed to the Vietminh leaders to find out what they were up to. Then, with Mr. Van, he planned the attack on Thaï-Nguyên and gave the team's equipment including a handy-talky and Captain Babineau's binoculars to the Vietminh. I heard him giving orders to the platoon leaders who were to lead the attack. The men and I could not sleep or relax, so to kill time we ate dozens of wild pineapples.

Thaï-Nguyên

At 2:30 a.m. on the 20th of August we received word that it was time to proceed toward our objective. Without the Major and Mr. Van, but with a group of 30 Vietminh guerrillas preceded by a red flag, we took the road to Thaï-Nguyên. Except for a large hole full of water in the center of the road and a deep ditch at the entrance of the town, the road was rather good. With our guns at the ready, avoiding street lights, we moved slowly into the suburbs of Thaï-Nguyên. As we reached an area close to a Japanese guard post the leader of our group told us to remove our shoes. One by one we passed by the Japanese guards and slipped into Thaï-Nguyên proper. We were so close to a sleeping sentry leaning against a wall that I could smell the sake on his breath.

Rounding a corner we ran into a lone woman who, seeing these strange armed men, began to cry. Because we were so close to the Japanese, our leader, fearing that they would hear her cry and investigate, asked her to shut up politely, but in vain. So they beat her up and left her unconscious on the road. Quietly we kept on moving, stopping at every noise, running quickly under street lights and proceeding slowly when in dark areas. Eventually we reached the front of a new-looking concrete building. Checking the area around it we discovered a 7 CV Citroën parked in the rear of the structure. We entered through the back door and went upstairs. Our escort, familiar with the lay of the building, went directly to a door and opened it. In the room were some very surprised and scared people who without explanation were chased out by our escort.

We were shocked by his actions and surprised to see real beds with springs and mattresses, an easy chair, a refrigerator, and all kinds of electrical appliances! Beer was brought in. We talked about our adventure, but soon we fell asleep right where we had collapsed.

Rifle fire nearby woke us up around 6:00 a.m. Wondering what it was all about, we stood up and waited cautiously to determine our next move. Our escort had left, we had no idea where the Major was, and we were alone between two antagonists: the Vietminh, and the Japanese with their Indochinese Guards. We were considering our next action when a runner brought a message from the Major who wanted to see Alan, Bill and I immediately. I did not go because I did not want to be involved with whatever he was doing, and in the process get in trouble. Later that evening, when he came to our building I was asleep and he did not awaken me. Alan, who had rejoined us, told me that he was with the major when he and the Vietminh chiefs talked to the Japanese representative. Believing that the Major was French the Japanese refused to surrender to him. To prove his American nationality the Major offered his identity card, a 38-caliber round, and a small American flag to the Japanese garrison commander. But the Japanese officer still refused to believe him. Disgusted he went outside and, waving his small American flag, walked toward the Japanese emplacement. Their reply was still "No". The Major admitted then that perhaps he should not have been there! Subsequently the Japanese did agree to surrender to the Vietminh, but not the French. Apparently the Indochinese Guards had their own ideas!

It seemed to us that more and more the Major was behaving peculiarly. At times he stared into the distance, talking to himself. As he spoke he often started laughing for reasons known only to him. His laugh was more a cackle than a laugh. When seeing a Japanese soldier his strange behavior and laughing increased.

But it appeared that peace had finally come into the area. From the balcony of our building Mr. Van addressed some of local people who had assembled in the street below. Afterward he left, with the Major in hot pursuit.

Meanwhile, I asked those responsible for our housing for larger quarters because we had so little room. They advised us that a house one kilometer away might be better suited for us. I suggested this move to the Major, but Mr. Van disapproved, suggesting that we should move to the local hospital. Of course the Major immediately agreed and by 5:00 p.m. we began moving our equipment toward the hospital with the help of several people. Suddenly all those following us vanished. Thinking that they had reason for doing so I was not overly concerned until someone pointed out that we had just walked across the field of fire of two Japanese machine-guns! Why didn't they warn us before we got there?

We continued toward the hospital, but first we had to stop by the quarters of the doctor who administered the hospital and who was to escort us to our destination. He was quite surprised when he learned that we were moving into his installation. Not only rooms were not available, but there was no bed, no water, and no electricity—nothing. Disgusted, I sent a note to the Major asking him to lay off the Vietminh and worry a little about his team. After eating our supper we returned to our former quarters where we found the Major sitting by himself in the dark. Without saying a word, we quietly retired to our sleeping bags. Suddenly we were awakened by the Major who walked in our room and gave each of us a blanket. We did not bother thanking him.

In the room next to ours, I clearly heard him and Mr. Van plan an attack on the Japanese for the following morning. They did not plan their move as military officers would, but more as two kids planning a war game with Indians!

186

Apparently the agreement between the Vietminh and the Japanese had broken down for there was gun fire through town all night long.

On the 21st of August the gun fire that had subsided in the early hours of the morning started again at 7:00 a.m. The Major advised me that a house had been found for us and that those in charge were going to take us to it. At 10:00 a.m., Bill Zielski and I left with Mr. Hon and a few of his men to check on the house. It was very nice, but it had few rooms and was in a terrible location. Behind it was a police station occupied by Japanese who were firing their guns every five minutes. We discarded that house and began searching farther on for another.

The next house was also located across the street from a building occupied by Japanese soldiers. A block away we came to a sand-bag barricade manned by two men armed with rifles. Probably Vietminh, they told us that the Japanese had been firing in our general direction questioningly. I looked at Bill who said: "Let's go!" I took off after him leaving our escort at the barricade. I barely made it across the street when two shots hit the road behind me. We ran across one more open area then crawled behind a 5-foot stone wall to the intersection and rushed through the garden into the house while the Japanese were still firing in our direction. Neither Bill nor I was nervous. We laughed and joked to cheer our scared escort sending him to fetch the other members of the team. While waiting for them we drank beer that was always available in all the houses we had so far occupied.

We were amazed by the quality of our new house and the size of the 9 rooms on one floor. We could not remain in the front room because it was facing the building occupied by the Japanese who kept on shooting in our

Vietminh defending a Thaï-Nguyên road crossing under attack by Japanese after the end of the war.

187

direction. The house, constructed according to French colonial standards, offered us excellent protection from small arms fire, but no safeguard against hand and rifle grenades or mortar shells.

Bill, Larry and I decided to check the front room to see what damage had been done, and determine if we could see the Japanese on the other side of the street. There were bullet holes in the wall and at 2:00 p.m., as we were examining the damages, all hell broke loose outside. An explosion from a mortar, a Bazooka shell or perhaps a rifle grenade hit close to the Japanese garrison and shook us. Shots from across the street peppered the building. One hit the wall above my head another missed Bill by a few inches. He ran to the back of house while Larry and I somewhat shakily followed quickly. Hell! The war was over, why take a chance on being killed now? I suggested that for the time being we all stay in the rear of the building. We waited for a while and calm returned. It was quiet and Larry and Bill returned to the front room, but again shots came from across the street. I had hoped that their curiosity had been satisfied. When would they ever learn?

By runner I sent a note to the Major asking him for news about the local situation. Instead of replying he came personally to report on his adventures. He told us that he had been fired upon at least one thousand times and had managed to escape unscathed. He looked more detached than before, his laugh turned into a kind of spasmodic bleating, and his thoughts were incoherent. He then returned to whatever he was doing, stating that it was so much fun, and he knew we were all safe. Apparently he was still directing the Vietminh operation.

Now we had a house staff to take care of us. There was a shower room in the house and a boy whose only job was to soap us from head to toes. All we had to do was stand while he scrubbed every part of our bodies. In the evening after relaxing we went to bed on real mattresses in queen-sized beds brought in from somewhere under the cover of darkness. These people could not do enough for us. Besides regular native food they provided us with French bread, beer, cigarettes and anything else we asked.

On August 22nd I was awakened in early morning by rifle fire in the street nearby. It was close to breakfast time so I did not return to bed, but listened to the fighting in the street that lasted all morning. Eventually we realized that the safest place for us and an ideal spot to sunbathe was in the court yard which separated the house from the kitchen and servants' quarters. Every once on a while we heard the whistling of bullets over our heads. But the walls around us were good protection. Although we were completely surrounded by the Japanese, the Vietminh managed to supply food, and an expert cook managed to fix the best meal we have had in a long time.

The Major did not come to see us that day. Unless he was with one of us we never knew where he was. Perhaps he found our area too unsafe for his travel.

Fifty yards from our house three men were wounded by rifle fire; one of them died. Around 10:30 p.m. the rifle fire intensified. Shots came close to the house. Perhaps it was the Vietminh offensive, but it did not last long, the shooting died away and we fell asleep.

On the 23rd of August when I got up at 6:00 a.m. all was quiet. As usual we sunbathed in the court-yard. We learned from the house boys that seven Japanese who had been in the building across the street tried to escape dressed as local people, but one had been captured. We were still cautious, and remained in the back rooms because some Japanese might still be holed up in the building. When it became evident that all hostile activities had ceased, I decided to check the outside wall of the front room for damages. The wall was constructed of the typical colonial bricks 10 inches thick. Two holes one inch in diameter indicated that two projectiles had penetrated the wall. We searched the room but found nothing.

Someone pointed at a hole in the headboard of the bed where I had slept the night before. It was located a few inches above where my head had lain. I had heard nothing, and neither had Hank who slept on the other side of the bed.

I received a note from the Major who wanted to know if we had heard anything from Poseh or Kunming. No message had been received from our two headquarters, nor from Holland who was supposed to be at Pho-Binh-Gia approximately 50 miles northeast of Thaï-Nguyên!

On the 24th of August we were again awakened at 6:00 a.m. by rifle fire. We were so used to it by then we did not pay much attention unless we noticed new holes in the wall facing the street, then we moved away from that room. Apparently there were still Japanese in the building across the street firing at anything that moved. Either they would be on their roof, or at times sneaked outside to climb the nearby trees and snipe at anything that moved. Some had managed to run away and once dressed in civilian clothes they were almost impossible to detect. To prevent their escape the Vietminh had set up an extensive system of passwords.

Rifle fire came from every direction. We could tell from the impact of the bullet or the noise it made through the leaves where it originated, but we never knew who was doing the shooting.

The Vietminh took three Japanese prisoners to a nearby house; one Japanese woman and two alleged Japanese intelligence personnel. We believed that they gave the 3rd degree to one of them because we heard loud voices and loud cries in the night.

A runner brought two messages from the Major, one for Poseh, the other for Holland. For the record I had sent the following one to Poseh:

"WE ARE NOW IN THAI-NGUYEN. THE MAJOR IN THE OUT-SKIRTS OF THE TOWN. THE REMAINING TEAM IS IN THE CENTER

OF THE TOWN. BATTLE BETWEEN VIETMINH AND JAP GARRISON STARTED MONDAY TWENTY STILL GOING ON. STREET FIGHTING DAY AND NIGHT. IS AMERICAN FORCES STATION STILL ON? SEND US SOME NEWS PLEASE."

Bill tried, but he could not establish contact with Holland.

After a good supper we relaxed on mats in the court-yard, but soon thereafter sniper's bullets chased us inside until 10:00 p.m. when we went to bed.

August 25th was a quiet day. Only a few rifle and light machine gun fire was heard in the distance. The hot sun prompted us to sunbathe and drink beer in the court yard.

In the afternoon the Major came with a Japanese civilian. After offering the Japanese a cigarette, he gave him a white flag and sent him across the street to discuss the question of surrender with the Japanese still holed up in the building. Shortly thereafter the Japanese emissary returned alone and declared that there were no Japanese in the building, all had skipped away during the night.

The Major told us that Mr. Van and Quang-Trung had left for Hanoï, and that he was now in charge of the Vietminh operation. He was as nonsensical as ever, speaking English to the Annamese and French to us. He appeared to be getting worse each day. Without telling us where he was going, he left behaving as a child. We had no idea how to get hold of him in case of need.

A message from Babineau of Poseh instructed us to sit tight a little longer. The Major came in and offered us souvenirs he had collected somewhere including a Japanese rifle. He stated that he had many nice souvenirs, but did not elaborate. After he left, to see what we could find we went to the house across the street from which the Japanese had taken potshots at us. They must have left in a hurry, and with very few of their belongings. I picked up a beautiful carved wooden box and a few trinkets. Later the Major returned and when he found out that we had been in the house he wanted to see that we had taken. He told us that we could take anything as long as we asked him. I did show him the box, wondering what Army regulation gave him control over the distribution of war souvenirs.

As the shooting was apparently over we decided to see more of the town we had been holed up in for six days. Many people milled around town, going about their business as if nothing had happened. We even went to a café and had a drink. For the most part people ignored us. When we returned to our house we were surprised to find that electricity, which had been cut off during the fighting, had returned.

August 27th began as a gloomy monotonous day with rain showers every couple hours and sun shine in between. When indoors our only entertainment were smoking, drinking beer and eating bananas. While we sat doing nothing,

190

Six members of the Deer Team resting in Thai-Nguyên.

to kill time Bill played with his radio, but this morning he received the best message we ever expected to decode. For him at least it turned out to be a great day. He had received the D.S.C. (Distinguished Service Cross) for his outstanding service in the European Theater. We were all very happy for him and wished we could do more than congratulate him. We decided to wait for a more suitable location to do so.

We returned to the building across the street to continue our search and in the process we discovered an ordinary radio receiver the Japanese had left behind. It was not long before Bill had it fixed and sweet American music was heard throughout the building. We almost went insane with joy. For the last three months we had heard no western music, only the horrible screeching and bell tingling of what the Vietnamese call music! It was a real treat. With our heads close to the speaker we ignored the static and savored every note. We even heard the news from San Francisco! We stayed up very late, not tired of hearing about our beloved country and our own people.

The following day, August 28th, the weather had not improved , and once again without electricity we were not able to hear the latest news on our radio. The Major came to stay with us, but when he showed up a wall of ice surrounded the team, a wall he attempted to break with his usual bleating laugh.

The gear we had left behind finally arrived from Kim-Lung. With the exception of two parachutes everything appear to be there.

191

A message from Poseh advised us to look for a suitable landing strip close to our position so that we might be picked up and flown to Poseh. Larry volunteered for the job and left to scout the area.

With our equipment were some of our cargo chutes. I decided that a bright red parachute would make outstanding pajamas. A tailor was summoned to our house by the staff and measurements taken. We stayed up most of the night in anticipation, not for the pajamas but for the next message from our HQ.

On the 29th of August the rain subsided. Larry, Hank, and Hoagy went to visit a Catholic mission managed by Dominican priests. When they returned they announced that they had invited one of the Fathers for the evening meal. After lunch we told the "Bep" ("cook" in Vietnamese) to fix something special for that occasion, and left for a stroll through town with Alan taking pictures.

Our guest arrived as expected and we tried to make him feel at ease. He spoke French adequately, but with a strong Spanish accent. The Major who was also present could not understand the conversation acted maladroitly, embarrassing all of us. We enjoyed a very good dinner served on flowered dishes over a table cloth, after which I spent at least three hours talking to the priest about FIC and what was going on in that area. Later that evening we escorted him back his Mission.

The following day Larry and I returned to see the priest and continue our discussion. Larry, who the day before had failed to locate a suitable landing field, came along for the real coffee served at the Mission. I wanted to get additional information about what was going on in this part of the world. The priest had better sources of information than we did. The Major only knew what the Vietminh wanted him to know, which was very little.

The area where we were had been neglected by the French because it was devoid of natural resources. However the Catholic church had found it to be a fertile ground for conversions to the faith. Strangely enough, the missionaries in that area were not from France but from Spain, mostly from the island of Majorca where most natives were rather light in complexion and some had red hair. I marveled at the comfort these missionaries had created for themselves. They did not live in bamboo huts, but in houses made of stone, European style, two to three stories high. The mission we visited had indoor plumbing! Not the flushing type but on all floors, at the same end, was a small room similar to the US or European farm's one hole out-house, but these were offset enough so that the top john was set off the one below and that one was off the lower one, thus allowing three people on three floors to use their respective johns at the same time. It would have been convenient enough if the john had been entirely enclosed, unfortunately for some reason the outer wall was not entirely closed so that if one was sitting in the lower john, things might pass him uncomfortably close!

We had to converse in French with the fathers, but it would have been easier had we known Spanish. When passing through villages I noted that several kids had red hair, in some cases curly, instead of the traditional straight black hair. I asked the Spanish priest if these had been the result of the French colonial army stationed in the area. He smiled and said rather quizzically, "No, but some of us missionaries who volunteered to serve in Indochina did not take the vow of chastity." I understood immediately the inference.

In the afternoon I stayed in the house not only because of the rain, but because my feet ached terribly. Having walked without shoes for so long I had trouble being used to my boots. The tailor brought the pajamas and I immediately wore them to the great enjoyment of the rest of the team. It was indeed a flashy outfit. To the Vietminh I must have looked very revolutionary!

On the 31st of August we celebrated Bill's birthday or perhaps the departure of the Major who left for Hanoï on a bicycle! He was such a tiresome person to have around that he was not missed. I was wondering how he would explain his trip to Hanoï to our Headquarters which had specifically ordered us to remain where we were!

During his absence a message from Babineau came in. It stated that Captain Patti, an OSS officer, was in Hanoï and had advised Kunming to order the Major not to proceed to that city. No reason for this order was given, but it came too late to stop the Major. We were certain that on his return he would have a lot to explain to our Headquarters, but we did not really care.

By the 1st of September, the Major had not yet returned. In town we were much surprised by the presence of many more Japanese soldiers who strutted arrogantly in full uniform, alone and in small groups, and in cases of officers with a sword dangling at their side. When passing by they gave us cruel stares or with disdain looked straight ahead. I had to admit we did not look so hot. Unshaven and in our undershirts we did not exemplify the invincible American military might. In downtown Thaï-Nguyên the Japanese looked more like conquerors than we did, and very possibly the local people took us for Frenchmen unless they had been part of our student group which by then had disappeared.

Close to 3:00 in the afternoon as we were sunning ourselves, a Frenchman came to our door. He looked terrible, very thin, emaciated and dirty. He told me that he had been in charge of a local mine, and that the Japanese had jailed him three months earlier. He had been released by the Vietminh five days earlier, but he had been kept in a room with only rice for food, not as a prisoner, but just about. He wanted to know if he could go to Hanoï. Unaware of the situation in Hanoï I suggested that he should wait for the Major's return. He might know what to do. The Frenchman left, inviting himself for supper, but then he returned too late to share our meal. Our cook gave him food that he ate ravenously. Intimating that he would like to share our table on a daily basis, I told him that we were guests ourselves. It that was not our food he was eating but that of our host. He left unhappy and never returned.

From the local Catholic Church, we received an invitation to attend a high mass in honor of the independence of Vietnam. Shortly thereafter the Major returned from Hanoï with pastries, and a story about the capture of Holland by the Japanese and the escape of Sgt. Stoyka. He did not tell us how he learned the story about Holland. We advised him of the instructions we had received from Poseh, but it did not phase him. He never shared his experience with us.

On Sunday, the 3rd of September, four of us went to the local Catholic church to attend the high mass. We were greeted at the entrance by a friendly individual and the parish priest, both Annamese. The priest had a perpetual smile and escorted us to a receiving room where a group of notables was waiting. They told us how glad they were for our presence which gave them reassurance that the United States was behind them in their struggle for freedom and independence!

After the high mass that included incense and all the pomp and circumstance they could muster, we returned to our quarters.

Alan and I accompanied the Major on a tour of the town. He was eager to show us where the fighting he had master-minded had taken place. We mingled with the thousand Japanese soldiers who had come to town the day before. They looked at us curiously, and when Alan tried to take their picture they showed their displeasure and refused to pose. We concluded that if it was the way they felt about it, why bother. When passing Japanese soldiers, the Major would whistle a tune to give himself countenance, or kept on talking English, mostly to himself, as neither I nor Alan were paying attention. Watching him was difficult for us. When it became impossible to maintain straight faces and we laughed, covering ourselves with excuses.

Later that day while sunbathing, we listened to the now improved radio broadcasts. The Major remained remote most of the day, busy at his typewriter. Only the meals brought us together, yet no one spoke to him. When he stepped into a room the rest of the team felt a cold wind seem to enter and silence immediately prevailed. He tried to break it by asking innocuous questions or making statements followed by his funny laugh. As a rule, to maintain a degree of civility, I responded while the others ignored him completely.

We were surprised by the arrival of Sgt. Stoyka who appeared from nowhere. After his escape from the Japanese, with the help of the Vietminh, he searched for us. When he reached Thaï-Nguyên, someone told him that Americans were in town and directed him to our quarters. He told us how

Holland, Burrowes and he had been captured by the Japanese. It was fascinating!

A few days after leaving Kim-Lung they were marching ahead of their escorting unit on a major road without the benefit of scouts or a point. Mike had been told earlier that there were Japanese in the area, but he paid no attention to that information. It was beastly hot and he was thirsty. Entering a small village he went the first house and asked the owner for a drink, preferably a beer. The owner left, and a short time later the beer arrived, but it was served by a Japanese soldier! The Vietnamese had vanished so only the three Americans were taken prisoner. Arriving at a small compound they were led into a room whose door had no lock. Their side-arms had been hung on a peg on the outside wall of the building not far from their room. Stoyka immediately planned an escape while Mike resigned himself to his destiny as a POW. After careful consideration Stoyka explained his plan to Burrowes and to Mike who reluctantly agreed to go along.

The plan was to wait until the Japanese took their siesta, then rush out of their cell and retrieve the weapons, then run for the hill nearby where the vegetation would hide them. Stoyka very carefully explained where they were to go after leaving the compound. At his signal they rushed out of their prison, grabbed their weapons and headed for the hills. Unfortunately, Mike and Burrowes did not follow Stoyka's instructions. Instead of turning one way they went to the other and into a blind alley. Stoyka managed to reach the side of the hill where there were bushes. Alerted, Japanese were quickly in pursuit of the escapees. Some distance away from the town, finding himself alone and realizing that only two Japanese were after him, he hid behind a bush and waited. When the first pursuer came close enough he shot him. The other ran the other way.

For days Stoyka remained hidden in the jungle living off the land. When far enough from the Japanese post he approached local villagers who turned out to be Vietminh. With their help he had finally reached Thaï-Nguyên.

We brought him up to date on what was going on including the fact that Holland and Burrowes had been released by the Japanese, and that they probably were in Hanoï. We firmly believed that his escape was the reason why the Japanese had not killed Mike and Burrowes.

After supper the following day, the 4th of September, I told the men about my training with the British, and subsequent operation in France. The Major commented that he had been to that school! Later on that evening he asked me to help him translate a message in French. After I was done he showed me the message I had sent on the 24th of August, stating that it wasn't fair. I replied that it was what I was told. Then we discussed how we should proceed to get our per diem and plan a program when we returned to Kunming. The members of our team were very happy that our leader was finally looking out for their interest.

The following day, September 5th, was no better. We remained indoors listening to the radio, still thrilled to be able to hear broadcasts from San Francisco and Los Angeles. In the morning I was working on a report when the Major told me that two priests wanted to see me. I recognized one of them as Father Perez, a Dominican missionary. He had just returned from Hong-Son the day before and wanted to tell us about Japanese atrocities in that village. Apparently they had buried people alive after the date of surrender. There was very little we could do about it but we invited them to lunch. When they were told that we would be leaving on Sunday without acting, they expressed great sorrow. They had hoped that the presence of American in FIC would be an important factor for the survival of Indochina.

Local bus running between Hanoï, Thaï-Nguyên and Hong Son. Author is sitting on the bumper while Major Thomas is standing with one of Vo Nguyên Giap's recruits.

The Road to Hanoï

The first part of the trip was relatively easy. To march on a hard-top road was a lot easier and faster than walking on a jungle trail. Shortly after getting underway we passed near a Japanese cavalry unit of perhaps 200 men in bivouac close by the road. We approached them to see our former enemies at close range. Some were on horses and it was there that I saw the tallest Japanese imaginable. During all the training sessions and subsequent briefings I had attended, Japanese had been described as small monkey-like sub-humans with thick glasses and buck teeth. When we moved close to one officer in particular, we could not believe what we saw. Compared to the Chinese ponies we had ridden, his white horse was much higher and he sat tall in the saddle. From his position, he looked down on us with disdain, while we stared at him with astonishment. He did not wear glasses, nor he did not have buck teeth; in fact he looked very impressive, even handsome, in his clean well-pressed uniform. We learned that this unit had been part of the Imperial Guard and that its members had been selected for their size and their skill.

As we walked along the road, the first and only good road we had seen in many months, people came to stare at us expressionless. They did not know who we were and they did not seem to care. We kept on walking until we reached the Red River. We crossed it by ferry because the bridge had been damaged by our own Air Force. We loaded our equipment into the ferry and down the river we went until we were close to the Doumer bridge. There, on the other side of the river, a few cars were waiting to drive us the rest of the way to Hanoï. One was a 1936 Citroën front-wheel-drive into which some of us climbed. We entered Hanoï and headed directly to the Governor's residence where we established our first command post in the bedroom of the absent Superior Resident. What a bedroom! It was huge, with heavy furniture made of tropical woods. A table in the center of the room must have been three inches thick and the bed was large enough to accommodate the five lesser members of our team. We all flopped on the bed and, looking up, we could see our reflections in a large mirror covering the ceiling above the bed. The resident of this palace must have had a great time looking at himself sleeping or doing something else.

This was to be the end of our adventure, but not before we had the opportunity to photograph our hosts. Mr. Ho, now referred to as Ho Chi Minh, had quickly become the most important individual in that part of the world. As for Mr. Van, we learned that his real name was Vo Nguyên Giap, the newly

Six members of the Deer Team resting in Thai Nguyên.

designated Minister of the Interior. Up to then, Ho Chi Minh had been reluctant to have his picture taken. Now he was willing and even eager to be photographed, probably feeling that he had now won and his days of hiding were over. The entire residence was Ho's headquarters and there he assembled his newly designated cabinet. A stream of people came to see him, some in their European dress, others in their native accouterment. One among the visitors received much attention from all those present. He was a small pudgy individual in sports clothes. Ho Chi Minh addressed him with respect and introduced him to us in French as "Mon Empereur" (my emperor).

Bao Dai shook our hands. I shall never forget his clammy paw. It felt limp, without strength, reflecting perfectly the character of Mon Empereur. Bao Dai was offering his services to the newly self-designated leader of his people before rushing back to the Riviera and his concubines.

Ho Chi Minh did not want us too close to him at this time. Not surprisingly, some of his people we had known and whom we cared for were not with him. One in particular, Quang Trung, had disappeared. He was to have been the Military Governor of Hanoï, a very responsible position. I wanted to know where he was, but my inquiries met a strange silence. A rumor spread that he had been eliminated because, as close as he was to the Deer Team, his allegiance was perhaps in doubt. He was the one that was the closest to us and rather than taking a chance, Ho or Van apparently took care of him in their own way. However I was to learn later that my suspicions were unfounded.

We were told that houses had been selected for our team and that it would be better for us to settle there rather than in the famous Métropole Hotel in the center of Hanoï. Three of us were driven to the house of a French functionary who had either left, or had been imprisoned by the Japanese. This

Ho Chi Minh, standing third from left, and Gen. Vo Nguyen Giap, in white suit, gavea farewell party for the Dear Team in 1945. Lt. René Défourneaux is standing second from left, with photographer, Alan Squires squating in front of him. Paul Hoagland is at extreme right.

house had been requisitioned by the Vietminh either for their own use or ours. In any case the servants were still there and once again we enjoyed the life of leisure to which we had become so quickly accustomed.

The Major and the others were not with us, and I had no idea where they were. Moreover, the first evening after we were settled, three girls in traditional Vietnamese dresses came to keep us company. Mr. Ho had been kind enough to send us a type of entertainment that was hard to resist. As the ranking one of the group I had first pick. I chose the tallest of the three girls, who spoke excellent French. After a sumptuous dinner, each one of us retired to our respective bedroom for the night.

This was a strange situation for me. Though when in England I had been in a house of prostitution, I had never been in bed with a prostitute, which this girl obviously was. Without hesitation she removed her dress, her slacks, underpants and bras. Then she stood before me stark naked her long straight black hair which reached her buttocks. In some way she seemed older than her looks; she may have been 25. Yet her breasts were rather small and her pubic area was almost bare. She smiled invitingly, but for some reason this ivory-colored body did not sexually arouse me. There was something strange about the girl. Unlike Caucasian girls that I had know she had no hips. She was absolutely straight from her shoulders to her thighs. I stood watching her as she lay on the bed saying: "Viens monsieur, viens." For me this encounter was a disaster.

The sun was up when I woke up and she was already dressed and on her way out. A rickshaw was waiting for her. She climbed aboard without looking back she was gone. I wondered if she would return in that evening!

The Métropole Hotel was the social center piece of Hanoï. That is where the few French women who had managed to escape the attention of the Japanese had come for news. And where we renewed our acquaintance with the now famous Captain Holland. He had been released by the Japanese and was making out with some of the French women whose husbands or boyfriends were still in Japanese concentration camps. No one appeared to be in a hurry to get the French out of prison!

Hanoï had not suffered much from the war. It was still the Paris of the East, and a truly beautiful city. Only the strategic roads and bridges had been hit by our Air Force. The shops and stores were intact but they lacked the merchandise and business they experienced in peace time. We walked around the city and occasionally passed in front of buildings still occupied by the Japanese. Some of these had sentries by the doors, and when we passed by they would turn around and face the wall, displaying their backs so that they would not have to salute us, I presumed. We discovered the best place to relax was by the lake where one could sit and eat ice cream while listening to popular French music.

By then, in accordance to the agreement signed by the Allies, the Chinese Army had moved into the Tonkin and the Chinese brass had taken residence in Hanoï, the Capital, while most of the their troops remained in the countryside. Rumors persisted that the Chinese were busy removing everything that could be removed and sending it back to China. Besides trucks, farm equipment, and entire plants, they even removed plumbing from private houses.

We knew that some American soldiers had been held prisoner in concentration camps some distance from Hanoï and it was imperative that they be picked up immediately and released to the U.S. Armed Forces. I accompanied the American officer responsible for the job. The Chinese Army was the official occupying force in the area, so we went to the Chinese General in charge. We located him in a villa which he used as his headquarters. General Lu Han met us in his makeshift office. He was a short rotund individual who did not appear to have starved much during this war. We presented our request and expected an immediate positive reply. Through his interpreter he conveyed his answer—"no." He could not spare any vehicles to fetch our prisoners! The only other group who had transportation was the Japanese, so we went to the Japanese Headquarters and made the same request. In two minutes we had our transportation, including a driver, and the mission was accomplished.

Late one evening, I was returning to the hotel when from the darkness in front of the entrance to the hotel I heard laughing and giggling, obviously from several women. As I drew nearer, I could see flashes of light as if someone was striking one match after another. When I was close enough, I realized that it was Lucien, an old friend whom I had not seen for a year. Surrounded by a half dozen giggling girls, every time he struck a match he would bring it to the face of one of the girls. Since there was no electricity as yet, he was making his selection for the night by match light.

I did return to our quarters and so did our guests of the previous evening. The three of us discussed our good fortune and hoped we would not get a bill for services rendered. When the time came to retire for the evening the procedure was easier because it was no longer new to me. However the result was the same and the girl told me that she believed that it was her fault. I assured her that it wasn't so. Again she tried her entire routine on me, but to no avail. Then she decided that perhaps I was too tense. She proceeded to give me a massage; first my back and shoulders, then my arms and legs. She was an extremely skilled masseuse. I felt so relaxed that I almost fell asleep.

But this time It worked! Wiping herself with a towel she turned on her side to face me and look into my eyes, but I could not read her thoughts. Was she proud of her accomplishment, or did she feel sorry for me? She left in early morning the same as the day before. It was the last time I saw her.

We were not the only OSS personnel in the area. Another OSS team headed by Captain Archimedes Patti had come while we were cooling our heels at Thaï-Nguyên. He set up shop in one of the best buildings in Hanoï, a former official residence of the French colonial government. Shortly after our arrival in the capital city, the Major and I were summoned to his office. When we arrived at the appointed time we were led to a long room, unfurnished except for a large desk at one end. Behind it sat an American officer in full uniform, medals and all. Seeing us, he stood up and, with his chin jutting out, looked disapprovingly at our dreadful appearance.

Finally face-to-face, we met Captain Archimedes Patti, an Italian-American who bore an uncanny resemblance to Mussolini. After what we had just been through the scene seemed out of place, unreal. I do not recall exactly what was said. It had to do with our return to be arranged by those who had just arrived from our Kunming Headquarters. I was glad to get out of Patti's presence, but I did not know why.

Eventually the Pont Doumer (Doumer Bridge) was repaired sufficiently to be passable for cars. This enabled us to go to the Gia-Lam airport which had been a military base and which, incidentally, was still occupied by the Japanese Air Force. Several Zero dive bombers with bull's-eyes painted on their sides sat on the tarmac. A Japanese maintenance crew fussed over one aircraft as if it would be taking off any moment. There were some American military people on the base, but there was no fraternization.

One day we were standing under a tarp to shield us from the hot sun when a Japanese officer came to talk to us. He was a colonel, the CO of the base. He spoke excellent English, having been educated in the United States. First he asked us what kind of bombs were used to cause such destruction in Hiroshima and Nagasaki. We were not very helpful; he knew as much as we did. Then he told us that his entire family, who resided at Hiroshima, had been killed and that he had nothing for him to live for. In fact he did not expect to live long because he was in the last stages of tuberculosis. We could see the hurt on his face as he asked us about the terrible weapon used against his people. Talking to him made us keenly aware of the power of the this super bomb, the "A-bomb" as it was to be known.

Eventually it was decided that I would return to Kunming, but that some members of our team were to remain a while longer. By that time I did not feel very good. I feared that I had contracted malaria again. During a big party given by Ho Chi Minh, he made a speech inviting us to return to his country and stating that we would always be welcome.

Back to Kunming

Soon thereafter, one of our men and I managed to hitch a ride aboard a C-47 returning to Kunming. We were the only two passengers on the aircraft piloted by a couple of real Air Force cowboys. The crew had spent the entire previous evening drinking at the Métropole and was still feeling no pain. The pilot

Deer Team in front of C-47

decided to give the people of Hanoï a sample of what American fliers could do. After a normal take-off, he headed toward Hanoï close to the ground, as if on a bombing run. Once over the city, he followed the main street and made a complete barrel roll while I held on for dear life in the bucket seat. Only the happy yells in the cockpit comforted me. I could see the people in the street waving at us or running for cover and, a second later, only the cloudless sky. Eventually we regained altitude and headed north for the Chinese border. During the flight I learned that our pilot had flown fighters and claimed that he could do rolls with any plane. I could not decide if I should be proud of him or complain. I kept the incident to myself, enjoying the thought that I had been on a C-47 that made a barrel roll over Hanoï. Not too many other people would be able to make that claim.

When I reached our Kunming Headquarters, I was disappointed to learn that all my gear, which I had stored in a warehouse, had been damaged by a flood. When I inventoried my belongings, I discovered that many items were missing including money and some gold leaves that I had purchased at a very good price. I was not the only one to have lost his possessions, but it appeared that we had no recourse even though the official story about flood was not very convincing.

Many of us had returned from our missions and were ready to go back home. That is when stories that would never be included in the official reports were told over cans of beer that were by then in good supply even if they were warm.

Our compound was too restrictive and boring. Most of us wanted to go to town and see any of the sights that were worth seeing and taste everything worth tasting.

Unfortunately the local war lord and the Generalissimo had to settle their differences before we could enjoy the freedom we so richly deserved. For a few days, street fighting left many corpses in the streets of Kunming, and it was deemed safer to remain in our compound. Eventually the Generalissimo prevailed and peace returned to the area.

One evening a group of us were about to leave for Kunming City when we ran into Lucien Coneine who had also returned from Hanoï. He had been in contact with French officials based in Kunming. They had asked about me, telling him that they were looking for me and that there was price on my head. Lucien advised me not to leave the compound. He did not know why the

---

HEADQUARTERS
OFFICE OF STRATEGIC SERVICES
CHINA THEATER
APO 627

2 OCTOBER 1945

SUBJECT: Letter of Commendation
TO: 2d Lt Rene Defourneaux, O-887913

1. I wish to commend you for your work with the SO Branch, Office of Strategic Services, China Theater.

2. Your actions in parachuting into French Indo China in July 1945 and your subsequent work in training a team of guerrillas are worthy of the highest praise. That this training was successful was proven in later action against the enemy. The success of the mission was due in large part to your ability and unselfish devotion to duty.

3. I wish, therefore, to take this opportunity to express my appreciation and commendation of your cooperation and outstanding contribution to the success of the mission.

4. I have directed that this letter be made a part of your permanent record file.

Richard P. Heppner
Colonel, FA
Strategic Services Officer

Letter of Commendation from Col. R. Heppner

French were so upset, but insisted they were serious and they planned to kill me. Remembering the warning from Lt. McCarthy, I took Lucien's advice and reluctantly stayed in the compound.

The good food served in our mess hall did not improve my health. I was hungry, but did not enjoy food. My urine turned darker and darker, and my stools became lighter and lighter. I went to sick call but the doctors could not decide what was wrong with me. I feared that I had contracted a venereal disease from the house guest of Mr. Ho. They treated me for dysentery, malaria and more, but nothing helped. They suggested that I return to the United States as soon as possible.

On the Way Home

It took a few days for my name to be included on the manifest of one of the C-52s making the runs between Kunming and Karachi, where I would board a ship for the United States.

The C-52, a converted DC-6 with bucket seats, had a range almost twice that of the C-47 and by now they did not have to fly over the "Hump." On that day several planes left Kunming for Karachi. Rather than heading west over the mountain ranges of Western China we flew south over Burma, then west over the Bay of Bengal and across to India. Over the Bay we lost an engine, but were told that we had enough power to manage with three. For some of us to be without a parachute was an uncomfortable situation.

We learned that we would be stopping at Calcutta instead of Karachi. Then, a short distance from our destination, we lost another engine. This time it was serious and there was talk about dumping some of our cargo. Again we were assured that we could make it with two engines. When we landed, we discovered that we had no more than two minutes worth of fuel! It was great to get back on good old terra firma. One of the planes that had left Kunming on the same day as we did not make it. It was assumed that it had ditched and that all aboard were presumed lost.

We could not continue our return trip on the same plane, so we had to wait for another flight to Karachi. About ten of us were housed in a huge office building where we slept on cots. It was hot and uncomfortable.

As usual we met people we knew and to break the monotony went to the well-known hotels and restaurants. The Great Western Hotel was one of the most popular, not only with Americans, but with the Allied troops as well. A few of us decided to go to the bar of a famous Hotel. We reached our destination in a taxi driven by a Sikh accompanied by his armed assistant.

Entering the lobby where drinks were served, I noticed Lucien Coneine sitting with French officers unknown to me. He had reached Calcutta ahead of us, and was already well acquainted with the best places of the city. He introduced my companions to the French officers and when my turn came, the French stood up and in loud voices declared that the stench was unbearable. We moved on and found a suitable place to rest. Soon thereafter, Lucien left the French officers and came to me to say that I had better lay low; the French now knew I was here and they may try to do me in. I took his advice and stayed away from areas frequented by the French.

The French military throughout the region were still upset with me for my role as messenger when it was decided to exclude the French colonial troops in south China in our plans. Even after my eventual return to the States, I continued to receive ominous warnings, cautioning me not to return to France. As a result, it would be 45 years before I returned to my native land. Not even during my later tour in Europe did I dare venture there.

In early October I was still in Calcutta. One evening some friends, including a couple of nurses from the local Army hospital, convinced me to join them for a good steak dinner at an American Officers Club. I was terribly hungry and looked forward to a good steak, something we did not have very often. I remembered ordering a T-bone, and was looking forward to it. When it was placed in front of me, my appetite left me and I could not force myself to eat. The others could not understand what was the matter with me. One of the nurses suggested that I go on sick call the next morning even though I was to leave for Karachi that day.

Calcutta Lay Over

I got up early and went on sick call to the dispensary where a very young doctor examined me. I described my symptoms which he carefully noted on the required form. Then, standing before me, the palm of his hand up and finger extended, he punched me just below the rib cage. The pain was unbelievable. He called to a corpsman to bring a stretcher and ordered me to lie down and not to move. I was not going to Karachi that day. Instead, I was going to the 137th General Hospital in the heart of Calcutta. The doctor suggested that I might have hepatitis. Blood tests would determine the type, and there was not much they could do for it except prescribe plenty of rest and lots of hard candy.

When I reached the hospital, they placed me in an eight-by-ten foot open-ended cubical and told me not to move. If I had to relieve myself, they would take me to the latrine in a wheel chair. Then began a daily extraction of blood. I was told that under no circumstances was I to drink alcohol. I was placed on a high carbohydrate diet.

Next to my bed was a box of hard candy that I was to suck continually. After one month at the mercy of the hospital staff, I was allowed to do things for myself. Apparently the treatment was effective and I was getting better. In fact I was feeling better than I had in years. I believe that I read everything in the limited library of the hospital, so I asked the volunteer Red Cross people to provide me with water paints and paper. I began to draw and paint and gave most of my new work away to the staff or the other patients.

I was in the officer's ward with some of the strangest characters. One of these was a doctor from Minnesota by the name of Reed. I believe that he was a descendent of the famous Dr. Walter Reed of Panama fame. I did not know what was wrong with him, however we had great conversations. Shortly after my arrival, the Commanding Officer of the Hospital joined us with a beautiful case of dysentery which he contracted in his own hospital. He was so proud that no one on his staff ever had this dreaded affliction that his condition almost put him a state of shock. All his meals had been taken at the hospital mess. He should have known the Russian doctor that I met in China who told me that one could take every imaginable precaution, boiling everything, cooking everything and washing one's hands every five minutes, and still get dysentery. All it takes is a fly taking off from a pile of human feces and landing on one's lips!

Another strange individual resided three cubicles away from mine. He was an American colonel who had been an advisor to the Chinese Army. A

Chinese lady visited him daily. He would close the curtains of the cubicle and judging by the noises coming from behind the closed curtains, something must have been going on! We did not see what the colonel and his friend were doing but the heavy breathing and the groaning left no doubt in our minds. This Colonel had a serious dislike for the hospital and for the nurses in particular. Our nurses were housed in the center of the compound. Their building was surrounded by a fence covered with tarpaulin so that it was impossible to see inside their small inclosure. This condition annoyed the old Colonel who claimed that as he was an officer, and by extension a gentleman, he did not have to be treated as a potential peeping tom. One day he asked me to make some signs which stated: "Off Limits to hospital Staff, specifically nurses". I made approximately six of these and he went placing them in various areas of the hospital. Of course it did not take long for the C.O. to find out and, as I was the only artist in residence, he appeared in front of my cubicle with the head nurse. I kept silent as he made his accusations, but it was obvious that I was going to be held responsible until my patron the Colonel showed up and compared dates of rank with the hospital administrator. That would be the end of the controversy.

There were three other officers with hepatitis in our ward. All three were very young pilots. They were being given the same treatment as I, but once they were able to move about they asked for passes and went to town. They could not resist the booze, and very soon they took a turn for the worse. Two of them did not make it, dying in the hospital; the third was sent home, but never made it. He passed away before reaching home.

The political situation in India was becoming very serious. The Hospital was surrounded with hostile elements and we could hear the masses outside our compound marching and reciting slogans. The British tried to maintain law and order with military or police patrols, but most of the time they were outnumbered. I recall seeing one of their trucks covered with strong wire mesh to protect them from the rocks thrown by the rampaging people.

One day, one of our ambulances was dispatched to pick up either an injured or sick American soldier. When it returned, the mob surrounded the ambulance and killed the driver. Only the medical corpsman escaped. The patient burned in the ambulance. It was a shocking incident for all of us. Perhaps the only reason why we were not harmed was because in the middle of the compound stood a Buddhist shrine open to worshipers, and cattle, which made the administrator of the hospital very nervous. As the situation deteriorated outside, we remained more and more within the safety of our compound. Trips to town were out of the question, and if it was necessary to venture outside, we went in groups escorted by our own military police or the British Army.

As time went by, my condition improved significantly. The staff invited me to their parties, and plays. Their favorite pastime was charades. Perhaps I was the only patient enjoying this type of diversion, however the staff of the hospital's Section 8, which was the psycho ward, were the most dedicated charade players. One doctor and one of his nurses were unbelievable. The two practiced telepathy, and the rest of us tried to stump them with words or phrases that we thought so tricky as to be impossible to describe by signs and motion. When it was the nurse's turn, she would read the message on the paper given by the opposing team, close her eyes and the doctor, closing his, would apparently read her mind. After a few tries, he would usually get it. When it was his turn to pass on the message to the nurse, he was usually more effective. She would get it faster and more accurately. This display of telepathy completely baffled most of us skeptics. Some of the other doctors were certain that there was some trick at play, but none could be found. Apparently this doctor and his nurse had been practicing telepathy for a long time.

At times, the evenings were so hot that our cubicles were very uncomfortable. I was on good terms with the staff so that when I asked to have my bed moved outside under the eaves which extended approximately 10 feet over the concrete walk, they agreed. I was the only one with this privilege and it was great to feel the gentle breeze moving the mosquito net covering my bed.

I had become very friendly with one of the nurses. When she was on duty at night she would join me between her rounds and slip under the mosquito net sit on my bed as we talked. The other patients kidded me about sleeping with my nurse, but I did not tell them that she was more afraid of the mosquitoes than of me!

Eventually I improved to the point where my blood was checked only twice a week. I was not getting any worse, but only slightly better. I had become very attached to my nurse and I feared that she was becoming serious. Only much later did I learn how serious she actually was.

Three months later, after consuming a ton of hard candy and having blood drawn every other day, I was released from the hospital and flown to Karachi, the first leg of my trip back home. There

The author, two patients and nurses of the 127 GH at Calcutta, India. The officer standing to the right of the author is Dr. Reed.

we were housed in a tent city pending our assignment to a ship bound for the United States. It was very hot and steamy. None of the other officers on the flight had been in my unit or even in OSS. We had very little in common, however we got along well because we were going home, and that was the most important thing on our minds. I missed the hospital, but most of all my nurse with whom I could talk, sometimes for hours. The days seemed very long as a result of the oppressive heat and the general boredom. The side flaps of our tent were lifted to allow in the light breeze, but only at night was the temperature bearable. When it rained, as it did a few times, the entire area was transformed into a lake.

Eventually we received our orders to report to the port of Karachi where the SS Santa Clara, a troop ship, was waiting to take us home. When we reached the port we joined a long line of U.S. troops climbing aboard the converted ocean liner. It seemed that the ship was filled to capacity. I shared a cabin on the second deck with four other officers. I did not feel well, probably because my liver was still acting up. However my companions were very kind. One in particular, Joe Minton, took great care of me. If and when I was not able to go to the ship's mess for a meal he would bring me something to eat, usually fruit. Joe was a pilot who had flown combat cargo aircraft in China and probably had supplied our team in the Tonkin jungle. Eventually I felt well enough to go on the deck to bask in the sun and enjoy the fellowship of the other returnees.

Our ship followed the southern coast of the Saudi Arabian peninsula. Past Aden, we entered the Red Sea and headed for the Suez Canal. Up to that point the sea had been calm, but it was even more so in the Canal. The coast-line on either side of the canal was only sand and rocks. From time to time, as we moved slowly under the expert guidance of a French pilot, we would pass near small buildings, the type one would see in France, and all around them green grass, a few trees, and of course a garden. No doubt a French engineer or employee of the Canal lived there as the French and the British still controlled this waterway.

Eventually we reached Port Said, the major Egyptian city on the Mediterranean side of the Canal. It seemed that the Canal was flowing right through the middle of the city. The buildings came right to the edge of the water and we could see into the apartments of the residents; some waved to us as we passed by. The sun was setting when we left the calm waters of the Canal and entered the Mediterranean Sea. The smooth sailing was abruptly replaced by a pitching and yawing that did nothing for our stomachs. We were told that it was always the case in that area, but that eventually a calmer sea would return. And it did.

We passed by an island off the cost of Sardinia, which was the only island captured from the Germans by our Air Force. It was said that its German occupiers had surrendered after a heavy Allied bombing, and without the involvement of our infantry. I kept wondering if this was a true story. All the pilots and crews aboard most certainly believed it. We reached the southern tip of Spain and slid by the Rock of Gibraltar which was barely visible though the squalls which pelted our ship. Our entrance into the Mediterranean Sea seemed a precursor to what was to come as we entered the Atlantic Ocean. When we passed the Rock, our ship became a cork bouncing up and down, rolling from side to side.

Ahead of us, all the way to our destination, waited a series of hurricanes. Originally, we were to reach New York within four, or at the most five, days. Instead we spent ten days circumnavigating one hurricane after the other, moving further and further south, until we were on the same latitude as Brazil. The winds abated and the waves, which had reached twenty feet, returned to normal. It was December. We would all be home for Christmas.

Back Home Again

As we disembarked at the port of Brooklyn, I could not help noticing that the plates of our ship's prow were buckled as if they had been smashed against a solid object. We had been told that the ship had suffered some damage, but I did not expect this much.

For once the Army was extremely well organized. At the port, processing was expertly handled. Records were examined and orders checked while a military band played welcoming marches. Representatives of the American Legion, the VFW and other military organizations sat behind small tables enticing people to sign up. The Reserve Officers Association offered me a membership that I promptly accepted, a move I have never regretted. My destination was not my home in New Jersey; it was Washington, DC, where I was hoping to line up a job with either the military or the State Department. While I was in the hospital OSS had been deactivated as a military organization by President Truman. I was not yet aware of its replacement.

Georgette Bennett the sister of Lowell, was a WAVE assigned to the Navy Bureau of Personnel in Washington. When I reached our Capital, we met and almost immediately decided to be married. I believe that I was more anxious than she. In any case, we went to Bethesda and found an obliging minister who conducted a very quick service, witnessed by his wife and a friend of mine. For me, the war was over but the battle for survival had just begun.

Our first night in bed was a disaster. Georgette did not have the technique of Mr. Ho's guest entèrtainer. The day after my marriage to Georgette I called my mother. She was very surprised and did not sound very happy. I suspect that she did not approve though she did not actually say so.

I was the first to return to New Jersey, because it took some time for Georgette to be released by the Navy based on her new status as a married woman. My mother-in-law, Marguerite, was happier about the marriage than my own mother. My father-in-law only growled: "She married a frog, and a damn Catholic?"

I am sure that he did not entirely approve of the marriage of his daughter to a "foreigner"—a Frenchman—and a Catholic to boot.

George Schlatter, with whom we stayed when we reached the United States, had given me my first job six years ago, now had his own company, a small shop employing two toolmakers. He again offered me a job and I immediately accepted. The salary was small but it was a job. To make things easier for me, George offered us an apartment on the top of his garage. The place was old and required much work to make it livable. George expected me to fix it as a consideration for the low rent!

Gertrude, George's spouse, and Georgette did not get along. Gertrude had hoped that I would marry one of their daughters! As a result we reached the conclusion that it would be best if we found our own apartment near the shop.

Our first apartment was close to the railroad station, making it very convenient for me to get to work. We shared a bathroom with another couple, and everything went well for us until the bed which came with the place, and whose spring was supported by several stacked books, collapsed. We knew we had to find a better place.

We looked into the possibility of buying a house through the GI Bill, and since both of us were veterans we had no trouble getting a loan with a minimal down payment made with the money mother had saved for me. We received the first home mortgage in the state of New Jersey under the then-new veterans' benefits which made the local headlines. We selected a multi-family residence so that the rental income would help pay for the mortgage. We occupied the first floor while tenants occupied the second and third floors.

The house was located in an old neighborhood in process of transformation. One of the houses at the end of the block had been purchased by a black doctor married to a former spouse of Jackie Robinson. When my father-in-law heard about this he predicted that we would lose our shirt. The house would depreciate so much that we would never be able to sell it.

Georgette found a job as a receptionist at a doctor's office not far from our home. We had no car, but public transportation was convenient and affordable. We spent most of our time fixing up the house. Strangely enough, given its generally bad shape, it had excellent plumbing, all copper, unusual for that type of house.

One day as I was visiting mother, she told me that a nurse who had met me in India had called. She wanted to get in touch with me. When mother told her that I was married and were I lived, the line went dead. I supposed she was more serious about our past relation than I suspected.

My job as a toolmaker with Schlatter was not very profitable. I decided to look for another place of employment. I went to the shop where I had worked prior to entering the service but they had no position available. They suggested that I go down the street and check with the Lionel Corporation. I made an application and was hired immediately. It was not as convenient to reach as the other shop, but the salary was a lot better. Occasionally I would get a ride with a co-worker and eventually I was included in a car pool.

Compared with all the places I had previously worked, this was the largest and the best equipped tool shop I had ever seen. The toolmakers were mostly German, Swiss and Italian. I was the only Frenchman.

214

Fortunately for me I was well liked and had no problems, especially after one of the fat Italians decided that he could beat me in a fair fight. He had escaped the army but fancied himself to be a good boxer. I knew that I could never beat him, but as he kept pushing me, one day I relented and in the solitude of the wash room we sparred. He came at me but instead of taking his first shot, I slid under him on my back, grabbed one of his legs with mine and twisted my body. Taken by surprise, he almost fell on top of me. Before he realized what had happened, I jumped on his back, took one of his arms and twisted it back. That was the beginning of a long friendship. Not only did his teasing stopped, he became my protector. That was the only time that I used the training the British had given me.

Lionel was a fairly large company manufacturing two completely unrelated products. They made the famous Lionel trains and an electric fence to control farm animals. I was involved mostly with the train, working on the huge white metal molds to manufacture the locomotives. This was a very tedious job requiring some skill. At times I was working with molds worth over $10,000. My greatest fear was making one mistake and having to work the next two years for nothing. One of my jobs was to make the dies for a project that can still be purchased in hobby shops. It was the platform for the milk deliverer. This item consisted of the platform, small cans of milk and an individual who moved the milk cans from the wagon to the platform or vice versa.

What surprised me the most about Lionel was the security. Access to the research department was closed to all except to those who worked there. If and when I had to consult with them, I also had to be escorted. All were under guard. It was tighter than the Pentagon's security. The enemy was American Flier, Lionel's arch competitor. In the past American Flier had sent spies to penetrate Lionel's plant and discover new developments for the following year so that they could copy them and perhaps beat Lionel to the punch. The production was fantastic. Two to three months before Christmas, truck loads of trains would leave for the various markets. They even had plane loads of trains going to South America.

After I was released from active duty, I had kept my Reserve status and was assigned to a reserve unit which existed only on paper. To maintain my status as reserve officer I was obliged to take correspondence courses on military science and to attend some active training as units were organized. I completed several courses and concentrated on cryptanalysis, so as to acquire an additional MOS (Military Occupation Specialty).

My basic MOS was Intelligence Specialist because the Army did not have spy or saboteur specialties! My secondary MOS was Infantry Unit Commander, a specialty even less in demand. Cryptanalysis is a fascinating science, and although I found it very difficult to master, I was amazed how by deduction I was able to break codes, not the most difficult ones, but codes just the same.

I had joined the ROA (Reserve Officers Association) which had a very active chapter in our area. I shall never forget some of the comments I heard during meetings. The topic was "Negroes in the Service". Several high-ranking officers made speeches asking the membership to write to our congressman about the need to keep the armed forces out of the reach of Black people. They predicted that if we allowed the unchecked enlistment of blacks into the military, the whites would lose control of the Armed Force and eventually this would lead to a revolution. Up to that time I had not seen many black servicemen in the military.

Although I was busy working long overtime hours for Lionel, I managed to become involved in a few outside projects. One of our neighbors was an engineer who had come up with an interesting idea. He had designed a rocket propelled by a cartridge of CO_2, the kind that was used to make seltzer water. His rocket was approximately 12 inches long, one inch in diameter and shaped similarly to the German V-2 rocket. The CO_2 cartridge did fit snugly into the head of the rocket. When punctured by a small nail protruding at the end a the wooden dowel used as a launching device, the rocket would fly straight up to 400 feet, leaving behind a trail of frozen gas. This was quite interesting except that the launching was too awkward and not realistic enough. What was needed was a platform with a launcher similar to those used by the Germans. That was where I came in.

I was instrumental both in designing the launcher, and in producing the mold to make the body of the rocket. I invested some money in the mold and in the purchase of a molding machine. Before completing the project, and before having a decent inventory, we decided to offer the idea to several toy manufacturers. I did not go to Lionel, which was my first mistake, but the second, even worse, was not taking the 3% of wholesale price offered by one company that saw the value of the toy. "They must think that we are stupid," we said to each other. We expected at least 25%. After all, we were the designers who had developed the idea. Our third mistake was to advertise the product in *Popular Science* magazine before we had the product in production.

When the mold was completed, in our basement, we began to make the plastic bodies of the rockets one at a time. The production rate came close to one an hour if we counted the rejects. Three weeks after advertising, we began to receive orders. One or two, then ten and thirty, then many more orders were received in the mail each day..

Many of the orders were accompanied by checks, even cash. One order from Israel was for 2,000. At our rate of production it would have taken twenty years to complete that order. Perhaps they saw some military value in our rocket. Could it be used against the Palestinians? We realized that our situation was hopeless and that it would take a miracle or a bundle of cash for us to be able to swing it. So we returned all the money and the checks with letters of apology.

About that time my philosophy of life of life changed completely. Up to then I took my wedding vow very seriously.

I had married Georgette for better and for worse, but I never dreamt that the worst was to come so soon. I accidentally discovered that Georgette was not true to her promise to forsake all others. From the very beginning I had trusted her implicitly.

I realized that she was not very careful in spending our money, but since she contributed somewhat it did not make too much difference. One day she told me that she would be going to New York to visit a friend she had met in the Navy. I thought nothing of it until I tried to get in touch with my rocket-design partner. I was told by his mother that he was also in New York! I found it strange that both would be in New York at the same time. I located the telephone number of Georgette's friend in New York and called her. Not only had she not seen Georgette, she was not expecting her! When she returned a day or so later, it was not very difficult for me to learn the truth, which she admitted readily. She never said that she was sorry. She could not explain why she had decided to accept my partner's invitation to go to New York and have sex in a hotel room. The only excuse she offered was that she did not enjoy it and that he was not very good at it. I was tempted to use the Japanese sword that I had brought back from Vietnam on my partner, but reason prevailed. He, being no fool, decided that it was safer for him to leave town.

But I was deeply hurt. The two people I trusted most had deceived me. It took me a while to recover and carefully plan my next move. Having taken the marriage vows seriously, and accepting this situation as the worst that could fall upon me, I believed that the better might soon follow. Believing that perhaps I could change her ways, I decided to overlook her transgression. Instead of telling her to go or leaving her, I said nothing and never mentioned the incident to her again.

Yet from that time on I never fully trusted Georgette, and often I used this incident to justify my own behavior. In retrospect I should have left her right then.

Shortly thereafter Georgette discovered that she was pregnant. Although I was trying to get her pregnant it might have been the result of her trip to New York with my partner. We would never know because on her third or fourth month she miscarried. Fortunately for us, one of our tenants was a doctor, and his spouse, though a slob, was a nurse. They took care of her when she had her miscarriage. I did not dwell on the past and managed to carry on as best as I could, but was aware that the trust on my part was gone when I wondered if the miscarriage might really have been an abortion.

To revive the past and perhaps improve the present we decided that a vacation was in order for both of us and selected Washington D.C., where both of us had been stationed and where we began our married life. We took the train to the Capital and stayed in a nice hotel. We visited museums, various sights and friends of Georgette who lived in nearby Virginia.

Before returning home I decided to stop by the Pentagon, a building I never had the time to see properly during the war. As I was strolling in the wide corridors, admiring the pictures on the walls, I came to the Ordnance Department section. As I passed by an open door, I noticed an officer sitting at a desk, an OSS friend with whom I had served in China.

After bringing each other up to date, he asked what I was doing. I gave him a brief description and casually mentioned our rocket. This piqued his attention and he wanted to know more. I supposed that I made it sound a lot better that it actually was. Nevertheless, he asked for my address and telephone number and we parted as old friends, promising to see each other again soon.

We returned home a few days later. When I opened the front door, I discovered a piece of paper on the floor. It was a telegram. I opened it quickly and nearly fell over as I read the contents. It was from the U.S. Army, recalling me to active duty and giving me one week to settle my affairs and report to the Aberdeen Proving Ground. I knew the installation well, having been stationed there during the War.

My parents took the news casually but Lionel was not as understanding. They had given me a promotion, rating me a First Class toolmaker, and I had a rather important project to complete when I told them that I was leaving. But when Uncle Sam calls, there is very little one can do but obey.

Recalled To Active Duty

We decided that I would report and scout the area before Georgette would join me. On November 16, 1947, I took the train in Newark and got off at Aberdeen where an Army truck drove me to the Proving Ground and the BOQ, my temporary quarters. After processing, I was directed to area of the post I had never before seen, the place where research was conducted on various weapons, especially on ballistics. Strangely, I arrived as one of the first computers was being delivered.

It was AVAC—a huge piece of equipment which occupied a large room.

I was lucky enough to see it briefly but was more impressed by the comments made by those who were to use it, especially those by a young lady who appeared to be the boss of the entire operation. I remembered that during the war my father had made instruments related to ballistic research for the Proving Ground. His were mechanical and far less complicated than this huge piece of equipment.

After things quieted down, I was interviewed to determine where I would be assigned. Until then I had no idea why I had been recalled to Aberdeen. As an officer my MOS were related to Intelligence and Infantry, not to Ordnance. However, because in those days there was no intelligence branch, and as all personnel for administrative reasons had to be assigned to a branch, I was officially classified as an Infantry Unit Commander. As I was recalled by the Ordnance Department of the Army, from now on I would be considered an ordnance officer. I realized quickly that they wanted me because of my toy rocket. They never took the time to check my friend's story.

They placed my name in the hopper and that was it. It did not take them long to discover that my knowledge of rocketry was limited and that I had no business in that area.

However, I was there and available, and there was a need to fill other slots. So they kept me, and assigned me to the correspondence course section of the Reserve Component. My job was to work on the tests given at the end of the various courses. First I had to complete all the courses, then take the tests to determine if these were indicative of the courses. This was the most boring job I had ever had! I looked forward to Fridays when I would catch the train home for the weekend. On Sunday evening, I was back on the train, heading back to the same boring job.

Christmas 1947 passed and the cold days began. One weekend I was about to leave Aberdeen when it started to snow.

By the time we reached Wilmington, Delaware, six inches of snow covered the ground. An even foot of the white stuff covered the rails by the time we reached Philadelphia. It was as bad at Trenton. When we arrived at Newark the train had trouble moving. We could not see what was going on outside because the station was covered. When I stepped out of the waiting room, I could not believe my eyes. This part of the city, usually busy with traffic, was completely empty.

Twenty-two inches of snow had fallen. Some had been plowed into view-obstructing mounds and all was deadly quiet. It seemed as if the city had died. Normally I would have taken a bus to East Orange and gotten off a block away from my house. But there were no buses in the street. So, I decided to walk to the Lackawanna station and take a commuter train that would stop at a station a few blocks from our house.

It took me over half an hour to cover ten short blocks.

When I arrived at the station, I discovered that I was not the only one with the same idea. Of course the train was late, but it finally arrived, filled to capacity. I and several others had to stand on the rear platform but, braving the freezing gale and the snow, we managed to hold on until we reached the East Orange Station. We did not see the conductor, who was blocked in the center of the wagon by the crowd. Thus this had been a free ride for most of the passengers.

I was wearing my jump boots, but snow came up to my knees. When I reached our house, surprisingly no lights showed in the windows. I had a key.

Opening the door I was shocked by the heat of the apartment, and by a strange odor similar to that of a barn or an animal pen.

As we had no dogs, I could not understand the nature of this smell. I flipped the switch and could not believe what I saw.

In the dining room, on top of the curtains hanging by his finger tips and his tail, was a monkey. He was rather small but had a very long tail. No one had mentioned a monkey to me. For a moment I thought that perhaps Georgette had been transformed. But reason took over and I called my mother-in-law, the most logical place for Georgette to be.

Indeed she was there, and so was her brother, Lowell, who had just returned from Brazil with the spider monkey. The monkey made the voyage from the Brazilian jungle to the freezing weather of New Jersey in Lowell's overcoat pocket. Now only a super hot house could help him survive. It took one week to clean the mess, and no one missed the spider monkey when he left with Lowell, for Berlin of all places.

I was expecting to pursue a career in the Ordnance Department when I received a surprising order to report to Fort Holabird, Maryland. I quickly learned that it was from the intelligence center and that I was being considered for the Counterintelligence School that would be starting shortly. I did not expect an immediate move overseas, so we decided to sell our house and Georgette would move to Baltimore, preferably in Dundalk, a suburb closer to the Fort. Georgette was responsible for the sale of the house while I attended school with little time to spare. Our class consisted of approximately 40 officers, one half male and the other half female, one of us with a rank of higher than captain. Most of us were World War II veterans, some with combat experience, and two of us were former OSS officers with intelligence backgrounds.

The school was tough because in some cases we were being taught things that were contrary to our own experiences by people who had none, only book knowledge. As a result, the ones with the highest grades were the women officers who memorized the book, and the last were those with the most experience. I might have flunked the course but for the determination of Lt. Ann Bray. She made damn sure that we all passed, working with us until late at night, making us repeat our lessons for the next day's test. We all passed and had a class party.

By that time Georgette had sold the house.

Contrary to her father's prediction, she sold it for three thousand dollars more than we paid for it. I had found an apartment at Dundalk within walking distance of the Fort. We moved in just about the time I was to take a Japanese language course. It was not the best apartment, but it was not the worst, except that our bedroom window was in line with the flight path of the Baltimore Airport. The landing lights of every plane approaching at night shone through the window and onto our bed. At first it was disconcerting because we believed that the pilots could see us, but we learned to live with it and forget it.

I completed the Japanese language course and fully expected to receive orders for Japan. Instead I was assigned to the Counterintelligence School as an instructor. As the assignment at the school was normally for two years I decided that we had to move to better quarters. It was almost impossible to rent a decent apartment in the area, so we did what many others had to do, we bought a house. It was a little further from the post than we had hoped, but public transportation was available and many of our neighbors employed at the Fort were willing to give me a ride if I needed one.

Actually I did not mind walking the 2 1/2 miles between our house and the Post. On the way I would pass by several huge warehouses and a distillery that smelled heavenly. I wondered at times if the smell was giving me a buzz. Unlike the other instructors who were somewhat subdued in the morning, I was happy and ready to go. It could have been the walk or the smell of the booze that was responsible for my good humor. In winter the walk was not as pleasant, but my warm three-quarter-length field coat left over from the war made it bearable.

My job turned out to be more than that of a classroom instructor.

I was a demonstration expert teaching the fundamentals of surveillance, the art of following someone without being detected and reporting the subject's actions thoroughly and accurately. Having been trained as an espionage agent by the British SOE, the Command of the School probably felt that I was qualified to teach counter-measures as well. The best way to teach the basic method of avoiding detection was to make the students practice what they learned in the classroom. Once they had mastered the various techniques of the trade, they went into the second phase—the tailing procedure.

This course of instruction was at times hilarious to us instructors but terribly embarrassing to the students. One time a student was tailing me rather closely because we did not have much time nor a good area in which to do the job adequately. I took him in an area of the Fort which was not used very much but which I knew well. He was doing fine until he became too impatient and did not pay attention as to where he was going. Casually I walked into the post gymnasium, went directly to the Ladies room and hid behind the door. Sure enough the student went right in after me. I closed the door and stood in front of it blocking his escape.

"What are you doing here?"

"I am not following you, sir."

"But what are you doing here?"

I concluded then that he was not aware that he was in the ladies' room and, opening the door, I pointed to the sign "LADIES". He shook his head in disgust but said nothing. The tailing was over for him and he was sure that he had flunked the course. We did not tell the student that we never flunked anyone for their mistakes. At the debriefing sessions we had a lot of laughs telling the other students what each had done either well or poorly.

Often I was the subject of the attention of the students from early in the morning to sometime late at night. They had to learn how to observe ordinary actions as well as extraordinary or strange activities under all conditions. The time and place of our exercises were constantly changed which meant that, at times, I had to be in place early in the morning. As a result I would not report to my section but go directly from my house to the area that had been designated for the day's exercise. I had to do the things that an average person would do in the course of the day. So I went shopping, went to the bank, the cleaners, and the like.

One day, needing nails for my house, I decided to go to a hardware store that happened to be next door to a bar. I had a student on my tail, so I first made believe I was going to the bar, but instead went through the hardware store door. It took a while for the student to realize where I was. A minute or so later he appeared. Immediately one of the clerks approached him and asked him what he wanted. The student replied, "I would like a six pack of beer." The clerk looked at the owner who was helping me. The owner looked at me, and we all burst out laughing. "The beer is next door," said the clerk to the red-faced student. He was so intense in observing my every action that he forgot where he was. I kept telling the students to take things easy. It is far better to lose a subject than to be "made" or identified as a tail.

One day I took the opportunity, while being followed by some students, to do some banking. This time some of the students were driving government vehicles equipped with radios while others were on foot. Their challenge was to coordinate their efforts and in doing so make the tail more effective and more discreet. The cars had out-of-state license plates. When they saw me enter the bank, they should have waited for me to leave and then continue their surveillance. They might have sent one student into the bank to observe while the others waited outside. Instead three of the students rushed into the bank right behind me pushing aside customers who were leaving. I was not aware of this, but one of the bank clerks, thinking that this was a holdup, pushed the panic button and before I had completed my transaction, the bank was surrounded by the police and our students were arrested. That was the last time I went to the bank during a training session.

I was given a direct order to stay away from banks when students were on a surveillance exercise.

My job was not what I would consider the best in the world. Everything was make-believe. It did not have the excitement found in real cases of espionage, but it was an important and necessary occupation. It was an easy job which allowed me to work on our house that was part of a block of four row houses typical in Baltimore.

In July 1948, I learned through the grapevine that the Army was looking for people to attend the Language School in Monterey, California. The Counter-Intelligence Corps (CIC) encouraged its personnel to take a second language even if they were already proficient in one. I had two languages, French my native tongue, and Japanese I had learned at the School, though it was only spoken Japanese, not the written language which took a lot longer. I applied for a new language and Albanian was my third choice.

Surprisingly I was immediately accepted. I learned the reason why later. It seems that no one else had volunteered for the one-year course.

The Presidio of Monterey

I took a few days of leave, during which we sold our house, packed our household goods and sent them ahead to California. We took the train and went to the West Coast via Chicago, Indianapolis, St. Louis and Kansas City, where we stopped for a few days to meet some of Georgette's relatives; then on to Denver, Salt Lake City and eventually San Francisco, where we stayed at the Pickwick Hotel in the heart of the city.

From there we went along the coast to Monterey and stayed at the Monterey Hotel, which at that time was the only decent hotel in town.

The Army Language School, as it was known, was located at the Presidio on the highest part of the peninsula. From there, one could see the bay and the usual two destroyers anchored close to the shore.

Before the classes began we were able to locate a first-floor apartment within Monterey proper on the road to Carmel. We had nice neighbors. One of them was an active duty officer stationed at Fort Ord. Another was a disabled veteran who worked as a tennis pro at the Pebble Beach Country Club. With him we were able to get into places very few people could, even occasionally into the Club itself to watch professional and amateur golf matches. Once I was lucky enough to watch the antics of Bing Crosby and Bob Hope prior to a game. I had my movie camera and captured both on film.

Monterey was a great resort area enlivened by its surrounding towns: Pacific Grove and its Cannery Row, Del Monte with its advance Naval School and officers club featuring an oval bar, sexy wallpaper and slot machines, and Carmel by the Sea with its Pebble Beach and the famous Lone Cypress. Time for us passed very quickly.

Prior to leaving Dundalk for school, we discovered that Georgette was pregnant. We went to the closest military hospital, at nearby Fort Ord, for her check up and all seemed to be fine. Then, when ahead of time she began her labor, some friends drove us to the hospital. I waited and waited but no one would talk to me. I kept asking, but they told me that the Doctor would explain. I knew then that something was wrong and indeed it was. If it was to be a girl, she was to be Danielle. It was a girl but she was stillborn. This was a shock to Georgette and to me, but there was nothing we could do about it. After a small funeral service conducted by a Catholic Chaplain and attended by two of our neighbors, we buried the small box containing the remains of the little Danielle in the Presidio Cemetery alongside the soldiers and officers who had been laid to rest there.

Georgette was crushed by this loss. When she learned about the stillbirth she became hysterical and had to be sedated. She blamed everything and everybody, including me, for her misfortune. It was a very sad period for me because I wanted a baby as much as she did, and inwardly I thought that perhaps I was to blame for the stillbirth. The doctors gave us no reason; to them it was only a statistic.

Georgette was released from the hospital a few days later and we tried to make the best of a bad situation.

Albanian was not as difficult as some other languages such as Chinese, Russian or Japanese. It had many words similar to French and Italian, and its Greek and Roman roots were quite apparent though sprinkled with Arabic. We had two instructors who came from two distinct parts of Albania. We learned very quickly that Moslems did not like Christians and vise versa, and that Tosks and Ghegs had no great love for each other either. Of course, one of our teachers came from one area where they said things one way and the other came from a part of Albania where they said the same things the other way. One was a younger individual who had come to this country very young; the other was a professor who was on sabbatical from Columbia University.

Initially our class consisted of four students including a Mormon from Utah. This was an ideal learning situation. We lost two of our students after six months, so only two of us finished the course. By that time I was eager to leave California despite the good time we had on the beaches and visiting Big Sur, San Jose and Salinas and its rodeo. We also left behind some good friends, in particular a couple in their middle 50's who had lived next door. They had built a motel with only a few rooms in the center of Carmel. Each of the rooms was decorated in the style of a specific country. One was a Chinese room. They asked me to paint some Chinese pictures to decorate the room, which I did. Unfortunately we lost contact with them and many others.

The Baltimore Field Office

Shortly before our graduation, I received my orders to report to Fort Meade, Maryland. I was assigned to a Counterintelligence unit of the Second Army. We traveled back to Washington on the train, and eventually to Fort Meade which lies between Washington DC and Baltimore. The closest town to the Fort was Laurel, known for its race track. In June 1949, I reported to the 109th Detachment at Baltimore Field Office.

The office was in one of the oldest buildings in the center of town. The Agent in Charge was a Captain and the first thing he did with new assignees was to check their driving skill. I was told to report to the examiner at Fort Meade to obtain a military driver's license. I had driven Jeeps and GM trucks, but never a standard sedan.

The sergeant in charge placed me behind the wheel of a 1948 Chevrolet four-door sedan and said, "Go ahead Sir."

I put the car in gear and killed the engine. I started again and, in fits and starts, managed to jerkily drive for half a block. The sergeant took pity on me and said calmly that I needed a refresher course. For one week I remained at Fort Meade and every day I took the sergeant or one of his helpers in the school Jeep for a ride. First we stayed on the country roads, then little by little he let me use more important roads with heavier traffic until I graduated to the interstate highway. Then we did the same thing with a GM 6x6 truck until I was able to park it properly. Eventually they allowed me to drive a sedan, and issued me a driver's license good for all military vehicles up to a ten-tons.

As a CIC agent, my job consisted of interviewing people who were either character references provided by applicants, or the applicant's former and present neighbors listed in their application. In addition we were supposed to develop sources of information from these interviews. The information we obtained was recorded in a very precise way as prescribed by current CIC regulations or instructions. Having graduated from CIC school did not necessarily qualify me as a suitable agent for that particular field office. I was placed under the wing of a more experienced agent not much older than I, and I acted as his helper until I was deemed ready to operate on my own. I learned several years later that I had been assigned to this agent because his report writing left much to be desired, and that the SAC felt he could learn something from me! For the next few weeks we worked together. When doing a neighborhood investigation he would take one side of the street and I would take the other side.

One early afternoon only one neighborhood interview was left to finish a case, a background investigation. The subject of the investigation had applied for a position within the Army that required a security clearance. He had given several names as character references and the address of the last one was in a very nice neighborhood. My associate decided to do this one quickly. He asked me to stay in the car and wait for him. I waited and waited, but after half an hour I decided that there must be something wrong; it should not take that long for an interview as this case had been a routine investigation up to that point. I locked the vehicle, and went to the door he had entered. When the door bell was pushed the door opened and a beautiful girl invited me in and directed me to what appeared to be a waiting room. The inside of the house was decorated in the Victorian style with a lot of red velvet and period furniture. She said that someone would be with me in a moment.

I replied that I was looking for my friend who had come in over half an hour ago.

"Oh! You are with him. He is in the kitchen with the matron," she said as she pointed towards the kitchen. I went in and sure enough, my buddy was sitting at a table with an older dame, both sipping beers. I inquired as to what was going on.

He advised me that we were in a bordello, a house of ill repute, and that the character reference was the head madam of the place. She was a very interesting lady who was running a very risky business, probably under the protection of some very powerful people in Baltimore. It is possible that the individual gave her name as a character reference not knowing what she actually did for a living. We stayed a while longer, talking to some of the girls who had drifted into the kitchen.

We were offered the services of the establishment but we declined and left laughing our heads off.

I wondered what the people who had to make the decision on this case would do. But this was not our concern. We could not hide what we had discovered very long because the typists who prepared all of our reports were not very discreet within the organization. News travels fast in a CIC field office and before long we had to tell the rest of the agents what we had discovered. I returned there a few months later but the house was empty and there was a "For Sale" sign in front! Very likely the madam and all the girls had moved to another section of the city and only their habitués knew where.

Baltimore was known to be a very rough city, the playground of Washington, DC. The Mob was known to operate there almost openly. Once I had to interview a character reference in a rather sleazy neighborhood. I located the house and knocked on the door. I waited a while until the door opened and out stepped a character from a Damon Runyon story.

He was wearing a hat, a striped shirt and a pin-striped suit.

"What do you want?" he asked.

I told him that I was a CIC agent looking for a certain person whose name had been given as a character reference. He waved me in!

So I entered and in a bare room behind a small desk was another individual, much bigger, but dressed in the same fashion.

"What do you want? Who sent you?" he asked.

I repeated what I had told the other individual. Then he inquired, "What do you want to know? What did he do?"

I felt that I was getting nowhere and should probably take my leave. I looked back, but instead of one individual there were now two blocking the door, and I could see their shoulder holsters and the butts of their pistols peeking from their lapels. I knew then that I better do some fast talking as I was in a nest of gangsters who probably thought that I was either the police or the FBI. As calmly as I could, I explained that this address belonged to a certain individual whose name had been given to us as a character reference.

"If you are this gentleman I am sure that you will know who I am referring to, if not I am sorry to have disturbed you."

This did not convince my interlocutor who said, "Who did you say you were with?"

I took my agent identification and handed it to him. He looked at it for about five minutes and then said, "You're not with the Feds?" I agreed vehemently assuring him that I was with the Army and had nothing to do either with the local police or the Feds. Apparently I convinced him, for he stood up and shook my hand. His two gorillas stepped aside and I left as fast as I could without showing my hurry. The incident was reported to the Baltimore Police who, to my knowledge, did nothing.

Occasionally I had to conduct interviews in predominantly black neighborhoods. Invariably the individual I would interview would disclaim knowledge of the subject of our investigation even though it was obvious that they had been neighbors and close friends. "I never heard of him," was the usual reply. We even heard that remark from his own relatives who did not want to talk to anyone wearing a suit and a tie.

We used a technique that usually worked. Once we received a negative reply we would say, "That's too bad. He inherited some money and we are trying to locate some of his friends and relatives." This usually did the trick and opened the door to further discussion and the information we needed.

At time CIC Special Agents had some very strange experiences. I had my share. One of these made a strong impression and added much to my knowledge of psychology and experiences as an investigator. On the second floor of an apartment building I knocked at the door of one of the neighbors of the subject of my investigation. He was a police officer. The interview was very easy because the officer knew exactly how to reply to my questions.

Then I knocked at the door of the other apartment on the same floor. A woman's voice said: "Who is it?" I explained to her who I was, and waited. She said that she did not want to talk to me. She did not know the individual and that was it. About that time the police officer left his apartment and seeing me talking before a closed door, said: "Marge. Open that f——g door and talk to the man."

Silence followed. Then I heard a security chain being removed from its slide. The police officer left. The door opened. A woman in her forties, wavering in her half-open robe, stood in the doorway. Underneath she was completely naked! Half smiling, her left eyebrow higher than the right, and her eyes half closed, she said: "Come in." I hesitated but she stumbled away from the entrance and, wrapping her robe around her protruding belly, flopped on an easy chair. I sat in the chair facing her and began my canned speech, watching her reaction. As I was talking her negligée began to open, uncovering her knees, then her thighs, and as she spread her legs slightly she exposed her pubic hair. She replied to my questions but her speech was not normal. She did not appear to realize that she was exposing her most personal attribute. After a while I was certain that she was drunk and completely oblivious of what she was doing or saying. I left the area and never reported that interview.

Probably due to my past experience as an undercover agent, I was eventually assigned to a special team responsible to the intelligence officer of the Command, known as the G-2. I was still member of the Baltimore Field Office, but was under the control of the detachment at Fort Meade. We handled the most secret and difficult cases of espionage and of alleged misconduct by members of the Army or their dependents. I was involved in several cases, none of which amounted to much, but all were deemed very important by the Command.

The G-2 of the 2nd Army had commanded a Division during the Normandy landing. He acquired a stray French bull dog that he named "D-day".

All CIC personnel were required to periodically go to the firing range to familiarize or re-familiarize themselves with certain weapons, primarily the .38 special revolver and the .45 pistol. This exercise is recorded in the individual's file and kept up to date. I had not handled a weapon since the War, and was due to go to the firing range along with some other members of our unit. I was on the firing line when along came the General with his dog. He knew me, having been introduced to me when I reported for duty at Fort Meade, and he was aware that I was from France. He recognized me and casually introduced me to his dog, "D-Day," saying that we had something in common! He had collected the dog on the beach at Normandy, so I spoke French to the dog, but he did not reply. Instead he darted across the firing range after a rabbit. That did it. Chasing after D-day went the General, running between the firing line and the targets. The range officer stopped everything until both the dog and its master returned to the safety of the range. Only after a half an hour did the firing range return to normal.

I learned very early to stay away from this General whose favorite sport was badminton. One day our paths crossed in a hallway of our headquarters close to his office. He asked what was I doing at noon. Thinking that he was inviting me for lunch, I said that I had no plans. "Meet me at the Gym at 1205 hours," he said. I reported to him and was surprised to see several other young lieutenants next to the badminton net that was stretched across the center of the basketball court.

"Frenchy," he said, "get yourself a racquet and get back here."

I did and with another junior officer was assigned to the opposite side of the net. The General served to me with all his might but I was not able to return his serve. He tried again and again and after a while, he told me to go to the corner of the gym and practice! Later, after he had worn out a couple of sets of lieutenants, he called me back. Fortunately for me I was as bad as when I began, so the game was canceled for that day. That was the last time the General asked me to play badminton with him. Some of the other junior officers who were good were not as fortunate. They ran out of excuses and spend many lunch periods on the badminton court.

If the G-2 was a peculiar individual, the Commanding General was even stranger. He considered CIC a private investigative agency that he could use for any purpose. He completely ignored the fact that he had a Criminal Investigation Detachment (CID) which was part of his own Military Police. When an incident did occur at Fort Meade which for some reason displeased the General, our detachment was called upon to conduct the investigation. For example, one day it was discovered that during the night the television set of the Officers Club had been stolen. The large and heavy set had been placed on an especially built platform in the main dining room. This was definitely a criminal matter without any security implication.

Nevertheless, our detachment was ordered to investigate. I was assigned to the job and went undercover as a resident of the Club, moving into one of the rooms reserved for transient officers. I spent all day long going from my room to the bar, to the dining room to the golf course, as soon as the Club opened until closing time. Because I had to be on the job when it opened for breakfast I remained at the club overnight. I became a familiar figure there and it wasn't long before it was common knowledge that "Frenchy" was "undercover" at the O'Club. Some of my co-workers would come to the Club to keep me company. One of them asked me what my plan was to actually identify the culprit. In a confidential tone, for his ears only, I said that I was waiting for the robber to return to pick up the antenna. The set would not work without it. It did not take long for the joke to be repeated. Many of the officers would ask, "Is the antenna still there?" It was.

During the month-long investigation it was revealed that sums of money were being stolen from the slot machines located at the Golf Pro-shop, which doubled as a coffee shop. There was only one individual who had access to these slot machines. Short of forcibly entering the coffee shop, one had to have access to the key. There were a limited number of individuals having access to the key; one was a Black assistant manager. Immediately we received an order from the commanding general to find him guilty. We did not suspect him at all, but the General did because the fellow had dropped a drink on his wife's new dress. While I was watching the TV antenna, some of our other agents were assigned the job of checking the pawn shops in the area. Nothing appeared in the immediate area, but several miles away in a small town, the TV set appeared in a pawn shop. The light blue convertible of the individual who had pawned it led to the perpetrator who turned out to be none other than the Club Officer and a good friend of the General. A more thorough investigation revealed that the same club officer had left a previous position in another military installation under almost identical circumstances. The matter was dropped abruptly by the command and the Club Officer was transferred.

One morning the reveille gun was fired and to the astonishment of the crew, chopped meat came out of its barrel, spraying the countryside as well as the side of a building located a short distance away. This was plainly an act of sabotage worthy of the attention of CIC. Again the Commanding General asked us to find the individual responsible for this reprehensible act. We did not know how much hamburger meat had been used—only the flies who had discovered this bounty could have told us. The mess officer checked his supply, but nothing was missing. Our investigation failed to find the culprit, but we had a pretty good idea who had done it. The Army cooks are a strange bunch. They work and rest at odd hours and have a pretty independent life as soldiers. When things don't go their way they can retaliate without fear, for no one fools around with the cooks.

A good illustration of the illogic exhibited by the SAC occurred when a truck hit my car as I was stopped for a traffic light right in front of the Baltimore police station. It was around noon. It was my first accident and it was not my fault, but just the same I felt bad. At least one dozen police officers passed by my wrecked car; as it was their lunch period, all declined to give me a hand. I went in and asked the officer on the desk if it was asking too much to have an officer investigate my accident. He assured me that at one o'clock he would have someone to check on the accident. I could not believe my ears.

Finally, after seeing my credentials, the desk officer relented and assigned an unhappy policeman to the job. It took a good half hour to complete the paper work and afterwards I returned to Fort Meade to face our SAC who was beside himself when told about the accident. He acted as if his own personal vehicle had been damaged and suggested all kinds of punishment for my misdeed. Fortunately for me the Detachment's ranking officer had a better idea as to what was a fair punishment. He ignored the incident entirely.

We had to do some unusual things at times, especially when involved in a surveillance. One day the subject of our investigation decided to take the train. I was following him in a vehicle that was registered in another state. In order not to lose him I parked it on the street and climbed aboard the same train. Two days later I returned and found the car gone. At the police headquarters I learned that I had parked the car in a limited parking area and that the vehicle had been impounded. In order to get it back, I had to pay a fine and the impounding cost which came to fifty dollars. Unless the Judge said otherwise that was what I had to pay. Of course this was not my car, it was a U.S. Government vehicle and the police cannot impose a fine on Uncle Sam. I decided to see the Judge.

After waiting my turn, I spread my identification and documents in front of the judge and explained what I was doing without revealing too much of the case. He listened carefully, scratched his head, and said, "Let's be intelligent about this, case dismissed." So far so good! At the pound it was another story. Unless I paid the twenty-five dollars, the vehicle would not be released to me. I told the individual in charge that as long as the judge had dismissed the case he had no reason to keep the car.

He thought for a while and said, "OK, you can take it." As a result of this incident I earned the respect of some of my associates who had found themselves in identical situations but without the same results. They had paid the fine out of their own pockets and then struggled to be reimbursed from special funds.

Later on I was involved in a very serious case with international as well as local, implications. The spouse of an army colonel was suspected of being a Soviet agent. This serious accusation came to our Detachment without explanation. But we had to prove or disprove the allegation.

The Special Agent in Charge (SAC) of the case was the same fat boisterous individual who bawled me out after my accident and who fancied himself a singer. At first I did not know his rank. In CIC, on the agent level, ranks were often ignored to make our working relationships more effective. This was especially true when an agent with of lesser rank had more experience than a novice with a higher rank. Only when one was unhappy with his superior did he go through the "Date of Rank" routine. It took a while for me to learn that our SAC was a sergeant with much pull and not an officer, yet he treated those of us who were officers as if we were dirt and got away with it!

The colonel's spouse, who was a suspected Soviet agent, was being watched without much success. On several occasions she and her husband had been the guests of the Soviet military attaché at Washington. That was enough to shake up everyone at Headquarters. When the decision was made to tap her phone the local telephone company helped with a line from their home in the Washington suburb to a listening post in Maryland.

Technically, a court order should have been obtained prior to the installation of the tap, but for security reasons this was not done. For one, this was in the early stages of the era of the "Communist Menace" and prior to the heyday of the American Civil Liberties Union, so there was more concern towards the threat posed by the Soviet Union than about civil liberties. This was true not only with respect to the intelligence community, but to the nation as a whole. Secondly, because the point of this exercise was not to obtain court-admissible evidence, we were not concerned with adhering to the letter of the law.

For technical reasons, the listening device needed to be located in the general area of the colonel's house. The home of a government employee who had been cleared and sworn to secrecy was selected. The headphones and recording device were located under a staircase in a damp basement approximately six by ten feet. A cot was placed in the small room, and a kerosene heater to boil water for coffee and maintain a comfortable temperature was included. The listening device sat on a narrow shelf fixed to the wall. There was no room for a chair or any other furniture. We took turns listening on the line which at times was silent for days while she and the Colonel were out of town. The tap began in early summer of 1949. The days were very long and no one was to see us entering or leaving the house, so we had to arrive before sun up at around five in the morning. For the same reason we had to leave very late in the evening. The tap was manned 24 hours a day. In the summer, those who had the night shift had a short time in the damp cellar, while those who had the day shift had a very long day.

This was the most boring job I ever had. Sitting or lying on the cot, breathing the musty air of the basement in summer or the kerosene fumes of the small heater in winter, the earphone covering your ears, was not what most would consider a very glamorous assignment. Most of the conversations we heard were innocuous, the subject calling her friends, or friends calling the subject to arrange get-togethers. The operations officer was determined to find something that would prove the allegation that the Colonel's spouse was a Soviet agent. Once the agent on duty at the listening post heard a call from the Soviet Embassy. The spouse of the Soviet Military Attaché invited the subject to an afternoon party. This caused a general panic at Headquarters. This was what we had been waiting for——a direct contact with the enemy!

The SAC decided that she must be followed to Washington using "loose" surveillance. This entailed keeping a discreet distance to avoid being detected. Unfortunately, the agents who were assigned the job of tailing her did not maintain a reasonable distance. She very quickly noticed her shadow and, using a trick she'd probably seen in the movies, she slowed down approaching a traffic light and at the yellow dashed through the intersection. Sure enough, in an attempt not to lose her the agent did the same, which is a no-no in a discreet surveillance. Then, spotting a Maryland State Police cruiser, she flagged it down and told the trooper that she was being followed, pointing out the car driven by our agents. That was the end of this phase of the operation.

Through our contact with the local and State Police we learned that she was very unhappy about being followed and we obtained a copy of her complaint.

One early morning around two o'clock, a friend of the Colonel who was passing through rang their telephone. After short conversation they decided to meet in a location a good distance from their home, but probably more convenient for both. This also caused a panic at the office. Most people are asleep at 2:00 a.m. However the SAC managed to round up two agents and send them to the designated rendezvous which was an all night diner. The "friend," who turned out to be a high ranking Army officer on his way to his assignment, and our suspect spent an hour talking while the two sleepy agents huddled in their undercover car parked nearby watched the diner.

As none of the agents were lip-readers, we never knew what the two discussed. However the SAC was certain that some nasty plot had been hatched.

Because nothing of significance resulted from the telephone tap, the SAC presumed that they were aware that they were being watched and so were careful about the subjects they were discussing on the phone. He decided that a listening device would be placed in their house at the first opportunity. When it was learned that the Colonel and his spouse were going to be way for a few days, the bugging operation was activated. Unfortunately none of the members of the Field Office was an expert in the installation of listening devices. Faced with this lack of expertise, the only recourse for the SAC was to go to the CIC School of Fort Holabird nearby and ask for the help of the department where this subject was taught. Fortunately or not, the head of the Department of Surreptitious Entry was willing to do the job for us. Entering the Colonel's house was not difficult and locating the best place for the listening microphones was duck soup. However, to install these properly was another matter.

Normally these devices were placed into the electrical outlets. But this was an old house with an outdated electrical system. The only way to resolve the problem was to enlarge the hole and replace the old unit with a new one using the same cover. This was done, but in the process plaster was loosened from the wall. Thus was required a serious cleanup job under difficult conditions, since the so-called expert was working with poor lighting. They left the target area, confident of a job well done. I was on duty at the tap when the wife was the first to return. She was not home ten minutes when she called the State Police. She told them that during their absence, someone had entered their house and wanted to know what they would do about it. Of course the State Police called us immediately and to tell us something that we already knew.

This was getting ridiculous. For months, we observed the activities of the Colonel and his wife without a shred of evidence that he or she was spying. To make certain that he would not reveal any secrets, they gave him a job close to that of a janitor, making him very unhappy. I often wondered what must have gone through his mind after having been an Attaché, only to find himself assigned to a no-work position! The tap was taking its toll of ill agents. One ended up in a psycho ward, another committed suicide. I survived, but barely.

Boredom was our greatest enemy. To alleviate this problem I decided to keep busy by doing something with my hands. One of the problems of CIC was its inability to support investigations in the field. Every time we had to have pictures developed, radio communication set up or fingerprints taken, we had to return to our headquarters for support. This took time and slowed down our operations. I decided that what we needed most was a lab that could be moved to a location close to the investigators. I designed an investigative unit which would fit into a converted ten-ton semi-trailer, and made a model out of wood, cardboard, and other material used by model makers.

While doing this I was smoking at least two packs of cigarettes per day, and drinking gallons of coffee to keep awake. By the fall of that year my stomach was continuously in a knot from the first cup to the last cup of coffee. I decided to go on sick call and the doctor diagnosed my problem as the start of an ulcer. I could not tell him what I was doing, but he knew that my job was probably the cause of my problem. He advised me to cut down smoking and to lay off coffee, or he would have me transferred! I did not want to lose my job then, so I did better than he suggested. I threw my half-full pack of cigarettes out in the back of our house just as it started to snow. It was Christmas Eve, 1949. That was my last pack of cigarettes, and I have not smoked a cigarette since.

Unfortunately I probably have inhaled a lot of second hand smoke. I spotted my pack of cigarettes the following spring; fortunately for me by then I was cured.

By then my model Truck-Lab was completed. I took it to the office and showed it to the Operations Officer of the detachment. He looked at it and seemed impressed. I had included a thorough explanation on how it should be used.

While he was examining the model, the CO of the Detachment walked in and, seeing the model, asked about it. The OPS Officer explained that I had made it and that it should be considered for implementation. After a while the CO got on the phone and said to the other party, "Sir if you have a moment I want to show you something." A full Colonel from the G-2 shop came into the room. "Look what our Detachment did," he said to the Colonel. The Colonel admitted that it was great, and left returning shortly thereafter with the G-2 himself. "Sir, I believe that you will be interested in what I have developed," he said to the G-2. That was the last I saw of my model and plan. Years later I heard that an actual full-scale lab based on my concept had been developed for Army Counterintelligence.

After the first of the year, an officer who had been stationed with the suspected Colonel was debriefed upon his return to the States. A completely different picture resulted from his comments. The allegations concerning the Colonel's wife came from someone who did not like her because she was foreign-born and therefore supposedly not to be trusted. The Colonel's association with his Soviet counterpart who was now the Attaché at Washington was part of his job. Their close relationship had resulted in the acquisition of information much appreciated by the Ambassador. Why these facts were kept secret all that time is hard to imagine. We were told to discontinue our investigation immediately.

I will never forget my last night at the listening post. I was told to remove the line to the house we occupied. It was a cold windy night and it was snowing when I reached the telephone pole. I looked up and saw the box I was to climb to in order to remove the two wires that permitted us to listen to the conversations held three miles away. I did not have the tools nor the equipment used by the telephone people who had set up the tap for us. I managed to reach the first foot hold, and slowly inched my way to the top of the pole. The freezing rain and wind were blinding. My hands and fingers did not respond properly. I managed to open the small box, and was shocked by the number of wires and posts inside it. Finally, after tracing our two wires, I cut both, hoping that they were the correct ones. Then I removed the wire, descended the pole as quickly as I could and left the area without looking back. I have never returned to that house since.

We had other incidents such as this but even more serious ones leading me to believe that these investigations were way over the heads of some of our so-called agents. Thanks to the cooperation of the U.S. Postal System the mail of one suspect was carefully scrutinized. Our subject's incoming and outgoing mail was given to us in one bundle for inspection. The envelopes were opened carefully by various means and the contents photocopied. This was not a very difficult job and one would think that with a minimum of care it could be accomplished. Normally, the agent responsible opened one envelope, copied its contents, re-sealed it, and moved on to the next envelope. One day, in order to speed up the operation after receiving a large pile of mail, the agent opened all of the incoming and outgoing letters at once, made copies of all and replaced the letters in their respective envelopes. At least that is what he believed until he was told that one of the correspondents had complained to the Post office when he received a portion of his own letter! Who knows what the other correspondents received. This is probably why this practice ceased entirely unless authorized by a judge.

About this time, a large military exercise code-named "*Swarmer*" was planned. The exercise's scenario was that one "friendly" force had invaded a foreign "aggressor" nation, played by the eastern portion of the United States. The friendly forces had penetrated the Atlantic coast and reached a line approximately one hundred miles inland and running from West Virginia at the north to Georgia at the south. All of the major US divisions including the 82nd Airborne were involved. Our CIC detachment was asked to create a resistance group within the aggressor's area to familiarize the friendly forces with the possibility of facing a popular resistance including guerrilla warfare in any future conflict. I was selected as the key resistance leader, the one who was to be apprehended or eliminated so as to break any possible resistance in the area.

In order to facilitate this task, the various CIC units assigned to the U.S. Army units were interrogating those of my men who had been captured. They were fed specific information about the aggressor's resistance activities and about me, including my description, future plans, as well as my photograph. Eventually they had acquired enough information to create a file on "Derringshoven", my assumed name. Through their interrogations, enough information was obtained for the friendly CIC command to print a wanted poster approximately ten by twenty inches with my picture and instructions as to what to do in case I was spotted. These posters were displayed throughout the four states where the exercises were held. Hopefully, they felt, this would lead to my capture.

When we discovered their scheme, we obtained a picture of Colonel William Westmoreland, then the G-2 or the top intelligence officer of the 82nd Division and later the commanding General of our combat forces in Vietnam, and printed our own wanted poster. Our poster duplicated the information on the other poster, but we added words to the effect that "this individual may wear the uniform of a high ranking U.S. Army officer". One night, we sneaked into the area where Colonel Westmoreland had his command trailer and placed our posters all over, on trees, doors and old buildings.

When Westmoreland stepped out of his trailer the following morning, the guard who had been posted nearby, recognizing the face from the poster, said to the Colonel, "Sir . . . you're under arrest." This shocked Colonel Westmoreland to no end, and I dare not repeat what he said upon realizing what had been done by the aggressor forces. From that time on and until all the posters bearing his face were collected and destroyed, he was not able to travel anywhere within his sector without explaining to those arresting him that he was not the notorious Derringshoven, but the G-2 of the 82nd Airborne Division.

In addition we also managed to steal his safe which made him very unhappy. Perhaps we were too eager to do a good job and to prove a point; we did everything that had been done in World War II during the German occupation of Europe and Africa.

We manufactured our own identification papers which, although they were not exact copies of the real military ID, were so good (or the people to whom we showed them so lax) that one of our men cashed a check at the bank at Fort Bragg with his phony ID.

We became so overconfident that we decided to tackle the headquarters of the entire friendly U.S. forces located at Fort Bragg. This almost finished our operation and could have killed a few of us. When planning such a daring operation, we should have been more careful.

The headquarters of the friendly forces was located in one of the Fort's major buildings. It was to be penetrated surreptitiously during the night, and in the morning we would alert the referees. That was our big mistake. We had kept this operation so secret that our own command did not know the details. We were not familiar with Fort Bragg and as a result we did not realize that the base headquarters was located next to a bank which had a very sensitive security alarm system. When the boys made their penetration they chose the wrong door, and before they knew what was going on the entire MP unit was surrounding the building armed with live ammunition and ready to shoot. That was the end of our great operation. But we had learned a lesson from our mistake. We did not intend to repeat it.

If we had some failures, I must say that we had several outstanding successes. One in particular was a copy of a WWII British operation in Tobruck during the African campaign. We dressed half of a group of twenty of our men in the aggressors' uniforms while the other half were dressed as U.S. Force personnel. Only those wearing the U.S. Army uniforms were carrying weapons, while the others had theirs hidden and were marching ahead with their hands clasped over their heads. They arrived unannounced at the Field Headquarters of the U.S. Forces and of course they were challenged. The officer in charge, one of our agents dressed as a lieutenant, explained that these prisoners had to be interrogated immediately, and that the G-2 section was the place where the interrogation would be conducted. Obligingly, the sentry directed the group to the most sensitive area, and in less than 10 minutes the place was ours. The referees who were always with us declared that the unit was a total casualty and that ours was completely safe.

The other very successful operation was conducted against the fuel supply of the Air Force command supporting the U.S. Forces. We knew the general area where the fuel reserves for the Air Force were located. One night we decided to investigate and two jeep loads of saboteurs went looking for the fuel dump or dumps. When we located our target we could not believe our good fortune. All the railroad tanks holding the fuel were not only unguarded, but all were bunched together on a railroad siding in such a way that if one tanker went up all the others were to follow. This would not be very good news for Air Force General who was responsible for this phase of the maneuver. Carefully we placed our dummy demolition charges in strategic locations, making certain that the referees would see our deed and report it. The next morning at the daily general briefing, the absence of the Air Force General was observed. He had been relieved of his command and was at that moment probably cursing us, himself and his staff profusely.

The fact that my picture had been posted all over the countryside resulted in some very funny incidents. Years later, I was recognized by soldiers who had seen it. Once on a bus a soldier asked me if I was still wanted. He thought that he should turn me in for the reward!

Germany

By the spring of 1950, while the war in Korea was going full blast, I received my orders for Germany. I expected to go to a country closer to Albania such as Italy, or perhaps Greece, but it was to Germany that I was assigned. Our household items crated and picked up by a shipping company, and our suitcases packed we left Baltimore. After a few days in New Jersey to say good-bye to our folks, Georgette and I drove our car to the Brooklyn Navy Yard for loading on a ship, and reported to Fort Hamilton near the Brooklyn port of embarkation. However, instead of leaving from the Brooklyn Navy Yard, we were driven by bus to Boston where we embarked on a U.S. merchant ship bound to Bremerhaven. Aboard ship we were separated because they did not have cabins for married junior officers. I bunked with several junior officers, some of them recent graduates of West Point. We had nothing to do since there were no troops to command on board. So most of the time we spent the daylight hours sunbathing on deck. At night we either read or attended old movies shown on a makeshift screen for the crew.

We reached the English Channel early one morning and slowed down to bring aboard the pilot who was to guide us to our destination on the North Sea. We followed the coast of England, admiring the white cliffs of Dover as we sailed by.

We landed at Bremerhaven, the busiest port on the North Sea. From there we took the train to Stuttgart in the Baden-Wurttenberg region of Germany where the headquarters of the 66 MI Detachment, the unit to which I was to report, was located. The northern part of West Germany where we landed was not a very picturesque area. From the train, it looked pretty dismal and drab. As we proceeded south, the countryside looked better and better and by the time we reached the vineyards surrounding Stuttgart, it appeared to be a very hospitable place.

At Stuttgart we were lodged at the Graf Zeppelin Hotel, apparently the only hotel that survived the heavy Allied bombing inflicted on the city. The rooms were adequate and the service was great. A pretty German girl was responsible for our room. She was very helpful to Georgette who by them was noticeably pregnant. I gave her some cigarettes—Georgette was not supposed to smoke. Alone with her in the room one day she asked me if I would like to "see the town" she would take me. I thought nothing of it and thanked her for her offer.

Although this was 1950, the streets were still full of rubble, the scars of war were much in evidence. Many people were wearing clothes made from

GI blankets, some with the "U.S." marking still visible at odd places. Our hotel was near what was left of the railroad station. Along the main street stores were non-existent except for Gast Houses, the typical German bars where music was played and beer consumed.

The MI Detachment to which I was assigned was divided into regions. I was told to report to Region IV located in Munich, the capital of Bavaria where a house had been prepared for us.

Our car, a 1950 Chevrolet, was to have come with us on the ship we came over on, but it did not. We traveled again by train to Munich where we checked in to a hotel under the control of the occupation forces as in the case of Stuttgart. While Georgette stayed at the hotel I reported to the CO, Major Aaron Bank an old OSS-China acquaintance. Prior to the War, Aaron had been a life-guard at Deauville, France. There he met vacationing Mrs. Delano Roosevelt, the President's mother. From that point and until Roosevelt's death, the door to the White House was always open to Aaron. It was just like the old days. I was still a first lieutenant and Aaron had made Major but was evidently expecting a promotion, because either he was already wearing his LTC leaves or they were of a very pale gold color. He told me that he was also expecting a transfer and that someone would soon take his place.

Before leaving for my overseas assignment, the CIC School of Fort Holabird had charged me with a project which on the surface seemed commendable and probably necessary, but was perhaps not as practical as it first appeared. Unfortunately the project was abandoned for "lack of funds", which is the destiny of most unpopular projects in the military.

This project consisted of giving a battery of tests to all CIC agents in the field. The people taking the tests were also rated by their individual supervisor and their co-workers. The results were to be compared and analyzed. Based on the correlation, the tests giving the most accurate description of the agents' field rating was supposed to be given to all future CIC recruits to determine if the recruit was CIC material before he entered an expensive training program. It was supposed to save a lot of money and effort by weeding out people likely to prove unsuitable for this type of activity, but the Army had to train a certain number of students, regardless of their potential.

I was familiar with the process, having been subjected to it when I joined SOE during the War. I was a firm believer in this research and did my best to help. Instead of reporting to my section immediately, for over one month I went to every Region to administer the battery of tests to our agents. Each session lasted approximately two days. I was accompanied by a sergeant, and was given a Jeep to carry the material needed for the tests. I began my tour with the northernmost Region of Bremen and went to each, including the one in Berlin. It was impossible for me to drive to Berlin, and the material I was using for the tests had to be shipped separately by official courier.

When I reached Frankfurt, after leaving my chauffeur I was to take the train to the East Zone of Germany. To proceed to Berlin was not as simple as it sounded. First I needed a passport and a set of orders that directed me to the U.S. Sector of Berlin passing through East Germany along a corridor prescribed by agreement between the Western Allies and the Soviets. Only a certain number of passenger trains were permitted to travel from Frankfurt to Berlin, and most of the time the trip was made at night with the curtains shut tight so that no one could see outside. This was rather stupid I thought, because there was nothing to stop any of the passengers from peeking through these curtains.

I was assigned to my own roomette and although I did not feel very well and probably had a fever, I was too excited to worry about it. The train left late that evening and all interior lights were dimmed. In the middle of the night the train stopped at the East German border. Incapable of resisting the temptation, I turned off the light in my compartment and lifted ever so slightly the thick curtain. It was very dark. The few lights on the platform enabled me to see that every twenty feet were soldiers with their weapons at the ready. I could hear people talking in German but could not see them. Occasionally English words were interlaced into the conversations and some were Russian. Probably the train conductor and the U.S. Army MP were negotiating or exchanging information with the German and Soviet guards. It took approximately one hour before the train finally moved on its way to Berlin.

This was a very slow train. By early morning it was still quite a distance to the Berlin enclave. It was mid-morning when we arrived at the American Zone train station. I was picked up by a staff car and taken to our Region Headquarters to meet the CO and report to those who were expecting me. Although the war had been over for five years, the damage resulting from it was still much in evidence.

When I was free I called Lowell, Georgette's brother, and moved in with him and his spouse Noëlle so that we could spend more time together. He was with the U.S. Information Agency and was very busy with the local situation. It was the next morning that I saw the monkey again. This time it had gotten loose and had found refuge in a tall tree next to Lowell's quarters. It took the effort of the fire department and many of the neighbors to recapture the primate and secure him properly.

I was very happy to leave this otherwise dismal city. The return trip was not exciting. I slept all the way to Frankfurt and felt even worse than I did on my way to Berlin. Back in Munich, I was told that my car had arrived at the port and that I should go pick it up as soon as possible. I traveled to Bremerhaven by train, and from Bremen I took the Autobahn and was back at Munich a few days later, but not before stopping at Stuttgart at our main Headquarters, and checking in the Graf Zeppelin Hotel.

The pretty German housekeeper was still at the hotel and when she saw me she smiled. I reminded her of her offer and that evening I picked her up at her home and we went to several beer gartens to listen to music and drank beer. I brought her home, and although I subsequently stopped at the hotel several times I never saw her again.

Back at Munich and feeling no better I decided to go on sick call to determine what was wrong with me. I was afraid that I had a reoccurrence of hepatitis because my urine was getting darker and all the symptoms of the disease seemed to reappear. Fortunately it was not it. I had a bladder infection. How and why no one knew, but it was easy to cure and a few days later I was as good as new. Of course, Georgette accused me of having contracted a venereal disease!

When I returned to Munich, Aaron Bank had been transferred to an airborne unit which was exactly what he wanted. He became the CO of one of the two Special Forces units created about that time. His unit was at Bad Toelz in the southern part of Bavaria not very far from Munich. Before the new CO had a chance to give me a job, I expressed my desire to be assigned to the record section where the files were kept. For a moment he said nothing, then looking at me strangely he said: "Why do you want to go to the files?" Such a request had never been made to him by a CIC agent. The file section was considered the pits, something to avoid. Again he asked me why I wanted a job that no one wanted. I explained to him that I had never been assigned to the records section in any of my previous assignments, and that I considered this area a very important function of CIC activities. He could not disagree with me. I did not tell him the real reason for wanting the files. My experiences at the CIC Field Offices in the U.S. had been such that I wanted nothing to do with operations. I felt that the leadership was so inept that I preferred to be in an area where I would not be told to do something stupid.

So to the files I went. The records section was on the top floor of a building located in the CIC compound known as Peterson Kasern. It was a former German Army installation located in the northern section of Munich. The file room extended for half the length of the building. The other half was designated as our physical activity room where weights and other equipment was stored for our use. The files were composed of two parts—card files related to individuals and organizations, and dossier files related to investigations and referred to by number only. Adjacent to the main room was a smaller room kept locked at all time where the Top Secret documents were stored.

In addition to my main duty, I became the Top Secret Control Officer, responsible for the storing, recording and securing of all Top Secret documents either originating at the Region IV level or coming to the Region from other headquarters. The safes in the smaller room had a three-way combination known only to three people, and the door leading to the room was also secured by a padlock. The file cards were in bins, each bin holding approximately ten thousand cards. The dossier file cabinets were the type used in most U.S. offices including the military. The cards were of an odd size because some of them had been created by the German Army and most were from the dreaded Gestapo which had carded practically the entire German population. The Gestapo did not have time to destroy all their files and as a result we inherited most of them, a godsend to our counterintelligence efforts in Germany.

When I reached the file room I had the opportunity to talk to those who preceded me, including a Captain who had a degree in library science. I discovered that for these cards to be effective and useful, they needed to be alphabetized and screened for duplication. That was the first job that I tackled in earnest. This was an 8:00 to 4:30 job giving me plenty of time to be at home and to explore our new location.

Having not been back to France for eleven years, and now being so close to my home town, it was difficult to resist visiting my friends and relatives. Georgette would soon be too far into her pregnancy for a long car trip, and so I decided to go to Switzerland to look into the possibility of going to France. My associates recommended against it because of the possibility that in certain circles in France I was still on a list for elimination.

We left one bright and sunny day and drove to Lake Constance, where we crossed to the Swiss shore aboard a ferry boat. Then we proceeded to the Jura mountains a part of the Swiss countryside with which I was very familiar. We passed the old family inn, the Cheval Blanc at the village of Cornol, and proceeded to the Swiss town of Boncour where I stopped to consider my next move. Rather than entering France at the official border crossing at Delle , I decided to remain on the Swiss side and drive to a farm-restaurant within walking distance to l'Enclos Roland, my Uncle Lucien's farm.

I parked the car and, with Georgette trotting behind, we walked through the orchard, across the border, up to the front door and knocked. I should not have done so! I was in uniform, and when my uncle opened the door he nearly had a heart attack, but he recovered very quickly. Soon we were surrounded with kissing relatives, to the great dismay of Georgette who had never received so much attention. We were treated to a feast—even the old rooster ended up in the pot in our honor, but was he tough! We were given the guest room. The bed was the old-fashioned type with huge pillows and fluffy eiderdowns, and was not very comfortable for someone in Georgette's condition. She did not take the situation gracefully. Thank God, my relatives did not understand English!

Big improvements had been made since my last visit. The outhouse had been replaced by an indoor john, and an old-fashioned four-legged bathtub stood in the hallway. Buckets of hot and cold water were brought in to fill it. My cousin Maurice, now a Douanier or border guard, came in while we had supper and tried to entice me to walk to town. I refused without telling him why. We talked about everything until the wee hours of the morning. The next day we walked back to our car and returned to Germany by way of Basel and the Black Forest.

By that time Georgette was showing her condition. She had her periodic checkups at the local military hospital and she seemed to be all right. December of 1950 had been very mild. It was close to Christmas when snow began to fall. On the afternoon of the 25th, after a quiet celebration at home, Georgette began her labor. I took her to the hospital and before midnight she gave birth to our first child, a girl that we named Noëlle. The hospital was staffed with Catholic sisters and there was a crucifix above her bed. Georgette had no religious training but she did appreciate the kindness of the sisters who could not do enough for the patients. Like all new parents, we found our first child a mystery to us, and every move she made and every cry she uttered worried us to no end. However we survived and managed to raise a healthy, normal young lady.

Munich was a fascinating city, a huge city, with all kinds of activities, restaurants and shops, opera, museums, and a zoo. Little by little the drab clothing made from old GI blankets disappeared and was replaced by more colorful accouterment. The dirndls and the Bavarian costumes worn by the men began to appear. Lederhosen were a fad and many of us bought them to wear to parties or on off-duty time.

The primary function of Region IV was to interview and/or interrogate potential émigrés; people who were refugees and considered stateless and provide them with a clearance permitting them to obtain a visa from the American Embassy. Some of these people had been investigated by the Gestapo because of alleged Communist activities or other suspected anti-Nazi activities. We were concerned mostly about their present activities and whether they could be agents for the Soviets or their Eastern European "allies". West Germany had become a refuge for many anti-Communist groups such as the Ukrainian Government in exile, and they had become a target of the MVD, the precursor of the KGB. For these and other obvious reasons, the West German Communist Party was a high priority target occupying many of our agents.

I was not fluent in German, but I was often selected for jobs requiring knowledge of the French language, regardless of whether they involved an investigation or some other duties. I recall two activities which brought me in contact with some very interesting people. One of these was as an interpreter during the intramural boxing games in Munich involving all the

Allied armies plus the Egyptian Armed Forces. Naser had recently taken over the leadership of Egypt from King Farouk.

The Egyptians, particularly the officers, were engaged in a fierce propaganda campaign directed at the Allied Forces. I could not understand the logic of it and I doubt if anyone else did.

My job was to be the official French interpreter and to translate the directions and information given over the loudspeaker. This was not easy for me because I was not an instantaneous interpreter. If I knew what was to be said ahead of time I had no problem. The most embarrassing moment came during a ceremony to welcome the French boxers. The Colonel in charge of the welcoming committee was told that I would be translating for him and to stop after every sentence so that I would be able to translate.

Instead, he gave a 15-minute speech without notes then he turned around to me and said, "Go ahead Lieutenant." Every one of his words was rolling around in my mind, I tried to remember his opening statement, but could not. So I decided to tell the assembled French soldiers that the colonel had said a bunch of complimentary words that I could not remember, but to be sure he was very happy to have you come and participate. It took all of one minute to say that and the French soldiers applauded, not for what I had said but for the "Culot" (nerve) that I had displayed. As for the Colonel, he said, "How did you manage to translate my entire speech so quickly?"

"Practice Sir, lots of practice," I replied.

The second job I was given was as an aide to a French General during an annual maneuver held by the Allied forces in northern Germany. This was probably the best job I ever had because the General understood English quite well but had trouble speaking. We became friends and we corresponded for several years until I was eventually transferred to another theater.

By early 1951, Georgette discovered that she was pregnant again. This called for a move to larger quarters. We only had two bedrooms in our first house and this was not enough room for four. This time we were assigned to a large house with a basement, two floors and an attic where we had rooms for the servants. The house was located in Gruenwald next door to a German liquor store, or I should say, beer store. They also had a small patio in the back with chairs where habitués (regular customers) would sit and drink their beer and tell jokes. In winter the patio was transformed into a curling alley where the same old boys were sliding their irons by sweeping feverishly ahead of them with brooms. They would play late at night under a special light set up by the owner. Thank God our bedroom was on the other side of the house. I bought our beer there because if was very inexpensive, the equivalent of 10 cents for a liter in an old style bottle with a ceramic cap and a rubber washer to keep it tight.

The Hollywood of Germany was located in Munich. The movie sets were less than a mile from our house, and at times we would walk to the sets whose streets looked more American than European. At times when the movie companies needed extras for mob scenes, they would call on the neighborhood, especially American dependents, to fill in. I never participated but many of our neighbors did.

Meanwhile I was still busy making our file room the best in Germany. The chief of CIC, Major General Gallager, arrived for his annual visit and, of course, the CO took him to the attics to see the best filing system in the detachment. His visit had been well announced, so this was no surprise. I was supposed to give him a two minute briefing and that was it. After all, what could I possibly have to say that he did not already know? I decided that we would make a card with his name and fill in information we had learned about him and his assistant chief of staff. When he came in I was very brief and told him an outright lie. I said, "We have a file card on everyone in Germany and very likely we have a card on you, General!"

He stopped and said, "You what? You mean that you have a card on me?"

"Yes sir," I replied and, going to the drawer in which the names beginning with G were filed, I took out a card with his name and handed to him. He looked, read it, and, smiling, gave it to his Chief of Staff. The General turned toward the Detachment Commander and said: "How come you don't have a filing system as efficient as this at your headquarters?"

At that point the Colonel said to me, "Get away from the General." The General had a reputation as a tough inspector, and on one occasion even threw a dirty typewriter out of a window to show his disgust. But he turned out to be human after all.

Georgette liked Germany because she had plenty of the free help provided to the occupation forces by Germany. For a while she stopped distrusting me, particularly when I returned from official trips.

Our first son, René, was born shortly before Christmas of 1951 at the same hospital as his sister. If the first few weeks of his life were to be any indication, he was quite different from her. From that time on, my nights were never the same. He consumed more milk during the night than a young calf. It was not unusual for me to get up three times during the night to give him a bottle. Each time he woke me with a cry loud enough to give me a heart attack.

The winter of 1951-52 was a rough one. We had much snow on the ground and lots of ice on the road. Yet we had no trouble going from one town to the other using our Opel Capitan, the four door sedan made by General Motor of Germany. This car had been created for Germany, while my Chevrolet had been designed for the U.S., and it made a big difference.

Occasionally I had courier duty. It meant that, wearing a side arm, I had to carry the Top Secret pouch to our Headquarters in Stuttgart and bring it back. I used a vehicle if the weather was all right; if not, I went by train. This was a very pleasant trip through great countryside. I would normally leave early in the morning and be back the same evening with the return pouch.

Hitler's Treasures

In the Spring of 1952, I was pleasantly surprised by my promotion to the rank of Captain. It meant that my job in the file room was over and that I would be assigned to another section of the regional office. However before receiving my new assignment, a special case from one of the northern regions came to our attention because they were in need of a French-speaking officer. They had coordinated this case with U.S. Army-Europe because it had ramifications in the French Zone of Austria. The French had agreed to cooperate, but they wanted someone they could converse with at the local level. Before I was involved with this case, the Operations Officer of our Region decided to go on site with a few of our men under the guise of a rest and recreation excursion. They went to the area, which was above the tree line, with individuals who had never climbed a mountain before. It was a disaster. One of the men became seriously ill with altitude sickness. Their effort had been a complete waste of time because our activities were supposed to have been coordinated with the French intelligence officer of the area from the very beginning. That was the reason why I was to be involved in the first place.

After a thorough briefing at the detachment headquarters, I set out to Innsbruck, where I was to meet the head of French Counterintelligence for that area and his assistant André Odekerken, an Alsatian. (At the end of the War, Germany and Austria were divided into zones, each of which was controlled by one of the major Allied powers. Innsbruck was located in the French zone.) His office was in a medieval castle with walls three feet thick, a moat and a draw bridge. The ranking French officer naturally was very arrogant at first, but André, turned out to be a very pleasant fellow.

I explained to him the reason for my involvement and that I was hoping to be able to acquire more information concerning an incident that occurred seven years earlier in a small valley located between Innsbruck and the Brenner Pass on the Austro-Italian border. The information that had been shared with the French high command had not filtered to him as yet except in general terms. Even I, up to that point, did not have all the facts.

However, I explained the situation basically as follows: Several months before, an Austrian presently residing in West Germany had, in the course of an interview, revealed that he had witnessed an incident about which he had never told anyone. Shortly before the end of the war the individual, who had been involved in the training of German mountain troops in the area, was returning alone one evening from a trip up the mountain when he heard people climbing the trail to an abandoned tungsten mine located above the tree line. As it was highly unusual for people to climb at that time of the day, he decided to hide and see who they were. They were young people in uniform, probably members of the Hitler Youth, who were carrying what appeared to be heavy metal boxes. They were about twenty under the command of an older individual, probably a member of the dreaded Waffen SS. They were laughing when they entered the opening of one of the mines, with their boxes. Then the group left the mine singing German patriotic songs. Our informant returned to his village by another trail.

The next morning the news in the valley was that a group of young soldiers had been discovered dead. It did not make a serious impression on the local population, but it did to the individual who had witnessed the incident the night before. He was certain that the people who had died were those he had seen on the mountain the night before. The war came to a close, the U.S. Forces came through the valley with their tanks firing their weapons at a few German positions and that was it.

The man left the area and settled in the U.S. zone in Germany, where people did not ask many questions. Seven years later in the course of an interview, the individual revealed the incident to a CIC Agent. The French agents were very much interested because this was their zone and if there was any validity to the report, they wanted to know the content of the boxes just as much as we did. Was it perhaps gold bars or other of Hitler's war booty?

First the French officer and I conducted a reconnaissance at the mine. For this first visit, we traveled on foot from the village below which was called Neustif. We left early one morning and began our climb. Already some of the farmers had cut the hay growing on the lower slopes below the tree line. We were approximately 6,000 feet above sea level and we had to climb close to the 10,000 foot level. Although the slope was steep, the trail consisted of switchbacks and so was not too difficult to manage. We passed a few farm houses hanging over the valley and by noon we were nearing our destination. We stopped for lunch that we had brought along and of course I shared the traditional bottle of cheap wine that my French companion had not failed to bring. When we arrived at the entrance of the mine shaft and looked back we had a view extending to the other side and the entire length of the valley.

That was the place where the German Army made their last stand. Nearby were the remnants of a cable system used to descend the tungsten ore to the village below.

We entered the mine and examined the expertly constructed make-up of the shaft. The first group of Americans from the CIC detachment had not examined the mine very closely because they did not know what to look for. The two of us were no better equipped, and for this reason we went only as far as we felt was safe and returned to the village where we had established a Command Post at the French NCO Club. We realized that we needed expert advice so I requested an Engineer from the U.S. Army. At the same time the four to five hour trip up to our target area was too long for us. I went to a small U.S. Army Engineer post close to Innsbruck and requested a Jeep. They did better—they assigned me a full time driver. The second time we went up to the mine, we were sitting in a Jeep that climbed the trail like a goat. The local farmers as well as the French troops shook their heads and I could hear they muttering,

Austrian Alps in search of Hitler's treasures.

"These crazy Americans, they climb mountains with their Jeeps."

A Major belonging to the U.S. Army Corps of Engineer came to inspect the mine. We drove to the entrance of the mine. We entered and one hundred feet into the mine the tunnel divided into two shafts inside the mountain. We examined the left shaft that was rather short, 50 feet at the most; then the right shaft extending over one hundred feet to a cave in. The shoring did not appear to be very strong. Water was dripping from the ceiling and we could hear creaking when we stopped and listened. The Major turned around and said that this was not for him. He was not staying there one more minute. He ran out of the tunnel into the open and said that he felt that the mine was unsafe and suggested that we get out before we were buried. We drove him back to the village and felt pretty disappointed by his comments.

French Intelligence Officer with US Army Corps of Engineer officer on the right.

Meanwhile, the French were doing some investigation on their own talking to the local people and hoping that someone would remember the names of the people who were there at that time, particularly the name of the commanding officer of the unit stationed in the village and at the mine. Some names came up and fortunately several of these people were still in the area. No longer in the military, they were either businessmen or government employees. I had the opportunity to witness the interview of an Austrian car dealer who had been a Colonel in the Wermart, or whatever troops were in the area, and watched him reply to the French agent. He knew nothing and remembered nothing; this was a complete blank. We even located the girlfriend of an individual we knew was there at the time; she knew nothing, remembered nothing, and suggested that we go home and forget the past. Although we were careful during our interviewing sessions not to mention the purpose of our activities at the mine, I had the feeling that we were being watched and the local inhabitants knew a lot more about what had happened than we suspected.

Since the mine was such a dangerous location, we decided that we should reinforce it and make it safe so that we might continue our search. A company of French mountain engineers was stationed nearby. We asked their opinion on this matter and it happened that the young CO of the unit, Captain Alfred Weber an Alsatian, was a mining engineer. Unlike his American counterpart he went into the mine, assessed the problem and told us that he would need lumber and tools and that he and his men, along with their mules, would secure the place in no time. At the same time we requested the presence of the informant, the individual who had provided the original information, to make certain that we were at the right place, and in the event he had additional details on the incident that might prove useful.

Through the same U.S. Army engineering unit I obtained a small generator and enough wire to place a string of lights up to the end of one of the shafts.

It took a while to arrange for the informant to come to the Fultmes Valley. The French mountain troops took advantage of the lull to begin the difficult job of transporting the construction materials up the mountain to the mine on their pack mules, a few pieces of lumber at a time.

Captain Weber, an expert in Jungle warfare, and I became close friends, sharing many war stories. Our work day was rather short because of the limited autumn daylight hours and because hiking in the mountains was quite dangerous after nightfall. We ate at their mess and in the evening we gathered at their small club where we drank beer and wine. Life was not dull despite the fact that there were no women around. I introduced the French troops to the true American drink, the Boilermaker. We had plenty of beer, but no whiskey. So I used cognac as a substitute. It was amazing what a jigger of cognac could do for a glass of beer! Before long this was the favorite drink at the French officer's club, the "popote".

When I had nothing pressing to do in the village with my French counterpart I would join the troops, following them and their mules, or sometimes hanging on to a mule to make my climb easier. The troops had installed a lighting system all the way to the very end of the right shaft and had reinforced the shoring along the way to the end. They were at the end digging so as to pass the area where the shaft seemed to end. At that particular area was an air shaft leading to the surface of the mountain. We could not determine how far into the mountain the main shaft went; only digging would reveal it.

Unfortunately the digging was painfully slow, not because the rock was so hard, but because the soil had the consistency of wet cement. For every shovel-full extracted, two would fall in its place. After a few days of digging, it became obvious that we were getting nowhere. We decided to wait for the informant, and hopefully for new information.

I was not aware that bringing this man to Austria was to be a complicated affair. As this operation was considered Top Secret, and transporting him legally would require telling many people why we were taking this individual without documentation to Austria, smuggling him in the trunk of our Opel Capitan appeared to be the best solution. We crossed to border at Garmish with our contraband and when it was safe we moved him to the back seat. He arrived late one afternoon and he occupied a room next to mine in the French Compound. The next morning we prepared for the trip up the mountain. The informant had left his room earlier and we feared that he taken off, but he returned as we were having breakfast.

We could have used the Jeep to reach the mine, but my French colleague and I wanted to see how well the informant knew the trails and the area in general. We meant to follow him which we did. The first hour was not too bad, but by the second hour his pace had remained the same while the two of us had slowed considerably. We had a rough job keeping up with that mechanical climber. By the end of the second hour he stopped, sat on a rock and opened his knapsack, which he had brought with him from Germany, and extracted a loaf of bread, a piece of cheese and a bottle of beer. With his Swiss Army knife he sliced a piece of his bread, cut a small piece of his cheese and, smiling at us, he ate. We stood there like dumbbells having nothing to eat, not even a glass of the terrible French wine the French Army gives to their troops. Feeling sorry for us he gave each of us a piece of bread and a piece of salami he had kept hidden in his knapsack. This helped us a great deal and we managed to reach the mine in a record time.

At the mine location we asked the individual to stand exactly where he had been when he saw the German soldiers entering the mine shaft. He looked around somewhat puzzled, because a lot had changed since he has last been there. The Germans had set up an observation post for an artillery battery, then our own troops had occupied the area before turning it over to the French, and there was a chance the local people had done something to the place.

Finally, after much concentration, he showed us where he had been and described what he saw. Indeed, he had seen more than he had previously stated. He told us that a 30-meter-long recess had been dug by the Germans into the left side of the shaft, that the recess began approximately 20-25 meters inside the entrance to the shaft. He claimed that the boxes had then been stacked in the recess, the shoring replaced and the loosened rock and earth replaced to fill the space. We had been looking at the wrong place all along.

The informant was returned to Germany by the same route while we began to check his story. By close examination of the shaft, it was apparent from scuff marks on the bottom surface of the lateral ceiling timbers that at some point these beams had been supported in their center. Certainly, for the Germans to have accomplished excavating the type of recess that our inform-ant described, it would have been necessary for them to first shore up the center of each horizontal member and temporarily remove the vertical sup-ports on the left side of the shaft. However the presence of the scarring did not in and of itself prove that the side of the shaft had indeed been carved out, or that there was anything secreted behind the left wall of the shaft. We decided to attempt to repeat this hypothetical construction process, beginning with adding supports down the center of the shaft. Unfortunately, the lateral beams were quite rotted and proving or disproving our informant's contention would first require a complete reconstruction of the shaft.

Before continuing, I suggested that perhaps we would be able to ascertain if these boxes allegedly metal boxes were there by the use of a metal detector. There were none in the area, however the local U.S. Engineering unit had a mine detector, actually a metal detector! They were happy to let us have it and we rushed to the mine, this time with our jeep. We took a reading at the entrance to the mine to establish a norm and began to scan along the shaft where the informant had indicated a possible location. When we reached 25 meters from the opening of the shaft the mine detector began to shriek and the needle bounced to the right side of the scale. We had located something big and not too far away. Hopefully they were not mines. This continued for approximately 20 meters, then stopped. For a mine detector to react in this fashion more than nails were present in the area.

Now that we were quite sure that something was there, the problem appeared to be quite simple. Unfortunately it was not. Our mountain engineers calculated that it would take a tremendous amount of lumber and that the best way to proceed would be to dig a new shaft, parallel to the old one. While this was a feasible strategy, we had one bigger problem. It was now late September; already the cold rainy days had begun and snow was falling at the higher elevations. The digging that was started proved to be useless. The rain transformed the mountain into a crumbling mass. We decided to postpone our search until the next spring when the weather would be more favorable.

My driver and I were the last ones to leave the mine. Before descending the mountain, we placed signs written in German at the entrance which read "Achtung Minen" ("Attention Mines"), hoping that it would deter the local inhabitants, who had watched us throughout our efforts, to start their own digging.

The snow began to fall as we left the mine and by the time we reached the village the entire valley and the dominant peaks were worthy of a postcard picture. The cows had been tucked away in their warm barns, all sounds were gone as if put away for the coming winter. The French troops had a small celebration before my departure and their Captain and I exchanged caps. The French Agent and I parted company promising to see each other the following spring for the opening of the new shaft. Unfortunately, before then, the Allies and Russians concluded an agreement granting Austria sovereignty in exchange for its neutrality and we were unable to return.

CIC Region IV-Munich

By the time I returned to Munich, snow covered the countryside, but I was glad to begin my new job as the Informant Control Officer, next to the Operations Officer, the most important staff position in the CIC field unit. The job consisted of keeping records on the informants, those who provide information to the unit either for money or because of their convictions. Most of ours were motivated by the money and those who informed because of their personal convictions were looked upon with suspicion because they might have been under the control of someone else. For this reason we tried to have them accept some remuneration either in money or in the form of goods such as cigarettes or whiskey. For this reason we always had a very good supply of both items.

Another function of the ICO was to maintain safe houses, homes or apartments where agents would meet their contacts safely and without revealing their own identity or their connection with the U.S. occupation forces. My job was to maintain these houses which for the most part were in the country side away from the city.

At one point I had an accident involving my car and a German truck belonging to an important firm. With the help of one of our German secretaries I fought my case and won which was rare in Germany. Liselote Thoene, who had been a legal assistant was the reason why I won. We became friends, and beside giving her cigarettes and chocolate that she loved, I occasionally took her as an interpreter in my inspection of our safe houses. Liselote was also an opera singer with a terrific voice. She would practice while we drove from one town to the other.

The other function assigned to the ICO was that of Technical Specialist, or the control and utilization of the technical equipment at the disposal of the Agents. This was by far the most interesting phase of my job. It was also the most difficult in terms of quality and effectiveness. When it worked, which was rarely the case, it was amazing and gratifying.

Bugging telephones was one of our activities, but bugging rooms and entire buildings was quite a challenge. We even had to bug the CO's office because he wanted to make certain that the conversations he had with certain people was accurately reported. This was during the McCarthy era when the military was under fire and Congressional committee members would drop in unannounced and ask questions about our activities. Fortunately for our CO and for the organization as a whole, we never made the headlines.

Every field office had an interrogation room that was bugged so that the interrogator did not have to take notes. However what was even more important was the way the individual who was being interrogated behaved before, during and after the session. Our room had a one way mirror permitting us to observe and take pictures of individuals without them being aware. This was a great asset to the agents who were able to detect peculiarities unnoticed during the interrogation.

The other tool used to determine the veracity of the statements made by informants was the polygraph or lie-detector. Several of our agents were trained in the use of this instrument, however I personally did not believe in its effectiveness, and only reluctantly agreed to its use. Our informants were generally people who led double lives—on the one hand they were ordinary family people and on the other, information gathering agents— forced to live a life of lies to survive. To accomplish their mission they had to deceive their friends and family. When debriefed, informants were required to revert to our side and provide us with accurate and truthful answers. The polygraph very often indicated a reaction which to me was understandable, but to some of our people this was proof that they were lying. I would have worried a lot more if an informant had passed the polygraph successfully as he had been trained to lie by his other masters.

We had people who crossed the borders and returned to Eastern European countries. They needed some means of protection against guard dogs trained and used successfully by most eastern European border guards. The best and most effective way was to use a product that is manufactured by the informant's own body — his urine. Unfortunately, when one has a pack of dogs on his heels, stopping even one minute to relieve oneself is easier said than done.

We had an effective alternate product but we never had the proof of its usefulness. The product was called SF. It was a liquid that evaporated quickly and left no visible trace in its container. For containers, we used beer bottles, the type with the ceramic caps, and instructed our agents that if they were being persued by dogs to open the bottle as they ran and spill the contents on the ground. The higher the air temperature and humidity, the more effectively it would perform. When the dogs reached the spot, one whiff and their sense of smell would disappear and they would stop and run the other way. The chemical didn't kill them but made then very uncomfortable for a couple of hours. It did the same for the individuals following the dogs. None of the FS bottles were ever returned to us. We believe that our people probably had doubts about its effectiveness and when in a safe area, would empty the bottle to see what would occur. As far as I know we never had a single complaint.

Dogs were always a concern of ours with respect to the safety of our informants crossing the borders. One day an individual whose identity was unclear came to my office and told me that he had a product that would eliminate this problem conclusively. He had the product in a small vial. He claimed it was enough to keep any dog a good distance away. I listened to him for a while and felt that the man was pulling my leg. We had a K-9 unit nearby, so I called them and asked if they had a mean dog available. They assured me that they had but I must promise that we would not hurt the dog. I drove the man to the kennels where they had approximately thirty dogs, each penned in an individual cyclone fence enclosure. The sergeant in charge escorted us to a pen where a Doberman was barking his head off showing his fangs as we approached.

The man opened the vial, rubbed his hands and forearms with its contents and opened the gate. Instead of jumping at the individual as I fully expected, the dog rolled into ball in the corner of the pen and began to whimper. The man took the dog's head and, lifting it, he said to the sergeant, "Is this your vicious dog?"

The sergeant was speechless, but he quickly recovered and asked what was this stuff the fellow was using.

That was the first test. The second was to determine if the best tracker dog would be able to follow and locate the man who had left for a destination unknown to any of us. He had left his jacket so that the dog would be able to get his scent. Ten minutes later the best tracker was released. The dog went approximately one hundred yards and returned. All the urging and coaxing from his handler failed to make it follow the scent left by the individual. This was amazing and bordered on the mystic. The K-9 people were shocked but I was still skeptical. I asked the man for the formula, but he refused to give it to me. Instead he gave me a sample that I promptly forwarded to our chemists for them to analyze. I never heard from them nor did I learned what became of this amazing substance. Neither did the maker of the product come to see us again!

Peterson Kasern was protected by uniformed police composed mostly of Albanian refugees. I had very little contact with them because they were under the command of the military police. However one day I was returning home and it was raining. I saw one of these guards walking so I stopped to give him a lift. I spoke to him in English, but he replied to me in German. Casually I greeted him in Albanian. The man looked at me with surprise his eyes almost leaving their sockets when fear seemed to take over. He did not reply, but when I stopped for a traffic light he jumped out and disappeared in the dark. I could not understand his behavior and mentioned it in our office to one of our agents who was familiar with the Albanian guards. He told me that these Albanians lived in fear for their lives because they were considered traitors by Communist Albania and that some had actually been murdered in Germany. This persuaded me to keep my knowledge of Albanian to myself.

On April 2, 1953, the day after April fool's day, Marc, our second son was born. I named him Marc after one of my favorite cousins, Marc Monnot, and gave him the middle name of Victor for my favorite uncle, the father of Marc Monnot. It is ironic that his initials would be the same as the dreaded Soviet organization we were facing, the MVD, the precursor of the KGB.

Occasionally we had to work on weekends, and this included our CO, Colonel Scherer. After work we headed for downtown Munich, and usually wound up at the Hofbräuhaus for a glass of good beer and a German sausage. Our boss was well known and well liked by the local people. One day, I believe that it was a Sunday, the colonel and a small group of us headed for the famous Hofbräuhaus and stood in line behind a dozen people. The person immediately in front of us was a huge, tall individual weighing close to 300 pounds. When he reached the door, several girls surrounded him and announced to the rest of us that he was the millionth customer and that everything he wanted was on the house. We were seated very close to him and between us we discussed this incident and agreed that this was a put up job. We felt that he was probably part of the management and we were laughing at the gullibility of the other customers. We were speaking English and noticed that the winner was watching us with interest. Finally he turned toward our table and said in perfect English, "Where are you from, boys?"

We told him, and he replied that he was from Milwaukee, Wisconsin, visiting some of his relatives in Munich. We could not believe our ears, but he was a for real. An American-born tourist who had been the one millionth customer at the Hofbräuhaus before our very eyes!

Our organization was supposed to be above board, every member carefully selected for their honesty, integrity and loyalty to the Army, our Government, the flag and the constitution, but not necessarily towards their spouses. One of our CO's had been transferred to France where he and his family settled. For several months we heard nothing from him. Then one day, during a routine check of the area, an Albanian guard surprised an individual making mad love to a woman in the back seat of one of the staff cars. When asked for his name, he gave that of the present CO, who as luck would have it happened to be out of town. The guard, believing that he was the actual CO of the unit, reported it and somehow the news got to his spouse before he had returned. Our CO had a lot of explaining to do to her. Fortunately, he had no trouble proving to her where he was at the time in question. As for the philandering colonel, he was promptly reduced to the permanent rank of sergeant, and returned to the U.S. by the first available means of transportation.

The other incident was even more ludicrous because it was the wife who caused the demise of her husband, a young Captain. During the visit of the Chief of Counter Intelligence, a Major General of a ripe old age, the wife of the young Captain, who wanted to improve her husband's chances for a promotion, decided to plead her case directly to the General. It so happened that she and the general were sharing the same floor of the same hotel. After waiting for the old soldier to retire for the evening, wearing only her raincoat and her shoes, she knocked at his door. He opened the door and she opened her raincoat. The following day the captain and his spouse were on the first plane out of Germany.

As I have stated previously, honesty was one of the most stringent requirements for admission into the sacrosanct CIC. Yet we still had instances of thievery by no other than the members of our own group. One day we were invited to the home of one of our captains. Only members of our organization and their spouses were present. Yet the captain lost several hundred dollars from his house during the party, and despite a thorough investigation, including the polygrahs of all present, no one was accused of the crime. Or I should say that it was thought better not to accuse anyone of the crime. We had a pretty good idea as to who did it, however he was untouchable.

After four years in Munich, I was finally reassigned to Fort Holabird. We had accumulated a lot of stuff but nothing big, so our household goods were easily packed. I had sold my car to one of the French Military Attaches, so I did not have to worry about a vehicle. This time we were not crossing the Atlantic by boat, but by commercial airline that turned out to be Pan Am. Noëlle and René, (we called him Sonny) were big enough to travel, but Marc was still feeding from a bottle and had a tendency to be fussy. During the traditional medical check up prior to departure, we talked to the doctor who suggested that adding a half teaspoon of whisky to his milk bottle would probably do the trick. Indeed it did. Marc slept most of the way, and when he would wake up between bottles, he would grin at the other passengers, who all commented on how well behaved our baby was. We had two refueling stops, one at Shannon, Ireland and the other in Newfoundland. On a crisp Fall day in 1954, we reached New York and went to see our families, whom we had not seen for four years.

Fort Holabird

After reaching Baltimore we purchased a new car, and locating an apartment, we moved in with all our furniture that had been in storage. After the birth of Marc I believed that it would be the total amount of children I would support. This was not to be so as Georgette became pregnant with our son Claude.

Baltimore had not changed much, and neither had Fort Holabird. The school was going full blast, and I was assigned to the unit responsible for providing practical demonstrations.

It was 1954 and the Cold War was in full force. I was back at my old job, except this time we were not training agents for peacetime activities. Instead, our training exercises were based on wartime scenarios.

Our job was to convoy a new class of between 20-25 students from Fort Holabird to an abandoned Army hospital at the Aberdeen Proving Ground each week and set up a CIC field office as if it were being done under battlefield conditions. The small unit was under the command of a Major and consisted of two officers and five enlisted men, all of whom were CIC agents, except for those in support roles who had other special skills. One member of the support staff was a black sergeant who had been General MacArthur's driver, and was in charge of the vehicles (primarily Jeeps, most of which were on their last legs) which made up our weekly convoy. Thanks to the Sergeant, we managed to get to our destination and return with our full complement of vehicles. My position was that of executive officer.

Once the students had set up their headquarters our job was to feed them information through prisoners of war, civilian refugees and any other means which would normally occur in the course of a military operation. Although the exercise was canned, the instructors had the flexibility to improvise and use their own ingenuity. Those playing the part of spies had to reveal just enough to alert the students that they may not be legitimate. Those who played the part of POWs behaved as POWs would, that is, refusing to say anything but their name rank and serial number. It was up to the students to use their imagination and somehow change the mind of the prisoner and make him talk.

The School was used by all the services including the Navy, the Air Force and the Marine Corps. All students were acquainted with the Geneva Convention that was part of the curriculum. The demonstration lasted several days, including night exercises. One evening we heard a commotion in the problem area. People were hollering and others were moaning as if in pain.

When we reached the area, we were aghast. Two Marines were interrogating a prisoner hanging from the rafters. Our demonstrator went along with the method, but when he found himself hanging by his wrists and stripped to his underwear, he called it quits and started to holler. From that day on we made sure that one of us was always present to observe the Marines at work.

This was a boring job but it had its moments. We were close to the Chesapeake Bay and the area was renowned for its crabs. While the students were driven to the Fort, some of us had to remain to clean up and get the area ready for the next class due to arrive the following week. Our CO, Henry Reinders, was a very accommodating individual and to recompense his staff for a job well done, he would detail a couple of our men to collect crabs at the Bay. Borrowing a boat from the recreation area they rowed to their favorite place. Their gear consisted of a strong nylon rope, to which every three feet were attached hooks fashioned from coat hangers. The hooks were then loaded with fat obtained from the mess hall. They would submerge the line, wait a few minutes and then draw it back to the boat. As the line came up, crabs would be hanging from the fat and our erstwhile fishermen would scoop them up with a net before the crabs broke the surface. It worked every time and in less than an hour our men had a couple of bushels of crabs.

The preparation was even more interesting. Using an old 55-gallon drum equipped with a false bottom, they first dumped in a can of spices which were a specialty of Baltimore. Then a six pack of beer went in before they placed the drum over a field kitchen range used by our cooks. When the aromatic steam appeared, the crabs were dumped into the drum and a lid was placed on top and secured. For a few minutes the scratching of the crabs against the side of the drum could be heard, then silence. A few more minutes and the lid was removed.

The aroma of the beer and the spices permeated the area and the green crabs had turned bright red. The crabs, still hot, were spread out on a long mess hall table covered with newspaper. Additional beer was brought in and the group attacked the crustaceans with determination, ripping away their legs and claws and getting to the most tender parts. Because of the small amount of meat in each crab I found this operation rather tedious and time consuming. However, it was the custom in the area, and when in Rome do as the Romans.

I was always amazed at the speed of those who collected the crabs. They let us believe that they had discovered a special spot that was unknown to the natives because they had never seen anyone crabbing in the area. This intrigued me and so I asked to go with them in order to observe. I sat on the boat while they rowed to their usual spot located approximately 200 yards from a large building on the shore. This was a sanitarium for TB patients. Indeed, in less than half an hour they had collected two bushels of crabs and we were on our way back. A few days later I asked an engineer about the area because we were going to use it for an exercise. While discussing our needs I said to him that just off shore near the Hospital was a fantastic crab nest. He agreed and told me why. It was at this point that the outlet of the sewer system for the hospital emptied into the Bay. That was the last time we had crabs.

The Officers Club of Fort Holabird was about the best I had seen in all of my times in the Army. Every Friday there were free oysters during happy hour. The bar was impossible to reach. The noise was deafening and the food was delicious. The club was making so much money that occasionally we had free drinks and at time free food. Of course the slot machines were responsible for this generosity. After all, Officers Clubs were not supposed to be for-profit enterprises but were supposed exist only for the benefit of the officers.

Although our jobs as demonstrators or instructors were very crucial, it was repetitious and boring. Fortunately, we had some people in our group who made life interesting by creating diversions, some of which turned out to be constructive and instructive. The Major in charge was an etymologist buff. He constantly played with words and for the fun of it would quiz us on the meaning of words and their origin. This caught on quite rapidly, and all of us carried a small stack of cards, each of which had a word scribbled on one side and the meaning and origin on the other side. I increased my vocabulary more during that period than ever before, and it was fun because the history of words is a fascinating subject.

To The Far East

(This chapter has been censored by the Central Intelligence Agency)

The stretched American Airline DC-6B looked a lot bigger and more impressive than the DC-6 I had flown in 1945 from Kunming to Calcutta. It was cold at Washington's National Airport. Instead of a uniform I wore civilian clothes including an overcoat and a felt brown hat. After presenting my boarding pass to the attendant at the stairs leading to the cabin, I went to my seat in the back of the aircraft. A curtain separated us from the tourist class.

Only a few passengers, probably businessmen, occupied the few seats. I was told by one of the slim flight attendants that, at the proper time, seats would be folded and berths similar to those found in trains would be lowered from the bulkhead and made up by one of the attendants before we retired for the night. Our flight was to take us to Alaska, then to Kiska, in the Aleutian Islands, and then to Japan and Hong Kong, where I would change planes. I decided to use my berth, finding it to be more comfortable than my seat. Early the next morning we reached our first refueling stop, the Island of Kiska, a deserted Aleutian. During the refueling operation a breakfast was served at a typical western restaurant.

After a few hours rest the crew was ready to resume our flight to Tokyo. The sun was bright and the attitude of the crew and passengers cheerful. We were flying in a southwest direction parallel to, but several hundred miles away from, the coast of Siberia, when the pilot casually asked us to look out on the right side of the aircraft. Fortunately for me I had the window seat on that side and a prime view of the Soviet MIG which was flying alongside us, perhaps one hundred feet away. The red star was plainly marked, and I could see the pilot clearly. For a few minutes we visited. The Soviet pilot slowly waved his hand and the planeload of Westerners waved theirs as if we were old friends. A moment later the Soviet MIG shook his wings then peeled off towards Siberia.

According to our pilot this was a common occurrence, but not for me. When I saw the red star, my first thought was that we would be forced to divert our flight to Russia. I doubt whether any of the passengers will ever forget that flight.

Members of our intelligence family were not allowed to use foreign carriers because many carried information that could be useful to Soviet intelligence. In the event of an emergency, foreign carriers might land on

Soviet or Communist China air fields, whereas American carriers did not have the same privilege. I felt relieved when the MIG parted company.

We landed in Tokyo and after a short refueling stop continued to Hong Kong where I found lodging at the Hotel International in Kowloon. This was my second contact with China, a China much different from the one I had seen during the war. In the evening I walked along Nathan Road, the main artery of Kowloon, admiring the store-fronts with every kind of product available in the world.

The next day a taxi took me to the airport for the last leg of my trip a flight to Vientiane via Air Laos. In those days the Hong Kong Airport was so small and so difficult that planes could only land and take off during the day. This time I was not traveling alone; a member of USAID was returning to his station after a week of R&R and joined our flight. We were ready at the appointed time, but the plane wasn't. Evidently this was not unusual. My new friend told me that the planes were so old that the airlines often ran out of spare parts, and that they had to use paper clips and chewing gum to hold them together. I was hoping that he was wrong.

Finally the old Strato-cruiser, a modified B-29, was ready. Unlike the plane I was in before, this one had a real bar, with a bartender! The crew, including the bartender, was French, but the two flight attendants were either Lao or Vietnamese and were in their colorful national costumes. Because the aircraft had no galley we would not be fed aboard, but we would stop for refueling and that lunch would be served at the Tourane (Da Nang) airport restaurant. This was fine with my friend and me. It was close to noon when we reached the Indochina coast.

We landed at the small airport of Tourane, south of the city of Hue, and while they refueled we proceeded to the sparsely furnished dining room. We settled at the table displaying the symbol of the airline which was paying for our meal. The crew occupied a separate table presumably reserved for them. We were served water and soft drinks while the crew, including the pilot and the copilot, were drinking wine! The meal lasted one hour after which we re-embarked and headed west toward the capital of Laos.

The view over the jungle-covered mountains was wonderful, but reminiscent of my flight to the Tonkin jungle back in 1945.

The flight was smooth. After a while the passengers moved about, mostly going to and from the bar with drinks in their hands. I very seldom drank during the day, so I was not interested. However I noticed that the pilot was also at the bar, and shortly thereafter, the co-pilot joined him. I pointed this out to my friend, who only shrugged his shoulders.

"Who is flying the plane?" I asked him.

"Probably the radio operator," he replied.

He was right, the aircraft was on automatic and the only individual in the cockpit was the radio operator. My friend said that this was the famous airline which, on the day of its inauguration, crashed their flagship on the only mountain within a radius of three hundred miles, killing all the guests and dignitaries aboard!

Hoping the pilot or the radio operator would miss the same mountain, I closed my eyes and recalled the series of events that brought me to this part of the world.

Southeast Asia Operation

When I was called to the Pentagon in the summer of 1955, I hoped it would be my ticket to a new duty station, away from Fort Holabird

The office of the Assistant Chief of Staff for Intelligence needed a French-speaking officer for a special job in Southeast Asia. Their search of the Army personnel record files had turned up my name.

The fact that I had been in OSS probably also influenced their decision. The Colonel who initially briefed me probably had never been an agent and or operated without the security of a uniform. I had the feeling that for him my OSS connection was a big deal, and that he felt that I should be treated with deference.

Eventually I learned that I was to go to Southeast Asia where Communist forces were gaining increasing influence over the area. For some time our military had been very unhappy with the quality of the information received from the region through the Central Intelligence Agency. In response to complaints from the military, one of our ambassadors suggested that the Pentagon assign a military person with an intelligence background to his Embassy. There were several problems with that idea.

For one, while the SEATO (Southeast Asia Treaty Organization) treaty had placed South Vietnam and Thailand under the wings of the U.S., Cambodia and Laos were to be under the influence of France. Except for our embassy's military attaché and his assistants, the U.S. could not legally have troops in countries such as Laos or Cambodia. For another, in order to be an effective intelligence gatherer, the new person should ideally be sent in with a cover identity not related to the military.

These restrictions posed a serious problem to intelligence operations. Only CIA personnel using government or civilian covers were able to operate effectively there, and at that time agents with a military and language background were not available. Thus it was decided, with the full concurrence of the Ambassador, to bring in an Army agent who would be undercover as a member of USAID program assigned to Laos, but actually under the operational control of the embassy. On the surface this seemed to be a very simple task, however it turned out to be a fiasco from the moment I reported to my duty station.

Officially, I was to be under the operational control of the CIA's Chief of Station. However, my Army superiors instructed me that I was to maintain a second, privileged and unofficial reporting link with the Pentagon, and that I was to provide them with copies of all of my reports. It was immediately apparent to me that this assignment placed me squarely between the proverbial rock and a hard place.

At any rate, because I was under the operational control of the CIA, the Agency insisted that I be trained as one of their agents prior to reporting to my duty station. For eight weeks I attended their school on trade crafts, but not before passing the polygraph test and sending a shock wave throughout the Agency. During the polygraph test I was asked if I had ever known or been associated with known Communists. I replied to the affirmative. After the test, one of their counterintelligence agents asked me who these Communists were and how and when I had known them. Of course the individuals I had know were some of my former OSS associates who had not hidden the fact that they were Communists, and had even bragged about it in 1945. It was now ten years later and the names of these officers were not permanently engraved into my head. So I gave the names that came to my mind. The agent appeared surprised but said nothing.

The next day I was asked to report immediately to an office where on a table were a number of pictures of people unknown to me. They asked me if I recognized any of them. Of course I didn't. They let me go, but that same afternoon called me again and showed me a different group of photos. I spotted one man I recognized and I said that he was one of the Communists that I had known. I could see relief on the face of the agent who then told me that one of the names I had earlier provided was the name of one of their most trusted agents. The individual that I had identified was truly a known Communist but he had different name. I learned later that my small mistake had caused a lot of concern to the Agency.

During the training period I had to remain in Washington DC. I stayed in the same rooming house in which I had stayed during the war. I did not have a car and, to facilitate my movements, I brought along the bicycle I had purchased in Germany. I would leave fifteen minutes before eight o'clock and be in the Pentagon office by eight. People who took the bus or who drove to work had to leave at least an hour before me. I could cut across the park, cross the bridge and, using walking trails, be in the Pentagon parking lot in ten minutes.

I even found a spot near the entrance closest to my office where I could tie up my bike. This was great until one day when I came to retrieve my bicycle. I found it surrounded by a half dozen security police. When I identified myself as the owner they wanted to know who authorized me to park in that spot. No one had, of course. They informed me that this space was reserved for an admiral who had been forced to park his car two blocks away. They directed me to a spot set aside for bikes almost a mile away from the entrance. I never did use it, but found other spaces, first making certain that they were not reserved.

This was during the time before the CIA built its headquarters at Langley, and had offices scattered all over Washington. I had to be both at the Pentagon and at the Agency, so I was glad to have a bike for transportation. I was able to cut my travel time in half, and when the traffic was light I could move pretty fast.

While I was going through the training and briefing for my future mission, my military record file was being changed to meet my new status.

Officially, I was placed on the Army retired list, and had been hired by USAID as a Far Eastern specialist. Then the day of departure arrived.

This was not a transfer in the same sense as those I had previously experienced. I was going alone and leaving behind a wife and four children. I was no longer in the military. I was traveling as a U.S. Government employee on commercial aircraft rather than military.

I had received a battery of shots for every possible disease. I had read a dozen books about Southeast Asia including *The Ugly American*, and I had scanned practically all of the dispatches coming from our Embassies there.

I had even taken a cure of psyllium seeds that I had purchased at the Homeopathic Pharmacy of Washington. A book by Supreme Court Justice William O. Douglas had described his efforts to prevent dysentery. He claimed that taking a teaspoon of psyllium seed daily for one month prior to going to Asia had prevented the dreaded dysentery so common in that area. Taking the cure was no easy task. When psyllium seeds enter one's mouth, they expand into a gelatinous mess three to four times the size of the dose. But I have never regretted doing this, and recommend it for anyone going to areas where dysentery is prevalent.

I had a passport identifying me as a civilian. My cover story was rather simple. For anyone who wanted to know, I had resigned my commission and had been hired by the USAID as a Far Eastern expert. Because of my French background I had been assigned to a Southeast Asian country where the official language was French. I traveled alone to my destination which had no place for dependents.

The Tricephalic Kingdom

I was very happy when we landed late in the afternoon in the capital's steaming airport. At the terminal, a small building in the traditional colonial style, my new friend and I were greeted by a representative of the U.S. Economic Mission, my cover organization. The man introduced himself as a USOM representative and told us that we were expected. He explained that he was alone to greet us because an official reception was being held at that moment at which all of the local dignitaries, including Americans, were in attendance.

Our escort advised me that even my boss was at the reception, but when we inquired as to who that might be, he gave a most unbelievable reply. Instead of naming the head of the Economic Mission, our overt boss, he named the second secretary of the Embassy, the Political Officer, who was in fact the CIA Chief of Station, our covert chief. We looked at each other and began to wonder who our escort was. He turned out to be the second in command of the Economic Mission, the Deputy Director! Back in Washington, during the several security briefings prior to my departure I was told that only the Ambassador, the Military Attaché, and the Chief of Station would be aware of my actual function. But, on the very day of my arrival, my cover was "blown," not only as a result of this USAID representative's remark, but also because of the comments made shortly thereafter by the Chief of Station himself.

My companion on the flight had been in the area before, so he just drifted away while I remained in the clutches of my escort. Rather than directing me to my quarters, the USOM Deputy Director took me directly to the on-going party. There, he introduced me to the Chief of Station, right in front a group of strangers! The Chief introduced me to the other guests as "one of his new boys." I could not believe what I was hearing. After spending months establishing my status as a member of the USAID project, before my first day on the job my cover for status was vaporized by, of all people, the chief of Station!

This was not a good omen. My supposed function was to give the station the military intelligence posture required in the collection of information for the use of the Army's Assistant Chief of Staff for Intelligence (ACSI).

The creation of my position had been requested by one of the preceding Ambassadors and had subsequently been accepted by all concerned. I was to report directly to the Chief of Station and coordinate my activities with him. At the same time, I was to have privileged communications with the Pentagon, through the Attaché with whom for security reasons I was to maintain a certain distance. My boss back at the Pentagon had cautioned me. His last words were indelibly engraved in my mind: "Don't you ever forget who you are and who you are working for. And keep this office informed of all of your activities."

After settling down I discovered in the following days that my job was to act as an advisor to a Major, the local G-2, the top Intelligence officer of the local Army. This was not exactly what I had expected to do as an AID employee.

However I realized that this was better than doing nothing, as those I was ostensibly working for at USAID had no idea what to do with me. So, taking my directions from the Station, I maintained a close relation with the G-2, going to his office and discussing various topics with him. He was very talkative, mentioning his escape from North Vietnam dressed as a Buddhist monk. He was bitterly anti-Vietminh, having been subjected to their attentions. Trained and well indoctrinated by the French, he was against Communism but at the same time he was not a supporter of colonialism.

The Major was an effective intelligence officer. He reported to the general commanding the local army, the alleged kingpin of opium traffic in the area. The G-2 did not smoke opium as did many people in the area. I never discovered the chink in his armor. He knew that I was there to help him and give him advice. However, it was silly to give advice to a person who obviously knew the area and the people better than I. Thus I concentrated my efforts in learning as much as I could about him and his staff. I reported all this to the Chief of Station, with whom I met periodically to discuss what I was finding and reporting. At the same time I forwarded the identical reports to the Pentagon, but I included my additional comments and related the activities of the station as they affected me.

As a result of the SEATO accord, the area had been divided into zones of influence. Thailand and South Vietnam were under the protection of the United States, whereas Laos and Cambodia under the tutelage of France. For this reason the presence of the French Army in Laos and Cambodia was a bona fide presence whereas ours was not. The French also had a more limited role in Vietnam. In our area the French were involved primarily in training the local army, whereas the U.S. had a logistical and funding role in support of the military. The entire army was financed, and therefore controlled, by the U.S. government. On the other hand, the French only had a mission with a small staff under the command of a general. It wasn't long before I met my French counterpart, a captain whose brother was the military attaché at the French Embassy of Pnom Penh, Cambodia. He was an officer of the colonial infantry corps with a long list of traditions. At that time his spouse and two or three of his children were in France.

The French military mission had a small compound which included a bar and a mess. Occasionally I was invited to share some of their cuisine, which was not the best in the world. The French captain and I began hunting periodically and would bring back a small fowl akin to the American snipe. After collecting these for a few weeks we would have a feast. We wrapped each one in a slice of bacon obtained from the American PX/Commissary, and then baked them until they were dark brown and impregnated with bacon grease. We enjoyed this delicacy. To me they tasted like bacon, but they were the delight of the French officers who partook in the feasts.

The French officers accepted me readily, happy to be able to converse with an American who spoke their language and knew their ways. We became so close that I spent more time with them than with the local army officers I was supposed to observe. However, through our association I learned more about my own targets than by doing it directly.

This was only two years after the fall of Dien Bien Phu. Most of the French officers had previously been in Vietnam and had been involved with the Vietminh, as they were called then. The general in charge of the French mission and I had occasional conversations, mostly dealing with the local situation, but also involving the role of the U.S. in Asia.

One day he said to me, "Ah Monsieur Défourneaux, we French have made a dreadful mistake in Vietnam, but I predict that you Americans will fail to heed our lesson and will make the same mistake. However, yours will be grandiose." I assured him that our intent was not to be involved, only to help these people maintaining their freedom. He did not believe me.

I was one of some fifteen local CIA personnel operating under AID covers, and we had our own compound.

Several of this group, who did not have their own housing, actually lived in the compound. Generally, all of us would meet there for our meals, although after a while the poor quality of the food led me to dine instead at one of local restaurants. Although it was well equipped with everything necessary to survive in this inhospitable environment, including paregoric (on the mess table to minimize the effect of dysentery) and a room full of medicine (most of it outdated), the station was still a hard duty post.

Reports written by staff members were usually rough—most of us were not editors. For this reason we had very competent writers who took our material and made it more presentable. One of the writers was a 50-year-old spinster who had been with the agency a long time. Milly was not only plain but unattractive, and I doubt if anyone ever had looked at her twice. We became friends because both of us were lonely and needed a confidante. We kept our spirits up and in the process learned much about each other.

Our station had a short supply of local maps. The French had a storeroom full of maps of the region. Having been in control of the area for many years the French Corps of Engineers had been busy making detailed maps of excellent quality. The French maps might not have been as accurate as the U.S. maps which were based on air reconnaissance photos, but they had a lot more useful information.

In any case I went to their supply room one day with the French captain because we needed a map to go fishing or hunting to some distant place. It was easy. The supply officer was very helpful; we joked and parted as friends. Subsequently I returned alone and collected more maps not only for me, but for the rest of our unit. This went on for months until one day when a member of the French group who knew me as an American happened to follow me into the store. I left before he did, but when I returned to get some maps, the fellow in charge accused me of having presented myself as a French officer. I had never done so, but from that time on, the French captain had to collect maps for me.

He was a well known big game hunter. While stationed in Africa he had killed three elephants; one came as close to him as twenty meters before he had fired his gun. He kept his superb hunting rifle in perfect shape. Unfortunately, the only big game in our area were a few elephants which belonged to the King and were therefore off limits to foreign hunters. Even the famous *gaur*, a type of wild buffalo, was very hard to find except in the deepest parts of the jungle.

The Meo tribesmen were known to kill elephants with a very unusual weapon. It was a wooden gun made from bamboo slats held together with animal skin. It was fired like a musket with black powder as propellant. The bullet, about the size of a 45-caliber shell, was made of tightly wound water buffalo hide. The Meo hunter tracked the herd of elephants until they stopped to rest and reclined. Selecting an elephant whose sole could be clearly seen, he would approach and fire his weapon into the sole of one of the elephant's feet. The bullet, lodged into the pleats of the sole, remained there without doing much damage. But as the elephant would tramp into the damp jungle floor, the bullet absorbed moisture and swelled. Eventually the elephant would not be able to stand on that leg. Incapable of keeping up with the rest of the herd, the isolated wounded elephant would actually lie down and starve, and if the hunter had survived the firing of his wooden gun, he would be able to kill the elephant by a more traditional means, his machete.

At first I was very skeptical about this unusual technique, until I saw in a Meo hut a wooden gun that had survived the firing of several rounds without blowing up.

On Sundays the Captain and I, along with one or two of the French civilians in the area, would often go on trips using our small Toyota truck and his Citroën Deux Chevaux.

Usually I supplied the gas, which was a very scarce item in the local economy but easily available in our compound. He had built a boat and had acquired a Johnson outboard motor, which he kept in good shape.

One Sunday we decided to go up the Mekong with two others. The Mekong is a powerful river which during the monsoon season can overflow its banks and inundate millions of acres of land. Yet during the dry season, the Mekong can be as gentle and attractive as a stream. Many sandbars diverted its flow and in some areas one could almost jump across. North of Vientiane, the Mekong narrows to less than one hundred yards. However it reaches great depths, causing whirlpools capable of taking an inexperienced swimmer to his death. This fate actually befell a French officer who had accidentally fallen overboard in that very spot.

We had taken some food and an extra can of gas with us to make certain we would be able to return. As we were going upstream, we knew that if worse came to worst we could always float down the river at a speed of 4 knots. We motored to a point where huge rocks blocked our way and the current overcame our struggling engine. We located a spot to anchor our craft and for an hour or so we enjoyed fine food prepared by one of the ladies who accompanied us. It was late in the afternoon when we returned and secured both boat and engine, which was removed for safe-keeping any time the boat was docked.

In those years, Vientiane, the capital of Laos, was a small town of perhaps 25,000 inhabitants with only one paved road. The other roads were surfaced with a red rock called laterite, a red ferruginous porous clay that holds up well during the dry season but which has to be replaced after the monsoon. Cars traveling over these roads would create a slip stream. This in turn would cause a washboard effect which did wonders for the suspension of the local vehicles.

Shortly after my arrival, the Chief of Station decided that I should have a car. I was told to look around town and see if one was available. I did find an Opel Capitan which belonged to a Chinese businessman. His price was three times what I would have paid. I was told to buy it and was given the cash to pay for it. The car was a nice vehicle, practically new, but not at all suited for the region. The best vehicles for that area were either a Jeep or a Landrover, sturdy and well designed for off-road driving. There were not many sedans in town. I am sure that I was not particularly inconspicuous. I had brought in my own bicycle which was actually a lot more practical, but for the role I had to play a bike was not really appropriate.

With the Jeep, I went snake-hunting at night in the center of town. The one and only electric plant was normally shut at night, and there were no street lights anyway. It was not recommended to walk in the street at night—not because of the crime rate, which was non-existent, but because of the snakes which came out in search of food such as rats or frogs.

During frog-mating season, so loud was the croaking of frogs along the banks of the Mekong that it was impossible to hear oneself speak. A flashlight was mandatory, unless stepping on a cobra was unimportant to you. With a Jeep, one was relatively safe, although snakes were known to land into Jeeps after being run over.

The trick was to have the headlights on high and slowly drive on the one and only black-top road through the center of the city. When I spotted a snake, I increased the speed of the Jeep approximately twenty miles per hour, and as soon as the wheels were close to the reptile, abruptly applied the brakes. This caused the wheels to lock and crush the snake. Merely rolling over a snake would not necessarily kill it.

In fact, I was returning to town one evening when at the last moment I saw what I believed to be a log across the road. It was too late for me to stop and I hit it rather hard before I realized that it was a snake, and a large one, probably a python, more than fifteen feet long. Later in broad daylight I rolled over a python that was longer than the width of the road. At first I thought that I had killed it, but he slowly continued meandering through the tall grass on the other side of the road. Snakes are not scared of people. They will leave you alone if you do not bother them. Unfortunately, one does not always know what bothers a snake.

One day my French counterpart and I were interviewing a couple of North Vietnamese guerrillas in the quarters above the French officers' club, a locally built building covered with a roof of palm leaves. We were taping the discussion and all of a sudden I looked up. "Look at that snake."

The talking ceased and everyone looked at a bright green snake approximately four-feet-long curling himself around the center post. The local people recognized the variety and immediately removed themselves from the premises. I followed, but the French captain, who was fearless, picked it up with a long bamboo pole and flung it out into the courtyard below. This did not kill the snake but a few blows with the bamboo pole finished the job. It was a banana snake, a type by which it is best not to be bitten.

A multitude of other reptiles were our friends and protectors. It was very common to see small lizards in houses. They served the very useful function of reducing the ever-present plague of mosquitoes. Occasionally their diet included fireflies which made their stomachs glow in the dark. Their large cousin, the gecko, was forever present behind the shutters and announced his presence with his distinctive "Ghek-Koh" sound.

Malaria was a constant danger in the area but, thanks to the mosquito netting over my bed, I escaped this malady. However I did manage to acquire another far more painful malady—a beautiful case of furunculosis, commonly known as "boils". This disease is common in the Far East, but how was I lucky enough to be the only European in our group to get it?

It started after a series of incidents involving my relationship with the French.

First I must explain that in addition to a military presence in the area, the French had an intelligence organization. While not as large, it was probably managed by more experienced agents than our own. Of course, since I was using my real name and had worked with the same French organization in Austria four years earlier, they knew exactly who I was. Periodically, our own Chief of Station met the French chief and they exchanged information or had a drink together.

Some few months after my arrival, the Chief of Station called me in and told me that the French were not happy with me around. "Be careful in your relationship with the French," he cautioned, without providing me with a reason for the warning. Later I learned that certain elements in the French contingent were attempting to orchestrate my departure from the scene. Their disfavor with me stemmed from my meddling with some of the intelligence resources developed by my French counterpart and others in the group. It is also not beyond reason that they may have learned of my activities during the war through the repatriated French colonial army men who had taken refuge in China when I was a member of OSS. The French did not care much for me, especially after they learned that I was member of the Deer Team who had trained and supplied arms and ammunition to the initial cadre of Ho Chi Minh and Vo Nguyên Giap, who later chased them out North Vietnam.

Sometime later our very upset Chief of Station called me to his office. He wanted to know why I had revealed certain classified information to the French, and indicated the time and place that I had supposedly revealed it and to whom. The particular information that I had allegedly revealed was news to me; I was not even aware of its existence. How could I have repeated something that I did not know, at a time that I was not even at the named location, and to someone I had never met? Unfortunately, it was very difficult to prove the negative to someone who trusted his French counterpart more than he trusted me. After all, I was a member of the other team, the Army. If I had a very friendly relationship with my French Counterpart and some of the other French military officers, it was mostly because we had much in common, and because my job required me to be in close contact with the local army being trained by the French.

In retrospect, the conditions under which we had to operate were insane and must have been planned by people who had absolutely no idea of the situation in that part of the world. The fact that Lao Army was supported logistically by the U.S. government, while the actual training was conducted by the French Army, was not an impossible situation, provided both the French and the U.S. agreed on a plan of action and coordinated their activities. This apparently was not the case. The policy makers and planners never met except at parties, and those who did meet had absolutely no power to institute coordination.

As a result, the French training of the local army emphasized unconventional warfare while at the same time the U.S. supplied them with trucks, tanks and heavy weapons which were difficult to move in a country without roads and impossible to use with the small amount of technical training they received. Without the needed logistical support to match their military philosophy the French completely failed; and without effective training in the use, care and maintenance of the weapons and equipment the U.S. provided, the material did not last very long.

I saw many trucks red-lined for lack of some very basic item such as a screw, only because the local soldiers did not know how to do basic repairs. This, of course, did not affect me because it did not relate to my job, but I heard many comments from the French, who loved to criticize the U.S., and from the local military who were caught between diametrically opposed military philosophies.

The town was truly an international village, not even a city. All nationalities were represented; some officially, and some not so officially.

The ICC (International Control Commission), composed of Canadians, Poles and Indians, was always present, either coming from or going to North Vietnam in an attempt to keep peace among the antagonists. The members of the Canadian mission were always helpful and provided us with some good information about our target, North Vietnam, and its allies. The Poles only parroted the Party line and Soviet propaganda. They wanted to give the impression that they were on our side, but it was difficult for them to maintain a friendly position. A member of the Polish mission decided that he would not return to Poland and gave the impression that he wanted to defect.

He probably did so merely in order to see how the U.S. would react. In fact, he did not defect and returned home after his tour of duty was over. The Indians spent most of their free times playing soccer. They remained absolutely neutral but leaned more toward the Poles than the Canadians, strange behavior for fellow members of the British Commonwealth!

There were many refugees in the area, mostly from North Vietnam, but some were from China, Burma and the northern provinces of Laos, Sam Neua and Phong Saly, which were under the control of the Pathet Lao. The largest group of refugees, numbering in the thousands, were the Black Thais of North

Vietnam. They had established a separate village close to the Capital under the leadership of His Excellency, Bac Cam Quy.

Many of these people had served in the French Army and had remained faithful to the French during and subsequent to Dien Bien Phu. Their presence did not please the local and U.S. officials who, for some obscure reason, wanted to exhibit a neutral position so as not to antagonize, I suppose, North Vietnam! I kept in contact with these people, hoping to be able to use their talent against our common enemy, North Vietnam.

In 1955 Laos had been invaded by the Communists who had advanced to the outskirts of Vientiane, but had retreated to the two northern regions for unknown reasons. The threat still existed and the official line held that the Lao army was capable of stemming the advance; however few believed that they actually could do so. In my discussions with Bac Cam Quy, the venerable old man said to me that the only way to stop the Vietminh was to do it in North Vietnam, using the same techniques the Vietnamese had used against the French. He told me that he could assemble three thousand of his men and form a guerrilla force that would volunteer to return to their homeland of Northern Tonkin. They had enough experience to be ready in a very short time and all they needed was logistical support from the U.S. I reported this offer but received no reply.

Even the French—who had left a few agents behind in North Vietnam—were surprised by our reaction, or lack thereof. They were on their way out, but they felt that someone should maintain the networks they had established before they had left Vietnam. Most of their nets were under the control of the Black Thais who hated the Vietnamese with passion. They had several radio operators hidden in the Tonkin area, but these agents no longer had anyone to whom to report. I was able to acquire some of these assets, but the Chief of Station never trusted the arrangement, believing that the French were just teasing us. It turned out that the material we obtained from these abandoned assets was both excellent and productive.

One of the ex-French principal agents we began to utilize was a local fellow who had contact with Vietnamese officials. These included Vietnamese Army officers who, in exchange for payment of medicine or money, did not mind cooperating and provided the agent with information about their units and their plans. The station firmly believed that either he was a double agent or that the French still controlled him, in which case he was only giving us what the French wanted us to have. There was a lot of skepticism at the station, but very little on the military side. Personally, I was not too concerned about the value of the information we were getting because it was raw information which in any case had to be verified by other means.

The situation in Laos was not as desperate as some wanted the world to believe. The United States Overseas Mission (USOM), a division of the U.S.

Department of State and the local USAID organization, was busy trying to improve the economic health of the country by any means. It was useless to lend these people funds they did not have the means to repay. Thus most of the help provided was in the form of grants to either government agencies or to businesses with some chance of success. There were many instances of corruption and misuse of funds and I do not recall a single one succeeding.

In those days, U.S. foreign aid policy towards Laos was a microcosm of our view of international politics. The local system in place for implementing that policy appeared to be under the control of the decision-makers back in Washington, but in fact was manipulated by local embassy bureaucrats whose aims were, to most of us, obscure. I shall never forget the frustration of one of the local authentic USAID staff, with whom I was friendly. He tried to do the right thing but was criticized and almost fired for trying to save the taxpayers' money.

His job was to organize, equip, and train a fire-fighting unit for the city of Vientiane. While the project was planned by Washington, he was given a large amount of funds and told to implement it.

After examining the project, based on American fire stations, he reorganized it to fit the local conditions. For example, the original budget included a massive ladder truck capable of reaching the top floor of a seven-story building when the tallest building in Vientiane was barely two stories high. The plan also called for the purchase of a large number of fire hydrants, when the city did not even have a water system!

In the process, he eliminated these and similarly other wasteful expenses that had been included in the original budget and presented his revision to those to whom he reported.

He did not have to wait very long for a reply. It came with a letter of admonition, criticizing him for having dared to modify the original plan. His plan had saved more than half the fund allocated to the project. He was told clearly to follow the original plan and to spend all the money. The Washington bureaucrats did not care how, just as long as all the money was spent. This was the logic resulting from our illogical federal budgeting system in which each governmental department knew that under spending this year's budgeted amount would likely result in a reduction of next year's allocation.

Reluctantly, my friend tackled the project, buying the material, the fire truck and the tools and uniforms needed to equip the fire-fighting unit of the capital. Eventually the day of the inauguration arrived with many foreign guests in attendance, including the U.S. Ambassador and visitors from Washington. This was a momentous day intended to show what a fantastic job we Americans could do when we set our minds to it and threw money at a problem. A typical native building was erected at the center of a large square. The plan was to set it afire and have the new fire brigade rush in and extinguish it as per the training they had received.

This was very serious business and my friend impressed upon the fire fighters that they had to make a good impression and have all of their new equipment in tip-top shape. This included their personal appearance and cleanliness. So in the morning of the demonstration, the entire brigade decided to take showers.

Of course in Vientiane there was no running water so one bathed in the Mekong River unless one had a good supply of water as we did. Our water was brought to us by truck tanker and pumped to our own reservoir, a large square tank located on a tower next to our building. The fire brigade also had a good source of water! Their truck held several thousand gallons of water because there were no fire hydrants to supply the needed water in case of fire.

Early that afternoon after the distinguished assembly had gathered in the demonstration area, the building was set afire. Someone alerted the brigade, and with siren blaring, the red truck came roaring in with its complement of thoroughly bathed squeaky cleaned fire fighters dressed in their bulky protective clothing which gave them the appearance of space creatures.

They began their procedure, unrolling their hose and, with the pump screaming, they opened the valve. Instead of the expected high pressure jet, the water only trickled out and soon even that stopped, as the pump continued its whining. First there was silence, than an uproar. All those present except a few members of USOM laughed uproariously while the building was completely consumed by the flames. My friend, who was in charge of the project, had a good sense of humor. He too laughed when he realized that the firefighters, so eager to be clean for the demonstration, had used most of the water in the truck while showering and had failed to reload it. So much for a very successful project! Incidentally, during my one year in Laos it was the only house that I had seen destroyed by fire and I have never heard of any since.

One would think that when a policy is expressed by the President, the entire Government structure, specifically those agencies responsible to the Executive branch, would follow suit; however, that is not always the case. In fact, in those days it was usually the exception. The Ambassador reflected the views of the President (to whom he reported) in his dealings with the King and/or his Prime Minister. However, the local State Department employees, those not politically assigned by the President, especially those of USOM, received their marching orders from the bureaucrats of Foggy Bottom.

One day I was flying with the Ambassador and several other people, including a State Department foreign service officer. I was only hitching a ride and was glad to be able to get to my destination in the comfort of a Cessna

280

instead of an Air America bucket-seat special. At one point during the flight, the conversation between the State Department official and the Ambassador turned to a certain policy to be implemented by the State Department. The official summarized the Department's position. Incredulous, the Ambassador asked the man from State to repeat his statement, then told him that this was exactly opposite of the instructions he had received from the President. The official replied that the White House did not know what was going on. The Ambassador was obviously shocked and most unhappy, and from that moment on the silence in the plane was deafening.

Until my tour of duty in Southeast Asia I was under the impression that foreign service officers were selected because of their impeccable background and their exemplary personal life. Their political affiliation surely was not a factor in their selection or retention. In the case of one with whom I became familiar, this was definitely not the case. He was in his mid-thirties, a good-looking and a potentially prime catch for any of the single female secretaries employed by the Embassy. He did not take long for him to establish a reputation as a swinger.

Because of his position he had acquired a rather large, newly built house in town. Unfortunately, its lower floor, which might have been originally designed as a storefront, had large windows from ceiling to floor. The curtains did not adequately hide the activities conducted in the lower floor of the house.

One of Lord Buddha's foot prints on a rock.

As a result, the kids of the neighborhood and others who had been alerted to the show would stand in front of the house and gawk. This infuriated the diplomat to no end. He would chase them and they would run away, only to return later. In desperation, he one day grabbed a rock and threw it at the "mob," hitting one of the kids. This was a bad move on his part because the kid he hit turned out to be the son of a high local Government official who did not waste time with his complaint to the Embassy. To avoid an embarrassing situation our diplomat was immediately transferred to another station.

In our area Buddhism was prevalent. I believe they practiced the rite of the low vehicle, one of the two principal branches of the ancient religion. They had a large contingent of bonzes (Buddhist priests) throughout the country because every male practicing Buddhism had to spend a part of his life as a Bonze. I was told that even the King had his head shaved and wore a saffron-colored robe, and in the morning went begging for his food when he felt it was required of him. That was the morning ritual. The bonzes would line up close to a local shrine, called a "vat", while women came to place rice and food in their bowls.

During my travel throughout Laos I occasionally came across special shrines watched over by bonzes and protected from the elements by bamboo sheds. One held a footprint of the Buddha. Legend had it that Buddha had walked across Asia in huge strides, leaving his footprints on rocks. This particular one showed the outline of a foot approximately five feet in length. It was surrounded with flowers and burning incense sticks. The bonzes were supposed to believe in a single God and believed that Buddha was a messiah, similar to the Christians' view of Jesus. Witchcraft was against the teachings of Buddhism, yet during the various holidays—and there were many—bonzes in booths predicted the future for a few coins in the local currency. They were supposed to be celibates, but often had reputations as women chasers. Lao women who could not get pregnant from their husbands would seek the help of bonzes.

Laos had many religious holidays; one in particular was the feast of fertility. A tradition of this holiday called for a parade where huge representations of the male sexual organ were dis-

Phallic prop used at the feast of the fertility.

played. Men disguised as women would dance to the sound of drums, and many carried wooden replicas of the penis.

One group carried an old-style box camera on a tripod with a flash attachment. They would stop in front of some giggling girls who covered their mouths with their hands as all laughing Lao women do. After a flash, the men would extract a series of pictures from the back of the camera. They then gave the photos to the girls who would hide their faces with both hands and run away. The pictures were shots of naked people having sexual encounters. The people observing this thought it great fun.

The climax of the celebration was the afternoon firing of

Bamboo rockets fired across the Mekong River.

rockets across the Mekong towards Thailand. Huge bamboo launching stands were erected at the site days before.

Rockets composed of large bamboo poles stuffed with gunpowder were placed on the structures and at the proper time they would be fired. The bamboo poles, decorated with designs of various colors and with phallic representations, were propelled to various heights toward the other bank of the Mekong. With few exceptions, none reached the other side, about a two hundred yards away, though the ceremony was meant to improve the fertility of not only the women, but of the ground as well.

Buddhism was thought to be a strange religion, one difficult for Westerners (who think of themselves as being more discriminating in their beliefs) to accept. Yet one of our CIA contingent, either to make points with his Buddhist friends, or out of personal conviction, wore a sacred Buddhist symbol around his neck to bring him luck. However, he was killed anyway, one of the early casualties of the Vietnam War.

One aspect of my job was to travel to meet people, either alone or in the company of a member of the G-2 section. One day I traveled to the high plateau of Bolovens, located in south Laos, with the executive officer of the Lao G-2 and his assistant. Our first stop was Savannakhet, a small regional capital located on the eastern bank of the Mekong. We stayed in a typical hotel without air-conditioning. As there was only one room available, we shared it. Our room had two beds and a ceiling fan. The temperature was close to 100, as was the humidity. My companion would not go to sleep; he kept talking until long past midnight. I was able to write a very comprehensive report on him. It might have been useful later because he became the army chief of staff in one of the many regimes which governed Laos in the years that followed.

The next day, borrowing a Jeep from the local military command, we proceeded first to Pakse, then on to Paksong on the Bolovens plateau, where he had relatives. The French had selected this area for a rest and recreation center for their colonial troops and bureaucrats. The climate was ideal, not only for people but also for growing all types of fruit and vegetables. Their strawberries, pineapples, leeks and cabbages were the biggest I had ever seen, and the tastiest. Their coffee was renowned all over Southeast Asia, so when I mentioned my fondness for coffee to my escort, his relatives made certain that only the best brew was served.

During that trip I heard all kinds of disturbing stories about the North Vietnamese coming to the small villages of South Laos and kidnaping young men. This had been going on for some time, but no one had done anything about it. Some of the young men had been politically indoctrinated and had returned changed, becoming very critical of the political situation in Laos. Others had never returned, which caused great pain and worry for their families. An old woman talked to us about her fear, and others voiced concerned about the North Vietnamese incursions into Laos. All this was duly noted in my report, which hopefully was sent to Washington for analysis.

We returned to our home base by local bus: a truck chassis with a home-made bus body covered with all kind of fancy designs and colors. I managed to get a seat in front next to the driver who handled his vehicle as if it were a Jeep, speeding along the washboard-covered roads with his passengers hanging on for dear life. The bus was filled to capacity with passengers inside and baggage and cargo on the roof.

Fortunately there was little traffic and the few vehicles we met carefully moved off the road to let us pass, waiting for the dust to settle before continuing their travel.

We stopped in every village, and each time young boys and girls came to the side of the bus to offer their barbecued chicken and bamboo sticks filled with sticky rice, some dyed red or blue. I tried the chicken, which was very spicy, and the plain rice, which was laced with coconut.

This was very nourishing and very welcome after several hours of bouncing down the road with our Kamikaze driver. After this trip, I decided that I would not take another bus trip while in Laos. Thus when I decided to go somewhere I waited until the opportunity to hitch a flight presented itself.

Once when I decided to go to Phong Saly, the northernmost province of Laos, I waited until a flight going to the same destination could take me. This aircraft had unusual features, engineered specifically for short take-offs and very short landings. It was a rather small plane, just large enough to accommodate four people without much baggage. The pilot was an old experienced pilot who handled the aircraft with a quiet and comforting assurance.

We started on one end of the runway and were airborne in less than fifty yards, after achieving a ground speed of only sixty miles per hour. We climbed steadily and leveled off when all of a sudden a loud bang sounded. I looked at the pilot, but his expression had not changed.

"What was that?" I asked.

"That's nothing," he replied. "Only the foils retracting in the leading edge of the wings."

It sounded as if the wings were about to go their way and we ours. These foils provided the aircraft with additional lift for short take-off.

We reached our destination where we spent several hours accomplishing our mission. On the way back, airborne a few minutes and at our cruising altitude, the pilot showed me the compass and said, "Take over and keep on this heading. Don't worry, this thing practically flies itself." I took control, fully expecting to somehow cause the craft to plunge to the ground, when I realized that the pilot was right. This aircraft was the easiest I had flown. After a few minutes, and for the duration of the flight, I noticed that my companion either quietly snoozed or watched me with his eyes half closed. He took over as we approached the capital.

When he reduced speed the same clanking occurred as the foils protruded from the leading edge of the wings, providing more lift. In line with the landing strip, he reduced the RPM to practically nothing and the plane settled down nicely, coming to a complete stop in less than fifty yards. The pilot commented, "This plane does not land; we use a controlled crash to bring it down."

The landing gear was also very strange. The wheels were built like casters so that when landing on rough fields they would conform to the shape of the terrain. This plane was designed for use behind an enemy lines in areas without landing facilities.

When I first arrived at the station, I decided that I would be very careful about what I ate. For breakfast, I walked or pedaled the bike I had brought with me, to the USOM cafeteria. It was quite a distance, close to a mile, which took me by the market where farmers sold their produce to the local inhabitants. I selected a fairly good size papaya, and at the USOM mess, asking for a knife, would eat it instead of ordering a traditional egg and bacon breakfast. I washed it down with a 10-cent cup of coffee, and went to work feeling very proud of myself for arranging such an inexpensive meal.

This went on for approximately one month. Then one morning the Filipino manager came to my table and said, "This is a restaurant, not a public dining-room. Unless you order a meal like everyone else, you will have to leave." I could not believe what I was hearing. I made him repeat it, and very politely reminded him that this refectory was a U.S. Government installation and I did not need someone to tell me what I could and could not do. This mess hall was used for other things besides eating. From that day forth he never asked me to leave and we even became good friends. I believe that some of our own people put him up to it, just to see what I would do or say.

The noon meals were taken at our USAID compound but were not prepared by native cooks. They were probably Vietnamese or Chinese, because I do not believe that local people were very good cooks. Their main diet consisted of rice and very hot pepper crushed into a sauce. They fed it to their kids when they were weaned from their mother's milk, probably accounts for the high infant mortality. The quality of our lunches was all right and they were pretty much the same every day; chicken and rice one day, rice and chicken the next.

On the dining room table was the ever present paregoric, as much a part of our meals as dessert). It was there either as a prevention or beçause it was needed by one or several members of our group. I never used it and, thanks to my weekly dose of psyllium, I did not get the dreaded "runs".

After a while, I decided to patronize a small Chinese restaurant located close to my quarters. I began with breakfast, which consisted of a couple of eggs and two or three slices of bacon. Later, I also took my noon meal there. If there were no Chinese food available I would order a "Bifteck" (the local pronunciation of a beef steak), a thin slice of water buffalo meat pan-fried and covered with a blanket of garlic. Thank God I loved garlic, which enabled me to ignore the shoe-leather-like consistency of the meat.

One morning I sat at my usual chair, which seemed to always be vacant when I came in, even if the place was full.

The owner came to me and said, "Ce matin, les oeufs ne sont pas frais. Je vais vous faire une omelette au fromage!" ("This morning the eggs are not fresh, I shall make you a cheese omelet!")

I did not quite understand the logic of this solution. I waited in anticipation, expecting the body of a small chick in the omelet. However I was wrong.

The restaurant was an excellent place for me to meet and talk to local people. Paul LeRoy, a Eurasian of French nationality, and his Vietnamese spouse, were regular customers. It was not long before we began sharing a table and exchanging views and comments over a glass of wine. He was a refugee from North Vietnam. His wife's mother was still in North Vietnam where he had been the owner of a large brick manufacturing operation and of several gold mines. He also dealt in cement and building materials. He was known as "Le roi des briques" or "the king of the bricks". He was trying to salvage some of his possessions and do odd jobs to survive. He and his spouse preferred Vietnamese food, so periodically they would order it and invite me to partake.

Despite the efforts of the head of local French intelligence to discredit me, my relationship with the French officers continued to be great. They would invite me to their parties and on their weekend trips into the mountains northeast of the capital, where it was cooler. The group included officers of the French military mission as well as some doctors who worked at the local hospital, which was staffed with French medical specialists. The group included a former military nurse who had seen combat in Vietnam prior to 1954, and all with years of experience in Southeast Asia. I learned a lot more from them than from my co-workers, most of whom until recently had never been in that part of the world. My previous experience in Vietnam was very helpful, even though during the war my association with the local people had been severely restricted and highly controlled by Ho Chi Minh.

On several occasions, my French friends and I visited the mountain villages, which for the most part were above the 2,000 foot elevation. Apparently these people could not live in the lowlands and those who ventured below the 2,000 foot level did not survive very long. We usually brought along our own food. I would purchase my portion from the commissary, including hot dogs, unknown otherwise in this part of the world. The villagers always offered us food, but we only accepted rice and "chum," a rice wine served from jars and drunk through a straw. Very often we gave them some of our canned food for their hospitality.

The French always brought along wine, and when the group was larger than ten people, a small barrel would be part of our supply. As long as we could get our vehicles on the narrow and at times extremely difficult trail, we were all right.

However, when we had to park and walk, the 20-liter barrel became a serious problem. On one of our trips, we drove as far as we could on a mountain road. The rest of the way we traveled on foot, approximately ten miles further to another village located on the side of a rather steep mountain. We were carrying guns because we had heard that there was wild game and that gaurs (wild oxen) had been sighted by the natives. We did not mind carrying our own equipment, but the wine barrel became a problem. That is until a young girl, approximately five feet tall, wrapped a piece of cloth around the barrel and hoisted it onto her back, then looped the cloth over her shoulders and wrapped it around the top of her head, using her forehead to carry much of the weight. With the barrel on her back, she trotted ahead while we struggled up the steep trail. She reached the village ahead of us and when we finally arrived, she greeted us, seated on the barrel with a big smile.

When we stayed overnight in a village, we were usually guests of the village chief, and this trip was no exception.

The grass and bamboo huts were large and roomy. The chief and his family occupied a corner of the hut while we stayed nearer the fire pit in the center of the hut. I learned very quickly that one's position within the hut was quite important, and the bottom of my feet had a significance until then completely unknown to me. On the wall of each hut was a small altar, not as elaborate as those in Chinese or Vietnamese homes, but just the same, an altar. When first entering a hut, we usually assembled around the fire located in a depression in the center of the dirt floor. The smoke filtered through the roof made up of dry palm leaves. After having prepared our meal, supplemented by our host's steaming rice, we prepared to settle down for the night, as it was already dark outside. As the evenings were cold high in the mountains we opened our sleeping bags and arranged them close to the fire banked for the night.

This was the first time that I had accompanied my French friends to a mountain village and stayed in a Chief's hut. I was about to fall asleep when I heard a commotion in the Chief's corner, and a lively conversation between the Chief and his bare-bosomed spouse. One of the group who had a smattering knowledge of the local language, said that the Chief's spouse was unhappy because one of us was pointing his feet at the altar.

This grave insult to their deity had upset the lady of the hut, however the chief was not inclined to get involved. It turned out that I was the culprit, the sinner who was pointing his tootsies at the altar. I moved around and brought my feet closer to the fire while my head remained cool all night long. The chatter in the chief's corner subsided and we had a peaceful night until the morning when we were awakened by the rhythmic chopping of corn stalks, used by the villagers as feed for their livestock.

It was the practice of the villagers in the morning to feed their animals before themselves. Afterwards they prepared the rice for the morning meal. After a quick breakfast we were ready for the trail. With our young wine carrier walking ahead of us, we left the village with all its inhabitants lined up to see us depart. The entire mountain was blanketed by a shroud of fog. During my entire stay in that area I never did see the sun rise in the morning. However, the sunsets were gorgeous, especially during the rainy season when thunderheads could be seen glowing up to impossible heights. As a rule, the Mekong River valley was covered with fog until mid-morning, when the sun would cause it to evaporate. Many times I had to wait at landing strips while the plane circled overhead waiting for the fog to clear in order to land. The mountain was always fresh at night and the few streams were clean and cool. We took

288

great pleasure in soaking in these shallow streams away from the flies and the pestilence of the jungle below.

During one of our trips into the mountain, we had stopped for lunch in a jungle clearing and were enjoying a glass of good wine when a Meo woman in her mid-twenties approached us. She wore a double silver necklace and her traditional costume and spoke Lao. Some of our people talked to her and offered her a glass of wine, which she accepted and downed in one gulp. She had a second glass and her face became quite red. She was laughing and chatting, telling us that she wished to leave with us and go to Vientiane, when all of a sudden a Meo appeared at the edge of the clearing.

Young Meo woman sharing a glass of wine

He was small but well built. He carried a long stick and, ignoring our greetings, walked directly to the woman and began pounding on her with the stick. She bent over to protect herself from the blows but said nothing. We were about to stop him, when one of our group, a doctor who had lived many years in the area, stopped us. He told us not to interfere, or we might not live to regret it. He explained to us that this was a domestic problem, and it would blow over very quickly. We should not get involved. Indeed, before long she was standing straight and proudly walking toward their village ahead of her husband.

Not too many members of USOM or the Embassy had their families with them. Ours was considered a hardship station and not recommended for people with families. Despite this, I decided to bring Georgette and our four kids to Laos. First we had to find suitable accommodations, and that was not easy.

The Station decided to lease a house for us. The one selected was in the process of being built close to our Bachelors Quarters. It was a typical house erected on stilts with a section built around a huge mango tree approximately four feet in diameter. The structure was constructed from local wood by a Vietnamese contractor. The outside walls as well as the room separations were made of woven bamboo strips. Access to the main floor was by a staircase through the center of the building. A kitchen was located on the

Native style house in Vientiane.

ground level and a small room under the stairs was the living quarters for our "Bep", or cook, who was provided with the house. This unusual house was airy with a view over the rest of the neighborhood. Periodically, mangoes would fall from the high branches extending over the house at heights up to 100 feet.

In the Spring of 1957, Georgette, Noëlle, Sonny, Marc and Paul arrived at Bangkok by commercial flight. I met them and took them to the best and newest hotel in town. We had a suite of rooms including a dining area where most of our meals were served. We remained in Bangkok until there was space available on the Air America flight. This was the beginning of a situation that would become more and more unpleasant as the days went by.

The C-46, utilized by Air America, was not a commercial aircraft. It was a cargo plane equipped with bucket seats. The space between the bucket seats was filled with cargo secured by nets and lines. Sometimes there was just enough room for the legs of the passengers. Of course, the bucket seats were not the most comfortable in the world, but the distance we had to travel was only approximately 330 miles and the flying time was less than a couple of hours. As usual, the plane was delayed. As we were boarding, the flight engineer invented something irregular that had to be fixed before we could take off. An hour or so in a super hot aircraft is not very pleasant. This was part of the job for me, but not for Georgette who started to complain.

We finally took off and the plane cooled off considerably as we gained altitude. The rest of the trip was uneventful.

When we arrived we were greeted by the Chief of Station and his spouse. Georgette immediately asked, "When do you turn on the air conditioning in this oven," for the temperature was approximately 95 degrees and the humidity 100%, which at this time of the year was normal for the region.

We drove to our house and when we reached it I knew immediately that bringing Georgette to this third-world country had been a mistake. The children of course did not care. This was new for them and that was enough, but Georgette let me know that I had committed the worst possible crime in bringing my family to this God-forsaken place. At first I thought that she would like the place as most of us did once we began to learn more about it. Unfortunately this did not happen with Georgette.

Sporadic electricity made it impossible to use electric refrigerators, so refrigeration came by means of gas-operated refrigerators and freezers. We had both, but these were full of bugs and malfunctions. They operated on kerosene not always of the best quality. When one of the appliances would work, the other was usually down requiring the transfer of food from one to the other.

Georgette did not have to perform kitchen duty as we had a cook, a small wiry little Chinese who, besides Chinese, could only speak very poor French. Every day he would ask what we wanted for our meals, but as he did not understand what we requested, he did his own thing, usually a mixed Chinese and Vietnamese menu. He did everything— shopping, cooking and the dishes. After the evening meal, with everything was put away, he would retire to his cubbyhole under the stairway. At first I did not detect the sweet aroma emanating from the area of the stairs. Then one night, curiosity got the better of me and I knocked at the door but received no reply, I opened it and knew exactly what our skinny cook was doing, lying down on a Chinese pillow. He looked at me with a blank stare, still holding his opium pipe. We had a drug addict as a cook!

Water was also in short supply. The 400-gallon tank up on our roof had to be refilled periodically with water from the Mekong. The water could not be consumed without boiling and treated with chemicals in order to kill any leftover bacteria. This was part of the cook's job.

The children were washed as best as we could and at times we even took them to the Mekong for a swim. Paul, the youngest, enjoyed a daily bath in a large pail next to the house.

Every day Georgette accused me of all kind of crimes against my family, continuously complaining. Our sex life had come to a complete halt. One evening, about two weeks after their arrival, we were sitting together in our living room when I noticed a huge spider on the wall behind Georgette. I said to her, "Don't move; there is a spider behind you. I will get rid of it."

She turned around and saw the four-inch black spider only a few inches from her. She let go with a yell and instantly became hysterical. I had quite a job to calm her down. The next day I took her to the doctor and from that time on her hysteria became more and more frequent. I discussed this with the Station Chief and we all agreed that for the good of the Station, as well as that of Georgette, she and the children should return to the United States. In order for them to be eligible for military transit back to the States, a medical waiver was required. Given the circumstances, the doctor had no problem providing it. A few days later, just six weeks after their arrival, they were back on the Air America shuttle, first to Bangkok, then to Japan and on to the United States.

This was a load off my mind, but it did not eliminate my worries. I did not know what Georgette would do when she arrived back in the States. She decided to stop in California to see her sister, Mimi. There she rented a house at Reseda in the San Fernando Valley. It was necessary for me to remain in Laos to complete the two years duty I had initially agreed to do.

The Beginning of the End

A few months after Georgette and the children's departure, I began to have a problem with my skin. I developed some 26 boils, principally between my knees and my navel. These began as small pimples, then grew in size until they reached the size of fifty-cent pieces. Our local doctor gave me antibiotic drugs, but they did not help. At times it was so bad that I could not move without experiencing excruciating pain. Sitting and moving was an ordeal. Even in bed I could not rest. It was decided that I should go to the Bangkok Nursing Home, a clinic where U.S. embassy personnel went when in need of treatment. The flight was a nightmare. Sitting in a bucket seat with a seat belt across my middle where most of the boils were located was so painful that I decided not to use it. I just held onto the seat with both hands.

The clinic was managed by a British company and staffed with Thai and Chinese personnel. I was placed in a private room because they suspected a staph infection, and was assigned a Chinese nurse, Suzanna Lee, whose husband was a very important businessman in Hong Kong. They even fixed me up with my own bathroom because they feared that I would infect the other patients. The tests they conducted proved that indeed I had a staphylo-coccus infection and that antibiotics were the only solution. They began with penicillin but without result. They developed a culture using my boils and to their amazement found that penicillin not only did not destroy the staphylo-coccus, but promoted its growth! After trying several other antibiotics, they settled for aureomycine. Three weeks later I was back on my feet.

I must say that the clinic was a very nice place. Unfortunately with the exception of nurse Lee and the Thai doctor, no one spoke English. I read practically the entire library of British magazines and books. The food was typically British: tasteless, in minuscule portions. I was always hungry and asked people from the Embassy and the Bangkok station who came to see me to bring me fruit such as bananas, mangoes or mangosteens, a local dark red fruit with a delicious pulp. Eventually I was well enough to leave the clinic and move to a hotel in downtown Bangkok.

It was on a Sunday that I checked in the Trocadero Hotel where I had stayed during my previous visits to Bangkok. They knew me and were very glad to grant my every request. Whenever I was in Bangkok on Sunday I made it a point to attend mass at the nearby Catholic Church. Each Sunday they conducted one service in French for the many French people of the area. It was too late for me to go to church when I reached the hotel, so I decided to go the following day. I asked the desk to wake me at 6:00 a.m. and went to bed unconcerned. I believe that what woke me up around 7:00 the following morning was the silence. Usually the traffic in the street would already be heavy by 5:00 in the morning and the street noise would reach my 5th floor room easily. On Sunday, the traffic was much lighter and the street less noisy.

However this was Monday!

Realizing that the front desk had failed to call me, I opened the window, looked out and, to my surprise, the street below was empty except for a few pedestrians moving rapidly along the sidewalks. I looked up toward the end of the street where I knew the Post Office was located, and saw two soldiers on their stomachs manning a machine-gun. "What is this?" I wondered. Getting dressed quickly, I went downstairs and asked the desk clerk what was going on. He replied, "We had a coup early this morning, but do not worry, it will all be over by noon."

Indeed he was right. By 12 o'clock the traffic had resumed, the soldiers and the machine-gun were gone, the prime minister had flown to Cambodia and life had returned to normal.

This was a typical Thai coup: no one got hurt and business as usual resumed, albeit with a different group in charge, while the previous group enjoyed the fruits of their corruption either on the Riviera or in Switzerland.

I returned to the station feeling a lot better. My friends, particularly the Vietnamese, warned me that someone had paid a witch doctor to cause my infection. I pooh-poohed the idea, figuring that only the French wanted to get rid of me, and they did not believe in witch doctors. I knew their methods, and they were much more subtle.

I was happy to see my French counterpart and resume my activities. In August or about, at the beginning of the rainy season, a group of French officers and I decided to go fishing on a tributary of the Mekong situated at the base of the mountain region. The French were glad to have me along because I was able to bring the big four-wheel-drive Toyota capable of going anywhere on or off the road. With our fishing gear and enough supplies for a few days, we left the capital as the clouds moved in from the West. Our destination was the Nam Ngun, a river that passed through a deep and narrow valley at a point where a long bridge had been constructed.

The center of the bridge was approximately 30 feet above the surface of the water. Built by the French Corps of Engineers, it was a metal structure approximately 300 feet long similar to a Bailey Bridge, placed on solid stone and concrete pillars anchored into the granite banks of the river. We arrived at our destination early in the afternoon just as it started to rain, and decided to leave our vehicles near the road and walk to the village, a quarter mile upstream.

The village was located on a narrow meadow approximately one hundred yards from the river, and all the houses were built traditionally on stilts.

294

The village chief invited us to his hut, giving us the enclosed porch large enough for us and our gear. Two members of our group, eager to try their luck, walked down to the river and began to fish. However the rain became so intense that they gave up and joined us to share a couple of bottles of wine before supper. Very pleased to have us as his guests, the village chief offered us the traditional rice and rice wine. We were looking forward to the following day when "the big one" could be caught. Night had fallen by the time we crawled into our sleeping bags and quickly fell asleep.

Suddenly I was awakened by the noises of animals and the loud talk of people. I looked at my watch; it was 1:30 a.m.

What was going on? My companions did not seem to have awakened, but I was curious by all the activities at this hour of the morning. Looking toward the entrance where the ladder reached the floor of the hut, I saw the head of an individual passing slowly in front of the hut. I knew that the floor was at least 10 feet above the ground, and so I assumed that either he was a very tall fellow or someone was carrying him. Hearing a sloshing noise under the floor, I spread the bamboo floor and took a look. I could not believe what I saw. Not two feet below us was the water. The individual I had seen was sitting in a dugout, floating in front of the house! I shook my companions awake and told them about the situation. One of them, a veteran of the area, insisted that this was not unusual.

We got up and went to the chief who was in the process of lifting bags of rice onto the rafters. Then he placed a nest with eggs and a cackling chicken on the rice bags. The animal noises we heard came from their moving their

Bridge over the Nam Ngun River prior to the flood.

295

livestock—cows, pigs and chickens—to higher ground. The chief offered us a bowl of rice and some tea and advised us to get our gear ready. Very possibly we would have to be evacuated to the road because the river was still rising. By this time the water was approximately three inches from the floor of the hut. Our local expert told us not to worry, that these people knew exactly what they were doing and that the river rose in this fashion every year—that was why they built their houses on stilts.

The Chief, seriously concerned with our safety, suggested that we should be taken to an area on shore approximately a quarter of a mile downstream, near where we had parked our vehicles. The only way to get there was by dugout canoe; but with all our gear, only two at a time could make the trip. I volunteered to go first with another member of our group.

We loaded our gear, seated ourselves carefully in the center of the craft and began moving. The current picked us up and carried us at full speed between trees and huts. Our guide was unbelievable. I fully expected to end up hundreds of miles downstream, but he beached us gently on the shore, which had been a road only a few hours earlier. Soon we were joined by the other members of our group and, carrying our gear to our vehicles, we decided to watch the dawn to see what would happen to the village.

By this time it was 5:00 in the morning and it was still raining. We walked to the bridge and noticed that the river was less than 5 feet from the underside of the 30-foot high span! Huge uprooted trees were floating down the river, some with animals clinging to their branches. By 6:00, pieces of the village began to appear on the surface of the water, then entire huts began floating under the bridge. A large hut, the one in which we had been soundly asleep only a few hours earlier, came floating down, and on its grass roof the little chicken was hanging on for dear life. So these people knew exactly what the river would do? Our expert had no answer for that question.

Amazingly, as we were watching, several people from a nearby village joined us. One of them approached me and in a serious way asked, "What is the value of the dollar today?"

Given the tragedy unfolding in front of us and this man's insensitivity, I felt like throwing him in the river.

We left the area extremely saddened by what we had seen.

While the people of the area were used to flooding, this was one of the most severe floods in some time. As we drove off, the rain still had not stopped. The road we had used from place to place had disappeared. In some areas the water was so deep that we had to stop the motor and push the Jeep and the other vehicle by hand so as not to take water into their engines. It took us twice as long to return and when we arrived we were thoroughly soaked.

The next day, Monday, I noticed a few sore spots on my thighs and on my lower abdomen. I cleaned them carefully and discovered on close examination that they appeared to be exactly the same as those from which I had just recovered. A few more days later the sore spots had developed into full blown boils. Our doctor did not have the antibiotics previously prescribed at the Bangkok clinic, but he did have pain killer which was all right with me. He gave me some without asking if I was allergic to anything, or warning me of side effects.

The following Sunday, after working on a report in the Attaché's office, I decided to go to church with other Catholics from our group. I was working with some top secret material and having no way to secure them, placed the documents in my briefcase which I took with me to church. In the middle of the service, probably because of my kneeling, I began to feel sharp pains in my lower abdomen and in my thighs. I was carrying the pills that the doctor had given me and I took one. But the pain did not subside entirely.

After the mass, my companions, including some members of the Canadian contingent of ICC, invited me to the Canadian officer's club (known locally, with pun intended, as the Canadian Club) for an aperitif. I accepted neither a beer nor hard liquor, but instead drank a can of chocolate milk.

It was cool and refreshing and I used it to take a second pill.

That was the last thing I remembered.

When I awoke, I was in a strange bed in a strange room and felt very tired and weak. I began to go over what I did and where I was before. About this time someone walked through a door into the room and, bending over me, asked, "Are you all right?" in a thick foreign accent. I recognized him as a member of the Polish delegation of the ICC, an individual suspected of being an espionage agent for the Soviets. I was certain that I had been kidnaped and that I was held as a prisoner. Yet I was not tied down and the individual did not ask me a single question. He walked through a second doorway, then reappeared through it a minute or two later and went on his way through the door through which I had first seen him enter the room, paying no attention to me. Then the wife of the U.S. military attaché walked in the room and asked me how I felt. I wanted to know the time and was not surprised to learn that I had been out for six hours in the assistant attaché's bed. Then it hit me. Where was my briefcase? She did not know, but she would find out. Soon thereafter the assistant attaché came in and told me that after I passed out at the Canadian Club, they carried me to his house and laid me out in his bedroom, took my briefcase to the embassy and locked it in the safe. I felt much better but the pains returned worse than before. The Ambassador, who was kept informed regarding everything in his organization, suggested that I should return to the clinic in Bangkok and offered to take me in his plane. The following day, I flew with the Ambassador and his spouse to Bangkok. They personally drove me to the clinic and made certain that I was properly cared for.

I was back in my old room and with the same nurse.

This time they knew what to do, but it took time for the antibiotic to take effect. The following day members of the Bangkok embassy came to see me. They wanted me to do something while lying in my bed. They suggested that I write down all that I knew about the people I had met and had been associated with since I came to Southeast Asia. They even brought me a typewriter and plenty of paper.

For several weeks I typed and typed page after page. Individuals from the local embassy would pick up the material and give me more paper. Within three weeks I was back to normal, and I returned to the station. By then it became obvious that this part of the world and I did not get along too well. I was spending too much time at the clinic and as far as I was concerned the assignment was a waste of time and effort.

During one of the many trips I had made to Bangkok and Saïgon, I met Col. John B. Stanley, a most interesting officer who commanded an Army intelligence unit in Japan. We had shared many ideas during our conversations and saw eye to eye on many things. He was aware of my function but he did not share the views of my Pentagon boss who had placed me there, nor did he care much for the CIA. When I told him about the problems I had encountered locally and with the Pentagon, he suggested that once I completed my tour of duty I should call him, and he would request that I be assigned to his group.

After it was officially determined that the local climate was not for me and that my health was more important than my mission, it was agreed by all concerned that I should return to the United States for reassignment. On my way back I asked for a layover in Tokyo without stating the reason why. I wanted to meet Col. Stanley and his staff and plan our strategy carefully so that no one would know our scheme. The difference between the Tokyo operation (USACRAPAC) and the Pentagon leadership was unbelievable. Unfortunately, the Pentagon (and at times CINCPAC) called the shots, and Tokyo had no choice but to submit.

When I reached the Tokyo office of Col. Stanley it was like meeting an old family friend. I was given the VIP treatment. They even introduced me to one of the secretaries who took care of me for a few days. We immediately took to each other. She had a car so we were able to go places and see Tokyo and its suburbs properly before continuing my return trip to the USA.

I left Southeast Asia a little over one year after arriving there, never dreaming that soon thereafter I would return.

The Waiting Game

As soon as I returned to the US, I spent a few days in Reseda, California, with my family. Georgette had rented a house there and soon after my arrival I met one of her closest neighbors, a single 30-year-old jock who seemed to know his way around the house. She told me that he had been very helpful and by the way she talked about him and his behavior, I had the impression that they had more than a platonic relationship. When I told her that I had to go to Washington and did not know when I would return, unlike other times she did not seem upset!

I flew to Washington D.C., and wearing civies, reported to the Pentagon for debriefing. When by taxi from the airport I reached the underground entrance, I phoned the office and asked for assistance in lugging my gear to my final destination. Lieutenant colonels and colonels were a dime a dozen in the Pentagon, yet I was surprised when a full colonel was dispatched to assist me, just as if I were a VIP. I suppose that someone had failed to tell him who I was, and so he probably believed that I was a dignitary. I said nothing to change his mind until after we reached my section's offices, at which point I remarked, "You know, colonel, this is the first time that a colonel has ever carried my bag. Normally, I carry a colonel's bag!" He got a big kick out of it.

We reached the offices located on the third level below ground, next to the heating plant. It was in this part of the building that some of the U.S. Army's most amazing intelligence operations were planned, and so it was super secured with sensors capable of detecting any movement including that of a fly. However, with few exceptions, the people working there weren't very smart and their dedication, if any, was primarily to their future and not so much to the success of the various missions. Many of Military Intelligence's civilian employees had been officers in the same department during their earlier military careers and had remained in the same job as civilians after retirement. They were the proverbial "double dippers," cashing in both on their retirement pay as well as their pay as civilian employees of the army if they were reserved officers. Regular Army officers did not have the same privilege.

I reported to the Colonel who had advised me prior to my departure to Southeast Asia. He was not entirely pleased with my reports he described as "vitriolic" or worse. He had specifically asked me to report everything to him so that his office could make an assessment of my activities. However he claimed that my reporting was too blunt, too critical and could cause serious problems if the CIA had learned of my remarks. After properly chewing me out he never mentioned my reports again. Afterward we went to lunch. While we were eating he casually stated that the CO of an intelligence unit located in Japan had specifically requested my transfer to his organization. He could not fathom why anyone would want me and he bluntly told me so. I innocently played dumb not letting him know that during my layover in Tokyo the Japan office had told me that they would make the request. His about-face concerning this operation surprised me. He was the one who specifically told me: "Never forget that you are in the Army, and the Army comes first."

Subsequently I learned that he was interested in a position with CIA, and was already looking out for their interests.

I also reported to the CIA to clear my financial accounts and work on my income taxes. Fortunately for me they had an agreement with the IRS, because I was receiving two salaries—one as a soldier and one as a civilian. I had to return my civilian salary to the Government, a situation very difficult to explain to someone outside the Agency. This was a nuisance for me and fortunately it was handled by people cleared to deal with such situations. However, in the end I always feared that I was the real loser because I couldn't comprehend their accounting methods.

After completing my report to both the Pentagon and the Agency I left Washington for California where I was told to wait until I received orders directing me to my next station, Tokyo.

Georgette's sister Mimi and her husband Larry resided close to Reseda where Georgette had leased a house. To be close to her kin was the reason why Georgette had decided to settle at California's San Fernando Valley.

After one week at Reseda I realized that the process for my returning to active duty status must be more complicated, problematic and time-consuming than the earlier procedure for my supposed retirement. Doing nothing was not exactly my bag. Fortunately, Larry was a house painter. He could always use an extra pair of hands. Thus I went to work with him for a couple of weeks.

By the end of the month, after several weeks without income, I decided to go to the nearest Army finance office, at the San Pedro port of embarkation. The finance officer in charge there did not believe my circumstances. He could not believe that I had been sent home to await orders. As far as he was concerned I was AWOL, and subject to immediate arrest! I tried to explain to him that I was on special assignment and that I was doing exactly what I was told. Failing to convince him, I gave him the telephone number of the Pentagon office and suggested that he call. He did so, and as he listened to the explanation on the other end, he kept shaking his head in amazement. He had never heard of such a thing in his entire army career. After I had collected my pay, he called me to his office and asked me: "How do I get into your outfit? Who do you have to know?

I replied, "It's who knows you, and not who you know!"

I do not believe he understood my reply.

I returned to Reseda and for two more weeks I painted houses until I received my orders. To my surprise these directed me to Okinawa, an island in the Ryukyu chain of islands still under the control of the U.S. military, and not to Japan as expected. All six of our family went to Oakland and boarded one of the ships of the Presidents' Line. We were traveling as a family, but because there were six of us, our two oldest, René and Noëlle, had to share a cabin with some other children, while Paul and Marc stayed with us.

The ship was large and quite comfortable. The first leg of the trip to Hawaii was uneventful. The second leg to Taiwan was quite rough, but not as bad as my return trip from Europe after the War. We had some time to explore the port of Keelung but we were too far from Taipei to visit the capital. The port was a dirty place without sewers, and in the harbor we saw American war ships as well as some R.O.C. (Republic of China) gun boats. Militarily, this region was a hot area, very hot. The U.S. Seventh Fleet was protecting Taiwan from the mainland Chinese. The two small islands of Matsu and Kimoy were under constant attack by the Chinese Communists, and the situation in that area was very tense.

Okinawa

We arrived at the port of Naha on Okinawa and were taken immediately to our assigned quarters. Okinawa is not a very large island, however it has always been considered a highly strategic outpost. During the War the Japanese used it, and after the famous battle it was occupied by the U.S. The house assigned to us, built of concrete slabs, looked more like a bunker than a villa. The entire structure—four concrete prefab walls covered by one huge slab roof—was bolted to a concrete foundation. The windows were small and very high on the walls. Heavy hinged shutters opened under eaves held by means of hooks, and all of the openings were covered with screens against mosquitoes. An air-conditioning unit cooled the entire house when necessary. Our housing area was located approximately half-way between Naha, the capital, and the Kadena Air Force Base. My office was approximately a mile away from our house, and as my car had not yet reached us, I walked to work every day.

After settling my family I flew to Japan and reported to our Tokyo Headquarters. I wanted to know why we were not in Japan as I had been led to believe. There was a typical Army problem of "slots!" Too many personnel and not enough positions to justify their assignment. My understanding was that I had been temporarily assigned to the the Army Liaison School (ALS) in Okinawa, but that I would be involved in intelligence work in Southeast Asia. When I returned to Okinawa I discovered that the Commandant of the School had not been told that my primary job was supposed to be that of an Intelligence Officer and that I was assigned to his school for administrative reasons while awaiting missions. Because I had been an instructor at the Intelligence School of Fort Holabird he was told that he could use me as an instructor. It turned out that I was the only officer who actually had been an instructor and the only one who spoke French. Because of my French ancestry, the commanding officer assumed that, of necessity, I must also be an expert chef. As a result, in addition to my normal duties, I immediately became the mess officer!

The school was created to teach intelligence and related subjects to foreign officers from Vietnam, Indonesia, Korea, the Philippines, Taiwan, Thailand, and Laos. Furthermore, many of these officers had been in military schools in France or England when these countries were their ally. These students were selected by the U.S. Military Attaché on duty in the respective countries from a list supplied by the country's staff officers responsible for training. A list of students for each group was provided to the school several months in advance so that a training schedule could be set. We had no language problem with the foreign officers, including the Vietnamese, except for those from Laos who spoke only French, the language taught in all Lao schools.

Shortly after my arrival on Okinawa I was ordered back to Laos because the individual who had replaced me was needed elsewhere. So, while my family remained in Okinawa, I was again on my way to Laos. Once there, I found the place changed since my last visit. Whereas during my earlier stay there was no presence of uniformed U.S. military personnel except for the military attaché and his staff, when I returned the U.S. Special Forces were there in force. The Lao Army had also changed quite a bit. Kham Hou, the former G-2, had been promoted and was now a battalion commander in the Sam Nua province close to the North Vietnamese border. USOM was still active and some of the old guard were still there, but many had been replaced. My Eurasian friends, Paul Leroy and his wife, had moved to Saïgon.

Very little was known about the situation in northern Laos. I was asked to go to the province of Sam Neua and the Plaine des Jarres in order to assess the situation. The U.S. Naval attaché of Bangkok, a Marine Major, was visiting Vientiane at that time. We had met earlier to exchange ideas and information about the situation, and when I was about to leave I suggested that he accompany me. With a young lieutenant from the G-2 Section of the Lao Army as our escort, we flew out on a Lao Air Force plane, an old C-47, to the Sam Neua air strip. Upon arriving, we borrowed a Jeep from the local command and headed for the forward headquarters of the Army. There I found my friend Kham Hou.

He received me with open arms, and could hardly contain himself when I asked him about the situation in his sector. He waited until the Marine Major left, then proceeded to announce his battle plan!

"What battle plan?" I asked. A large map of the area hung on the wall. Marked on it in red were the positions of the North Vietnamese troops, and, in blue, the location of his own troops. Apparently the North Vietnamese were making periodic incursions into Laos in order to grab food—and at times recruits— retreating to the safety of their territory before the Lao Army had time to react. This had been going

The author eating sans chaise.

303

on for some time and Kham Hou, responsible for that region, was by now very tired of it. He had decided to do something about it.

His plan was very simple. He had identified the location of a large Vietnamese supply dump inside North Vietnam close to the Lao border. The Vietnamese always used the same route to enter Laos, so Kham Hou had prepared a trap. He would allow the Vietnamese to enter Laos as usual, but as soon as they returned to Vietnam he would send his troops after them in hot pursuit. They would ignore the border, hit the supply dump, knock it out and return to their base near Sam Neua. This sounded extremely simple and feasible, until he assured me that his success was guaranteed!

"How?" I wanted to know.

That is when he told me the strangest story I have ever heard. A few days earlier, he had been thinking about this plan, wondering if he had taken into account every possible factor. As he was leaving his office an old *bonze* walked up to him when he reached the center of the compound and greeted him with clasped hands. Without being asked, the *bonze* told him that his plan would work and that he should not worry. He recognized the *bonze*, a high priest who belonged to a monastery located approximately 200 miles south of his headquarters. Kham Hou was very familiar with the Buddhist monks of the area. A few years earlier he had escaped from Vietnam dressed in the saffron robe of a monk. How could this old man have walked this long distance without showing signs of weariness? In a moment of inattention, the *bonze* vanished.

At first he thought nothing of it, but the more he reflected on the appearance of the *bonze*, the more he believed that there was some strange force at work. How did the *bonze* get into the compound without being challenged by the guards, he wondered, and where did he disappear to afterwards? So Kham Hou phoned the military installation closest to the monastery where the old man supposedly lived and asked them to check if in fact that particular *bonze* was there. Several hours later, he received the reply. The *bonze* had never left the monastery! Kham Hou was convinced that the *bonze* was capable of transporting himself anywhere anytime, and that he possessed magical powers. He was certain that someone was looking out for him. This was a good omen, he felt; his plan would work!

So much for the "common sense" of Kham Hou. Now it so happened that our escort was a native of Sam Neua. His family still lived there and he knew most of the people in the area. We had planned to meet him at a certain point below a shrine. When I arrived at the designated spot, I saw our escort and a *bonze* squatting and facing each other. The *bonze* was speaking and our escort was listening intently. At one point, our escort gave something to the *bonze* who held it in his clasped hands. Then, after rocking back and forth on his heels and shaking, faster and faster, he finally stopped as if exhausted, and returned what appeared to be an amulet to our escort.

"What was all that?" I asked our young lieutenant. He replied that he had just received a guarantee that he would not be injured on the field of battle. In the event a bullet struck him it would merely feel like the prick of an ant.

"You don't really believe this, do you?"

Instead of replying, he took his pistol, a 45-caliber semi-automatic, and handing it to me he said, "Here, shoot me. I am certain that you cannot kill me."

I was dumbfounded. I assured him that I believed him and that I did not need proof.

The author standing beside one of the mysterious stone jars on the famous Plaine des Jarres.

This was enough for one day. We stayed in the area overnight and visited the famous Plaine des Jarres, where large mysterious stone jars lay scattered over a large area. No one has yet come up with an explanation for the use of these jars, but many have speculated that these were probably either used as storage bins for grain, or as fermenting pots for rice wine. We spent the night at Sam Neua and the next morning we awoke to find the entire area covered with a thick layer of fog. Usually the fog would lift by 9:00 a.m., when the sun became hot enough to burn it. On that day it was past 10:00 when we heard the plane flying overhead. It could not find the landing strip and was looking for an opening to land. Finally, around 10:30, the fog dissipated enough to allow the C-47 to land.

Because of the tense situation in the area, many military men were sending their families to the capital or to their hometowns. There was a line of women, some with children, some with live chickens, some with small pigs and all with bundles of clothing and God knows what else, waiting for the plane. The pilot was a crack Laotian officer who had been trained at a U.S. flight school. When the time came to depart, the plane was loaded first with the women and children and livestock. When our turn came and we entered the aircraft, we discovered that there were no bucket seats. Everyone was sitting, or squatting as is customary in Laos, on the deck. My friends and I did the same, and when the door was closed, the plane taxied to the end of the strip and we took off.

The plane was probably overloaded, for it took a while for it to lift off the dirt runway. I felt that we were not climbing very fast. We had not been airborne a minute when I heard a clanking outside the door, as if someone was knocking to be let in. I brought it to the attention of a member of the crew who went to the door, listened and, shaking his head, returned to the cockpit. Looking closer, I realized what it was. The plane had recently been on drop mission. One of the static lines had slid under the door and the end with the metal ring was still floating loose alongside the plane as the air flow caused it to bang against the side of the aircraft. We were very happy to reach our destination.

That same afternoon, I reported to the U.S. General responsible for the support of the Lao Army. Without mentioning the bonzes, I told him that I had been briefed on one of the most unusual battle plans that I had seen in a long time. Making use of his own maps, I described what Kham Hou had related to me. As I was speaking, I could see the General getting redder and redder in the face. Finally he said, "This is absurd; this is crazy! What are they trying to do? Get a hold of the Lao General and bring him over here! I don't care how you do it; just get him here immediately!" I left and started searching the town for the Lao General, the one who commanded Kham Hou's sector.

I finally located him. I told him that my General had something very important to discuss with him and that he should come with me immediately. He agreed and we both drove to our compound. When we entered the office the American General said, "What are you trying to do General; start World War III all by yourself?" The Lao General looked at me with his mouth open, then looked at the other General speechless. I translated the comments of the U.S. General and told him that I had just returned from Sam Neua and had seen Kham Hou who had shown me his battle plan against the North Vietnamese. The Lao General assured us that he knew nothing about this. I believed him, but I doubt if the American General did!

What surprised him the most was the way the U.S. General had reacted to all this. He said to me: "Why all the fuss. Aren't we supposed to fight the communists?" I had no answer to his question, neither did the American general. Failing to receive a reply to his logical question he left shaking his head, promising that he would countermand the battle plan of Kham Hou immediately.

The Naval Attaché and I were also interested in the southern part of Laos. We decided to pay a visit to the local command and see what was going on in that area. We flew to Pakse, this time without an escort, and obtained a Jeep from the local command. The road from Pakse to Paksong was a good road, well maintained, but not heavily traveled. It climbed through jungles to the Bolovens plateau. We were about half way to Paksong when we passed a column of troops marching on our side of the road. They were heavily armed and wearing a type of uniform we had not seen before, but the Lao Army had been supplied by several countries with different types of uniforms. They looked at us, we looked at them; we waved and they waved back. They looked sharp, and we remarked to each other that they appeared to be the best troops we had ever seen in Laos. We reached Paksong and reported to the local Lao Command.

After the amities, I told the Colonel that we had seen some of his troops along the road south of Paksong. He replied that we must be mistaken; he had no troops in that area. I assured him that both of us had seen these soldiers and that they were no more than five to six miles from town. He asked for a description and while listening to our reply he became pale and said: "Messieurs, they were not Lao soldiers! You have seen North Vietnamese troops."

This was 1958 and it is very likely that we were the first Americans to see North Vietnamese troops in Laos. Shortly afterwards, I returned to Okinawa to resume my duties as an instructor.

When the time came to instruct the first class of Lao officers the school commandant decided that they would be taught in French. Instructions had never before been given in that language and not too many instructors were capable of doing so. Several officers and enlisted men were recruited from other units to do the job. I was supposed to be in charge of the translation that was to be done at Fort Holabird, Maryland. I flew back to the States carrying the entire course in a cardboard box. A group of us from various assignments met at the Fort. Some officers were old friends. We tackled the translation of the material that I had brought from Okinawa, a stack of paper approximately two feet high. At first we believed that the job would be impossible because even many of those who spoke excellent French had no idea how to translate some of the military terms. They could speak the language with their relatives and with people on the street, but writing complex translations properly, using the accurate equivalent of military terms, was another matter. Fortunately for us we had the help of an excellent French/English military dictionary. For two months we struggled until the entire course was completed in the French language. I had strong reservations about making available to the students some of the material, which dealt with techniques we should have kept to ourselves. However I was overruled by the school commandant, who was more interested in the curriculum than in the real purpose of the school. Unbeknownst to him and hopefully to the students' respective governments, the school was to assess these students so that eventually many of them might be recruited to work for us as intelligence assets.

Except for a few including one Captain, I did not know these Lao officers. We had no way of checking their backgrounds and true allegiance. We had to rely on the counter-intelligence capabilities of their own service, which was nil. When the time came for the Lao officers to begin their eight weeks of instruction, I was assigned the job of looking after them. Those I knew had been with Kham Hou, G-2 of the Lao Army when I was his advisor. I had no idea as to the others. Before leaving their country the students were to have had thorough physical examinations. However, a few days after their arrival, several developed physical ailments. One of them was so sick I took him to the local hospital myself. After a lengthy examination, the doctor decided to keep him for a few days of observation. When I returned to the hospital to drive him back to his quarters, I asked the doctor what was wrong with the student. He replied: "He had all the venereal diseases known to me, plus a couple I have never seen before." Then he prescribed antibiotics. It turned out that except for three students, the entire Lao class had some kind of venereal diseases plus tropical diseases just as serious. We were wondering who was the doctor who had given them a clean bill of health in Laos! I knew a Lao doctor who did practice a brand of voodoo although he had graduated from a French medical school!

However the course of instruction went well. We managed to persuade the cooks to prepare a lot of rice and to serve as many hot peppers as possible so that our Lao students would feel at home. Some were homesick, but the majority of them seemed to enjoy themselves, and it was not long before they made their way to the local town and visited the areas where prostitutes gathered. Some of those girls very likely acquired some of the rare venereal diseases imported from Laos. I would joke with the students, asking them what they thought of the Okinawa girls. Laughing, they would say that they had ever seen so much hair on a body. Apparently they discovered that the pubic region of the native women on Okinawa was extremely shaggy, just as the men have very heavy beards. The Laotian men and women are almost as hairless as the Chinese and Vietnamese. They could not wait to let me know their discovery!

While the school was in session, my instructional duties kept me well occupied, but during off-duty hours, often I would invite a few select students to my home for a meal and talk. At times I would bring one student to a distant part of the island where we could have serious discussions, mostly about the situation in Laos and about themselves, their family, and their feelings toward their job and their future in the military. The information I collected was carefully recorded and sent to our Tokyo office for future reference. This did not please the school commandant. On several occasions I was reprimanded because he did not want "his" school to be used as an assessment and recruiting base for future "spies". Of course, the school commandant was not an intelligence officer; he was an artillery officer who only saw action—or I should say inaction—in Alaska during the war. He was close to retirement, so this assignment would be his last before returning to the United States.

I must admit that the old boy was in very good shape. His favorite sport, next to golf, was squash, which he played extremely well. To stay in shape I would go to the gym with him and join him in a 45-minute session of squash. That was the only place where I could get even with him and hit him numerous times with a fast ball. He knew that I was not very careful, even though it was generally accepted that the opponent must get out of the way when it was the turn the other player to serves the ball or play. He, in turn, would occasionally hit me with his racquet, once right between my eyes. I recovered and said nothing. I felt that it was fair trade for the many welts to his back which I had caused.

Father George

At the Intelligence School at Okinawa, to the displeasure of the commandant, I was often asked to fly to Tokyo or elsewhere to participate in special operations. In mid-1960 I received one of my most memorable assignments. It was to investigate an individual who had puzzled all of the American intelligence services for some time. He was known as Professor Paul J. or G. Mathew and by us as Professor Paula yet neither of these names were his real name. He had come to the attention of our Tokyo office because he was organizing young Japanese people into communes and teaching them various trades. We knew very little about him and his supporters except that prior to coming to Japan, he had conducted a similar operation in India, where he had supposedly excellent results. A few months earlier while on one of my many trips to Japan I had been introduced to him by one of our agents as a French businessman.

Colonel Stanley, our commanding officer, became very interested in the professor operating in Japan as Professor Paula, aka Professor Laura and probably under other aliases. What the Professor was doing in Japan intrigued him for this reason the Colonel decided that I would go to India to see for myself what he was up to in that part of the world. I was to meet him in Calcutta and go with him to his base in South India. There I was to observe his operation and supposedly report my findings to a group of businessmen who were interested in contributing financially to his organization.

Prior to my departure for India, during an operational briefing I learned that he was very fond of Scotch whiskey, and that he suffered from a heart condition. So I took two bottles of Ballantine with me. I landed at the Calcutta airport one evening around 7:00. I was one of the last passengers off the Air France plane. My papers were in order and I had no

Col. John B. Stanley, CO 500 MI Det. Tokyo Japan.

problems with the Indian Immigration inspector. However, when I reached Customs and opened my suitcase, the two bottles of Ballantine attracted the attention of the agent, who said that I could not bring more than one bottle of whiskey into India. I said that I was passing through and that I needed the whiskey for my health. He said that it did not matter; I could only bring in one bottle. I said that was fine with me, that I would just pour the contents of one bottle down the drain outside.

"No, you cannot do that," he replied.

"Well, what do you want me to do with it?"

"I must confiscate it," he replied.

"All right," I said, "but I want a receipt for this bottle because I want to pick it up when I leave tomorrow."

"Sorry Sir, but I cannot give you a receipt."

"Well then, I shall drink it and we will forget about it."

"No, sir. You cannot do that."

I was getting upset. All the passengers by now had left on the one and only bus. It was now around 10:00 p.m. and I was quite far from the city without any means of transportation. About that time a supervisor walked into the Customs area. He asked what the problem was. Before the Customs agent could open his mouth, I told him the problem. With a generous gesture, he said, "Let him go." I was stranded just the same.

Except for a van waiting for the flight crew parked close to the entrance of the terminal there was no means of transportation available. When the pilot and his crew came out I explained, in French, my predicament, and of course they would not leave a compatriot stranded. So they gave me a ride to their hotel—the same hotel where several years earlier, French officers had threatened to kill me!

The Professor had checked into the same hotel earlier that day. The next morning we met to discuss the mechanics of our next step, which was to go to Trivandrum, in the Kerala province of South India, where Communists had taken over the state Government. I was quite surprised that at the airline ticket office when purchasing my fare for our flight, I was asked by the clerk what was my religion. I thought that perhaps it was in the event of an accident they would know my preference for burial services.

I learned the real reason when food was served. I was sitting next to a turbaned Indian who was served a beautiful plate of hot curry. Expecting the same fare, I was already licking my chops when I was served a piece of smelly fish with fried potatoes. I asked the flight attendant to explain what this travesty meant! She replied that her manifest stated that I was a Christian and as such fish was the meal she was obliged to serve me! I could not believe this. Of course, this was India!

I recall a conversation I had with another passenger during a trip on a flight with India Airways. He was an attorney who, as soon as he realized that I was an American, began to criticize the United States, the country that had just donated shiploads of corn and wheat to India to prevent a famine. It was rumored that this food had been repacked and shipped to Russia in exchange for military hardware. I kept my cool and said very little, but I felt like punching this fellow in the nose. While it would not have changed his mind, it would have made me feel better.

We landed at Madras to change planes and proceeded on to Trivandrum, where a small truck picked us up for the final leg of our trip to Cape Comorin, the southernmost tip of India, close to our destination, Bhakta Nilayam. I was housed at a hostel run by the Indian Government, not far from the commune run by the Professor and several of his associates. They included Georges Angelade, a Belgian doctor, Helene Moreau, a Belgian nun who was also a nurse and several young Indians in their late teens and early twenties, including Rita Ihverah. The compound at Bhakta Nilayam where the community lived was composed of several buildings. Approximately fifty young people lived and worked there. The girls learned how to weave material, while the boys studied the art of raising cattle. The operation appeared to be run professionally. The material produced by the weavers was sold and the money used to operate the commune. The milk and meat produced on the farm was consumed by the commune and the surplus sold to produce additional revenue.

At that time, the Indian Ocean had been on a rampage. The local fishermen were unable to go fishing. This was their main source of food and livelihood and there were incidents of starvation all along the coast. None of the food generously given to India by the United States had reached these people. Professor Laura was conducting his own humanitarian effort in his own way, with funds from European industrialists, principally Belgians and Italians. He had purchased a large amount of corn that had been milled and bagged locally. The corn meal was stored in a warehouse, and with the help of a few young Indians, he personally distributed the corn meal, going from village to village.

In addition to the corn meal, the Professor would supply the people with tools and/or labor in order to repair their houses, agricultural implements or fishing nets. I accompanied him to one of the villages that had been particularly hard hit by the storms, a village of fishermen composed of about fifty houses and huts.

With us was a crew of young men carrying the corn meal and a measuring can, and one assistant taking notes. He entered every house and, after greeting the owner, would ask several questions pertaining to the number of people in the household, what they had eaten that day and the day before, when the last time

312

was that they had been fishing, the state of their nets, etc. All the replies were duly noted by the assistant. Meanwhile, he looked over the conditions of the house, giving instructions as to what should be done, such as repairing the roof, fixing a door, etc. After this was completed, he ordered the corn meal carriers to give the family a specific number of measures of corn meal, and instructed them on how to prepare it.

These people lived almost entirely on fish. Corn was unknown to them. To make the transition, he suggested to the people that they mix palm honey with it. The palm honey, with which they were familiar, would hide some of the flavor of the corn meal. The big problem in India was the caste system. Apparently every caste had its mores, which included food. Those who were affected the most by the lack of food were the fishermen and their families, even though they were less than a quarter-mile from fields of sweet potatoes grown by a group belonging to another caste.

In villages where they grew manioc, the roots from which tapioca is made, he showed the farmers how to improve their yield, resulting in an increase in the size of the plants' roots from the size of a large carrot to larger than my arm.

However, I was most amazed by the man's ability to change the attitude of people everywhere he went. India is a nation of beggars. "Baksheesh" was the name of the game. Throughout India kids would run after Caucasians, who were mostly tourists, with their hands out, asking for rupees. One had to hold on to his belongings very well or someone would grab it and run with it. In all the villages where Professor Laura or Father George had been, not once were we asked for a handout. Not only were we not pestered by the kids, who followed us everywhere, but the loaded truck would drop off a hundred-pound sack of corn meal for one of his many helpers on the side of the road in a village, and half a day or more later, if the helper had not yet retrieved it, the sack would still be there, untouched.

The Professor was a miracle worker. He was so successful helping people that many of the churchmen of India took a dim view of this outsider doing a better job than the fat and lazy priests sitting in their comfortable rectories. Because of his reputation he was intensely disliked by the Catholic hierarchy of the area who had declared him persona non grata. The western coast had been Christianized by the Portuguese. Before Christianity was considered a religion, one of the apostles, St. Thomas had roamed the area. His body is buried in the cathedral of Trivandrum where I attended church with other members of the commune. In some of the villages where the Catholic church was dominant the Professor would assume his status as a priest and as Father George would check with the local church officials for information about their parish. The priests only reluctantly cooperated, and for good reason he did not trust them anyway. Once the sacks of corn meal he had left at the rectory of a Church mysteriously disappeared.

Eventually I learned that Father George was not a freelance do-gooder. In fact he had the blessing of one of the highest authorities in the world, the Pope himself. The French Cardinal Tisserant who was the titular head of the Eastern Rite of the Catholic Church was his sponsor. Father George was a Croatian priest who had been in German concentration camps, and after the war was the unwilling guest of Russian concentration camps. He was on their wanted list because while in jail he converted some of his guards to Christianity, which in those days was a crime. Through Cardinal Tisserant, Father George managed to acquire the tacit authorization of the Pope to conduct undercover activities in the Communist world, in Eastern Europe and the Far East. His method of operation was simple. He needed people, young people, to do his work. So he set up assessment programs through the communes he had organized in India, as well as in Japan. Among the people he helped, he would find the one he needed to accomplish his mission.

The funds he received from European industrialists and the presence of European doctors and the volunteers who accompanied them, were for humanitarian purpose. I doubt if any of those people knew exactly what Father George had in mind.

Unless father George was with Catholics aware of his ecclesiastic title in India he was referred to as "professor." In Trivandrum, he introduced me to an Indian Catholic doctor who occasionally helped him and looked after his health, which was not the greatest. This doctor was bitterly anti-Communist in a state that was run by them. I learned a lot from him and was able to report some interesting bits of information to our office. He resided in the suburbs of Trivandrum. His rather large house was surrounded with many trees, including cashew trees. I learned that the cashew nut was part of a very poisonous fruit and that only the nut was edible.

The commune was located on the very tip of the Indian peninsula close to where a memorial to Gandhi had been erected. This simple memorial, composed of several rooms, overlooked the Indian Ocean. An interesting phenomenon was incorporated into the design of the structure. It manifested itself once each year on the date and time of the birth of the Mahatma Gandhi. In the center of one of the rooms stood a cup in the shape of a lotus on a stone stands approximately four feet high. On that date, at a specific hour and second, the rays of the sun would penetrate a six-inch hole in the wall and shine on the cup. This phenomenon was the result of the efforts of well-educated Indian scientists who merely duplicated the work, centuries before, of the Egyptian designers of the pyramids and those of Stonehenge.

Mahatma Gandhi's memorial at Cap Comorin.

Nearby the commune, on a cliff overlooking the ocean, was a swimming pool fed by a spring. On hot days this was the best place to cool off. The men of the commune and I took advantage of this luxury. As was the practice in India, girls did not participate.

After several weeks at the commune, Father George decided to go north, where he had a similar group of people in the Darjeeling area, and I was to accompany him. We decided to leave separately for Calcutta, where we would meet at the Intercontinental Hotel and continue our journey to Darjeeling. I went ahead and was the first to reach the hotel, and waited a couple of days.

I shall never forget the meeting we had to discuss our next move. We learned a great deal about India on that day. When he reached the hotel, Father George phoned me and stated that he and Hélène Moreau, who was his nurse, would come to my room to discuss our trip. I was quite surprised to have a nun along, but I said nothing. I knew that Father George had a history of heart trouble, and so he was seldom far from medical care. As a result, among other thing's air travel was potentially deleterious for him. In fact, one of my fears in accompanying him while undercover was that if he were to become incapacitated or die it could put me suddenly in an awkward position.

They arrived at my room and, before saying anything, he took the telephone from the bed table and placed it under the pillow of the bed. He informed me that one could not be too careful in India, that the walls have ears. I recall thinking that he was only kidding when there was a knock at the door. I opened it and a house boy came in. Walking directly to the bed, he reached under the pillow, replaced the telephone on the bed table and left.

The Bentley on the road to Darjeeling.

We looked at each other amazed. How did he know that the telephone was under the pillow? We searched the room, but found nothing. In deference to the other members of the commune we usually spoke in English. All three of us could speak French, so we decided to speak only French from that time on.

We had met in order to plan our next move, which was to fly as close as possible to Darjeeling where the other commune was located. Because there was no airport in that city, we had to fly to Siliguri and make the rest of our journey by taxi. Then we discussed the amount of baggage we would carry so that we would travel as light as possible. We could leave what we did not take at the hotel. Then Father George said that we should leave everything behind, but take our suitcases anyway. That is when he told us that we would be taking supplies to Darjeeling and that was the best way to take them there.

He left the room for a while and returned with some of his supplies, a stack of pamphlets written in Chinese. I did not ask questions, just stuffed the materials into my suitcase, but kept a sample for future examination by our own Chinese experts. By the time my suitcase was loaded, I could hardly lift it. The same was

Hélène Moreau at Darjeeling.

316

true of my two companion's luggage.

Then we went to the India Airlines offices and purchased our tickets, making sure that we registered as new converts to Hinduism. The following day when we checked our bags, the clerk wanted to know if we were carrying coats of arms, so heavy were our suitcases. We did not want him or anyone else to know that we were carrying propaganda material to northern India.

After a relatively short flight when we reached Siliguri early that afternoon Tamaw Sangay, and his Bentley, was waiting for us at the airport. He had been dispatched by the Civic Motor Service of Darjeeling alerted either by the Professor or his Bengal headquarters. Although the Bentley had seen better days it ran well and climbed the steep hills rather easily. Sangay who appeared to know the professor was an excellent chauffeur. We could have used the railroad that ran between Siliguri and Darjeeling, but the cars were miniature in size and there would have been no room for our luggage. We did cross the rails a couple of times and in one area the railroad made a complete 360 degree curve passing over itself to reach a higher elevation.

It took us approximately three hours to drive to Darjeeling, where we checked in to the Everest Hotel, a structure built in the old English style during the British occupation of India. After dropping us off at the hotel, the Professor left alone taking some of our luggage. He did not tell us where he was going, but the sister and I decided to do some sightseeing in town. By that time clouds began to gather over the town. We could see very little of the surroundings. We walked the narrow cobblestone streets and explored the dirty shops for souvenirs, but there were none worth buying.

We were approximately two miles from the hotel when it started to rain. First a soft and kind rain, it slowly increased its intensity and, dodging from store to store, we retreated to the Everest. When we reached the lobby both of us were drenched. My suit was soaked and I had nothing dry to wear, so I asked the hotel clerk for a fire in my room (each of the rooms was equipped with a fireplace). I spread my suit over a couple of chairs in front of the hearth, hoping that by morning it would be dry. The bed, a high European type with an eiderdown comforter, was welcome because the room was not the warmest.

I woke up early in the morning and, looking out from my window, I could not help marveling at the sight. The sun had not yet quite revealed itself from behind the peak of the mountains, the valley was still dark, but high above the range of peaks shone a bright rose-colored diamond. It was not Mount Everest—it was Kachejunga, the second highest peak in the Himalayas. Fog was rolling into the valley when I decided to take the trail that passed in front of the hotel and climbed toward the nearest mountain range. It must have been five or six o'clock in the morning and the town was beginning to awaken. The rough trail, which climbed up the side of the mountain, was deserted. I climbed steadily until the fog lay below me and the dark blue sky embraced the mountains around me. The trail kept winding up the side of the mountain until it reached a flat step at the base of a wall, the wall of a monastery.

I had never before been inside a Buddhist monastery, even in Laos. Normally, no one went into the monastery except those who intended to stay. The door was ajar, so I entered and was surprised to note that the place was empty. Huge rugs hung on the walls. A line of bronze bells

Father George and Mrs. Thundup visiting a Tibetan pottery factory in Darjeeling, India.

and several prayer drums sat motionless. The room was dimmed and strange.

I was about to leave when a voice called to me in English. "Good morning, Sir. What can I do for you?" I looked around in the direction of the voice, and in the penumbra I spotted him. The man was sitting on a stand approximately five feet in height. I approached while he remained sitting cross-legged, covered by a brownish coat over his saffron robe. The colors of his apparel blended beautifully with the wall decorations.

I excused myself for invading his domain, but he ignored my explanation and asked a multitude of questions as to what I was doing there, where I had come from, what my job was, etc.

Father George with Princess Coocoola of Sikhim.

I replied as best as I could without revealing the truth. Then he wanted to know about the places I had been, and soon we were discussing all kind of subjects. I wanted to ask him questions but every time I thought of one he would ask something else. The prayer gong sounded, and he left without saying goodbye. By that time I was ready to return to the hotel, because my early morning promenade had given me an appetite.

When I reached the dining room, there were only a few people having breakfast. I ordered something and as I sat there waiting, an elderly lady walked into the dining room, acting as if she owned the place. She wore a nineteenth-century-style dress including a black choker. She appeared to be in her late 60's or early 70's, but her voice was strong. She spotted me immediately and walked toward my table. Standing before me, she said in a booming voice loud enough for everyone to hear, "And you, young man, to what intelligence organization do you belong?"

At that moment, I would have welcomed a hole into which to crawl. I introduced myself as an American company representative stationed in New Delhi on a holiday. "Come, come," she replied, "no one comes to this place on a holiday at this time of the year." I learned long ago if you do not want to answer questions you had better ask some quickly, which I did. I learned that she was the American widow of a British Colonel who had spent much of her life in India with her husband. She came back periodically on vacation and to visit the people she had known. Actually, she was a delightful person, but very inquisitive and well informed.

My two companions joined me later and we planned our next move, which was to visit a rug factory run by the sister-in-law of the Dalai Lama. The area was full of Tibetan refugees who had escaped to India following the Chinese communist takeover of Tibet. In order to support themselves, the refugees, led by a relative of the Dalai Lama, had organized a rug-making operation using the Tibetan method. The factory building was dark and dismal. The vertical threads of the rug were stretched on huge frames, ten or twenty feet tall, leaning against the wall. On a scaffold erected in front of each frame, two, three or sometimes four artisans, sitting cross-legged on a shelf in front of the rug, wove incredibly beautiful designs of silk and wool, typical of Tibetan artistry. Amazingly these workers, working together, were able to knot in place one thin fiber at a time and end up with such intricate patterns.

Mrs. Thundup, a Chinese the sister-in-law of the Dalai Lama, appeared well in charge of everything within the Tibetan refugee camp. When I was introduced to her by the professor, she was accompanied by Princess Coocoola of Sikkim, the sister of the Maharajah or Prince of Sikkim. She openly expressed her dislike for the Indians. With them was Mrs. Dodje, a striking looking woman whose father, the Prime Minister of Bhutan, had been murdered by the Chine during their invasion of Tibet. Mrs. Thundup impressed me as another Madam Chiang Kai-shek. By this I mean that she demonstrated a tenacity, assertiveness and persistence similar to the fabled spouse of the Nationalist Chinese leader. These were very unusual characteristics for Chinese women of that period, whose society traditionally discouraged their independence. When Father George introduced me as a businessman to her, she tried to convince me that I should purchase her rugs and sell them in the West. They were very efficient manufacturers, but had no sales force. Unfortunately, I was not able to help much, although I promised that I would try my best.

Father George did not want the nun and I to visit his Darjeeling operation, supposedly for fear that we would disturb its tranquillity. I believe that he did not want us to see what he was doing. He let us help him bring the last of our stuffed luggage to a point approximately one-half mile from a Catholic monastery, where he exited our taxi, but he would not let us carry it to the end. Our taxi dropped him off at the turn off to the monastery, and we returned to Darjeeling and waited for him there. During the day, the nurse and I continued our investigation of the stores. I bought three items—a prayer wheel, a prayer bell and two beautiful cashmere scarves.

The hills on the outskirts of Darjeeling were covered with tea plantations. Unlike the Ceylon tea bush, the leaves were smaller, as was the bush itself. The flavor of the tea served at the hotel every afternoon at four was far superior to that of Ceylon, later known as Sri Lanka.

Father George decided that he and I should go to Kalimpong located on the border of Sikkim, a small kingdom and a protectorate of India. He wanted to go to Kalimpong, but the situation in that area was very tense. The Chinese had invaded a portion of India, and they were in control of Bhutan and Sikkim. The Indian government-controlled newspapers were making claims that everything was under control; there was so little to worry about, they claimed, that the Indian Army Chief of Staff, General Tit Maya, was at that moment on vacation. When Father George and I reached Kalimpong, again by taxi, we found the place buzzing with activity.

We went to the one and only hotel and asked for rooms. They told us that we were in luck. General Tit Maya and his staff had just left (contrary to the official news he had not been on a holiday), and there was room for us. The owner of the hotel, who spoke excellent English, told me confidentially that the General had slept in the bed I was about to occupy! He must have thought this a true honor. I only hoped that the sheets had been changed!

We ate at the hotel, and afterwards, as I was a visitor and a stranger, I was initiated into the local drink, which was made of fermented millet. It was served in a bamboo "glass" and was sipped through a straw. As the imbiber drew the fermented content through the straw, he would add water into the cup, maintaining the same level of liquid, so that eventually the mixture was diluted until it was only water. Then it was time to reorder. The taste was rather pleasant, but what a headache the next morning! At breakfast I requested tea, hoping the be served a cup of darjeeling brew, but I was served Tibetan tea

Bridge over the Tista River on the road to Darjeeling.

with floating twigs, and a spoon full of rancid yak butter floating on the top. This was fine if you were very thirsty and liked rancid yak butter!

As we were not returning to Darjeeling until that afternoon, we decided to see the town, the last village before the Sikkim border. We were the only Caucasians in evidence. The marketplace was full of individuals who decidedly did not look Indian or even Tibetan and who wore trousers and boots of the same exact style and color. This was strange because they appeared to be parts of uniforms, but their blouses were definitely civilian attire, mostly ill-fitted. We returned to the hotel and asked the innkeeper who these people were. He told us confidentially that these were Chinese army officers who routinely slipped across the border on buying expeditions. I asked him if General Tit Maya knew about it. "Everyone knows, but they do nothing about it. They do not want to make waves and start a war again with the Chinese," he claimed.

We returned to Darjeeling with our taxi and the next morning went down the mountain to Siliguri for a flight to Calcutta. When we reached Siliguri we learned that the regular India Airlines flight was not due for a couple of days. Fortunately for us we discovered that a privately owned airline did have flights to Calcutta and that one would leave in an hour or so later. Since we had no reason to remain in Siliguri, we decided to take advantage of this return travel possibility. We asked where we should go to buy tickets. They advised us that we had to pay cash immediately before climbing aboard the plane!

"Cash before boarding," we asked.

"Yes," was the reply. "They do not have an office at Siliguri, but they do fly regularly, weather permitting."

We found an old DC-3 (probably a surplus C-47 because it still had a few of its bucket seats) waiting on the grass next to the runway. A young man took our money, approximately half of what India Airlines had charged us on our way over. Promptly at the designated time, the plane rolled off the grass and, after revving engines, took off towards Calcutta. We had been flying for approximately one hour when the door to the cockpit opened and from my position, I could see the left seat of the cockpit where the pilot usually sits. Instead of the typical male captain dressed in a jacket and tie, there was a beautiful, young Indian woman dressed in a light blue sarong. I nudged the nurse, and she nudged Father George who was snoozing away. He opened his eyes and seeing the object of our attention, he said, "It's OK, she owns the airline." Apparently this airline was the only privately owned airline in India, and it was the property of a woman, the spouse or a daughter of a Maharaja. I had never flown with a woman in the pilot's seat, something largely unheard of at that time in commercial aviation. However, I must admit that she handled the plane as well, if not better, than many male pilots with whom I had previously flown. Her landing was smooth and regulation perfect.

I returned to our Tokyo headquarters and reported my findings about Father George and his operations in India. I do not believe that my associates were as impressed with my report as were the Psywar (Army Psychological Warfare) people, after they reviewed the propaganda material I had brought back.

According to them, it was the most clever propaganda they had seen in a long time. After reading it one could not but question the Communist system under which they were living. If this fell into the hands of people who had doubts, it would positively reinforce their determination to fight the system.

I would not see Father George again until several years later in Tokyo, after he had returned from one of his expeditions along the Chinese border. He had approached the U.S. government for assistance. By that time, he had begun recruiting and training volunteers to penetrate communist China on foot for the purpose of denouncing communism and proselytizing Christianity to the populace. This was in response to the imprisonment and slaughter of missionaries by Mao Tse Tung's forces during the revolution, and the subsequent outlawing of religious practices.

The life expectancy of these agents after penetrating China was very short. Reluctantly Father George accepted the fact that if his agents were to have a chance to survive they would need to be armed. He requested arms, communications equipment and a number of other items that would enable his people to succeed. In return he agreed to let U.S. intelligence debrief, if and when they would be back from their mission.

Because I knew Father George, who by now had become aware of my true affiliation, I was asked to meet with him. After hearing his story, I and several others in our unit felt strongly that we should provide this assistance. We felt that if, on his own, he was willing to undertake activities supplementing our own efforts and in doing so fulfilled the intelligence requirements of our own organization why not help him! Unfortunately, someone on the upper echelon of our government chose to decline the arrangement.

Typhoon Alley

My lengthy absences to India and other areas were not appreciated by the school commandant, because while I was away Georgette had been giving his organization a bad name. Georgette was upset with my absence, and to break the monotony, she would write letters to the editor of the local newspaper, criticizing the management of the school and making the commandant very nervous. When I was ordered on a mission I could not tell the nature of my work to either the Commandant of the school or to Georgette. I am certain that it annoyed both to no end, because she believed that the Commandant knew where I was going, and he would not tell her, and at the same time he was convinced that I told her where I was going, and she would not tell him. Of course when I would return, he would call me and tell me about the dumb things she had done in my absence.

Once, a general was inspecting our installation when the newspaper published a particularly vitriolic letter from Georgette. A copy of the letter found its way to the General probably with the help of the School Commandant. What surprised everyone was that the General was very sympathetic to my position, and instead of bawling me out he offered what he believed was sound advice on how to handle my "situation."

"René," he told me, "I sympathize with you because I have the same problem with my wife. Do you know how I handle the problem? When she starts complaining I buy her an expensive gift or take her on a trip." Had I received a General's salary, I would have gladly followed his advice. Unfortunately, the pay of a lowly captain did not allow for much extravagance.

It was on Okinawa that my fellow officers gave me the moniker of "The Fox". Occasionally I would be away on confidential assignments for weeks at a time. Each time I returned from a trip I would have to make up a story to explain my absence. Some of my colleagues found it difficult to believe. They assumed that whatever I did, it had nothing to do with my official duties, and yet I never seemed to catch flack or be in trouble from my superiors. They firmly believed that I avoided being reprimanded by manipulating my superiors.

This is probably why they originally referred to me as The Fox. They never missed the opportunity to tell Georgette what a crafty individual I was, a fact of which she was already convinced.

At the intelligence school, many documents relating to my overt activities as an instructor reached my desk. It was customary for me to initial each document to indicate that I had read it. I had a local engraver make me a chop (a Chinese character used as a mark of personal identity and as a seal by many in the Far East), not with my initials or a Chinese/Japanese character, but with the face of a winking fox, which I felt was more befitting of my local reputation. After all, I was not a very serious fox, I only appeared to be.

This undeserving reputation followed me to the end of my military career. The only fox-like characteristic that I felt truly reflected my persona was flexibility. Foxes will live anywhere and will make the best of an unfavorable or adverse situation.

When I would return from either Thailand, Vietnam, or Laos, if time allowed I would bring back delicacies such as pineapples, coffee, litchi nuts and thin round rice leaves used to make egg rolls. I would bring these in stacks of fifty from Saïgon where the best were made. Once I brought back a fifty pound sack of green coffee beans from Laos. I had to change planes in Hong Kong. When I reached Customs, through which those with American passports were merely waved through, an inspector stopped me. "Please follow me sir" he said, guiding me to a room where my belongings including the sack of coffee were. They did not search my belongings, but they dumped the entire sac of coffee into a tub. Of course, they found nothing but coffee. Coming from Laos, I was immediately suspected of carrying either opium or some other contraband illegal in Hong Kong. They apologized and helped me reload my bag of coffee.

This did not surprise me, because during my stay in Laos our own ambassador had been subjected to the attention of the Hong Kong customs and the narcotic police. Periodically, Air America as well as Lao military aircraft were taken to Hong Kong for maintenance because that was the nearest point where it could be performed. When the plane was scheduled to go, Embassy personnel would go along on R and R, on a shopping trip or on Government business. Occasionally, Lao guests would also fly to Hong Kong.

This particular time, the Ambassador, the Military Attaché and his spouse and other members of the Embassy were aboard. When they landed in Kai Tak airport, the aircraft was directed not to the terminal, as it normally would have been, but to an isolated area. The passengers and crew were detained by the police and the plane searched. In the tail section, behind a bulkhead where converged all the cables controlling the tail section of the aircraft, a large package containing opium was discovered. The location of the opium immediately exonerated the pilot and the crew. No one in his right mind would have placed this heavy package on the command cables. Furthermore, no one aboard would have been in the position to do so. The passengers and crew were released, but the opium and the aircraft were seized until the investigation was completed.

It was rumored and generally accepted that the commanding general of the Lao Army was the head of the opium trade in Laos. The night before leaving Laos, the plane had been stored in the military area of the Vientiane airport, which was under the Lao military, who were responsible for its security and safety. Therefore the opium must have been loaded by someone under the control of the military, who had no idea about aircraft safety. The Hong Kong police did not act on a hunch. They were tipped off by someone from Laos but they did not know who the informer was or would not tell. We speculated for a long time, but were never able to conclude the identity of the informant, except that it must have been someone who did not like the head of the army or someone under him, and that included a lot of people.

During the time we were in Okinawa, while I was on one of my many intelligence missions to an area where I could not be contacted, my father passed away. I learned of his death upon my return, several weeks after he was buried. On one of my returns I learned that Georgette was pregnant again. That would make an odd number family. I was also gone when Alain, our fourth son, was born in a new military hospital on Okinawa.

During the summer we spent many hours on the beaches, skin-diving and collecting sea shells. There were so many beaches and the water was so clean around the island that it was possible to see marine life in its undisturbed state. We would all go to the beach where the water was calm and float on a large tube at a distance from the shore.

Protruding from the water near the beach were a number of skeletons of ships from the battle of Okinawa. They were rusting and slowly disintegrating in the salt water. Natives would regularly collect the cartridge shells that would wash up on the beaches. I discovered that even in winter, while the air temperature was in the fifties, the water temperature on the China Sea side of the island was a comfortable 70 degrees, while on the Pacific side (where no one swam) the water would be five to seven degrees colder.

We quickly learned that Okinawa was on the path of hurricanes and that when they occurred there was very little one could do except batten down the hatches and wait for the eye of the cyclone to pass and the winds to begin blowing in the other direction. We experienced several cyclones during our stay on Okinawa. I can still remember the worst one. The alert sounded as if for an enemy air raid. With all other activities on the island, our school and offices closed by order of the command and everyone was sent home to secure their residences and take care of their families. All the aircraft of the Kadena Air Base were evacuated to nearby islands or to Japan. Ships lifted anchor and sailed away from the storm. The heavy shutters were released and bolted against the outside walls as were the doors. Everything loose was brought in or secured and the bath tub was filled with water in case the water supply was shut off. Candles were made ready, and everyone was glued to the radio and the TV.

By mid-afternoon, it was so dark outside that it was impossible to see more than 100 feet ahead. The wind was blowing at 120 miles an hour and its speed was increasing by the minute. Peeking out periodically, I saw corrugated sheets flying through the air. The leaves of all the trees were gone in no time. The electricity went out, but fortunately we had a battery operated radio. We listened to the news for the direction of the hurricane. The sound of the wind was terrifying. In some places, the wind had reached a speed of 180 miles per hour. Our block house did not even shake. Suddenly, the noise stopped and the wind died down to nothing; it was eerie. Stepping outside, the sky above us had a pink glow, but was still overcast. We were in the center of the cyclone. After one to two hours, the wind again slowly increased in intensity, except now it blew in the opposite direction. The storm lasted a couple more hours into the night and fizzled out by morning.

The sunrise was spectacular. I went around to check on damage. Our house had been spared. The military housing area had very little damage, but the natives did not fair as well. Their houses, covered with corrugated sheets were roofless. Many electric and telephone poles were down, some sheared by the corrugated sheets. In the village next to us I saw pieces of straw imbedded in a telephone pole.

The most unusual occurrence was in the countryside, where the Okinawa farmers and fishers had built their typical homes with thatched roofs for hundreds, perhaps thousands, of years. Not a single of these houses was lost! The greatest damage was on the newest structures built along the new roads. The old Okinawa natives must have known exactly where to place their home so as to avoid destruction.

We were not always in the direct path of hurricanes. Sometimes they would skirt the island, or at the last moment change course and head for Korea, Taiwan or occasionally Hong Kong, where they would cause devastating mud slides.

Although as far as I knew night beach landing missions on mainland China were not conducted from Okinawa, and so far as I recall we never instructed the students in this type of activity, periodically we practiced it ourselves. Okinawa was an ideal location for this type of activity which consisted of approaching the coast at a predetermined location, searching for a signal by a waiting party and beach the boat to put someone ashore or to pick up a passenger. It is well within the realm of possibility that others in our group were training for specific missions, although due to the compartmentalization of operational information, I was not aware of it.

To conduct this type of training, we had a boat very similar in appearance to a typical Chinese fishing boat; but that was the only similarity. The boat was powered by an inboard 350-horsepower Gray Marine diesel engine that enabled it to reach speeds of 20 knots, three times or more that of a Chinese junk.

When we used the boat for practice, we would normally position someone on the beach with a black light. This light can not be seen with the naked eye, but with a special viewer the light appeared as a bright green dot. From our mooring point it took a while to reach our destination on the other side of the island, where the shore was better suited for our purposes. When we left it was daylight; but by the time we arrived at the other side of the island, it was usually pitch dark. In the event the fish were biting, we would hang a couple of lines from the side of the boat.

We ran with lights until we were ready to begin the simulated landing. Then one of us would stay on the bow and watch for any obstacles in the water. One night, we were moving along at a fairly good speed with our diesel cranking at top RPM, when a dark shadow loomed ahead. A huge freighter without lights was coming right toward us. The helmsman swung the boat just in time to avoid a collision. No one aboard the freighter had seen us. We reported the incident, but we never learned the name or the registry of the ship. Perhaps it was a ghost ship without a crew!

It was not unusual to notice a small flickering light on the water in the distance. As we approached, we would invariably find a lone Okinawa fisherman, sometimes several miles from shore, fishing in the dark, with a small kerosene lamp hanging on a pole. At times there was no lantern, so we had to be very careful not to collide with a native fisherman. The size of our engine was so great that there was no room on the boat for anything else except for the radio which connected us with the island.

One evening we were making a practice landing on the eastern shore of the island near Buckner Bay. In the distance, we could see the bright lights of the Naval base and of the villages along the coast. At approximately 11:00 p.m., we reached our point of approach. We reduced our speed and began scanning for the black light signal on shore. We knew that we had to cross a coral reef but did not worry about it because it was high tide. We passed the reef, and slowly made our way to the shore. Somehow the current had pushed us away from our expected landing point. We lost our beacon and were trying to establish contact with the waiting party. We must have been way off because we never were able to make contact, so we decided to return to our port and call it a night.

There were two of three openings in the reef through which a boat could pass even at low tide. We realized that we had missed our intended pass when our boat suddenly stopped despite the groaning of the diesel. We had hit the reef. "All Stop" was ordered and we tried to back up, but no luck. We shut down the engine and we tried to check out the problem with a light. The boat was sitting on the reef, which was rather flat at that point. We radioed our position to the island, hoping that someone would come to rescue us. Their reply was rather blunt, "Wait till the tide returns. Have a good night. Ha, ha!" To get stuck on the reef was a sure sign of ineptitude and poor sailing.

Slowly our boat began to list as the water receded over the reef. The deck offered no level area upon which to rest. We listened to the local military network station on the radio and waited for the tide to return. Each of us had our regular assignment at which in the morning we were expected to be. We knew that the School Commandant would be very unhappy about this, but it could not be helped. As the sun came up, the tilt of the deck became less and less until we felt our boat drifting toward the shore half a mile away. Once we were certain that we were safely off the reef, we started the diesel and hightailed it to the base. From that time on, the boat exercises were canceled.

Because I made many trips to Southeast Asia and I was very familiar with the situation in the area, I was occasionally asked to brief the commissioned and non-commissioned officers of the 3rd Marine Division that was based on Okinawa. The officers and top sergeants would assemble in a theater and for a couple of hours I would tell them about the political and military situation as I knew it.

After the briefing, I would be invited to lunch by the General who would ask questions to satisfy his own curiosity. One of his questions was, what should we do to prepare ourselves to fight in that area. My recommendation, which was probably not what a Marine wanted to hear, was not to become involved. I also pointed out that the Marine-issue foot gear, just as that of the Army, was not suitable for this area. I explained to the General our problem with shoes in the Tonkin area when I was with Ho Chi Minh and his boys. I told him that within weeks, the soles of my paratrooper boots were gone, that the leather became a green velvet and that I had to go barefoot to keep up with the native troops who were also barefoot, with the exception of those who had kept their French military hobnailed boots.

My association with the Marines of Okinawa was not with the 3rd Marines alone. A squadron of helicopters was located close to our school, and some of their pilots resided in our housing compound. One day, a pilot suggested that I accompany him on a training flight in which he would be practicing landing and some other necessary maneuvers, about which he did not elaborate. I sat in the co-pilot's seat with earphones on. We took off and headed for the ocean, flying a few feet above the water then along the shore, scaring the local people collecting octopus. Then we climbed to approximately three thousand feet, and headed for the southern tip of the island.

The pilot remarked that this particular aircraft was fantastic; it would fly without power, and he then shut off the engine. We fell like a rock, but

UNITED STATES MARINE CORPS

HEADQUARTERS
THIRD MARINE DIVISION (REINFORCED), FLEET MARINE FORCE
C/O FLEET POST OFFICE, SAN FRANCISCO, CALIFORNIA

IN REPLY REFER TO
7/wes
1650.1

24 OCT 1960

From: Commanding General
To: Commanding Officer, U. S. Army Liaison School, A.P.O. 331

Subj: Letter of Appreciation

1. It is with great pleasure that I express my appreciation to Captain Rene J. DeFORNEAUX, a member of your Command, for his assistance to this Division by his instruction on the military and political situation in South East Asia.

2. Captain DeFORNEAUX's knowledge of the Laotian situation was presented in a highly professional and most informative lecture delivered to eight hundred Officers and senior Non Commissioned Officers of this Division on 11 October 1960.

3. His intense interest and vast knowledge of the terrain, government, people and political situation in this country were very apparent to his audience.

4. Captain DeFORNEAUX's highly professional and intelligent presentation of this knowledge greatly increased understanding, on the part of his audience, of the current critical situation in this country.

5. I commend Captain DeFORNEAUX for his personal efforts, interest and a professional job well done.

DONALD M. WELLER

Letter of Appreciation from United States Marine Corps General Donald M. Weeler

my heart remained at 3,000 feet. The fall seemed to last an eternity, I was ready for a crash when somehow our fall seemed to slow down and was about to stop when he restarted the engine and maintained altitude a few feet off the ground. My friends explained that periodically they had to practice this so that in the event they lost the engine they would know what to do. Why he decided to try it while I was aboard, I'll never know!

My life in Okinawa was not improving; in fact it was getting worse. Not only was Georgette making my life miserable by her constant griping and complaining, but some of my associates gave me a hard time because they felt that I was privileged and was favored by our Japan headquarters.

Students from all the friendly nations of our area were now attending our school. Their ranks varied from second lieutenant to general officers. Some were very sharp and well equipped. Others were not so gifted and had trouble with the English language. They made use of an interpreter which usually accompanied them. The Indonesian officers were the most fun because they were great improvisers, and ready to sing or dance at the drop of a hat. At the parties periodically given for the students we could count on them to entertain the rest of us. Some of our Vietnamese and Lao student officers were well versed in French Popular songs. During one of our parties, surprising everyone including myself, I and a Lao captain sang a duet in French. The success was immediate. For me these parties were an excellent way to assess the potentiality of the students.

From a strictly educational point of view, the purpose of the school was to instruct the students in the American Army concept of intelligence, so that in the event of a conflict they would be familiar with our systems and methods, hoping of course that they would still be on our side in the event of a conflict!

However, from a purely security point of view, this concept was a dangerous one. If it were true that some of the students may be recruited and used as a secret agent, there was an equal possibility that a number of these student may be used by the opposition as was the case with the Lao students when more than half of the class went on the side of the Pathet Lao who were under the control of the Vietminh.

Unlike the other instructors who were not involved in intelligence operations, but contrary to the policy set forth by the School Commandant, I made a point of maintaining a close and friendly relationship with the students. It was amazing how quickly they realized that I was their man, their ombudsman, the one who would relay their requests or grievances to the authorities, the one they could trust.

For me this was not always a very enviable position. Once a group of students came to me with a serious complaint. One of our officers, a captain from the Southern part of the U.S., seemed to have very little sympathy for our oriental students. He would refer to them as "little brown bastards," an expression he believed was cute. On more than one occasion, he had utilized this slur in my presence and that of other officers. Unfortunately, his comments had also been overheard by several of the students who re-

From left to right: Major James van Fleet, Col. J. B. Stanley, the author and Capt. Robert Lehman.

331

Lt. Col. McIntyre checking on the author running the length of Okinawa.

ported them to me and asked that the officer apologizes, be reprimanded and made to discontinue these references. Obviously I was not in a position to do so, but I made an official report with the full support of some of the other officers who had overheard the captain's offensive remark, and who were supposedly my friends.

In filing my report, my intent was merely to cause the commandant to reprimand the captain. Instead the commandant forwarded my report to headquarters. As a result, the complaint became a matter of record, and our Tokyo Headquarters appointed a board of officers. Roughly equivalent to a pretrial hearing in civilian criminal courts, a board of officers was convened to determine the veracity of an allegation prior to a full court martial, if the board determines one is necessary. These Boards were always conducted *in camera* (closed session) by officers of equal or higher rank from another com-

Col. John B. Stanley and the author.

mand, with the accused present during the deposition of the witnesses.

When my turn came to testify I stated under oath what I had heard the captain say, assuming that all of the other officer/witnesses would testify forthrightly. As it turned out, I was the only one who told the board the truth in terms of the accused statements. All the others claimed that they had never hear him making disparaging remarks about the students.

I learned then and there that in the military, the truth is purely a relative concept—relative mainly to rank. The higher one's rank, the higher is one's perceived credibility, and the greater the likelihood that others will help confirm your lies. The accused was a 33rd level Mason, a Sojourner, and so were the others. I was not, and therefore not a member of the fraternity.

Some of the officers assigned to the School were outright rejects. One of them was an alcoholic. His behavior was so bad that under normal conditions he would have been kicked out of the Army. Instead, he was protected by the

---

UNITED STATES ARMY, PACIFIC
THE COLATENDATION RIBBON WITH MEDAL PENDANT
C I T A T I O N

Captain Rene J. Defourneaux, 0887913, Ordnance Corps, United States Army, distinguished himself by outstanding meritorious service with United States Amy Command Reconnaissance Activities Pacific Command from 13 April 1959 to 15 October 1959. He served as a member of a special training team in which he demonstrated an exceptional degree of professional skill and leadership in materially contributing to a pilot course of study, His constructive planning and tireless efforts in laying the groundwork for the project oontributed to the development of a highly specialized and technical training project and effectively met an urgent military requirement. This service required tact and diplomacy in relations with officers of Southeast Asia. Through his informed leadership, professional skill, and selfless devotion to an extraordinary task, Captain Defourneaux has been singularly instrumental not only in greatly facilitating the mission of the organization but also in engendering goodwill and creating a friendly atmosphere of genuine rapport with select military representatives of Southeast Asia, Captain Defourneaux's significant efforts directly aided in raising the prestige if his organization to an outstanding level, and reflect great credit upon himself and the military service.

Citation, US Army Commendation Ribbon with Medal pendant.

Commandant, who took no action because he felt sorry for the drunk's spouse, who was an invalid. Once, during a party at the Commandant quarters, he disappeared until someone discovered him stone drunk, but only because his feet were sticking out of the bushes lining the garden.

Although he was powerless to do anything about the state of things at the school, the only individual who understood my views was the Executive Officer, a lieutenant colonel of Chinese decent named Chung. Whereas the CO was short, and pudgy, unlike most Chinese, Col. Chung was tall and good-looking. After the completion of the translation of the course into French, he proposed the Army Commendation Medal for those who had done the translation. It was presented during a formation to those who received it, but casually given to me by the commandant upon my return from one of my many trips.

About that time, the CO was getting close to retirement. normally, when an officer is about the retire, he is reassigned to the States for his last assignment, usually close to his hometown if at all possible. However the CO had other plans. During the last year of his command, he carefully created a new civilian position for an assistant to the CO. Pushing it through channels up to the Pentagon, he drafted the job description and requirements in such a way that only he would fulfill them all. Shortly before he retired, the civilian position was open to the public. He submitted his application shortly thereafter, and he was quickly judged most eligible, and of course got the job.

As a result, he never left Okinawa, remaining in the same house and, in addition to collecting a fat retirement check as a retired Lieutenant Colonel, receiving a salary as a GS-12 or 13, the equivalent of a Major or Lt. Colonel's pay. The new CO of the school, his successor, needed an assistant like a hole in the head, but he got one just the same.

Fuji-San/La Revanche

This was more than I could take. When I was offered the opportunity to transfer to Japan, I jumped at the break.

In January, 1960, Georgette, our five children and I flew to Tachikawa Air base near Tokyo. While we awaited the arrival of our belongings we were housed in a downtown Tokyo hotel. We stayed there until quarters were ready for us at Grant Heights, a housing compound close to the camp. I found my new associates and co-workers to be a much friendlier and more sympathetic crowd than those of the school at Okinawa. Although the group had its share of duds and incompetents, at least we were all pointing in the same direction, if perhaps not all with the same intensity. Nevertheless our goal was the same.

While in Laos, through my French contact, I had acquired a principal agent who reported to us periodically through an American contact, a member of the organization to which I had been assigned. Wang, the principal agent, had been originally recruited by the French and now controlled a very valuable network of informants in North Vietnam. Apparently incapable or unwilling to support this effort, the French had given me this asset when I returned to Laos the first time. By the time I was transferred to Japan, the situation in Laos had deteriorated considerably. There had been several coup attempts and one, staged by Colonel Phoumi Nosavan, had partially succeeded. He and his rebel army were in Central Laos at Savannakhet, not in the capital of Vientiane. The link to our principal agent also happened to be at Pakse. If the situation in Laos deteriorated any further, as it had every indication of doing, we stood to lose the link to our North Vietnamese nets. If all U.S. personnel had to leave Laos, we might not be able to reestablish contact.

It was decided that we needed a new line of communication as soon as possible. This would require that someone who knew Wang go there and contact him. I was the only one who had met him, so I was to leave immediately for Savannakhet to try to set up a new line of communication to Thailand, where it was easier for us to operate, and where we had people to service the net.

Of course there was a problem. A rule within the Pacific Command stipulated that all official travel to Southeast Asia by intelligence personnel had to be authorized personally by CINCPAC (Commander in Chief—Pacific), Admiral Harry D. Felt, a four-star admiral. This meant that, technically, we had to wait for three weeks or more for an authorization before orders could be issued for my travel. By that time, the situation in Laos might be so bad that no one would be able to get near the place. The Operations Officer decided— without the concurrence of the CO, who was away—that I leave immediately. The request for permission to travel would be made to CINCPAC, but I was to proceed under my true identity without the authorization which would hopefully arrive in Bangkok where we had an office and where I was to check in prior to going into Laos.

I reached Bangkok, reported to Colonel Homer Bagley, the intelligence officer assigned to JUSMAG, the U.S. support organization to the Thai Army, and briefed him on the reason for my trip. He had not yet heard from our Tokyo office, but agreed that I should proceed with or without an OK from CINCPAC. He wished me luck.

I left Bangkok that afternoon on the Khorat express. I shared a sleeper compartment with an ordinary Thai individual. By nightfall, after a quick meal in the diner, we both retired to our respective berths. Neither of us spoke until we were close to Ubol in the morning. When I returned from the lavatory I found my companion dressed in the uniform of a high-ranking Thai police officer! In perfect English he asked me where I was going! He was the regional police chief! We both got off at Ubol, the nearest railroad stop to Pakse, my ultimate destination. There I was to meet Mr. Wood, an American advisor to the Lao Army. I spent the rest of the day at Ubol searching for transportation to take me to Pakse. It seemed that no one wanted to go there. The bus had stopped running in that direction and the commercial traffic was practically non-existent. Finding no means of transportation to my destination, I stayed at Ubol overnight, and the next morning decided to go by bus to Mukdaharn, a Thai village located across the Mekong from the Lao town of Savannakhet. From Savannakhet I hoped to hitch a ride to Pakse. The bus trip to Mukdaharn with an assortment of pigs and chickens was not great, and the rickshaw ride to the western shore of the Mekong was no fun. After searching in vain for a suitable ferry to cross the river so late in the day, I finally settled for a dugout canoe to take me on the Lao side.

After a wild ride across the swift Mekong the canoe dropped me on the at the Savannakhet landing. It was dusk when I walked in the police station. The lone customs inspector insisted in looking into my small suitcase but found nothing interesting. I completed the necessary immigration formalities and checked into the nearby Samsabai Hotel.

Later on I went to the only decent Chinese restaurant on the main street of Savannakhet. After enjoying a good Chinese meal at the sidewalk café, as I was settling my bill with the waiter a military Jeep passed by. The driver, a Caucasian, caught my attention. He looked very much like Mr. Wood, the individual I was to contact at Pakse! What was he doing in Savannakhet? I decided to locate him immediately because I doubted he was aware that he would play an important part in my mission. I had no trouble finding him after I spotted his Jeep parked in front of a large building, the local HQ of the PEO (Programs Evaluation Office) the U.S. Military Advisory Group to the Lao Army. He recognized me immediately because we both had been in OSS during the last war and had met several times since then. However, he was surprised to see me standing before him because he had not been alerted of my coming to his area. I leveled with him quickly, explaining in general terms the purpose of my visit, and asked him to keep my presence to himself and not to inform his Vientiane headquarters. I did not have to emphasize the importance of my mission to him. He understood exactly what I had to do. At the same time he provided me with a thorough briefing on the local political situation and the reactions to the recent coup.

The following day I returned to his office. Another individual, obviously American, was there! The presence of the stranger worried me and I sensed that there would be trouble. He introduced himself as "Jim Moran," a temporary occupant at the PEO Residence, but he did not indicate his function. The name rang a bell, but I did not connect him immediately. J. M. knew exactly who I was. I realized then that he belonged to the agency I had been with in Laos previously. He was a CIA representative! Unable to do much about this turn of events I kept quiet while Mr. Wood did most of the talking. J. M. was very loquacious, claiming that he had read some of my reports and that he was in full agreement with them. I listened carefully to his remarks concerning some of the people I had known while in Laos, including a few of the students we instructed at ALS, our Okinawa school. He asked me to locate one of them—Lt. Somelith who allegedly had been fired by Siho, the present G-2 of the Lao Army.

J.M. wanted to know why I was in Laos, but neither Wood nor I told him. Obviously Mr. Wood was not very happy about this encounter; unfortunately it was too late to worry over it. I spent the rest of the day trying to locate agent Wang, but in vain. That afternoon I ran into Lt. Nou, a former ALS student who was surprised to see me.

The following day in a restaurant Capt. Eckarath, and Lt. Nou and Capt. Mock, the two former Okinawa students, came in. They wanted to know what I was doing in Laos. I told them that I had business in Thailand, and being so close, I decided to come to see how things were in their country. I knew they would believe me, but also that they would tell the other former students who had followed General Phoumi to Savannakhet. Finally, close to noon that day while coming to the PEO Office, I spotted our principal agent. He saw me and looked startled. He passed by me casually once, probably to make certain that it was I, and as I reached the street corner, he came closer and whispered a rendezvous place and time for that evening, then moved on.

Before meeting Wang I decided to check on McFadyen, the "cut-out" who received the material from Wang and forwarded it to us. He was unknown to me, recruited by my successor to replace the cut-out I had originally selected who had left Laos. When I asked McFadyen about his last meeting he stated that had not seen our principal agent for over a month! I told him to stand by until further notice, and that I would get back to him before returning to my headquarters. If Wang had something for us I would handle it personally.

Having time to spare before meeting Wang, I was walking around town when a Volkswagen stopped alongside of me and a voice said: "Get in, Mr. Défourneaux." Startled, I almost ran away when I recognized Massini, a known Eurasian police informer. I had almost recruited him before leaving Laos but did not have the time to complete the vetting [our word for a critical investigation]. With a peculiar whisper as if afraid that he might be overheard, Massini stated that after meeting my successor, had decided not to become involved with him. Now he had changed his mind and he was offering his services to me! Skeptical and fearing the possibility of provocation by the French or the Lao police, I suggested that he contact the French who would appreciate whatever he had to offer more than I. He stated that was still working for the Lao police and when asked, promised to provide me with a city plan of Savannakhet which he would deliver the following day at the same time. He dropped me off in front of the restaurant where I had planned to go before being picked up!

It was difficult for me to move about Savannakhet without running into someone who knew me, and many of these I did not want to see. I was happy to get away from Massini and later that evening I was almost finished with my supper when Capt. Eckarath, Lt. Nou and Capt. Mock walked in the restaurant. Apparently Eckarath was a special assistant and advisor to General Phoumi. Lt. Nou was a former student of ALS and Capt. Mock was Phoumi's chief of transportation. We did not discuss the present situation in Laos, but talked about the school days in Okinawa and the people they knew there. After the three officers had left I went to the prearranged meeting with Wang. He was very glad to see me because the situation in the area was becoming tense and it was increasingly more difficult for him to meet his agents. For a month and a half he had failed to receive their reports. Normally he met his agents near the Lao-Vietnamese border. Unfortunately the local police and the Army were very suspicious of those moving about. His lack of private transportation made it very difficult for him to keep appointments with his agents. He was upset by the lack of communication with my replacement who was to supervise him and finance his operation. He painted a very bleak picture of the local political situation and was looking for the guidance his present handler was not providing.

Secure lines of communication were adequate as long as American personnel were in the area. Once all the Americans had left there might be a few remaining French people. I knew some who could have been used, but their days in Laos were also numbered. Through Thailand we would have to establish a system of communication with Laos that would be secure under any circumstance.

I asked Wang if he had any information related to the coup and if he knew what the French were doing about it. He stated that he had learned from a very reliable source that the Souvanna Phouma government was under the complete control of the French, and that Kong-Le and Phoumi Nosavan had been involved in the coup from the very beginning. His reply was quite unusual but it did not surprise me.

His version was as follows:

Phoumi had planned the coup some time ago and had ordered Kong-Le who commanded an airborne unit in the capital—to create an incident in Vientiane when the key personalities of the Lao government and of the Army had left town to attend the preparation of the King's cremation at Luang Prabang. Once Kong-Le had taken over the city Phoumi was to return to Vientiane and assume control of the coup. However, this was not what happened. When Phoumi flew to Vientiane after Kong-Le's diversion, the tower at the airfield refused to give him clearance to land. He ignored the tower and landed anyway, but when a group of paratroopers rushed his plane at port arms, he panicked and ordered the pilot to take off in the direction of Savannakhet. At the Seno Air Base near Savannakhet the same situation occurred. The tower refused to clear him to land and when he did soldiers came rushing towards his plane. Again he took off, but this time he landed at Ubol in Thailand. By then he knew that something was wrong. At Vientiane it might have been an honest mistake on the part of the tower who might not have been advised of Phoumi's participation in the coup. However the Savannakhet incident confirmed his suspicions that someone had taken control of the situation. Strangely, both the Vientiane and the Seno air fields were under the control of the French! Wang stated that the French had penetrated Phoumi's coup-planning committee and had been aware of each phase from the very beginning. When Kong-Le did his part, they prevented Phoumi from returning to Vientiane and took over. Souvanna Phouma might not have been involved in the planning of the coup, but he was under the complete control of the French, and was placed at the head of the Government. The French at Seno had received orders to kill Phoumi if he attempted to land at the base. Another source told Wang that he had witnessed the following incident that tends to substantiate the above version. At the time of the coup, Mrs. Phoumi had been placed under house arrest in Vientiane. Subsequently she was escorted to the Thai border by Kong-Le. Kong-Le was seen crying and had supposedly said to Mrs. Phoumi: "Madame Phoumi, I am sorry for what happened; believe me I had nothing to do with it. I had no control over what happened. Tell the General that I am very sorry." This version of the coup might have seemed strange to an outsider, but Wang was convinced that the French had engineered the situation into a counter-coup, an act which very few people realized at the time. Wang had also learned that the French had intensified their intelligence collection against the FAL [Force Armée Laotienne]. They had asked their agents to obtain information about the movements of all FAL units, the Lao army officers, American and Thai personalities, in and out of the Savannakhet area. They wanted to know what Phoumi was up to. The traffic between Savannakhet and Mukdaharn was carefully monitored by the French who had placed so-called "fishermen" on the Mekong to observe the people crossing the river near Savannakhet.

I was not surprised nor shocked by what Wang told me. This was a typical French operation designed primarily to embarrass the United States, and get even for our having handed FIC to Ho Chi Minh in 1945. Now while we were supporting the FAL financially, we had established a good relationship with the upper echelon of the Lao Army. The French, responsible for the actual training of the units, had a more direct contact with the troops. It was easy for them to penetrate FAL and control the Lao Army from within. I doubt if PEO had anyone capable of keeping an eye on the French. Although I was close to the French in Vientiane, I might have learned about their plans, and then again I might not have.

After the meeting Wang and I planned to meet again on the following day. Wang suggested that we meet at his house again and I concurred.

Before returning to Tokyo, I wanted to talk to Lt. Somelith. He was a friend and apparently he was in trouble. I knew where to find him, and when I did he was glad to see me, although he looked as if he had lost his best friend. He confirmed the fact that Siho, who was the top intelligence officer, had kicked him out of the FAL G-2 section. Thanks to General Ouane Ratikoune he had escaped an assignment to a line unit and instead was transferred to the office of the Lao Army Attaché at Pnom Penh, Cambodia, not as an assistant, but as a secretary! In this capacity he did nothing. He appeared very dejected and acted as if for him it was the end of the world. I asked him about his views concerning the situation in Laos, pointing out the possibility of a takeover by the Pathet Lao. What would he do if Laos became communist? He did not know, but he emphatically stated that he would never be a communist and would resist any coercion. I remarked that he owed his allegiance to his country and in the event it did go communist, what would he be doing. He did not know. Would he be willing to help the U.S.?

He did not reply to the question, but wanted to know how he could be of help. After all, as far as the FAL was concerned he had been demoted, and very possibly he would never be utilized in the capacity for which he was trained. I indicated to him that the U.S. had spent a lot of money, time and effort training him, and we hated to see it go to waste. I pointed out to him that his present position was far from hopeless. In fact, from an intelligence point of view, he enjoyed a very desirable position. In Cambodia, a country open to communist block nations, he might come in contact with all types of people, and Cambodia was a logical place to operate against North Vietnam.

All he needed was some guidance and perhaps a little support and I was certain that he could effectively capitalize on his present situation. I explained to him that we could help him develop something that would demonstrate to his people that, despite what Siho did to him, he was a capable officer. The results of his efforts would be passed on to his own government if he wished to do so. He knew that my main interest was only the communist military forces and that I had no direct interest in Laos as a country. While in Laos the year before he and I had discussed this many times. I suggested that he keep my offer in mind and let me know later. He could contact me through my Okinawa address. He assured me that he would. When I told him that Moran was looking for him he begged me not to reveal his whereabouts to him. I gathered that Somelith did not care much for CAS. We parted on good terms and promised to keep in touch.

At 2100 hours I returned to Wang's house to continue the discussion we had begun the night before. He explained why he believed that a Jeep was necessary for the conduct of his clandestine activities. Public transportation was subject to close check by the Lao police who usually allowed private vehicles to go through the many road blocks. However, they paid close attention to the passengers of buses. Well equipped with French travel orders, Wang could travel alone, or with someone without any problem. Anyone else not equipped with this type of documentation might be subject to the scrutiny of the Lao police who paid attention to the language of the occupants of public vehicles. I told him that I would take up his request with my chief, but could not help him now. I did not want to pursue the question of the Jeep but wanted to discuss the communication system that I had to set up before leaving Savannakhet. We considered many possibilities to respond to the various situations that might occur in Laos. Wang seriously wanted to work for us, but what he wanted and needed mostly was guidance. He stated that the way we had worked last year was much better. Now, he did not know if he was doing the right thing. The previous year, shortly after my departure, as per my instructions, he brought one of his agents to Savannakhet. Unfortunately, I had left before he was able to arrange the meeting with my successor. My replacement failed to come to Savannakhet to meet the agent and had never contacted Wang who had kept the agent at his own home at a great risk. Because I had to leave the following day, Wang and I spent the evening planning dead letter drops and setting up emergency communication systems in the event the local situation deteriorated further. I left him shortly after midnight.

When I saw Mr. Wood the following day, he advised me that the main bridge on KM 86 north of Pakse had been destroyed by the Pathet Lao and that the military situation was deteriorating rapidly. How would I ever reach Pakse now?

I was writing my report in Wood's office when J. M. came in and handed me a piece of paper, saying: "I did not show this to anyone. It came for you."

It was a message from Col. Bagley. It said: "Make no contact. Return immediately. S/Homer C. Bagley." J. M. added that the telephone communication was so bad he was not been able to understand the rest of the message! I told him that there was no need to worry. I was told to return, so I would return. He suggested that perhaps he should help me do what I was supposed to do. I told him that he was too late—the road to Pakse had been cut, there was no need.

I knew immediately what had occurred. J. M. had reported my presence to the Chief of Station at Vientiane who immediately objected to my presence in his territory because he had not been advised. CIA did not want the Army meddling in an area they considered their own. When I told Mr. Wood about this turn of events he, who was usually a very cool individual, became very upset. He wanted to have it out with J. M. who was half his size! I talked him out of it. Instead he sent a message and a copy of my orders to his commanding officer, explaining in detail the reason for my being in Laos. Then casually Mr. Wood said, " By the way René, General Phoumi heard that you were in town. I think that since you know each other, you should pay your respects." I had known General Phoumi Nosavan when he commanded a military region of Laos. I had no direct dealings with him except for occasional social encounters, but he knew who I was and, because of my association with the military, he believed that I had contacts with the U.S. Army on a high level. As it was impossible for me to hide while doing my job, he had quickly learned that I was in Savannakhet.

After what had happened so far I thought that it would be best if I did not see Phoumi. However, Wood insisted and said that he would arrange a meeting and would accompany me.

Together, at the appropriate time, we went to Phoumi's residence and waited, and waited. Eventually we were told that he was in conference and we should return the next morning.

The next morning, 10 September, I waited for Mr. Wood to pick me up at 0730 hours to see General Phoumi. By 0800 he had not appeared. As I was checking out of the hotel Capt. Eckarath and Capt. Mock came in. Eckarath had two packages for me and a letter to be hand-carried to the Lao Ambassador at Bangkok, His Royal Highness Tiao Khampane. Eckarath was surprised that I had not accompanied Mr. Wood who had gone to see Phoumi as prearranged. I told him that I had a train to catch and had to hurry to the Thai side of the Mekong. Eckarath insisted that I go the see the General because he wanted to see me.

Thus, escorted by both Lao Officers I went to see General Phoumi. When we arrived at his house he greeted me as a long-lost friend. This surprised the hell out of me because I had never been chummy with him. He took me to his office and locked the door. After we were alone he said: "I want you to take a message to CINCPAC, preferably to General I. D. White. I know him, he will act. Tell him that I will start something tomorrow and that the U.S. should seriously consider helping me. Recently I had a long talk with the King. I believed that I had convinced him, but he changed his mind and backed up Souvanna Phouma. In short, I have been double-crossed by the King who now wants me to come to Vientiane, where I will not return unless there is a more representative government, one without the Pathet Lao. As long as the Lao Army is not unified there is no chance for a stable government in Laos."

I told him that my primary concern was not for the internal problems of Laos, but rather the communist efforts in that country. He then stated that the Pathet Lao had been extremely active in northern Laos and that the Vietminh were helping them. In the South he estimated the strength of the Pathet Lao to be between two and three thousand men. Bridges had been destroyed and communication between Savannakhet and Pakse had been cut. He added that the situation was very grave and unless something was done quickly it might deteriorate irreparably. I assured General Phoumi that I would pass on his message to the intended as soon as I returned to my headquarters. I did not want to offend him by saying that very seldom I had a tête à tête with I.D. White, the commanding General of the Army in the Pacific theater. I repeated the essence of his message to make certain that I knew it. Ten minutes later, Eckarath drove me to the police station to have my passport validated and returned me to the boat landing on the Mekong. I boarded the first boat out of Savannakhet and reach Mukdaharn at 0930 and waited for the bus to Ubol that left at 1130. I reached Ubol at 1600, and boarded the train that left for Bangkok at 1845. Lying on the berth, alone in a sleeper compartment, I went over in my mind the five preceding days until the rumbling of the wheels on the track lulled me to sleep. The next morning I awoke shortly before the train reached the Thai capital at 0900 and I rushed to JUSMAG HQ to report to Col. Bagley, and face the music.

The Music

When I saw Colonel Bagley at his Bangkok office, he was not laughing. He was extremely upset when he told me that there must have been nearly a hundred telex messages between Washington and Tokyo mentioning my name. He further recounted that during a Security Council meeting at the White House the CIA representative had asked ACSI, the Chief of Army intelligence, what this man "Défourneaux" was doing in Laos without authorization. ACSI didn't know who "Défourneaux" was. That started a series of questions down the chain of command and no one, with the exception of our office and our CO, knew about my activities. Colonel Bagley offered to serve as an alibi, suggesting that he had told me to come. He did not worry over the consequences, because he was close to retirement. I declined his offer, believing that my office would straighten out the mess promptly.

How wrong I was! To start with, our CO was away on an official trip. Those left in charge decided that Défourneaux was expendable. When I reached Tokyo International Airport, Major King, a friend of mine, was waiting for me with a sedan. He was to be my escort to our headquarters! Perhaps they believed that I would run away! It quickly became clear that this was a classic CYA (cover your ass) exercise.

At our Tokyo HQ, the first question I was asked concerned the whereabouts of my travel orders, which were usually issued in multiple copies. My "friends" had decided that all orders directing me to Laos were to be destroyed so that they could deny having anything to do with it. I gave them the copies that I had left, but they wanted to know what I had done with the rest. Copies of military orders were used to obtain commercial air tickets. The issuing airline always retained a copy. This annoyed them to no end, as this incriminating piece of evidence would make their cover-up impossible. I couldn't imagine how they had overlooked this paper trail. How had they expected me to travel? Pay for my own tickets? When I told them that I had given a copy to Mr. Wood to attach to his own report, they were really shaken. This was a serious blow to their attempt to cover up the fact that my travel had indeed been authorized by our own office, mistakenly perhaps, but by my supervisor just the same.

The second bit of news given to me was that there was a plane waiting for me and my escort at Tachikawa to take us to Okinawa where General I. D. White was waiting for me. The sedan took us to Tachikawa Air Base where a C-130 waited for us on the tarmac. We got aboard and discovered that we were the only passengers and only cargo. The C-130 was probably the loudest aircraft we had at that time. After a painful trip to Okinawa, we landed at Kadena AFB where another waiting sedan picked us up by the aircraft steps.

The meeting with General White was to be held at ALS where I had been so miserable for a couple of years. I was certain that some of my former associates were gloating at the prospect of my big trouble. After all a three star general does not order a Captain to report immediately to congratulate him. Défourneaux must have done something really bad this time. My escort felt worse than I did. He suggested that I get an attorney to protect my rights. I pooh-poohed the idea because I felt confident I had done nothing wrong. We reached the school and were greeted by the General's aide who immediately informed the General of our arrival. He had a dozen high-ranking officers—generals and colonels—with him in the office of the CO of the school. I entered the room feeling a little like a pigeon in a shooting gallery. All eyes were on me: some with surprise, others with pity.

General White, who came up to my chin when standing up, told every one to get out. In two seconds the room was empty and we were alone. But to make certain that he was not overheard, we went into the next room, the office of the Executive Officer, which was also empty, and he closed the door. Then, looking at me, he said, "What are you trying to do, Captain? You have caused me a lot of trouble. ACSI has been after me for an answer, but no one knows anything. What in hell were you doing in Laos?"

After swallowing hard a couple of times, I explained the nature of my mission and how, because of the deteriorating situation in Laos, we felt that it was imperative that I set up a new line of communication with our principal agent Wang. He looked at me surprised and said, "Is that all there is to it?"

"Yes, sir."

"Why didn't someone tell me this before? All of this ruckus could have been avoided."

As long as I had the attention of the General, I decided that I might as well give him the message which General Phoumi had given me. He listened carefully and thanked me. Then, placing his hand on my shoulder, he said, "Now son, I appreciate what you are doing. You're doing a great job. But the next time you have to take off in a hurry, what are you going to do?"

"Exactly the same thing, General."

"No, no, you're not. You are going to call me directly and tell me about it."

"Yes, sir."

He escorted me to the CO's office, then called to his aide who was waiting on the other side of the door. When I reappeared with the General and he and I shook hands, I could see a sign of relief on the faces of those present, including some from our Tokyo office who could have been blamed, as well as those who just didn't like to see the General upset. Several of the officers came up to me to ask what the General had said to me. I declined to answer. I felt that if the General wanted them to know he would tell them himself.

My escort was overjoyed. We returned to Japan on the shuttle, a C-47, and the next day I was invited to give an account of my encounter with the boss of the army of the Pacific. My explanation was very brief. "He told me that the next time I go on a trip to give him a call." The CO understood perfectly well what I meant; that regardless of technicalities, I would continue to perform my duty as best I saw it. He indicated that I had his full support, but wanted a full report by the following week. Two days later my 18-page report was on his desk.

Le Roi Des Briques

I continued to make periodic trips to Southeast Asia. Every time I stopped in Saïgon, I would see my Eurasian friend Paul Leroy, who was now doing odd jobs to survive. He was employed by USOM's South Vietnamese AID office, until he spotted some irregularities in its operation and reported them to his superior. Then he was promptly fired. He had holdings in France and was well known among the North Vietnamese refugees because he had been a prominent businessman in Hanoï prior to the defeat of the French. His mother-in-law, a Vietnamese, was still in Hanoï, which worried his wife a great deal.

One day when I stopped in at his house, he informed me that he had been approached by a French firm which wanted to hire him to replace a mining engineer who was about to retire. This mine engineer had a very interesting job. He spent a good deal of his time in North Vietnam in the area of the Hong Gai coal mines, where he was responsible for checking the quality of the coal being loaded into ships.

After Dien Bien Phu, the French and the North Vietnamese had reached an agreement which stipulated that a French company would be responsible for the sale and the shipping of the coal mined at Hong Gai. At first, the Vietnamese loaded a lot of rocks and dirt with the coal which resulted in some very unhappy customers. The French insisted that unless they inspected the shipments, they would no longer handle the coal for their former enemy. The North Vietnamese agreed to have all shipments inspected, and allowed a Frenchman to conduct the inspection. My friend Paul was now selected because he was French, spoke Vietnamese, was familiar with the mine and was a mining engineer.

What luck! Paul would be smack in the enemy camp in the most strategic location near the port of Haïphong. He agreed immediately to cooperate with our needs. But when I presented my plan to our operations officer suggesting that Paul be trained in Saïgon, it was denied in favor of training in the Philippines.

"Why the Philippines?" I asked.

"Because we would have better security at one of our own bases," was the answer. Our huge base at Subic Bay was selected, and we coordinated with the U.S. Navy, which provided support such as a room with a bunk bed and access to a mess hall.

I had warned our own Chief of Operations that what we were doing was dangerous. Paul's disappearance from the Saïgon area for several weeks would be noticed, and one never knew what assets the North Vietnamese had in place. They knew that he was the one who would be taking over the mine engineer's position. They were to issue him a visa, so in all likelihood they would be watching him carefully before letting him travel to the North. "René, you worry too much," they told me.

Using money we had provided him, Paul flew to Manila on a commercial aircraft, and for the next five weeks I trained him in the art of clandestine operations. Afterwards, we discussed the targets which we wanted him to cover and devised our lines of communication.

From the day we decided to utilize him, Paul was to receive a salary which would be deposited into his account at the Paris branch of a large French bank. The money was to be laundered so that no one would suspect that he was working for the United States. Paul was not privy to our methods of transferring funds; he was told only that money would be periodically deposited into his account at the French Bank he had designated, and that the deposits would be reflected on his bank statements. The payments were to begin approximately two months before he left for North Vietnam.

A few days after he returned to Saïgon from the Philippines, he walked past the Saïgon branch of his Paris bank. An officer of the bank who happened to know him said, "Ah, Mr. Leroy, you are working for the Americans now?" My friend denied it, but the teller continued, "We have just received a check for you from the U.S. Government. I am sure that it is for you. It is addressed to Mr. Paul Leroy." Paul denied that he was employed by the U.S. and insisted that there must be another Paul Leroy in Saïgon, which incidentally there was; a man by that same name with a very bad reputation did live in Saïgon.

When he related this incident to me, I could not believe it! Checking our records, I realized that the finance people of our own organization had goofed. Noticing that Leroy had a Saïgon address, they decided that the reference to the French bank must have been an error. Instead, they sent a check directly to a Saïgon bank rather than to the undercover organization through which we transferred funds, thus concealing the identity of our sources. Under normal conditions my friend and the check should never have been connected, but the banker knew him. To make matter worse, most of the bank tellers were Vietnamese, and God only knew how many of them were also working for the North or the Vietcong!

Our operations division still did not believe this to be a serious breach of security. Only six months later, when my friend failed to receive his visa from the North Vietnamese and was completely ignored by them, did our office realize that, as I predicted, his connection to us had been detected by the North Vietnamese and that he would now never be allowed to go to Hong Gai. And he didn't. Fortunately, he was able to make his way to France shortly before the North Vietnamese takeover of Saïgon.

Counting the Days

Our operations division was slowly shrinking. The immediate post-war era was now at an end and I felt that the day would come when we would no longer be welcome in Japan. We returned some of our offices to the Japanese for use in their planning for the 1964 Olympic games. Several of our offices located at Washington Heights were moved to Yokohama and thus some of us had to commute from Tokyo by train every day. This was a real thrill. There was very little for me to do except write operations plans, all of them soon to be rejected or various reasons. My immediate supervisor did not want to spend money. Every time I would suggest a plan and present a budget, he found the project too expensive regardless of its value to our overall mission.

I regularly met with several people, each of whom had some passing interest for intelligence purposes but none of whom I could use as agents, because none had access to my assigned target—North Vietnam. There was a large community of Vietnamese refugees in Tokyo. One that I met had emigrated to Japan and had married a Japanese woman many years before. He was an electronics engineer who had contact with other Vietnamese refugees, some of whom were pro-North Vietnam and had links with Japan's communist movement (which was quite strong and a real concern to the U.S. at the time). I suspected that he might know some of them.

This fellow had many patents on electronic instrumentation. Of his many inventions, the one which intrigued me most was a powerful amplifier, no bigger than a cigarette pack, capable of activating a 12-inch loud speaker. I saw a potential for its use in our psychological warfare program.

I designed a receiver that could be dropped behind an enemy line not by parachute, which is easily spotted, but with a rotary propeller (similar to that of a helicopter), which would be released before reaching the ground. In this manner the receiver could be camouflaged and difficult to spot. The receiver, coupled with the Vietnamese inventer's powerful amplifier and a loud-speaker, could be controlled from a high flying helicopter or from a remote ground location to produce the sound of animals, such as tigers, or announce "orders" in Vietnamese to guerrillas hiding in the jungle. I gave these plans to our Psywar people to play with. They were impressed or amused, but did nothing with it until years later when it was actually used during the Vietnam conflict.

In 1961 we had an addition to our family—a girl born at the Tachikawa Air Force Base hospital. I named her Gisele, after the daughter of a friend of mine who was killed by the Nazis during the War. Everything seemed to be all right until a doctor decided to keep her in the hospital after her birth, pending the results of a test. He suspected Cystic Fibrosis. When she heard this, Georgette became completely unglued. She blamed everybody and imagined the worst. I could not believe that this little girl, who three days after her birth was lifting her head and looking around, could be sick. In fact, there was nothing wrong with her; the diagnosis was in error. She was the healthiest of all of our children, and the easiest to care for.

When I was home, I loved to take the kids to the Kumotori mountain range, known as the Western Alps of Japan. The roads in that part of Honchu (the main island) were not the best in the world. As a matter of fact, at times they were just plain dirt roads. We used our family car, a 1958 Chevrolet, for these jaunts until one day, several hundred miles from our home, we lost a tie rod. One wheel went east while the other went west. We were stuck in a small village on the top of a mountain.

After discovering that there was no telephone in the village, we learned that the forest rangers had a station nearby. I went to their cabin and explained as best as I could our predicament. They did not have a telephone either, however their two-way radio connected them with other stations located in or near other villages in the valley below. I wanted them to contact any American base so that they could send someone to pick us up. Instead they called for a garage mechanic who came with a pickup truck better equipped than a garage. It even had a welding torch. In a half-hour the tie rod was welded even stronger than before, and when I asked what the cost of the service was, the man refused to take any money. This was the way most Japanese treated us, particularly those of us who had children.

At other times we would take the train and travel to the end of the line. Then we would climb aboard an overloaded bus and ride to a village below our favorite mountain, the Kumotori Yama. We would stay with some people who rented rooms to tourists from the big city. We stayed there several times and would come equipped with all kinds of food, mostly cans from our commissary. We would ask the people to warm up the contents of our cans, while we watched them eat some mighty tasty Japanese dishes. We learned very quickly that they had never before seen the types of food that we were used to. As we always brought more than we needed, and preferred not to have to lug home cans of food, we gave them to our hosts.

Eventually we gave them our cans when we arrived. In return, we would share their food which was a lot tastier than ours. We would usually arrive on a Friday and return home on Sunday. Our Saturdays would be spent climbing specific mountains and hiking on trails. On one of our trips, René fell or jumped into a ravine. That scared the hell out of me. When Paul was with us he was so fast that at times he would reach the top, double-back to us and then again run to the top ahead of us before we could finish the climb.

Marc was always the mischievous one. He would throw toilet paper down the mountainside and watch it unroll. It was great fun. Returning to the inn, we would relax at the hot bath next to the house. The only unpleasant aspect of our stay was the Banjo, the world's smelliest john, but we got used to it. At first, the children didn't care for the device which consisted of two foot prints on either side of a hole in the floor. The kids were used to a comfortable sitting-down position instead of squatting.

We climbed practically all year long except when the snow became too deep to allow a safe trip. One weekend in late fall we decided to go to one particular mountain that we had heard was great. We were to stay at a refuge which had a spa fed by a hot spring which would be great for weary mountaineers. We drove to the base of the mountain and, leaving the car and grabbing our rucksacks, we began our climb. It had snowed and the temperature was around 20 degrees F. René, Marc and one or two of their friends were with us. The going was very tough. In some areas the trail narrowed down to a foot in width with a drop of over a hundred feet on one side and a shear cliff on the other, with very little to hang on to. I wore a pair of climbing shoes, but it did not prevent me from sliding on the ice which had accumulated on the trail.

We reached the refuge early in the evening and were given thick heavy comforters which seemed to have been filled with pebbles, so heavy were they. We believed that our sleeping bags would be sufficient, however that night we learned better. The refuge was a large room with a raised wooden floor and a square stove at one end where we could heat water for our food. The room could hold approximately twenty five people. The other unusual thing about the room was that ropes were dangling from pulleys attached to the rafters. At one end of the rope was a large hook. Later that evening I would learn the purpose of the ropes.

After supper, we decided to go next door to a shack where there was a large square tub, approximately three feet high, filled with water from the hot spring. These were the hot baths everyone had been eagerly awaiting. We undressed in our cabin and, wearing only our coats, entered the bath house which was full of steam and lit by only one dim light bulb. Feeling our way, we hung up our coats and towels and entered the hot tub. What a thrill! The sulfur-smelling water was heaven for our tired sore muscles. The boys were ecstatic. René declared that he would stay in the tub the rest of the night.

After a while, as the cold air warmed up and the steam dissipated, we could see three people standing close together on the other side of the large tub. Like us they were naked, and . . . they were girls! In a flash the boys jumped out of the tub, grabbed their towels and coats and rushed out into the freezing night to the safety of the other building. I had never before seen the boys move so fast.

Meanwhile the girls were laughing, but not without first covering their mouths, which to them was more important than covering their bodies. The three women were the wife and two daughters of the manager of the refuge. They lived there all year long, keeping the place in good order.

Back in our sleeping quarters, we noticed that the other visitors had suspended their rucksacks (which held their food and other belongings) on the hooks and pulled them as high as possible to the rafters. I thought that it was to provide more room and so I followed their lead, but later that night I found out the real reason. The temperature was dropping by the hour. By 10:00 the stove, which was constantly refilled with wood, could not keep the place warm. So we went into our sleeping bags and covered ourselves with a couple of the comforters they had given to us when we arrived. I fell asleep almost immediately, but was suddenly awakened by something which seemed to be on top of me, moving over the blanket. I open my eyes and approximately six inches from my nose was the nose of the biggest rat I had ever seen. I jerked the comforter and all those next to me did the same, as it bound from one sleeping guest to the next. I had trouble falling asleep after that.

That same night we were awakened by a lot of noise. People were talking and gathering around the stove which was red hot. Water was boiling furiously, sending steam into the cold air. I got up to see was going on. One fellow, an elderly Japanese whom I had not seen before, told me in perfect English that he was a professor at a Tokyo university and that he came late because he had been delayed. It was 2:00 in the morning. He had climbed the treacherous trail in the dark with a flashlight! I couldn't believe it. He told us that a fellow Japanese was following him and would be coming soon. We talked for a couple of hours and returned to our sleeping bags. In the morning when the professor's friend failed to materialize, the professor alerted the manager of the refuge who contacted the police down the valley. They discovered the man's frozen body at the bottom of a crevasse.

Strangely, on these trips we would often meet people we had met before, and we soon established relationships with them. All were Japanese because very few American ventured into those mountains. The fad among Americans was to climb Fujiyama. There were several other volcanoes whose climb was more interesting than Fujiyama. We got to know a young Japanese student who spent much of his spare time in those mountains and was familiar with many unusual areas. For example, he told us about a cavern not far from one of the refuges.

One day we decided to go with him. I expected an entrance with a welcome sign electric lights along the way, as in the Kentucky caverns.

Instead, we had to look for an opening, no bigger than a foot and a half, between rocks. Our Japanese friend found it and, equipped with flashlights, one by one we crawled on our stomachs through the twenty-foot-long passage. Then the hole enlarged a bit so that we could crawl on our hands and knees. Then another tunnel, barely large enough to squeeze through, led to a huge chamber that was over one hundred feet high. We were directly under the peak of a hill. René, who we called "Sonny", Marc and Paul were with us. On our way out, I was behind Marc and noticed that in one of the smaller chambers he was lighting a match. All of a sudden several bats came flying out of the tunnel. I realized that Marc was trying to touch the lit match to them in order to cause them to fly. We got out of the cavern and were glad to see daylight. We returned to the same area several times after that but never again ventured into the cave.

While in Japan, Sonny belonged to a boy scout troop and occasionally I would attend the meetings or go on field trips with the troops. Eventually, I was asked to become the troop's assistant scout master. Once each year scout troops from all over the region would gather in order to improve their scouting skills and allow them gain merit badges. I accompanied them on one of their outings to the mountains in the northern part of the main island. We lived in non-waterproof tents and got soaked until the weather became acceptable.

I shall never forget climbing a very steep extinct volcano with our troops. Sonny was moaning all the way up. He said that he couldn't make it to the top. He complained that he was "so-o-o tired." Ironically, in later life he became an accomplished outdoor man. Eventually we all reached the top and found the view fantastic. The return trip was difficult but we promised the scouts that we would take them to a local spa for a hot bath. Late that afternoon we reached the hotel where the spa was located. We all undressed and, just as the Japanese did, we soaped and rinsed ourselves well before going into the communal bath, a large swimming pool no more than four feet deep. We were all sitting or standing in the water when through the door came a small naked wrinkled Japanese grandmother. All hell broke loose. Shielding their private parts with their hands, they rushed to the safety of the dressing room and their clothing, while the little old lady laughed along with the Japanese men in the bath house.

Once, returning to Tokyo from Vientiane, for some reason I stopped at Pnom Penh, Cambodia. When I reached Saïgon, from where my flight to Tokyo would depart, I felt miserable and decided to check in to the Continental Hotel, where I usually stayed when in Saïgon. I spent a terrible night, feeling hot one moment and cold the next. I went to the U.S. Embassy where they had a clinic and a doctor, who immediately diagnosed my problem as Dengue fever. He said that there was nothing he could do for me and that I should go to bed and stay there. I asked him to call or cable my office so that they would know why I would not be returning as planned. I went to my hotel room and barely made it to the bed. I woke up in the middle of the night and, having had nothing to eat since the morning before, felt hungry. I decided to go out and have a bowl of noodles.

I got dressed and walked out into the hallway when it hit me. I felt completely drained. I could have laid down right there on the floor and been happy. I managed to return to my bed and to relax a little before falling asleep again. When I woke up it was mid-morning. I felt great and raring to go. I got dressed and was looking forward to a big breakfast. This time I made it as far as the front door of the hotel. Again, I returned to my room and to bed. It was early evening when I woke up, again feeling fine and ready to go. But I had learned a bitter lesson.

Rather than leaving my room, I decided to ask for room service. However, when the hotel manager came to check on me he informed me that the employees, knowing that I was sick, would not come to my room for fear of contracting what I had. I told him that I had "La Dengue" and that only a mosquito can give it. "I don't sting, and I don't bite," I assured him. He managed to convince a small Vietnamese woman to periodically bring me a bowl of noodle soup. I spent a week in that hotel room—alone, perspiring at times, freezing at others, at times so depressed that I wanted to die. Alternating periods of depression and euphoria are a prime symptom of Dengue fever. Eventually I recuperated and was able to go out to eat more than a bowl of soup. No one had called my office; no one was aware that I was sick. I returned to Japan twenty pounds lighter!

The CO, Colonel Stanley, introduced me to Lieutenant General Trudeau who had been ACSI some years before. The two were old friends and when the General wanted a briefing on the situation in Southeast Asia during his visits to Tokyo he would call me. General Trudeau was in charge of an Army Research and Development Agency. It was a dead end position that he did not deserve, but one to which he had been appointed as a result of his outspokenness and the fact that he was a very controversial officer. He was a man with ideas and a great motivator, but not a politician. I usually met him in his room at the Sano, the officer's club of Tokyo.

Le Monde

The French were not very numerous in Japan, however they were well liked, probably due to the one man who did more for Japan than most other foreigners with the exception of General MacArthur. Marcel Giuglaris was a small wiry individual with a large forehead and piercing eyes. Born in Nice, France, in 1922, he attended Saint-Cyr military school. During World War II, while involved with the resistance in Italy, he was captured by the Italian Security Police and turned over to the Gestapo. While in a concentration camp he learned Russian from Russian prisoners who were in the same camp. Under various pseudonyms, Giuglaris served several French News Services as a special correspondent in the Far East. He married a Japanese theater actress.

When I met Marcel Giuglaris, he was the Tokyo correspondent for Le Monde, a French newspaper. He was probably the only western foreign correspondent who not only spoke Japanese but who could read and write it. He was an amateur archaeologist who became fascinated by an ancient Japanese religious sect which claimed to practice "self-mummification." An avid reader, he had read old Japanese manuscripts which made reference to this type of life-ending process. With the help of some of his Japanese friends, Giuglaris researched the activities of the sect, found the possible location of their monastery and excavated the area. They stumbled across an underground room and found many large ceramic jars. Each contained the desiccated body of a monk. His research was fully documented and written in Japanese and possibly in French.

I was fascinated by this individual who was able to do things that very few people had the guts to do. We became good friends, although he did not know exactly who I was. Giuglaris probably believed that I was with a French intelligence organization, but he never pried into my own activities. He was happy to get a few bottles of good whiskey and American cigarettes. Although Japan was his territory, he traveled all over Asia including Siberia. When he returned he discussed his experiences, some of them quite fascinating, over a cup of tea.

Fluent in Russian, when visiting Siberia Giuglaris was able to escape his Intourist guide and go places where he would otherwise have not been allowed. One evening in Irkutsk he was passing a university campus when he heard a ruckus in a courtyard which was surrounded by student housing. There in the center of the courtyard stood a school official arguing with the students who filled every window of the buildings. All of a sudden they began pelting him with light bulbs. They had a grievance against the school and that was their way of voicing their displeasure.

His book *Visa pour la Sibérie* had a wealth of information for American analysts, providing, of course, they could read French. In his last book, *Le Jour de l'Escalade*, he described the futility of our involvement in Vietnam and predicted the eventual end of the struggle including the winner.

I periodically visited Giuglaris' office at the headquarters of Asahi Shimbum, one of the local newspapers. There I met many of the people with whom he was involved in various ways. One of his many women friends was a Japanese girl named Kioko.

In her late twenties, she was allegedly the mistress of a well-known Japanese actor. The fact that he was married did not please her. She was hoping that some day he would leave his wife and marry her, a very strange attitude for a Japanese. Kioko spoke excellent English and she seemed to enjoy speaking with me.

As we occasionally met at the offices of Le Monde, she suspected that I was a reporter. Perhaps Giuglaris had told her that I was working for him. I leaned a great deal about her including the fact that her father had been killed at Hiroshima. Kioko told me that she had been selected to go to mainland China as a representative of a Japanese art society. I felt that this was an excellent opportunity to have someone on Chinese soil who could collect first hand information. As far as she knew, my interest in China was strictly that of a reporter. The more that I checked into her background, the more I became convinced that she would be perfect for the job, although some of her friends and associates were not entirely pro-American. Some belonged to leftist organizations and some of these included members of the Japanese Catholic clergy. It was decided to recruit her, but after much planning she decided that it would be safer for her to remain in Japan, and we did agree with her.

Giuglaris was invited by the North Vietnamese to tour their country, probably because the Vietminh wanted to tell the world something through the French press. Before his departure, I had asked him to bring me a few souvenirs from Hanoï. I wanted to take a look at products made in North Vietnam in order to determine their quality. I also asked him for samples of rice, for which our analysts had given us a standing request. While in North Vietnam, in order to get a sample directly from a rice field without attracting the attention of his escort, he asked to relieve himself while passing by rice fields. He stepped off the road and, while urinating at the edge of the paddy, he grabbed a handful of rice which he stuffed into his pocket. When he returned to Japan, he gave me the grains and I turned them over to our office for technical analysis. That was the first time our experts had seen North Vietnamese rice. From this small handful, they were able to determine the composition of the soil, the type and quantity of fertilizer used and the yield. It was determined that they would have to import rice that year and they did.

While in Hanoï, Marcel met a French lady named Colette who was teaching at a French school as part of an agreement between the North Vietnamese and the French Government. She told him that she would be returning to France within a couple of months at which time she would be replaced my a man who would spend a year or two at her school. We found this very intriguing because she was very observant and had revealed things to Giuglaris that were of great interest to us. Apparently the foremost Russian laser expert had visited Hanoï and had spent much time with some of the North Vietnamese scientists and military people.

I wanted to learn more about this, but I couldn't actually ask Marcel without jeopardizing my position. In any case, I obtained enough information about Colette to know that she would soon return to France. I also knew that she would have to pass through Pnom Penh on her way there because there was no other way to get from Hanoï to the West. I knew within a week when she would be leaving.

Marcel eventually left Le Monde and became Japan's representative of the French cinematography industry. He displayed French films to potential Japanese buyers, reducing his usefulness as a source of information. As a newspaper man he was of great interest to me; as a movie agent, he had lost his appeal.

A Do-It-Yourself Operation

While most of my associates were happy doing nothing except showing up on time in their office, I could not sit behind a desk without doing what I was being paid to do. I wrote a multitude of operations plans which were regularly rejected for various reasons. The most common reason as that I could not guarantee results, the second was that funds were not available. I could not understand why there was enough funds to pay all of us for doing nothing, yet not enough to do what we were supposed to do!

One of the operations plans I presented to our Ops Officer was promptly rejected. He decided that it was impossible to implement it, that it would never work and that it would be a waste of time and effort. I became upset with the fact that those directing me had never done anything except sit behind a desk. I was convinced that I could make it succeed and decided that with or without their authorization I would contact Colette and get the information we badly needed. After examining all of the options, I decided that I would send her a cable in care of Air France at Pnom Penh. As she was a French Government employee, I felt certain that she would be flying via Air France, a government-owned airline. So, advising Air France that she would be arriving from Hanoï any day on her way back to France aboard one of their planes seemed logical, and I felt sure that they would give her the telegram.

My method of delivery was a gamble, I knew, but that was the easy part. The rough part was to write a cable enticing her to return to France via Tokyo instead of through Cairo which was the other possibility open to her. I drafted and redrafted the cable until I was satisfied. Basically it stated the following: "We have heard that you are returning to France. We are expecting you in Tokyo for a great time. Please advise Air France's Tokyo Office as to your flight number and the date and time of arrival. Signed, Your friends."

I knew that there was only a remote chance that she would bite. Giuglaris had described her to me so well that I was certain that she would come. I knew the schedule of flights from Pnom Penh to Tokyo. I waited a couple of days and checked with the Air France Tokyo office. They had not heard from the lady. The following week, I was certain that my plan had failed, but I continued to check with the Airline office anyway. I was about to give up when they advised me that they had received word from Colette; she had sent them her flight and time of arrival which was the following evening at the Tokyo Airport. When I announced the news to the Ops Office they refused to believe me.

I wanted to get a room at the best hotel and hire a limousine to transport her from the Airport to the hotel. I was refused the funds to do it but I knew the American manager of a local three-star hotel. He owed me a couple favors, so he let me have a suite for a decent price and gave me the use of the hotel limousine and his driver. I arrived at the terminal about the time the passengers were debarking.

I spotted her immediately. A typical French school teacher in her fifties, she was wearing a flowery dress, and white cotton gloves. Too well dressed for a tourist. I addressed her in French to which she responded immediately giving her name.

"Suivez moi, s'il vous plait," I said so that we would get out the terminal as quickly as possible. Together we approached the Japanese immigration, and I presented my identification and her passport requesting that the lady be allowed to leave immediately as she was a VIP. It was easy to impress the Japanese in those days and she looked rather impressive herself. I could tell that she had no idea as to what was going on, but did not give her the opportunity to ask.

After picking up her luggage, I guided her toward our uniformed chauffeur who opened the door and both of us climbed into the back while all of the people standing in front of the terminal gawked, wondering who we were. We left the airport and joined the heavily traffic on the highway to Tokyo. I asked her how her trip was, but she did not reply. Instead she said, "Who are you? Who told you I was coming?"

I acted surprised and said that I was sure that her friends had told her that they were expecting her.

"I do not have friends in Tokyo, nor in Japan," she replied.

"Where are you taking me"

"To the hotel where you made your reservation."

"But I never made a reservation."

"We shall see. Have you been to Japan before?"

"Never, but I always wanted to visit. But who are you?"

"I am just following orders."

We reached the hotel and to her surprise she did have a suite reserved with a magnificent view of the city. On a table was a bottle of the best French champagne and a bouquet of flowers with a note reading "Welcome to Tokyo," and signed, "Your Friends."

I was about to leave when she stopped me and said, "Tell me now, what is going on? You seem to know me, where I come from and where I am going, but I do not know you nor do I have any so-called friends in Tokyo."

I decided to tell her the partial truth. I told her that I belonged to an organization which was very much interested in North Vietnam. We knew that she had spent several years there and had acquired a lot of information about the general situation, the people and the conditions in the area. Would she mind spending a few days with me and talk about her experiences at our expense? I would escort her any place she wished to go in Japan, and while we toured Japan, we would talk. I would ask questions and she would answer them as best as she could.

She agreed with a smile, and said, "Why didn't you say so before?"

First, we did Tokyo and its suburbs; visiting pagodas, shrines and the major important sights. Then she wanted to see the old capital of Kyoto. Finally convinced, the Office managed to get tickets on the high speed train to Osaka and from there, using tourist buses, we went from one city to another. When we reached Kyoto, we remained there a couple of days. One evening, she told me that she had heard that the Japanese had the most unusual striptease artists. She had been in many countries and was fascinated by the "art," as she called it. I inquired and sure enough Kyoto had some of the best striptease joints in Japan. After finding out where they were, we hired a taxi and went looking for one.

Our driver was most reluctant to take us to the area which was not exactly the best part of town. However, we insisted so he drove us to one theater. But when we tried to enter we were stopped because they didn't believe that we foreigners should see the show. We insisted to the point that the manager came to see what the problem was. Lucky for us, he spoke excellent English. We told him that the lady was a professor doing research on striptease, and that she wanted to see a typical Japanese version. This did the trick. Not only were we allowed to enter at no charge, but after the show we were accorded an interview with the girls in their dressing room.

The way the girls expressed their feelings was just marvelous. Most of them were married and had children. They were not prostitutes, but actresses who actually did very little stripping compared with the American strippers. A girl's kimono never left her body. She twisted around her kimono, allowing it to flow away from her body, but never really revealed anything. The audience, mostly men drinking sake, were gawking, laughing and bending low, trying to see underneath the kimonos.

Occasionally a member of the audience would hand over a sake glass to the dancer who would grab it and down it in one gulp. The music did not have the typical bumps and grinds which accompany the American stripper. They were playing Japanese music, which made the scene even more interesting. We left and returned to our taxi, which had not moved an inch. Our taxi driver sighed with relief when he saw us walk out of the theater in one piece.

Her visit was not all fun. We spent hours in her room discussing her experiences in North Vietnam—talking about the personalities she had met, the rumors she had heard, the problems she had encountered. I knew that she was expecting me make a pass at her but I did not. What I was doing was too important to spoil it by making it personal. So I refrained from making any inappropriate advances.

Then we discussed her replacement. She provided his name and a lot of information about him and his family. He was to report to Hanoï in late August for the following school year. After her vacation, she and her husband were to be assigned to Brazil. After one week of thorough debriefing, it was time for her to take the plane back to France. I escorted her to the airport the same way I had brought her in.

We parted as great friends; she, wondering who I really was, and I, hoping she would forget about me. I was almost certain that she had been working for a French intelligence organization and that when she reached Paris, someone would ask her if she had met anyone interesting and that she might well describe me. I felt fairly certain that she had me pegged as French intelligence and might remark to her controller back in Paris, "Oh, by the way, I ran into one of your people in Tokyo!" She did not know my name, as I was using an alias. The French knew that I was in Japan, and very likely could easily identify me.

After she left, I never heard anything more about her.

The Best Laid Plans of Mice and Men

This unorthodox operation turned out to be a lucky break for our collection effort. We obtained a large quantity of timely information about North Vietnam, but it would be much more advantageous if we have had someone on site to report to us in real time. For this reason I decided to write an Operations Plan to that effect. I had written many plans before, but all were rejected in our own office by my various immediate superiors, usually Majors, or Lieutenant Colonels, who did nothing for fear of making a mistake. Every time I was able to involve myself with something interesting it was because I jumped the chain of command and went directly to the CO, or because the CO wanted me to do something, usually over the displeasure of my supervisor. This occurred when Col. J.B. Stanley was the CO.

Now, even though Stanley was gone, I felt that what I was proposing was a good enough plan to succeed.

But, when I presented the plan to my immediate superior, he laughed and said: "You're crazy René. It will never work. Who in his right mind would try a stunt like the one you are proposing?"

He had forgotten the one that I had pulled off with our Lady from Hanoï. My new idea was no more outlandish than that, but this time I could not do it alone. I had to have some solid support. The Major stated that in order to prove to me that my plan was insane, he would let it go to the top. The new CO reluctantly endorsed it, and to the Pentagon my plan went. Two weeks later, surprise of surprise, our office received the order to implement it. Suddenly everyone higher in rank than I decided to volunteer to carry it out, including my once-doubting superior.

When those who were to implement the plan had been selected and the plan was returned by the Pentagon, a very brief reply was received, "We want René to do it." From that time on I was in the dog house with the new CO and his cronies. I was accused of having close friends at the Pentagon, of playing politics, etc. About that time I was supposed to return to the United States because I was getting close to retirement. It was decided that Georgette would leave with the children and go to my next station but, as I was still assigned to Japan, I did not have one designated.

As long as I was away, the command preferred not to have to deal with Georgette. By that time Col. Stanley, my protector, was no longer with our unit. He had retired and stayed in Japan instead to accepting a promotion which would have necessitated his returning to the United States for a new assignment. As the godfather of our little Gisele, he was the only one who was able to handle Georgette. We decided that she and the children would go to California and wait for me there until I was finished with this operation which would take at the most three months.

In August, 1963, I left Tokyo for Washington D.C. to implement the operation that I had planned. To my surprise there were not many changes made to the basic concept. However because of the fact that I was known to French Intelligence, it was deemed necessary for me to assume a different name and nationality. In addition, I was to start the operation from a foreign country so it was important that I not be linked to the U.S. For this reason Germany was selected as my starting point because we had good control there and all of the necessary support facilities.

I was given a fake passport from a South American country with a logical cover story to account for the fact that I spoke French and English but not the language of my country of residence, which was difficult to explain. My story was that my mother had been French and my father, who was deceased, had been South American. I had been born in my father's native country, raised in France, lived in England for a time and had never returned to my birth country. I was a businessman who traveled considerably as indicated in my passport.

I realized that I had better watch my step, because one false move and I could end up like the three French Intelligence agents who had recently been caught and imprisoned in Egypt. Because my complexion was rather light, it was deemed necessary to dye my hair, which I had let grow out for a while, a darker shade, as well as my mustache. I submitted myself to the experts who did a great job making me look like a South American gigolo.

I began my trip at Frankfurt after a thorough briefing by our Counter-Intelligence Office, which had obtained the fare for me. I was to board a French ship and travel from Marseille to Hong Kong, making several stops at various ports in between. I took the train from Frankfurt to Paris for the first leg of my trip. Reluctantly, I gave my passport to the conductor who would handle the formalities at the border when we entered France. I prepared myself for all eventualities in the event that the French authorities questioned the document. But I fell asleep and woke up one hour out of the French capital.

This was my first visit to France since the war. In Paris I had some time between trains so I visited Notre Dame on my way to another railroad station, the Gare de Lyon, where I boarded a TGV (high speed) train to Marseille. At Marseille, I checked in at a hotel and, having a couple of days until the ship left, went over to the old port where I had the best Bouillabaisse I had ever tasted, and sat on an outdoor terrace of a cafe on the Canebiere watching the girls go by.

The ship was a medium-sized vessel, making the run between Marseille and Yokohama. She took approximately 35 days to make the trip. I was taking this boat because the individual who was to replace Colette, the Lady of Hanoï, was to be aboard and I would have 30 days to recruit and train him. I had a general description of the man and his family, which consisted of a wife and a child. Coming aboard, I received a list of the passengers. His name was on it, which was reassuring. I kept watching the people arriving and those who were already there, but did not recognize any of them. My cabin was on the second deck and had a porthole which was much better than an inside cabin.

The ship left the dock early in the afternoon for our next port of call, which was Barcelona. Perhaps he was not able to get aboard at Marseille, maybe he would be picked up at Barcelona. The next morning we entered the part of Barcelona where we were to stay the entire day. Some of us left the ship for sight-seeing. Returning late that afternoon and looking over the passengers, I realized that my worst fear had been realized. My target had not come aboard. Why? I had no way to contact my office, however they could get in touch with me but hadn't.

Perhaps he would join us at Alexandria, prior to our entering the Suez Canal. I debated whether I should stay on the ship or get off at Alexandria and fly back to the United States. I would have done so providing I had a good excuse, but I did not. I didn't even leave the ship at Alexandria or at Port Said, where many people left to see the Pyramids and the Sphinx. Upon leaving the vessel, the passengers' passports were handed over to the Egyptian authorities, who were checking all passengers very carefully. In those days, the Russians were their main suppliers and several attempts by the French and Israelis to secure information about Egypt had been at the forefront of the news. French intelligence operatives who had been caught were lingering in Egyptian jails awaiting trial. I decided it was safer for me to stay put and remain aboard until another opportunity presented itself, or stay on until Hong Kong and fly to Tokyo from there.

We stopped at Aden, a God-forsaken place, then Singapore, where I was almost thrown off of the ship. Each passenger was assigned to a particular dining room table and during the entire trip those at each table became a family, sharing their meals and entertainment together. We had the same waiter throughout the voyage, a Spaniard who spoke both excellent French and English. We became friends and when we reached Singapore we decided to go sightseeing together. Upon returning to the ship, passing by several fruit merchants displaying their merchandise along the dock, we noticed a stall selling Durian, a tropical fruit which, like Limburger cheese, was known for its extremely fetid odor but great flavor. We decided that it would be fun to serve it to our table, because most likely none of the passengers knew what Durian were.

When the time came for desert, I told our table companions that I was supplying the dessert and that our waiter would serve it. About that time, a strange odor, reminiscent of that of an outdoor john, floated toward the dining room from the swinging doors of the kitchen. I was facing the back of the ship's captain who had his table a short distance from ours. When the odor permeated the dining room, every passenger seemed embarrassed, probably thinking that their neighbor had passed wind. The Captain, of course, knew better. I could see his neck getting redder and redder, until he called over the Maitre D, who rushed to the kitchen to investigate.

He returned promptly and, although I was too far away to hear, I could see that he was explaining to the Captain that a certain passenger had brought the fruit aboard and had asked that it be served to his table for dessert. The Captain turned around and looked at our table, and at me in particular, with daggers in his eyes. He let it be known through his staff that he was not pleased, and that he would make certain that I would never again be allowed on board his ship. Our waiter was also severely reprimanded, but he had a good laugh over it and we enjoyed the rest of the trip, talking about it and planning other mischief.

There was a swimming pool on the upper deck, and when the weather permitted, many passengers would go for a dip. I was no exception, but I should not have gone in because something very strange and difficult to explain happened to me. When they dyed my hair, the makeup expert didn't tell me that salt water would affect the dye. When I climbed out after my first dip, my hair turned a bright red, almost the color of my beard when I let it grow. My fellow passengers had a good laugh. I laughed with them, but fortunately no one asked me why my hair had changed color.

From Singapore we went to Bangkok and then on to Saïgon. There I was on familiar ground. Having not heard from me since I had left Frankfurt, a member of our organization, David Carr, assigned to Saïgon came aboard to determine if I was all right. We left the ship to check in with the local Chief of Station who turned out to be Lucien Coneine, my old friend from OSS days. He was now second secretary at our Embassy. This was a short time before the assassination of President Diem and Lucien was later accused of having masterminded the plot to kill the President of South Vietnam. I doubted that he did, but someone had to take the blame.

At Singapore an attractive Chinese lady approximately 30-years-old named Miss Wong came aboard, bearing a striking resemblance to the Dragon Lady of "Terry and the Pirates" fame . She lived in Hong Kong where she worked for an American university doing research funded by a grant. We became acquainted and, having nothing else to do, engaged in long conversations on the deck. I suspected that she was more than a researcher and to verify my suspicions I decided to see her when we reached Hong Kong, as she had given me her address.

At Hong Kong I was to revert to my true identity. Before doing so I decided to accept her invitation to attend a party given by Miss Wang. She lived on the island in an apartment building overlooking the port of Aberdeen. When I arrived at her place the party was in process. Most of the guests were British men who were apparently old friends. None of the guests appeared to be involved in activities other then academia. I had obtained enough information about her to begin the "vetting" process which might lead to her recruitment by some other agent. If she was successfully recruited and utilized my trip might not have been for nothing.

As planned, I turned in my fake documentation to a representative of local CIA station, and assumed my true identity. I flew on to Tokyo where I reported the results of my trip to the Operations Officer, who was not very happy with the results of my cruise. I learned then that the individual who was my target did not make the trip because at the last moment his daughter was hospitalized with an undisclosed malady. This had delayed his schedule considerably, and as a result he decided to fly to Pnom Penh instead of taking the ship to Bangkok.

I could not understand why, if they had known, they didn't send me a message advising me that a member of my family was dying to provide an excuse for my leaving the ship. I explained to them that had I left the ship at Alexandria, the Egyptian authorities would have collected my passport and given it to representatives of my assumed home country. It would not have taken them long to find out that it was a fake. My explanation was grudgingly accepted.

Before leaving Tokyo for the States I learned that my new assignment was to be Omaha, Nebraska, which, according to some of my friends, was the end of the world. I stopped at San Diego to see Georgette and the kids. She had bought a house in a new development. There at a party I met several of her friends. She had also purchased a car. She informed me that she was not about to move again. I knew none of her friends and from what I heard they were giving her many favors. I was wondering what she was giving in return. I left very uneasy, suspecting that something was wrong. When I reached Washington, I discovered that my assignment had been changed and that I was to report to the CIC Indianapolis Field Office. One of my associates said, "You must have really screwed up to be assigned to India-no-place!"

The Pasture

I left San Diego and flew to Washington D. C., where I reported to the OPS office, located in the basement of the Pentagon. The brass there was disappointed that the operation that I had planned had not materialized. I checked in with those who had provided the necessary physical support for the mission and told them about the results of their efforts. They were pleased with the report on the documentation, but not with the results of the hair dye they used on my scalp.

By that time—October, 1963—we were completely out of Laos, and Vietnam was in a turmoil. While in Washington, I stayed with Lowell and Noëlle, Georgette's brother (who was employed by the U.S. Information Agency under Edward R. Morrow) and sister-in-law.

Lowell was spending a good deal of his time at the White House. He would return home late in the evening and after a few drinks would tell me what was going on in the presidential palace. Lowell was not a prude, but I had the impression that he was not entirely pleased with what he saw. He mentioned the skinny-dipping parties in the White House pool which apparently were common occurrences.

At that time I was more concerned with my future than what was going on in the White House or even with the state of the world. I was given access to the dispatches from our Military Attaché in Saïgon. They were not encouraging. Mrs. Nu and her husband were blamed for the deteriorating condition there. Buddhist monks had cremated themselves in the street in protest of the Diem Government. The situation was most unfavorable for Diem and his associates. Because President Kennedy felt that North Vietnam did not represent a threat to Laos or to the rest of Southeast Asia, and therefore there was no need to protect them, he had "neutralized" Laos. The nets that we had maintained there with so much difficulty were abandoned.

While in Washington, not entirely happy about the prospect of being assigned again to a CIC unit, I decided to explore another career path, which at the time appeared to me a bit more attractive than my imminent exile to the "boondocks." I made an appointment with Bill Colby, an OSS acquaintance who I had met in Thailand, and who was now the CIA's Chief of Far Eastern Affairs. His reaction was not particularly encouraging, probably because my dealings with the Agency in Laos had not been the best. He assured me that I would hear from him one way or the other. It turned out to be the other, which was probably for the best. Bill eventually became the Director of Central Intelligence, probably the most qualified that we ever had.

I realized then that my chances of remaining in the military were slim unless I was transferred to an agency requesting my presence, and only then if the transfer was acceptable to the Army. After my reception at ACSI following my return from Laos, my popularity with the Army as well as with CIA left much to be desired. As a reserve officer, my active duty time was limited to twenty years. In a couple of years I would have to become a civilian.

Having exhausted my leave, I decided that I might as well report to my new post and flew off to Indianapolis.

Looking out the window of the plane, I was thinking about my destination when, around noon, the stewardess announced our landing in Indianapolis. I looked out and saw nothing but empty fields and clumps of trees with a few houses. I was sure that these were the boondocks about which I had been warned. As the plane taxied to the terminal, it seemed that the airport was deserted. There were no other aircraft visible on the ground, and when the terminal appeared, it was smaller than some of the smallest I had seen in my travels to other boondocks. We disembarked down the steps, a good distance from the terminal.

I called the CIC office because there was no one waiting for me at the airport. An hour later a member of the field office arrived to pick me up and take me to Fort Benjamin Harrison. It was November, a lot colder than Washington and much colder than the Southeast Asian climate that I had just left—and I was still wearing summer clothes. I reported to Lt. Colonel Petti, a small but dynamic officer who oversaw the CIC detachment office, which was responsible for a region consisting of Indiana, Michigan and parts of Kentucky, Illinois and Ohio. Our office was at the Finance Center at Fort Harrison.

Col. Petti was kind enough to offer me a bed in his home until I was able to get a room at the post BOQ. He was a staunch Catholic who never missed mass on Sundays or the Catholic Days of Obligation. I had several meals with his family and established a good relationship with them from the very beginning. The billeting was short of rooms for assigned personnel. I was not considered to be permanently assigned to Fort Harrison because, although I was on duty there, technically my permanent assignment was to the army Headquarters at Fort Sheridan at Chicago.

Shortly before he was to go on leave, Pat Cannon, an enlisted man I had known from a previous assignment who was working at the Finance Center, asked me if I would mind house-sitting for him. His home was located in on the northeast side of Indianapolis, not far from Fort Harrison. He even offered to give me the use of one of his cars with which to commute between his house and the Fort. I accepted gladly and stayed there for two weeks until he returned and I was able to obtain quarters at the post BOQ.

One afternoon at a staff meeting the telephone rang. The secretary answered the phone and shortly thereafter she interrupted the meeting to tell the Colonel that his wife was on the line with an urgent message. He picked up his phone, listed for a while and then said, "Gentlemen, someone has shot President Kennedy! He is presumed dead.... "

"That's the best news I've had in a long time."

We all sat there dumbfounded. Our boss was glad that his Commander in Chief was dead. We did not know his reasons, and only found out later why he disliked Kennedy so intensely. Col. Petti was from Massachusetts and he knew a lot more about the Kennedy's than we did. After what Lowell had told me I could see why a devout Catholic would take exception to JFK's personal behavior. He looked with disgust at the fuss which the Catholic Bishop of Boston made over this "philanderer".

I had only met Diem once, but I was very familiar with his Minister of Justice, who I had escorted to church during his visit to our Japanese Headquarters. He was such a kind gentleman, I could not believe the accusations against him (that he was responsible for multiple acts of criminal barbarism toward dissidents) were factual. Perhaps many were pure fabrications on the part of those who hated him and the President.

As far as Diem was concerned, up to that time he was calling the shots. However, the General in charge of the U.S. military support of Vietnam, General Hartkins, gave the impression that it was he who was in full control of the situation and that Diem did as he was told. One of my friends happened to serve as the interpreter for the General during his meetings with Diem (Diem did not speak English and the General was not particularly fluent in French). One day the General was to meet Diem to discuss a very important matter related to the General's mission.

Upon arriving at the Presidential Palace, the General and his interpreter were kept waiting. Finally, Diem called for the General. Upon walking into his office, the General said, "Mister President ....." Before he could continue, Diem cut him off and began a long monologue, to which the General could only say, "Yes, Mister President." One hour later the meeting was concluded. Diem had done all the talking and the General had done the listening. Afterwards, the General was discussing the meeting with other officers. He told them, "Boy, did I give Diem a piece of my mind!" I have no reason to doubt the words of my friend. This was pretty much the way we conducted business with other countries' leaders, despite the general impression within our own government. Within our government, the conventional wisdom was that when it came to our client states, we were in full control.

I needed a car for my personal transportation because although I had access to a staff car for official business I didn't want to have to rely on others to take me where I wanted to go. I bought a Corvair, which was small and economical. I kept in touch with Georgette, who was very unhappy to have been left alone, but who did not want to come to Indianapolis because all her friends were in San Diego. She called me often, making all kinds of threats.

Around December, I met Ginny. She was a Major with a local Army Reserve medical unit. She would attend unit meetings on weekends in Fort Harrison's old hospital. Because I had very little to do in the evenings, I would often go to the Officers Club to kill time. One evening I was at the bar talking to a Red Cross representative that I had known in Japan, when Ginny and a couple of nurses came in. We were introduced and talked for a while. We decided to go out for a hamburger to a nearby restaurant. I did not have enough money to treat anyone as I was on a very tight budget.

It turned out that I did not have to pay. The girls, probably Ginny, were nice enough to treat me. They will never know how much I appreciated their kindness. From that time on, Ginny and I became good friends. I would tell her about my family problems and she would encourage me and keep up my morale.

About that time, there was to be a reorganization in the CIC regional unit. It was decided that the Indianapolis regional office would be moved elsewhere. The Colonel responsible for the move was to select a new location. Two options were available to him: Fort Custer near Battle Creek, Michigan, or Fort Harrison. The Colonel was a native of Michigan, so not surprisingly he selected Fort Custer, even though Fort Custer had very little support capability in terms of space and maintenance facilities. Furthermore, Fort Harrison was offering all that was needed at no cost. This was a stupid move on the part of the military because shortly thereafter Fort Custer was closed.

Indianapolis slowly reverted to a CIC Field Office and I found myself appointed the office's SAC (Special Agent In Charge), with twelve agents working under me, doing exclusively pre-employment investigations. Our territory was basically central and southern Indiana from Kokomo south to the Ohio River. Little by little, through attrition, the agents left and were never replaced. I had very little to do. Technically, as a Major I was supposed to be in charge and remain behind a desk, bored to tears.

To break the monotony, and perhaps make a few dollars on the side (I was getting desperate having to support two households), I placed an ad in the local newspaper offering French lessons. I received a few replies, one from two employees of the Finance Center. They wanted me to come to their house and teach them there. They lived in an old home in Woodruff Place, one of the oldest historical sections of the city. Theirs was a beautiful home and it was a pleasure for me to be in such surroundings. Unfortunately, my two students didn't have a very good ear for languages. At times, it was rather painful to hear their attempts at speaking French. One day they realized that they were wasting their time and canceled their lessons entirely.

As a result of the ad, I also received a call from a lady who put forth a strange proposition to me. She suggested that she call me once or twice a week and for fifteen minutes we would speak French. At the end of the month she would send me a check. What did I have to lose? I agreed, and from that time on she would call me, usually during the day, and for fifteen minutes we would talk about all kind of subjects. She spoke French well, but she wanted to practice and be up to date on certain expressions. She had learned French long ago; where and how, she never told me. Every month I would get a check which was great. Yet I had never met her nor did I know who she was, except for her first name which was Sonia, an eastern European name I presumed.

As we were losing personnel, it became necessary for me to get involved with the day-to-day work of our office which consisted of conducting pre-employment investigations. We were to interview people whom the applicants had offered as character references as well as their current and former employers, and to develop other sources of information about the subjects of our various investigations. We checked police records, court records and credit records, but most useful were our interviews with the subjects' neighbors, those who were not listed as character references.

This would take me all over the state, often to farming areas, where I learned a great deal about Indiana. I came to the conclusion that those who considered Indiana to be the boondocks had never bothered to visit the state. In the course of my investigations I talked to many farmers who were far better informed about the world situation than many of my own associates. They were anxious to express themselves and had opinions very close to my own. They reminded me of the people I had left in Europe such as my uncles, who were also farmers, but who were much more interested in what was going on in the world than were city folks.

What amazed me the most in the farming area of Indiana was the trust of the people. I would walk up to a farm house, find the door open, walk in and find no one about. Looking around the farm I would see people in the distance who at times would wave me over to them. I would conduct the interview while they kept at their chores. If they invited me into their home, they would always offer me something—coffee or a piece of the best pie I ever tasted. Invariably I was greeted by a group of dogs, not mean ones but friendly pups with their tails wagging.

One day I stopped at a farm, left the car close to the road and was walking toward the house when a German Shepherd came towards me, tail down, head down, as if he was about to attack. Having learned how to defend myself against dogs, I removed my jacket, rolled it around my left arm and waited for the dog to jump. The closer he came, the more convinced I was that he would attack. I was about to grab his jaw to twist it when he licked my hand and whimpered. About that time, the farmer, who had seen me, came out and said, "Don't be afraid, he's old and blind, come right in." I felt like a fool. The more I traveled throughout Indiana, the more I liked it.

My room was located in one of the BOQ (Bachelor Officer's Quarters) on the officer's row section of Fort Harrison. In the basement was the Class 6 store where one could purchase beer, wine and liquor. I could easily walk to my office or to any part of the post. I didn't have a telephone, however I could use the pay phone located in the hall outside of my room.

I was getting close to my retirement date. It seemed that every month I was losing more and more of my agents, yet the work load did not diminish. In addition to being required to maintain liaison with the local police, the State Police, the FBI and the CIA (which had an office in the Federal Building), I had to maintain contact with the major industries in the area such as RCA, Ford and Chevrolet.

Occasionally I would receive a call from Georgette who was more and more unhappy about her situation. Once she called me and told me that she would kill all the kids. She told me that she had a lot of problems with Sonny and with Marc who were now 13 and 12 years of age. She wanted to get rid of Sonny, so I suggested that he come to Indiana and stay with me. I arranged for his fare and he arrived one day on a big wide body jet. His idea was that we would live together alone, spend our time fishing and forget about the rest of the family. He entered Belzer Junior High School in Lawrence Township, and was picked up and delivered daily by a school bus from Fort Harrison. He immediately adopted me as his constant companion and did not care much to share me with others, particularly with Ginny, with whom by now I was occasionally spending time.

One day, shortly before Christmas, the temperature was down to nearly 30 degrees and he still insisted on going fishing. I had to go somewhere, so I took him to his favorite fishing hole and left him there, telling him that I would pick him up later. Close to noon I decided that perhaps he had had enough. I told Ginny what I had done. She told me that it was a dumb thing to do and that I should go after him immediately. So together we rushed to Geist Reservoir on Fall Creek Road.

Close to the dam we saw this frozen body dragging a fishing pole along the road. By the way he looked, we knew he was in trouble. He could hardly talk. His hands were blue, close to being frostbitten. We stuffed him into the car, Ginny placing his hands under her armpits to warm them while we drove hurriedly to my room where we dunked his hands in water, gradually increasing the temperature. Sonny was sure that he would lose his fingers and perhaps his hands. After a while he recovered and swore he would never do that again.

At the end of 1964, Georgette continued to make threats.

One day after receiving a telephone call from Georgette advising me that she would kill the children, I went to see Ginny and broke down. I was devastated. I felt so helpless and did not know what to do. I was seriously considering giving up and joining the French Foreign Legion, or become a mercenary as several of my friends had done, but Ginny convinced me that the kids were more important and that I should go to California and bring them to Indiana. I rented a house, asked for leave time and, leaving Sonny in the care of Ginny, flew to San Diego to see what was going on. Georgette picked me up at the airport and, on the way to the house, informed me that she was suing me for divorce and presented me with an settlement agreement drafted by her lawyer. I was taken by surprise because I had planned to have her bring the kids to Indianapolis and had arranged for a mover to pick up our household goods.

The evening before our departure she dressed as if going to a party. She had a tight red dress and was wearing a string of pearls I had given her. She informed me that she had a date and that I should feed the kids. She described her date and said not to wait for her she would spend the night with him. "You are never home. Why should I wait for you?" she said. This was more than I could stand. I grabbed her, wanting to pound some sense in her head. In the process the string of pearls broke and all the pearls went to the floor. While I was gathering them, she left.

All I could find in the cupboard was peanut butter. I talked to the kids who told me the kind of life they had with their mother, who hardly fed then. Their diet was mostly peanut butter. That night I slept on top of one of the bunk beds. She returned home in the early hours of the morning and informed me that she had slept with someone better than I. Right then, I decided that I had had enough and would not continue living this kind of life.

The movers had come and were loading the van. All of the kid's clothing had been packed and loaded into the car, when I told Georgette that I had to get some gas. The kids came along for the ride, and after filling the tank I asked them how they felt about taking off directly and leaving Georgette behind.

It was unanimous. All five said, "Leave her behind, leave her behind." I realized then that we had to move fast and get out of California (before she realized what had happened) where she could have had us stopped. So we took the most direct route to Arizona.

When we crossed the border and reached Yuma, I felt relieved that we made it that far and were all right. We drove through New Mexico, Texas and eventually reached St. Louis and I-70. We stopped overnight, but the next morning it started to snow. We moved in and out of snow squalls as we drove through Illinois and by the time we arrived in Indianapolis it was snowing pretty hard. But Georgette had beat us there!

I had rented an unfurnished house from a local doctor. When we checked in with Ginny she informed me that Georgette had preceded me by one day. Ginny had been cleaning the house when Georgette walked into the house prior to our arrival. I do not know what transpired then, but her presence complicated things greatly. Waiting for the van and our furniture which was to follow us, we stayed in a motel where Ginny had made reservations. Georgette, who had taken a bus, had arrived ahead of us and was staying at the Post guest house. She had obtained the address of my room from my office, and the key from the housekeeper. She had gone to my room and rummaged through all my belongings and had found letters that Ginny had written to me while she was in reserve training.

Eventually the van arrived with our furniture. We moved into the house and began a routine which at first appeared to be accepted by the children, but was later proved to be not so by one—Noëlle, the oldest. I made plenty of soups, salads and rice which they liked. Georgette had returned to California, intent on pursuing the divorce. That winter, Indianapolis had the worst winter in many years. Twenty inches of snow had fallen one night and the next morning the city was at a standstill. Our neighbors had car problems. We all stayed home awaiting the street cleaning crews.

Meanwhile, I decided that for my own protection I better have an attorney. When I explained my situation to him, he suggested that as long as Georgette was suing for divorce in California I better do the same in Indiana; which I did. Georgette returned in the Spring and obtained a local attorney.

Both of our attorneys got together and, in 1965, came up with a possible solution. I did not want to take everything away from her. The house in San Diego was to be hers and, after discussing the situation with the children, Noëlle decided to return to California with her mother, as did the two youngsters, Alain and Gisele. I turned over the station wagon to her and, renting a trailer, stuffed it with as many household items as we could and they left.

The Final Blow

The presiding officer ended he meeting telling me that I would hear from the Board shortly. Too numb to say anything I saluted and left the building. Shaken, apprehensive, and very much alone, on a cold January afternoon I left Fort Sheridan and headed for Indianapolis where I was to wait for the verdict. Oblivious of the heavy traffic out of Chicago I drove wondering why people who did not know me had repeated a story told to them by Georgette! What did they have to gain by going to the FBI? What was Georgette's motive? She had asked for a divorce. She got it. If I was court-martialed and was drummed out of the service I would lose my retirement and she would lose her alimony and the kid's financial support.

Having reached the end of my military career I was looking forward to my retirement day, when I received a strange phone call from a friend who was an FBI agent at the Indianapolis field office. One of my duties was to make official visits to the local FBI office to maintain a good working relation.

I arrived at his office believing that his call had to do with an official matter. Instead, he assured me that what he was telling me was off the record, and that it concerned me! I could not believe that I would be the subject of an FBI investigation at this stage of my career. He explained that he had received a call from the San Diego office of the FBI which had been visited by a couple who stated that I had revealed top secret information to them.

As it involved a member of the Armed Forces, technically FBI-San Diego couldn't take any action, but when they learned that I was the SAC of the CIC office in Indianapolis, they contacted the FBI's Indianapolis office to determine if indeed I did exist. Of course the local agents knew me and wanted to warn me that the San Diego FBI office had to report this incident to the Army through channels, and that it would reach my boss shortly. I remembered meeting a husband and wife couple who were friends of Georgette, but I didn't even remember having a conversation with them, let alone discussing classified information. The man was the one who sold the station wagon to Georgette.

It did not take long for the other shoe to drop. A day or so later, I was told to report immediately to Chicago without any indication as to why. I knew the reason, and was preparing in my own mind a reply even though I had no idea as to what the allegation was. I left early one morning. There were six inches of snow on the ground and I could hardly see the road. By the time the sun came up I had only reached Lafayette only sixty miles away.

I arrived at Fort Sheridan around 10:00 am and learned that I was to appear before a board of officers on a charge of having violated the Secrecy Act. After twenty-two years in the Army, with most of the time in intelligence, I had supposedly violated the Secrecy Act! The board was made up of five officers who knew me and treated me with compassion, probably because they felt that they could be in the same predicament some day.

Up to that point, the board had not yet told me about the accusation. They wanted to know who Virginia Edds was. I could not understand the connection between my alleged violation and Ginny. They were quite surprised to learn that she was a member of the Army Reserve and a nurse. They wanted to know if I had ever discussed classified information with her and if I had sex with her. Of course I had not. How did they know about Ginny? Georgette must have told someone about her because she had met Ginny at the time she was contacting her attorney in Indianapolis.

Then they asked if on a given day I had stated that Mrs. Nu, the sister-in-law of South Vietnamese President Diem, was the mistress of an American diplomat, a high-ranking attaché at the Saïgon Embassy. I did remember telling that story to a group of people, all friends of Georgette, at a party that I attended when I returned from Japan on my way to Washington two years earlier.

I had read this in a French tabloid on the plane as well as in many other French newspapers, which at the time took great delight at highlighting the Americans' inability to control the situation in the former French colony. It was common knowledge that Mrs. Nu had other love interests besides her husband and that she had a strong influence over President Diem. Some in fact considered the "Dragon Lady" to be the real power in Saïgon. At that time, Vietnamese Buddhist monks were immolating themselves in protest of the Diem Government. When asked about this, Mrs. Nu bluntly stated, "Let them barbecue themselves." I had made a casual remark which should not have surprised anyone with a basic knowledge of current events. However, to Georgette this was hot stuff which she planned to use against me for some obscure reason.

She managed to convince two of her gullible friends to report this to the San Diego office of the FBI. It seems that the members of the board were just as ignorant of current events in Vietnam as were Georgette and her friends. They had to check with a higher authority, probably the local press, in order to learn that this so-called top secret information was common knowledge within the U.S. press, which was not inclined to publicize it because it originated from French sources!

On the icy road to Indianapolis I wondered about my future. What a way to end twenty-two years of faithful service to my adopted country! I had sacrificed all these years for something I believed was important, important not so much to me, but to the world, especially to the United States. I had joined the Army not because I had to, but because I wanted to, and I remained in the service because I felt that I could, in small way, pay for the privilege of being a U.S. Citizen. Having been brought up by the Swiss side of my family I understood the responsibility of all able-bodied men for the security and defense of their country. I watched the Swiss farmers periodically changing from work clothes to green uniforms. To my great surprise, some were high-ranking officers. Like those ordinary people, citizenship to me meant more than maintaining a basic familiarity of the three branches of our government and of the U.S. Constitution—I defended it.

I had assisted in the defeat of Nazism and fascism, and saw communism rise up to become an even greater threat to world peace than the others. The Korean conflict ended in a stalemate. There were neither winners or losers. We had taken on France's obligations in Southeast Asia, but did not know how to carry them out. Two of our presidents had given the wrong message to the North Vietnamese. We violated the international rules of warfare by fighting first and applying sanctions later. We refused to help our friends and made it easy for our opponents to manipulate not only U.S. public opinion, but that of the world. Winning was no longer part of our vocabulary.

Why had I been so anxious to do a good job when the result of our efforts were completely ignored by our policy makers? As I reached the end of my military career I sensed that intelligence and counterintelligence had become expendable. No one wanted to hear the truth, no one seemed to care. Unlike many of my contemporaries, who had retired as I did (with the exception of those who had remained in the military as civilians), I felt relieved. I was free to do what I pleased. Unlike in the military, where it seemed to me only those who do nothing succeed, I could enjoy the fruits of my efforts.

On the 9th of February 1965 the good news finally arrived. All charges against me had been dropped. The following day I drove to Fort Custer the last time for a farewell party given honor of my retirement. During a short reception in my honor the CO gave me an engraved silver plate as a memento for my twenty-two years (to the day) of faithful service, and a set of orders providing me with a pension equal to 55% of my pay as a Major. It was not much, but it would keep bread on the table until I could find another job. I was offered a retirement parade, but I declined. All I wanted to do was return to the half of my family waiting for me in Indianapolis, and try to make up to them for my years of neglect. I was forty-four years young. Already I missed a few of my military friends, but not the Army. On the surface the Army was an efficient organization led by great leaders. Everything about it was ably planned, well organized and its members superbly trained. Seen from within the Army was not that proficient. It was wasteful, and the planning seldom went much farther than the length of the tour of duty of the planner. In fact the Army, perhaps the entire Armed Forces of the United States was extremely political. Politics was the name of the game. If one did not mind getting his nose brown, he might attain great heights. It was not what you knew but what were you willing to give to others higher than you that made the difference.

The Fox had survived twenty-two years in a cage. No more need for my fox chop, no more documents to read, to write, and mark, yet I wanted to keep the chop as a souvenir of the difficult times that I had endured. I decided to make a ring so that I would have this symbol with me all the time. At the hobby shop of Fort Harrison, using the lost-wax method, I created a lasting reminder of the past, a silver ring bearing my emblem—the winking fox.

Index

Pictures included into The Winking Fox

Documents included in The Winking Fox